THE EXPLORER RACE

MW00581874

ET Visitors Speak

Vol. 2

THROUGH
ROBERT SHAPIRO

Other Books by Robert Shapiro

EXPLORER RACE SERIES

1 The Explorer Race

2 ETs and the Explorer Race

3 Explorer Race: Origins and the Next 50 Years

4 Explorer Race: Creators and Friends

5 Explorer Race: Particle Personalities

6 The Explorer Race and Beyond

7 Explorer Race: The Council of Creators

8 The Explorer Race and Isis

9 The Explorer Race and Jesus

10 Explorer Race: Earth History and Lost Civilizations

11 The Explorer Race: ET Visitors Speak

12 Explorer Race: Techniques for Generating Safety

13 Animal Souls Speak

14 Plants Souls Speak

15 The Explorer Race: ET Visitors Speak Vol. 2

MATERIAL MASTERY SERIES

A Shamanic Secrets for Material Mastery

B Shamanic Secrets for Physical Mastery

C Shamanic Secrets for Spiritual Mastery

SHINING THE LIGHT SERIES

Shining the Light: The Battle Begins!

Shining the Light II: The Battle Continues

Shining the Light III: Humanity Gets a Second Chance

Shining the Light IV: Humanity's Greatest Challenge

Shining the Light V: Humanity Is Going to Make It!

Shining the Light VI: The End of What Was

Shining the Light VII: The First Alignment—World Peace

ULTIMATE UFO SERIES

Andromeda: UFO Contact from Andromeda

Zetas, Hybrids and Human Contacts

SECRETS OF FEMININE SCIENCE SERIES

Book 1: Benevolent Magic & Living Prayer

Book 2: Disentanglement & Deep Disentanglement

Book 3: Disengagement, Engagement & Connections

SHIRT POCKET BOOKS SERIES

Touching Sedona

Feeling Sedona's ET Energies

THE EXPLORER RACE

ET
Visitors
Speak

Vol. 2

*   *   *

ISBN-10: 1891824783
ISBN-13: 978-1891824784

Light Technology Publishing, LLC
Phone: 800-450-0985
Fax: 928-714-1132
PO Box 3540
Flagstaff, AZ 86003
www.lighttechnology.com

Table of Contents

The Continuing Adventures of Visitors to Planet Earth

Zoosh

July 1, 2009

or those of you who've always wanted to meet somebody completely different, here's your opportunity. This book contains the continuing adventures of visitors to planet Earth. In a strange sense, you might include yourself as one of those, as the human race does not really claim the title of full-time, permanent Earth citizens. So when you're reading this book, think about it as if you were visiting another planet. What would you say in reaction to the local population, their habits and so on? Put yourself in the picture so this isn't just a meaningless travel log from various beings that you don't know and may never meet. Make it personal this time because the time is coming—maybe even in some of your lifetimes—when you might just meet one of those extraterrestrials on another planet. So you might as well practice now and get your lines down right.

The End of Fifty-Year Earth/ET Secrecy Agreement

Zoosh

January 20, 1998

Now for a brief commentary on the recent sightings of lights in Phoenix, Arizona. I will reiterate my previous position, which correlates to this sighting. These lights are caused by ground-based vehicles associated with a highly secret project in the military of the United States. I will also say, in reference to those who call the Air Force base and speak to whatever hapless individual is unlucky enough to pick up the phone, that the average personnel has no knowledge whatsoever of this. It is supersecret, and these vehicles will be flying over more cities in the future.

I also wish to say something else. The cities will be mostly in the U.S., but there will be a few flybys over foreign countries if it is felt to be safe. Generally speaking, though, they are not on any military mission, in the sense that it is not exactly a wake-up call, but it's more to get people used to the experience. There is, then, an arrangement. For a long time insiders within the military and political arenas of stable governments worldwide (certainly the U.S.) have had an arrangement whereby when a certain year came—which was 1998 and beyond—that it would be a good thing if stable governments, utilizing technology provided by extraterrestrials, could begin flying this technology over their own towns and cities in order to get people used to the idea of UFOs as a benevolent phenomenon. This is not to suggest that a lot of UFOs that have been sighted over other cities and countries and over the ocean are all from ground-based aircraft. But some are, and I use the Phoenix sightings because this is a typical example.

Pacts with ETs in the 1940s

This arrangement between the military and extraterrestrials goes way back. Early in the forties the extraterrestrials made this arrangement with various high-placed individuals, the military and the political establishment of the time. These were relatively stable governments, and although they shared some of this with governments that have changed since then, these governments and systems have largely stayed in place, though personnel has changed. The arrangement was that sharing the technology would ultimately provide a more benevolent technological expression for the peoples of the Earth—meaning that what you are now experiencing as a day-to-day phenomenon of electronics, computers and even biogenetics was to some degree greatly speeded up by this process.

From the extraterrestrial point of view, it was not only to help you along in your motion toward becoming universal citizens, but also to do what they could to help you on Earth to keep from self-destructing before you discovered that you were not alone, that there was lots of help available, to say nothing of friends you haven't met yet (at least most of you haven't), and that there would be available to you a common ground. Now, it was felt by certain beings (extraterrestrials and their teachers) that it would be best if most of the flybys in the late eighties and now the nineties would be done by them. But they also felt that as time progressed (especially after 1995), it would be useful if you had developed some ships or rebuilt some they lent you to fly some missions yourself, as long as the missions were totally benevolent (they would monitor you, by the way, to make sure they were).

So what we have here in recent days in Phoenix, Arizona, is another one of these flybys. In this latest circumstance the lights were lined up in such a way as to be clearly perceived as individual lights. (There was some confusion last time: Was it one vehicle or was it many?) It was the same thing both times: many individual, singular vehicles. So you are being prepared. Now, I grant you that not all ships that fly through the sky and are manufactured by various secret governmental or military organizations are entirely benevolent. Some are not. But this project I am talking about is benevolent.

Can you describe these vehicles?

If you were to see them, some are disc-shaped, and some are shaped like this [draws an upright rectangular shape].

I saw one of those earlier tonight on **The Learning Channel** *on TV.* **It looks like a rectangular column.**

Some of them are disc-shaped. Some of them are not quite circular, but roughly have that kind of a context. (When I say disc-shaped, I do not mean a flattened disk, but what is typically referred to as a disc shape. A lot of the so-called ET technologies are involved.) The reason they're usually seen at night is that without having the light-gathering instrument activated, the vehicle itself tends to give off light through its skin. This isn't like someone flying around with a searchlight. The vehicle itself tends to radiate light. It is possible, of course, to draw that light in with an instrument that is rare but available to some secret establishments. If that is done, it is possible to intentionally mask the vehicle, but if that switch is not activated, it is intended that the vehicle be seen.

I would also say this to big cities who have helicopter policing and so on: If a helicopter should fly over to where the ships are, it is possible that its instruments could be affected, so give yourself a degree of boundary. Don't fly any closer than three miles if you can help it. That's part of the reason the lights usually appear in places where they are not likely to encounter many airplanes or helicopters. I mention this as an aside to the occasional pilot and reporters who might be able to use a helicopter: It's probably not safe to get much closer than three miles because of the electrical radiation that would unintentionally interfere with instruments. Three, maybe three and a half miles, is probably safe.

How high can these vehicles fly beyond the orbit of the Earth?

If you are talking about going to the Moon, they might have capabilities like that, but in terms of who is going to fly them, they don't have the life support required for such missions, in terms of ground-based ships.

How many of these ships are there?

Oh, I should think that at any given time and place, seeing more than seven would be unlikely, though at the outside, even eight or nine. However, seeing three to five is most likely.

Are the nine available as the total, or do different bases each have nine?

You have to understand that if these vehicles are seen, they are not coming from a local air base. No, they are not located that way. They are centrally located.

Okay, in the place where they're based there is a total of possibly nine or ten, and then they go to different cities?

Well, some of them are being parted out, as it were. At any given time on a good day (as is said in some technological circles) you might get nine up in the air, but five can get into the air pretty much anytime, and a few more are iffy.

Okay, how much can you say about this? Is it wide open right now, or do you have to be discreet?

I am being a little discreet. As you notice, I haven't said anything much about this in the past except my rather cryptic referral to the last Phoenix flyby. I am mentioning this to the degree that I can talk about it now. I don't wish to say where they're based. I don't want to say too much about who is onboard. I will just say that it is, for the most part, strictly benevolent and is really intended to gradually bring you to consciousness about extraterrestrials. I might add that as it becomes more common, it will be normal for the press to report it as if it is reporting anything else. It would be said, "Oh, more lights in the sky. How about that?" No negative comments, no laughing up their sleeves.

The whole editorial position of derisiveness about such sightings is becoming very much passé now on the official level, though on the more colloquial or anecdotal level, from person to person, it is still somewhat entrenched. It's going to take time to gradually eliminate the head-in-the sand idea—"it can't be, therefore it isn't." This attitude was promoted for a long time, and it's going to take a little while to eliminate that in this country. It will take less time in other countries because there has been a lot of what I would call official and unofficial propaganda, especially in this country. The conditioning of the average citizen has been very thorough. People in this country have been conditioned for a long time, not with a rigid hand but with an almost overly paternalistic hand. But now this is gradually being removed from you as a steady influence.

The 1947 Contract

Are these vehicles totally in the control of an arm of the U.S. military or some benevolent multinational group?

This is based on a contract that cannot be broken. The contract was originally sealed (I am using that term advisedly for those of you who understand that word) in the late forties. It was between the U.S. and some of its allies' governments and the extraterrestrials, and this contract would last for x number of years, basically about fifty years, during which the extrater-restrials would have certain rights to have clandestine contact with citizens of Earth without any interference. For that there would be trade-offs to the various governments. At the end of the contractual time (it wasn't exactly fifty years, but that's a ballpark figure) there would begin to be a public rela-tions experience whereby the governments that could afford it would begin to help wake up the citizenry to the actual fact of extraterrestrials. This would be done as gently as possible. I might add that the insistence that it be done gently was promoted by the extraterrestrials, not Earth-based governments. Extraterrestrials understood that after many years of denial, it would be neces-sary to make it gentle.

Were these extraterrestrials Zetas, or were they a group of beings from various ET civilizations?

More of what I would call a group of beings. Zeta Reticulans were involved, but there were also some Pleiadians, a representative from Andromeda and Orion representatives. A Council of Sirius was represented through the Orion representative, the Council of Sirius being, loosely, a group of philosophical/scientific individuals. And several of the extrater-restrial star systems were involved.

Can you say what year the contract was sealed?

It was officially recognized as a contract in 1947.

And who signed it for the Americans? Who represented the Americans?

I am loath to say who. I would rather not. I would rather say it was three citizens of influence: one a private citizen, one a citizen associated with the mili-tary and one a public citizen, meaning in service as a government representative, all of whom represented the United States at the sealing of the contract.

The Crafts and ET Engineering Help

The crafts themselves: Are they reverse-engineered? Are they gifts? Did we manu-facture them?

I will say a little bit about that because it is an interesting question. Some of the vehicles represent accidents, not shoot-downs. This whole idea that vehicles were shot down—this is not so much the case. I'll grant that a couple of vehicles were shot down, but it was because of what I would call a lack of communication. You know, if someone's communicating on one band and you are communicating on another and you can't reach each other, there are going to be mistakes like that. The ETs recognized that it was a mistake. A lot of the vehicles were knocked out of the sky because of your experimenting with radar and other such reflective electrical instrumentality, which in the beginning used huge amounts of energy. The tools were not as refined then and people didn't know they could use less energy. This created fields that were disruptive, not unlike what I mentioned before—where if you fly a helicopter into a massive electrical field, it's going to mess up your instruments even if they are shielded.

That's what happened then. But then there was one gift, what I would call a rudimentary craft (it could do this but not that) and there was also some assistance to you. Some parts and assistance were provided to help you rebuild ships. In a couple of cases the assistance was provided as long as the citizens inside the ships were returned—and they were. It's true that sometimes citizens were held, but in these cases the citizens were returned. Alive or dead, they were returned.

Then there was help (physically). Representatives would come and tell you, "This goes here and that goes there," and why. Sometimes they wouldn't answer a question, and that would be that. At other times they might help. Let's say you are the ground technician and you have these bits and pieces and don't know where they go, or you don't know what the circuitry (if I can call it that) will do once you assemble it. You are a little shy about assembling it, not knowing what it will do, which is reasonable because sometimes this "circuitry" has more than one way to be assembled. If it is assembled one way, it will self-destruct the vehicle, not unlike switches. If it is assembled another way, it will be very useful in transporting this or that. If it is assembled still another way, it might be a weapon. What would be given is the way to assemble it, for instance, whereby you could use it as a device to transport something; you could use a field effect to move a heavy object from one place to another.

That kind of help was granted, and it was always done in such a way as to teach the technician something on a spiritual level as well as a mechanical level. We are not talking about only mechanical guidance here.

On **The Learning Channel's** *program "Alien Secrets: Area 51," I just watched a man who's probably in his seventies saying that for sixteen years he worked alongside a Zeta who assisted him and others in modifying these vehicles for humans. Whenever he had a question, the Zeta would already know it and would answer in his mind. He said he had been permitted to come out and say this on this television show by his employers. You are confirming exactly what was on television tonight.*

Trial Balloons in Educational TV and the Press

I would say that it's a worthy thing that it is coming out. You see, it's coming out on legitimate stations. I don't want to say that some television programs are only sensationalist, but some are a little more tabloid than others. Now you have programs that are basically educational television, which are perhaps a little more legitimate in the eyes of the average viewer, and this is important. So you won't think I am heaping scorn on so-called tabloid television, sometimes tabloid television and newspapers perform valuable functions by putting out stories that would not get into the conventional press and into the public eye. Sometimes it is speculation presented as fact, but at other times it is actual eyewitness testimony. Now this information is beginning to move from that trial-balloon position into the more educational press, and it will continue from there.

It is really not such a big move to say that something is benevolent. You just have to understand that ships from other planets might be very benevolent with benevolent people in them. The ships that are not benevolent (which are very few indeed) are held at bay these days. They can't get to you; they won't get to you, as it's not possible. By the time you have ships of your own and you can get to them, those individuals will be benevolent. Everything is on track so that when you meet people they will be benevolent and will be looking forward to meeting you. I am saying this largely for those of you out there who are convinced that some ships are dangerous, with dangerous beings on board. The greatest danger, as you have discovered in your own personal history on this planet, is ignorance.

It's been a couple of years, but the last time you discussed this, the secret government had technology that kept all ET ships away from the planet. Have the ETs gotten around that? Are ships able to come and go more freely?

The spectrum of light in which they were approaching your solar system has been modified to a different wave. That's all I want to say, because the Sinister Secret Government can hear me too, you know. It is a different wave that I do not think is possible to block. I am not going to give the formula, for obvious reasons, nor am I going to give any hints about the method, but the method is now in place so that extraterrestrial ships can come here only if they need to be here and if it is acceptable for you people on Earth to have them near. Those are the main qualifiers, though there are a couple of others. They can be here now, which is why you are getting more sightings and why there's press about it. It's becoming a regular thing and more people are realizing that it's a real thing. I might add it's nothing to be afraid of. As a matter of fact, it's a great adventure. It will be a lot of fun for most of you, and it's not too far down the road where extraterrestrials will be introduced to you on television and they will be benevolent beings.

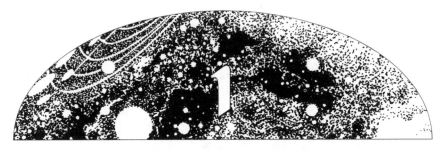

ET Greeters to Future
Mars Earth Colony

ET from a Future Version of Saturn
September 27, 1999

reetings. I am a visitor from your immediate surroundings. In the future we will be a colony on the planet Mars, a thriving colony initially started by Earth visitors from about the year 2025 and peopled by other individuals from other planets. Initially, the colony will be up near the polar icecap on Mars, but very soon you will discover how to create and regenerate the oxygen you need. My companions and I will be some of the first individuals from other planets who come to visit with you.

The Beginning of ET Contact

At first when you see us, you will be alarmed because of the suit we wear. You will be frightened because the suit is skintight and you will think that the way the suit appears is the way we appear. But in fact, before anyone has a chance to reach for a weapon, I will hold up my hand and say, "Don't worry," in your language. Some of you will hear me in French, others in Japanese, one in Chinese, some in English and so on. I will say, "Don't worry. It's just the suit we're wearing. This is not how we look. We look like you." And then people will lower their weapons.

We're also the first emissaries who come to help you get settled on Mars so that you can have a good life there. A younger member will say some of the usual things people say when they are nervous and excited: "Oh, I have hoped for this for so long. We were looking forward to it. We didn't know when you'd come." Then you'll be outside, the people there will be outside and we'll talk for a while.

Eventually, one of you will sort of nervously say, "Well, why don't you come in?" And we'll say, "Well, we'd be happy to do that, but why don't you come look at our ship first," because it will be parked behind a hill and you won't see it. Then your group will walk around [to the ship]. There will be about twenty-seven or so of you. We'll all be outside. There will be two or three of you who will have to stay inside but wish they could come. Those people will be working with instruments and so on, so they have to stay and monitor things. But the rest will come around.

You'll come into the ship and we'll show you how the ship works. Of course, everybody's going to want to go for a ride, but we'll say, "We'll come back and do that another day. First we want to give you some equipment." At that time you'll have discovered how to generate and regenerate oxygen, but it won't be a lot. Plus you will have discovered by then that the inclusion of a few other gases will be good for not only improving health but for perpetuating longevity. We'll give you some generators for those. They will look just like small rocks, but in fact they are compressed from elements. I'm sorry I can't reveal them right now, but in time they will come to be known to you. That would be one of the ways that your peoples of Earth learn how to live longer while also learning how to maintain your population at a level that Earth can sustain. Then there will be a pleasant meeting that will go on for about six hours, after which we'll leave. But there will be many other times we visit.

I realize that I am not exactly a visitor to Earth in your time, but I will come on a mission at a later time and visit the people of Earth. By that time, around the year 2030, you will have established something not unlike the United Nations, but it will be in another location, probably in Europe. The new United Nations will be a place where people focus less on government and problems and more on intercultural studies and exchanges in order that one culture help out another and practice goodwill toward one another. In short, everybody will help each other. That's where I'll go and that's where people will meet. It will really be the beginning of Earth contact with extraterrestrials in a most benevolent way.

Can you say where you're from?

I will be at that time a resident of the future version of Saturn.

How far in the future?

In terms of your now calendar, it's a bit distorted, but for the sake of a general figure, let's say about 1,200 years.

But you're a human? You look like us?

My people will look like you, but internally we will be a little different. One difference is that you have your heart here on this side of your body.

On the left side.

Yes. Our heart on that side is a little smaller. We have another heart about half that size on the other side. Also, our lungs are shaped a little differently, which allows us to be more flexible in the atmospheres we breathe. Our internal organs are quite a bit different, but externally we will look very much like you. Not exactly, but very much.

You said that at that time you will be a resident of the future Saturn. Did a colony from Earth go there?

No.

Where did the Saturnians come from?

From inside the planet.

They're inside the planet now?

Well, that's where the colony is in that time. It's the colony inside the planet.

What about now? There's no colony there now?

Our people aren't.

Where are your people coming from? Where is your home planet?

I was born on Saturn.

Okay. Who colonized Saturn, then?

I think it is difficult to explain, but the colonization occurred in the future of my time and came back into the present of my time. So the colonization occurred in the future of Saturn; it was colonized from, I believe, Sirius.

So it was colonized in your future, you were born there and then you came into your past, which for us is thirty years from now?

Something like that.

Chosen for First Contact

How did you get chosen to be our first contact?

I had done human studies for a long time and found it most interesting, although I was always alarmed and upset by some of the violent patterns of the past. You have to remember that I'm making this contact twenty-five or thirty years in your now future, and many of the violent patterns you have now will not be as extreme in the future.

But you've studied our now and previous time?

Not much of the previous, but I will have studied your social structure as much as we could understand it from about your calendar year 1985 up to the present moment of the contact.

2030. And how do you study us from afar? Where do you get your data?

We have a small stone. It is not quite as hard as a diamond and not perfectly square—more of a rectangle, a cubelike thing—and we are able to communicate with it. It is able to project an image we can see—not into the air, but in our imaginations—about anything we've ever asked. I don't want to say that this stone can literally do anything because I can only say that it can do anything I've ever asked it to do in terms of providing information. I do not know what it can't do, but I expect it has its boundaries. That's what I can say about it. The stone was given to us by a very advanced civilization from Andromeda who wanted us to learn more about our environment and the environments of other peoples so that we could initiate you and eventually others into a circumstance of social acceptance with other cultures.

You've studied a lot about us, but we don't know anything about you. How do you live inside Saturn 1,200 years from now?

Living Underground

We live in an underground colony. It is not something that is drilled or mined, but a vast underground open space. We do not drill or make any holes in the planet at all, but we have moved portable structures into the space and live in those structures when we need to. At other times we explore this cave. It's huge inside the planet. It has many extraordinary crystal veins, some of which seem to be lighted somehow from within. We are not clear whether this is some kind of a microbiological luminescence or whether it has something to do with the consciousness of the stone itself, but we do not feel compelled to know the answer. It is a huge and vast network of underground caves. It is like being in a crystal palace, it is so beautiful. During the time my people have been here, which is many years, the total amount of exploration of these caves and tunnels amounts to just a tiny fraction of what's available, as far as we can tell.

How did you find the cave?

We are, you might say, kind of futuristic geologists. In the future, geologists do not mine or take anything out, but rather look for and discover mineral life forms such as crystals. They inquire of the crystals what knowledge or wisdom they can pass on to us—what they can do that might be compatible with us and, conversely, what we can do for them if they need anything. Of course, they practically never do, but in short, it is a study of the life form as itself rather than a study of the life form disconnected from its home environment.

That's fantastic! Why did your people choose Saturn? How did they find these caves? What's the story with that?

The Andromedan Connection

I don't have all that information. I can only tell you that the original quest was encouraged by the Andromedans in order to get us closer to the Earth people, and that they recommended this place because they knew of my people's love and appreciation for beauty in many forms.

So the Andromedans have been behind all this—initially, anyway.

The Andromedans have some kind of overall affection for the people of Earth, although they do not seem to approach you directly.

Because they don't look like us?

No, I wouldn't say that was a great issue. They really didn't tell us why, and we didn't ask. For some reason they do not approach you directly, and we are happy to do the job.

What dimension are you in?

We are able to access anything from seven through four, but sometimes we can stretch into three and a half.

In thirty years, we should be a little over three and a half.

I cannot say.

Zoosh got to you.

No, we have our own guides.

How long do you live? What is your society like, your families? Do you live in a way we would understand?

Only partly. Our society has a great deal to do with music and tone, which is part of the reason we're attracted to crystal life forms—because they are connected to color. We generally do not produce more than one child per family in order to maintain our civilization at a certain level of population. We do not have a marriage ceremony as you do, but we tend to take a life mate. We live anywhere from 1,200 to 1,700 of what you now measure as years.

Have you always been on Saturn? Are you all exploring other places, or is Saturn your home and that's what you're exploring?

Saturn is our home and that's all we feel the need to explore. Occasionally, we have visitors from the home world, but we are émigrés, and as most immigrants know, once you accept and appreciate your new world, you don't really feel much urge to go back to where you were from.

Is your home planet a water planet?

Yes.

Conditions Inside Saturn

So are you comfortable in a cave with no water?

There is water.

There's water in the caves?

There are places where there are vast lakes and reservoirs of water and some water creatures. Not like the ones on Sirius, but it's kind of nice to have them there.

Water . . . so are there plants?

There are some plants, mostly in the water rather than around it.

And is Saturn like that right now?

I think it is not completely that way now.

Is it going to change radically in thirty years?

I can't say. This is not my field. I was born there when things were established.

So there's no one on the outside of the planet in any other dimension?

I cannot say, but I am not aware of anybody living on the surface of the planet. It is possible, but I am not aware of them.

How do you live? Do you grow your food or do you make it? What is your lifestyle like? Do you live in houses?

You have to ask one question at a time, because I will usually only answer one. As I said, we brought our own buildings and they're inside the caves. We have some food that we grow, and it is sort of a synthetic substance but it sustains us. We draw quite a bit of sustenance from the water and certain crystals that give us some energy. We do not eat as much as you do and have nowhere near the complexity of the food that you eat. It is a sort of a staple diet of a simple, bland foodstuff.

What about education? Do your children use these stones to learn what they want to study?

No. They have cultural studies, much as you do, but instead of studying facts and figures and famous people, they study values—our values. They study cultural values as well, and morals and principles and how to live, things like that. This is what your educational system will come to once it becomes more universalized—once it faces what I believe is the inevitable fact that an educational system needs to prepare somebody for life, not prepare them to be separate from life.

Well, I think our system has been set up to keep us from knowing anything. You know, it's part of the whole experiment.

Well, at some point it will change completely. Someone will say, "Well, that's it, I've had it," and teachers will just rebel and say, "We're not going to teach English anymore. We're going to teach you how to balance a checkbook." And where do you go from there? By the time the children graduate from high school, they'll completely understand how to get along, and they won't have any illusions that everything is supposed to be like the movies. They'll understand that it's give and take and there are up days and down days and all that. They'll be prepared to live in life.

In the real world.

In the world as it exists. And they'll also be prepared to work toward creating a better world within real opportunities, not unrealistic mythologies.

So did the Andromedans pretty much prepare you about what you should take to the Earth colonists on Mars, or did you devise that yourself?

No, we devised that. The Andromedans don't oversee us. They just gave us a few things and suggested that we do a few things, but they do not oversee us. No, we just took what we felt you might benefit from. We didn't give the people we found, the colonists, everything we brought because we brought a broad spectrum of things in case it felt right to give them this or that. We wound up giving them some things, but not everything, just as you might go on a trip and bring many things but not use everything.

Are you the spokesman for the group?

No, but I'm the one who's talking tonight. I do not claim to be a leader, but when we approached the colonists, I spoke because I just happened to be at the front of the group and I was closest to the closest colonist. That wasn't the person who went for the weapon, but it felt appropriate for me to speak, so I did.

Three Genders

Were you all men or both men and women?

Men and women. There is another group of us, an equal group, that is something that is neither men nor women, but humanlike.

Is it what Zoosh has called the third sex?

No. I cannot find terms that describe this for you.

They're totally like you except for gender.

Yes, they have a different gender. They do not reproduce. They are born just like anybody else, but they do not reproduce. They are equal citizens like anybody else.

And there's nothing different about what they do? They don't have special jobs or anything?

No, they're not smarter or more foolish. They're just another group. Not a man, not a woman. I do not have a word for them. Our men and our women are a little different from your men and your women, but they're similar.

In what way? In physiology or culture?

Physiology. A little different.

But you all have equal jobs? There's no gender bias or anything like that?

No. It would be a waste of energy, wouldn't it?

Right. How old are you now?

Length of Life, Past Lives

Oh, about 600.

You're not even middle-aged yet.

No, but we don't really think that way. We don't have an aging process like you do.

You keep your vitality and . . .

We keep our vitality up to about, using your time measurement, a week to ten days before our life ends.

Do you choose the time that your natural cycle ends?

We don't mentally choose it, no. It just happens. We just notice. It's quite obvious when you've been vital your whole life and you suddenly start to feel tired and more like you're resting. This is not really unusual, but we can tell that it is our time.

Do you remember your past lives?

Not readily. We can access them if there is a reason to, but we do not access them for curiosity's sake.

For instance, if you had learned something that would be lifesaving or if you had some talent or skill?

If there is something that is needed and it is unavailable, then people will search their past lives, but only then. We believe that it is not good to search past lives because it is easy to get involved in them and distract yourself from your own life and the lives of those you care about.

The point I was getting to was that you're really aware that you've had past lives, so obviously you'll have future lives. Therefore there's no problem with the end of the natural cycle.

We know that there are past lives and we search them only for the reasons I stated.

But that gives you the confidence that there are future lives.

We don't need that confidence. We know there are future lives.

So you don't have what we have, the fear of death and the trauma.

Well, that's only because you're cut off from more of your good and know-ingness, but that's going to change soon.

You're aware of the whole concept of the Explorer Race?

Not the whole concept, but some.

What would you like to tell the people who will read this?

Just know that there are so many people who are interested in you, not only as a species of Earth humans but in your capacity to survive such difficult situations. Equally, there are those who care about you and want to help. We would have approached you to help long, long ago, but we were guided by our teachers and advisers that the time wasn't right. But the time is coming, and those of you who are very young will probably live to hear about our con-tacting you. Don't fear extraterrestrials. There's nothing to fear but your own fears. The contacts between you and extraterrestrials will be benevolent. The worst it will ever be is boring, but it won't be hostile. Good night.

Thank you very much.

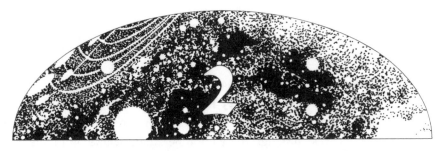

Harmony Is a Way of Life on Future Earth

Tuwass, a Visitor to Future Earth
May 7, 2001

reetings. I have visited your planet about six times, but in your future, not in your now time. On my last visit, I decided to take a chance and extend from your future time. The calendar you use now is no longer in effect, but it would be roughly 480 years experiential time in the future.

I have been studying past Earth civilizations and I have extended in a capsule from that future into the past. The capsule protects me from harm, which would happen were I exposed to the entities you have to deal with. People in that future on Earth no longer have the shielding that you have now to interact with such energies.

Do you mean the veil? You mean we're not veiled?

The shield you have physically, your body, is quite different. I am not of Earth, but I have visited there quite a bit—in the future, you understand.

So we are in a more supple body at that time, we are not as dense physically? Is that what you mean?

No, what I mean is that there is no structure to deflect anything. Your body now has something that this being who contacted me thought you might like to hear about. He calls it "creation connection." He will talk to you about that—his name is Speaks of Many Truths. But he and I have been talking for many experiential years. He thought it might interest you to hear from me.

Yes, I'm delighted that you're here.

Your Future Time Will Be Peaceful and Benevolent

It is a fact that in the future of your Earth time, future Earth people look much like yourselves, although there are others here who look different. Future Earth people feel like they are of substance. If you were able to see future Earth people from where you are now—perhaps I can show you later—you would see people who look rather like yourself, except I believe the arms might be a little longer in some cases, and then there are the others. I have come today to tell you more about that future. I realize that most of your so-called extraterrestrial visitors speak to you about other things, but I thought perhaps there might be some interest in what future Earth looks like. Speaks of Many Truths felt you might be interested.

Absolutely! Yes, please.

The physical bodies of these Earth people in this future time are on average no more than 5 feet 10 inches tall. There are no real tall people anymore. They are not all skinny, but in your time would be considered, perhaps, slim. There is no more consumption of what you call "animals." Diet is made up almost exclusively of fruit and vegetable combinations. Sometimes they even grow in combination—say, for example, some fruits and vegetables grow together. For instance, what you call a daikon now would in the future be combined with strawberry to make a pleasant flavor.

Genetically changed?

No, allowed to combine.

By their own choice?

Yes, and if comfortable with that, allowed to continue to grow that way. This is not exclusive. Daikon and strawberries still grow, but no food is harvested in the same way anymore with big farms, machineries, none of that. Rather it grows where it would feel most welcome. As a result, food grows in optimal ways. What is picked for human consumption is never all that is on the plant. The person who picks feels the plant offer that one but does not pick everything, and the plant is thanked. This is what I would call more heart-centered farming. All people pick their own food. Food grows where people live, so they go out of their shelter into the surrounding territory and pick food because their food grows in such a welcomed way.

A little bit is sufficient, and it does not require much to satisfy and also to nurture.

Hard labor as you know it does not exist anymore—no factories, no brutal hard work. Looking around the planet, government structures are nothing like you have now; they're much more benevolent and comfortable. They're not quite casual, still formal, but more friendly and, in comparison to today, more loose knit. They're not exactly tribal, because the government structure is global, but it has the friendliness of tribal. So there is a comfort zone around government people. Their main function is to keep things running smoothly should there be any problems and to interact with people and cultures from other planets.

As you can tell, it's very peaceful. There's lots of time for people to pursue arts and beauty, and get to know each other and the best of past cultures. Celebrations of previous wars no longer exist. Children do not know about war. Adults, if they choose, are allowed to study it, but not its brutal nature. They can only study the nature of conflict, with a bias in what they can study toward resolution of conflict—meaning that conflict does not come up between individuals or groups of individuals in that time, but it might be a factor for visiting cultures occasionally. Therefore, adult citizens are allowed to study it somewhat so they understand it and are not frightened should they observe it.

What if they're observing it on some recorded database or something?

No, that is not allowed—if they observe it from a visiting culture. Perhaps people will be visiting from extraterrestrial places and the visitors will have an argument, even a disagreement—not coming to blows, not heated like you have now, but compared to what they are used to, it would be almost violent, maybe raising voices, like that. Adults are allowed to study this so that when they see it, they will not be alarmed and can direct children to do other things, to not stare. Children stare all over, not just on Earth in your time.

There is almost no need for medical practice because food is so compatible with the human body and the human body so welcoming of that food that there is almost no disease. When I say "almost," I mean that sometimes visitors from other planets might have some discomforts. So there is a facility where they might receive any medical treatment they might need, but medical treatment is not necessary for Earth people in those times.

There Are Very Few People in Your Future Time

How many people live in that future time?

Very few compared to your current population. The population is controlled to about 1.4 million total.

On the entire planet?

On the whole planet. The permanent full-time population is about 1.4 million.
Do not be frightened and think this means plagues and dying out and all
that. It's just that as time goes on, more understanding will take place of what
is balance and how to live in the best balance. As there is a more benevolent state of being in governments and so on, there will be distinct and clear
understanding of what supports and nurtures life and what does not, of the
acknowledgment that other life has much to offer when it has space to give
that—meaning plants, animals and humans sharing the planet but no one trying to dominate it. There are 1.4 million approximately.

Are they scattered all over the globe?

Yes, all over. But some places that you now think of as where people
live, islands that have a landmass roughly half the size of the island you are
visiting now [in Hawaii]—none of these islands are populated. They are all
left for plants, animals, fish, all of that. Beaches are allowed to be visited
by visitors from space—let's call them visitors, meaning people from other
places—but the permanent population does not, to allow it to be strictly
for the animals. By then, of course, there is understanding that animals are
people from other places.

Have many of them come back? So many of them are leaving now or have already left.

A good question. Quite a few will return—that's why they'll need the
space—some of whom have not been seen for a long, long time, at least in
number. One comes to mind, who you call coelacanth. Another one you
have no name for in your time, but it is a long being, a water being, that used
to be seen in a famous Scottish lake. This is a long water being from a natural
state; naturally it is forty to sixty feet long, maybe eight to ten inches thick.
Sometimes, if the being is old, it can be up to twenty inches thick, even seventy feet long. This is a very nice, very friendly being.

What about a dinosaur? Do any cheerful dinosaurs come back?

I do not think they are present.

*What about the people? Supposedly at some point, instead of being white, yellow,
brown, purple, we're all sort of a light chocolate brown. Has that happened by then?*

Not quite yet.

There's still some variety?

There's still some variety: light-skinned people, dark-skinned people, a color you do not have in your time, a skin color blue. Some people are called that in your time, but this is a skin color more in the spectrum of what artists might call blue. Blue people used to exist on Earth in times gone by, so this is like the return of what you call animals.

Then, of course, there are the others. The others are beings who now occupy a different dimension. These are the beings you know about who came from that difficult planet in the Sirius galaxy, who occupy a slightly denser dimension than you are in now on Earth. But by that time, some of them (not all) have assimilated into Earth culture but still look different, have not taken up the form. Some of them you see now, but now most of them do not, in my perception, do not . . . well, it depends. Some of them are changing and beginning to look like Earth humans, but some of them are still looking humanoid in that future time—a darker color, but humanoid, not human. But this is a complicated topic, separate really. I will not go into that.

You mentioned several times "the others."

Those are the others.

Oh, those are the others. I see. I thought you meant visitors. So there are many, many others?

To give you an idea of how many others, mixed into Earth's population, there would maybe be total a few hundred.

Oh, that's all. What do they do? Do they feel separate, or are they students, or are they teachers?

No, they're like everybody else—fully assimilated.

Wonderful. That's only because they have sort of gotten their lessons quickly?

Yes, they moved quickly into adaptability. It's not lessons so much as adaptability.

That's right. Lessons are over.

And they were able to quickly move. They will sometimes—but it is a one-way trip—choose to return to that denser place and be with the rest of their people. But if they do that, they cannot come back. So it requires absolute dedication. I have observed or heard about two individuals who have done this to help the others in that other place.

How many are there of the ones who are Sirians in the denser dimension of the future? Hundreds? Millions? Thousands?

I'd say I would not speak of that matter. I'm speaking only about this future time.

What dimension are the beings there in? I'm talking numbers—like we're almost at 3.50. Is it dimensional at this time?

Nothing is dimensional, including in your time. Those digits are used to support your sense of separation and individuality, but dimensions do not exist. Nevertheless, to continue that support from your perspective, dimension is first observed. One sees a flat surface, then around the corner sees other surfaces, notices three dimensions. That is how dimension came to be used. So from your *perception*—this is like a hint for the reader, especially a physicist reader—the dimension would be 4.7.

The Explorer Race Has Moved On

So the Explorer Race people have gone. They are out exploring, right?

The Explorer Race has moved on. Fortunately, certain people in your time, people who have the wanderlust or nomadic people in your time—who are not always welcomed, I might add, in your time—have permeated your culture and assimilated more in your time and in the future of your time (just a little bit into the future), which prompted an even greater desire by your culture to explore planets. It won't be too long into your future from your time that citizens—not just military, but citizens—can fly up in space. Once people start doing that on a regular basis, everyone will want to do it. But this is largely supported by certain nomadic peoples in your time. I have observed this. These nomadic peoples, their energy supports the desire to do this. I know *you* have a desire to do this, but not everyone does. You think you hear about people wanting to fly up in space and see things, but most people don't. You don't know that, do you? Most people on Earth have no interest in flying up in space and seeing things, none at all. This is a surprise to you now.

Certain people in your time are of a nomadic nature, actual cultures such as the Bedouins and the Roma. These cultures were always intended not to remain separate, even though they have tried because they have been made to feel so unwelcome that those remaining kept contained amongst themselves . . . I digress here, but it's important. When they would go out and be amongst others, they were often threatened.

But in the future of your time, they become more welcomed. And their infusion into other cultures is what prompts the vast population on Earth to want to explore. The fact that these groups and other nomadic peoples have managed to maintain their existence is what allows this desire to build on a global basis.

So is that where the humans went, then? They went off to colonize other planets?

Not to colonize, but to explore. Once it becomes feasible, everybody wants to do it. But other things are happening, not the least of which is the awareness that you cannot have billions and billions and billions of people living on one planet and expect that to work. And your former method of reducing the population is not acceptable.

War, yes.

Or disease—that's not acceptable either. So scientists, governments, heart-centered people and religions gradually formulate this awareness. Some resist, but others embrace the fact that harmony cannot be a philosophical idea only, that the example of the plants, the harmony of plants, is intended to suggest a means by which human beings can live—observing nature, yes?

The fact that plants do not always get along in your time is because humans have, intentionally or otherwise, moved plants into places where they weren't intended to be. This is intended to show humans in your time how your lack of balance can be reflected by a world that you think of as balanced. So-called alien plant species—meaning not alien where they're from, but alien where humans have inadvertently or intentionally put them—are a lesson for you, and many people have observed this. What I'm saying is not new, but it becomes more and more an ideal. The message soaks in, how you cannot choose who will live and who as a species will be allowed to die out.

The observation of how plants grow in harmony, even same species—not how humans plant them, but how they naturally grow when they are welcomed in the Earth and grow in the wild—more observation about this and more dissemination of that observation is likely in your time. The observation in recent years has been scientific and therefore has had almost no bearing for the future. The scientific is unnecessary. If a scientist observed human life, family life, and reported on it in scientific terms in a scientific journal, the average citizen would most likely be offended—at the very least, disinterested.

So this needs to be done by heart—by shamanic people maybe, but at least by people who lovingly, in an honoring and respectful way, observe, notice and report. That becomes more of a goal that societies work toward. This has been done by many people already, but it is not the current theme that governments and peoples are striving toward. It will become this, however. I did not mean to digress. Let's talk about the future.

No, no, this is very important. It's very interesting, how we got from here to there.

Travel Is Not So Common

Okay, in the future there are a million people?

There are 1.4 million approximately—a little more than that, but I am rounding it off.

So what about transportation? How do they get around? Do they have airplanes, automobiles, ships, trains, boats?

No.

What do they have?

Nothing.

How do they get around?

They walk. By that time, it's understood that the need to travel . . . it's like those so-called alien species (that's why I talked about that in your time), plants that are at home in one place are brought to another place, not at home. And they either don't do well, or do too well and take over and are not compatible with local plants. People recognize that where they are born is where they may be the most compatible.

There are other means to discover that are understood and embraced in those times. If an individual would be more comfortable elsewhere, there is a method of transportation that will take them there when they are old enough to make such a journey, meaning in young adulthood. They can have some time there and see if it feels better or if they like it better. Usually they return home, even if they like it better in the other place. But they might return there when they get to be an adult.

What is that method of transportation?

It is a vehicle, what you might call today a "flying ship." It does not consume energy to travel but rather floats about. It generally travels maybe about three to four hundred feet off the ground. It utilizes energy by acquisition, pulls it in from the atmosphere, and if the atmosphere is cloudy, then it has a means to store, like a battery. It can also acquire energy from the Sun, but not solar as you understand it.

Each community has one of those, then? Or is there only one? Or does the government have it?

They are not owned. Ownership is unknown. Rather, they are available. It would be like in your time having bicycles parked, and people just ride them to where they need to go and leave them for the next person. But there are pilots—not automated, but pilots who are trained—and that's what they do. So, generally speaking, there are no more than four or five of these vehicles operating at any time. Not that many people need to travel.

What about technology? Computers?

No, but there are small objects, not much larger than a fingertip, that are sometimes carried and can produce, if necessary, information—or, in connection with other objects, can guide a person to where he or she needs to go to. These are very small objects—they're not computers; they do not display words. But a person would pick one up, hold it in the palm of his left hand, grab it if he didn't know where to go to get something or something like that. Then he would just know in his mind where to go. Or if it's too far, it would come to that person, someone would bring it in one of those vehicles. Most often, everything you need is right in your nearby area. One might think that people don't need to walk anymore, but it's understood in those times that being physical—walking, going places—is good.

Art, Language and Education Are Very Different

What about language?

There's a homogeneous language.

One language?

One language. It is not too much like the languages you have right now. I can do script perhaps—let me try. I have seen this. [Writes.] It looks something like this—I make a couple of lines. It's curvy, like that.

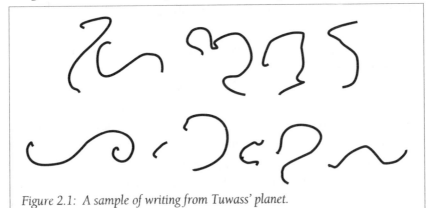

Figure 2.1: A sample of writing from Tuwass' planet.

Left to right?

Left to right.

How interesting. What about trade? If there are artists and they do crafts, they would want to trade with others on the planet, wouldn't they?

What for? What you need, you have. Art is created for the pleasure of all. Think about it in your time—what is used to make art? Tell me some things.

Oh, well, there's paint, board, there's chalk, there's ink . . .

Where do those objects come from?

The store.

Where did they come from before the store?

Somebody had to make them.

So they come from nature.

Oh, I see what you mean.

It's nature. Are those natural beings asked, "Do you want to become this material?" Most likely, no. So in that time, art is only created with complete permission of that which is found. That's why often one finds art at the beach. Sand is happy to be formed into something as long as it is close enough to the waves so that it can re-form in its natural way when the tide comes in. So impermanent forms of art are much more common.

Permanent forms of art only happen when all material wants to be part of that art. Should any of it not want to . . . after you've placed something into the art creation—whatever that is, maybe a stone or something else—you as the artist would be permanently responsible for that which you placed, would have to check on it regularly to see how it feels: "Do you want to stay here, or do you want to go someplace else?" So the artist has responsibility—he or she can't just grab something and put something on it. There's no more art without permission.

So how are they taught, then? What's the form of education, if they have no communicative devices?

They know what they need to know. They have so-called "vertical wisdom," as your friend calls it. Here's where the government comes in. Should visitors bring wisdom or information of their own, it must be exposed through the government to see if it's compatible with the population on Earth. What is compatible is allowed to be stored. The information storage system is not unlike that little object one might hold in a hand or put in a fold of the fabric one wears. If it is something of beauty that is comfortable for people in that time, it's allowed to be shared, but it is first screened, you might say, by government people.

These government people sound like another total class of people.

They are wise; they might be called "elders" in some populations. They have people amongst them who are trained to be able to interact, not unlike your diplomats in your time, statesmen. But the further their training goes that allows them to be exposed to visitors, the less contact they are allowed to have directly with the population. So it is a sacrifice to be a member of government. If you have this exposure, then you will have thoughts, feelings of that exposure that will affect everybody. Thus government service is truly a service and to some extent a personal sacrifice. That is the case somewhat in your time, but it is more so in that time.

The Future Is a Place of Utter Harmony

What is the point of this enforced simplicity? The souls who are incarnating there . . . they sound like vacation lives or something. What is it that these souls are looking for when they incarnate in these bodies?

To live in a place of beauty and utter harmony. Can you think how many people on Earth now in your time would love to live a life there?

Oh, yes.

It's not as simple as you think; it's just utter harmony all the time. One can do many things. It sounds to you at the moment as if it would be restrictive, but think of how you have felt when you are completely open on a spiritual basis. It means that all things, experiences, possibilities and so on that are compatible with you as an individual in that open state anywhere in the universe can be experienced by you at any time should you focus in those directions. You do not just get your interactions with others from visitors but are wide open all the time. This is not unlike some planets in your time in your universe now. So this future on Earth is similar to cultures on other planets in your time now.

So it's very simple physically but very rich spiritually and emotionally and interactively with people.

Well said. It is simple physically, meaning things are done in a certain way. If you are not sure how to do something, you just follow your natural feeling, which is a warmth, a harmony feeling. You cannot make a mistake as long as you follow that feeling. You will know when you are making a mistake because you do something and that feeling goes away. Then you stop, retreat a little bit until you find that feeling and then do whatever you are doing in a different way so that feeling remains.

How wonderful. Why do the alien visitors come? What are they looking for? They're not trading—they just come to go to the beach or something?

They come to visit as people travel on other planets in your time, planet to planet—just for pleasure, for interest, for curiosity. It is the same in that time. There is a visitor greeting center. People are met in the visitor greeting center, which is on a long . . . it looks like a jetty, but it is an actual landmass and the visitor's center is out in the water. That's where a ship might land. It's far enough away from the general population centers so that the natural radiation of the ship and its occupants does not affect them.

There is a form of energy isolation around the visitor's center for two reasons: one, to protect the population of Earth, and two, to allow visitors to have their own energy reflected back upon them so that they feel welcome. They feel like they are landing someplace safe that will support and nurture them with their needs. That is where the medical facility is and so on. It will support their needs, and it is also a place where there is a permanent government establishment to interact with. Vehicles that might land are directed to that place, and there is more than one such place around the Earth—there are three or four.

All Your Infrastructure Will Be Gone

So in the next few years, there is an incredible physical, material, technological thrust to get people off the planet, and then by this time all of that is just . . . what happened to it?

It's not a thrust so much, to be specific here, but an attraction. Nomadic peoples who are in your time beginning to integrate more with the general population and infuse that energy . . . the nomadic is not part of the masculine, it's feminine, thus the attraction. It will be as if people of Earth will notice stars and get interested in planets for the first time. In your life, you think that most people you meet have that interest; in fact, only about half, or fewer than half, do. But that is your way of thinking as an individual. Most people on Earth now—other than children, of course—do not have that interest, but that will change. Yet until that changes, the desire for the Explorer Race will not be present. Right now you have been given this information about the Explorer Race, but other than its history and the present dynamics, the actual desire to go out and explore planets is only desired by very few. But that will change.

I'm thinking that if you look back 450 years ago, you see physical structures on Earth that were built. There are things that go back several thousand years. So 480 years in the future, I'm just wondering, what does the planet look like? Are all the tall buildings gone? Are all the ships gone?

In the future, you mean?

In 2480, yes.

What does it look like? Completely different. There are no tall buildings at all. Tall buildings don't last.

But then you have rubble, you have metal, you have infrastructure.

One does not see any of that. I am not speaking as a citizen of those times; I'm speaking as a visitor. I do not live on Earth in that time—I am a visitor; I have visited. I have never seen a building, as you call it, that is more than maybe fifteen feet tall. That's as big as they get. Shelters are not fully enclosed. All have at least one or two walls completely open to the space. Weather is very benevolent all the time.

All over the planet?

All over the planet. Some places have more rain than others, but it's always green and lush. Nobody cuts plants. Plants grow only so far as they feel welcome, then stop. Just like people—people only grow to 5 foot 10, maybe 10½, then stop. There is harmony, no competition for space. Harmony does not have competition as a factor.

But we've got churches from 1,000 B.C. and A.D. 1,000, and they're still there. We've got pyramids, we've got structures on the planet that nobody's maintaining, they're just there.

There are no pyramids.

No pyramids?

No. As I say, nothing over fifteen feet tall, period.

Future Garments Are Much Simpler

Now let's talk about the future. It is not my desire to be time captain to explain all of this.

Okay. [Laughs.] That's a good phrase.

I can only tell you about the future, but I'm not here to say how it got to be that way because that is not my interest. I have studied past civilizations, but I have not studied many civilizations as far back as you. I only know about Speaks of Many Truths' civilization because we have a spirit connection. I have not studied the population that built the pyramids or other artifacts in your time. I can observe some of these artifacts and they are very interesting, but they are not in my field of interest. My field of interest is populations that have striven toward harmony.

Oh, I see. So if people choose to be born along a seashore, then that's where they live. Are there deserts anymore? Are all the deserts lush now?

There are a few deserts, yes, because there are beings, even in your time, who like to exist in deserts. So there are some deserts—not many, but some. No human beings live there, and no others live there either. There are only what you call animals living there.

So the humans live where it's lush and green. What about mountains? Are all the mountains still here? And do they still have snow on them?

Yes, there are mountains here and some tops of mountains where there is snow. There are even a few outposts for people who like to experience snow, but they do not go everywhere where there is snow. They just are there to have the pleasure of the change of temperature. It is warm and comfortable and lush down below the mountains, but there are a few places up on some mountains (not all) where one can enjoy cold and snow if they like. Not many people go there, but sometimes they do. Especially young people like to see what it's like, what it's about, and experience the fun of snow.

But if they go, they walk.

Oh yes, they walk and walk slowly, very slowly, so as to assimilate gradually to the change of condition. There are no outer garments. They must assimilate the body so that their body becomes warm based upon spiritual and physical means. This adaptation is now known to some people in your time. Mystics and some monks can change their body temperature so that they're comfortable with only slight outer garments even in the coldest environment. This is known in this future time, so youngsters, young people, young adults do that—they walk slowly. It's not vertical steps; the road goes back and forth, back and forth.

Like switchbacks, yes.

There are places for them to stop and camp and eat on the way up. It takes time, but by the time they get to the top, it can be cold and snowing and they are comfortable in their usual light garment.

Oh, they do wear something.

Everybody wears something. It is like a light outer garment, loose fitting.

Pants or a tunic?

It is like pants and a . . . what is a tunic?

It would be something that came from the shoulders maybe down to the knees and is just loose fitting—no sleeves or anything.

No sleeves?

No sleeves.

There are sleeves.

Oh, okay, in this case sleeves, like a long shirt or something?

A long shirt, yes. It sort of comes down and then tapers back a ways. There is sometimes sort of like a gold line around it, but otherwise it is sort of like white but not white, an off-white color. Then it's loose fitting and somewhat billows—it sort of billows here on the sleeves and then is loose fitting through the upper body. There are no collars and no buttons—like a fabric sash and loose-fitting pants, no belt. There's the same kind of cuff on the pants, sort of slanted, sometimes with a little gold-colored decoration, sometimes not. There are no shoes.

No shoes?

No shoes. No one has shoes. In your time, you do not put shoes on your hands—am I correct?

Right.

That's because hands need to touch, explore. But in your time, feet are exactly the same. People put shoes on because they are used to it, but although feet have different duties and capabilities, they are just like hands. They need to touch the ground. This is not always compatible in your time because the ground is not allowed to be its natural self usually. But in that time, people know that feet are like hands and wouldn't even consider putting on light fabric over feet. That would be like putting on light fabric over hands. You would not do that in your time either, unless of course you're protecting them for some reason.

If it's cold, yes. Oh, how interesting. Who creates these garments? Does everyone make their own, or is there bartering within each little group?

I say again, bartering does not exist. There is no such thing. If someone makes something that others need, you make more than you need so you always have extra in case someone comes along and says, "Oh, can I wear that for a time?" Then you say, "Yes, I have extra," for example. So not everybody weaves, but some people like to weave. But remember, where does fabric come from in your time?

Nature.

So in this time the fabric only comes from—there's no silk, okay?—a relative of cotton. Cotton in that time is very silky soft. There are some types of cotton in your time like this that are very soft, but it's even softer in that future time. It's very carefully and lovingly gathered by some individuals. They gather it in the same way one might pick a fruit or vegetable from a plant. So this is an ongoing process from plants that have it to offer, though not year-round.

So this material is available, and then is spun the old-fashioned way onto looms. Nothing that makes up the loom, or any so-called machine, is there because . . . all parts of it are there because they want to be part of it. Should a portion of the loom want to go someplace else, it does. This means that the person who uses the loom is responsible for all parts that make up that loom. If some part wants to go back, perhaps, to be with its ancestors, then it must do so. So one often has spare parts around. Some people do the weaving of garments—not others. The difference is that garments themselves, as I say, with this variation of cotton, last almost indefinitely. So the idea of handing down a garment to a youngster . . . hand-me-downs are considered desirable.

I have studied this; I've gone into the future of this time as well. There are some garments that have been and will be around. Occasionally they pick up decoration on the way, not unlike the garments of your time. I am aware of some garments . . . 700 years the same garment is passed along and still worn. This is not unknown in your time. There are some people who wear ancient garments in your time that are hundreds of years old but still serviceable. There is a similar situation in the future but in greater harmony.

So the people work part-time at something they really want to do?

If they like. Work is not required. Do you think you'd fit in?

It would be really difficult. So how many people live in one place? Do they have an extended family or people who come to be there?

Extended family is not at all unusual. You find that often. Sometimes there are enclaves of young people, not unlike in your time.

Like communes or something like that?

No, not communes, not just living together in the same building. There are no buildings in that time, no big buildings unless it is to greet visitors or for government structures. But there are no big buildings to house large groups of people; there are small structures only. An enclave would be . . . maybe some young people would like to live together for a time, so they live in the same general area but in small structures.

I Am Here to Study

How did you get to know so much when visitors can't interact with the people?

I study from afar. I have not interacted with anybody in this time except government contacts. But because of my field of interest, I'm allowed to use something like a view screen. I am not allowed to observe life as it actually goes on, but I'm allowed to see records like that. So I can see what has gone on. This is so as to not interfere with life.

But if they have no technology, how do they make records?

They do not require the technology. I have it. I think they have some technology like that, but they have no use for it. But I do not require it. The reason I say this is that they have facilities in their government and visitor's center that I have not used or even seen. I think they might have some things like this, but I do not need it.

You said at the beginning that they might be allowed to study their history but not the violent aspects of war.

They might have something like that. But when I come, I stay in the visitor area. I am made welcome. I have friends now who are government-contact friends, and I enjoy having time talking to them. They explain their culture to me. If I want to communicate with them, they are very friendly and helpful, but I have no direct contact with the population.

You understand that I am here to study. Some visitors, I believe, are allowed to interact directly with the population if harmony is compatible. But I am here to study. I am interested in civilizations that have striven toward harmony, whether they have achieved harmony. But my civilization has not done so yet. Therefore, my personal harmony is not equal to the task of interacting with people in this time. However, when I interact with government contacts and generally when I visit this place, I am wearing like a suit. It is not like a space suit, but it is a suit that covers me and keeps my natural energy from radiating out to others.

I would not be comfortable in your time—too dense, as you say. A few hundred experiential years in the future—then I would be comfortable. But in this future time I like to visit, from which I'm talking to you, my energy is not comfortable for them, just as your energy is not comfortable for me. I have not gone that far yet. I am not that much in harmony as these people.

So you're speaking through Robert only from a distance—you're not feeling his energy or my energy?

I do not understand. Is that important?

Well, you said you couldn't interact with humans here.

I can't interact with humans in that future time directly—no direct contact.

But you said we'd be too dense for you in this time right now.

I could wear my suit and be in your time, but I have not. I am in an extended capsule that entirely protects me from density in your time— I'm in your time in that capsule. I can see around in your time but I do not feel.

Oh, so you can speak through Robert but you can't feel him or me. I see. Have you channeled through him before?

Not through human being in your time.

In the future? In the past?

We don't call it channeling.

What do you call it?

A form of communion—not the only form, but a form. I've done this occasionally.

The Soul Leaves the Body When It's Time

So there are 1.4 million people—how many of the people, then, are government people?

I will inquire. [Pause.] Roughly 700. There are currently 749, but they say there are no less than 700 and no more than 749. There have never been more than 749.

So when they retire, do they have their own little retirement area? They have to live amongst themselves?

If they are no longer able to interact with the general population, then they must have an area where they stay near where they have been working, near where the visitor's center is, the government area. They retire, as you say, in that area, but retiring is almost unknown.

They work until they are ready to leave the body, then?

Pretty much. There's no disease as you know it. In a culture of complete harmony, the soul leaves the body when it's time to go on. The soul is needed elsewhere, so it goes on. There's no struggle to stay in the body—that would not be harmony.

About how long do they live, then?

In terms of your time, their life cycle is approximately 149 years. Understand, you have the option: You can live 149 years, but some people live close to (I'll give you the exact number) 247 years, anywhere in between that. Generally, one does not live less than 149 years. In your time, it's possible for a soul to come and live just a few years—that's not possible there. If you are born there, you are going to be there for at least 149 years.

Then what happens? They die and the soul goes on—then what do they do with the body?

When the soul is ready to go on, you walk out in a special area. You're often accompanied by friends, family. In that special area, the body is assimilated into the ground. If you were to see it, you would say . . . let me see. They don't want me to discuss this too much, but let me say this: When there are no more life signs, then the soul has gone on, and people can observe the soul going on. They don't want me to discuss it, but the body is returned to Earth in a certain way that is actually a way that exists in your time—part of nature. I do not know why they don't want me to tell you. It seems completely reasonable to me and natural. But for some reason they don't want me to tell you, and I must honor that.

They Can Follow the Feeling of Harmony

So they can literally move in consciousness? If they want to go visit someone on another planet, they can just expand or connect or do . . . what?

Yes, not unlike spiritual people do in your time. They are open all the time. But because of the nature of their openness and harmony, it's not a two-way road. They can go to other places, always following that feeling of harmony, that pathway along the feeling of harmony—not just like telephones, but the extension always going along that good, warm feeling in the body. They can follow that one way, make contact and come back on a similar warm route. But not the other way—not people radiating to them like that, no. They can go out, but others cannot come in.

Do you know why?

I already explained that.

It wouldn't be harmonious.

That's right. They cannot because others may not come in using the same harmony method. Harmony is not just a goal; it's a way of life. It's a given. It is like for you the Sun, the Moon, the stars. Harmony is a given.

It sounds like there must be a waiting line—it sounds like an absolute paradise.

It's paradise, but it does require what you would now call spiritual mastery. That's why not too many people are there. Lots and lots of soul journey is necessary. You understand, the Explorer Race have had some . . . ah yes, they tell me that no one is allowed to come in your time without having had one life of spiritual mastery, yes. So you would all qualify, those of the Explorer Race, but there's no Explorer Race there in this future—they're out exploring.

So there's no government?

There's no authoritarian government.

Is there something that represents them to the outer world?

.No.

They have no what we call policemen or military or . . . ? I can see that. So there's total truth because everyone knows everything about everyone else, right?

Yes, there are no secrets. Let's right now see if I can create a means by which you can see, because I cannot do this much longer. You have the capacity to see lights sometimes, so relax and try to put yourself in that space. Don't suppress the imagination. [Long pause.]

Well, I didn't see anything, but it's like I heard words that weren't mine: water, lush, green, warm, loving. I had feelings and heard words, but I didn't see anything.

Good, that is something. Sorry you could not see, but perhaps you will dream.

Well, it's because I don't sit and meditate a lot.

But you had words, so that is something.

Well, the thing is, the feeling was so beautiful.

You had the feeling, then. That's what was most important. The feeling is adequate. Relax and enjoy the feeling for a while.

It was wonderful.

We Look Quite a Bit Different from You

Can you tell me a little bit about where you're from? Is it in this universe or some-place else? What kind of civilization do you have?

It is in this universe. My people do not want me to tell you exactly where, but I will . . . no. The Explorer Race will be making a stop there.

So it is someplace we've heard of before?

Yes, sometimes not everyone wants to . . . my people are shy. But you will be making a stop there, so it is to our advantage to have some idea of you, yes.

Can you say anything about yourself, about your life or anything without disclosing where you're from?

I do not look like you. If you were to see me . . . I don't think I could go so far as to say "humanoid," no. I look quite a bit different—I have an exoskeleton.

Oh, how interesting. Are you tall? Short?

I'm not sure it applies, but in length, in size, I'm smaller than you. When your people come meet our people, you will probably not see us directly but will meet . . .

Diplomats?

Yes, diplomats who look more like you who interact with us.

How can they look more like us if they're one of yours? Have they been created to be diplomats or cloned or something?

They volunteered from other planets.

From the Pleiades?

Yes.

So you do you have a tail?

Yes, but not wag-wag, like dog or cat. But it would look like a tail structure to you. You would say, "Well, is that a tail or an extension of the body? I'm not sure."

So the exoskeleton comes all the way down to the floor in the back like that. It's very sensitive, right?

If you don't mind, I will not say too much what I look like.

I've Traveled All Over the Universe

So you are a scholar of some type?

Well, I like to think of myself as a scholar. That's a nice term. I study, not books, but through accumulation of observation . . . extrapolation, yes?

So how many planets have you been to before this one looking for harmony?

Ninety-three.

Ninety-three, all in this universe?

Yes, all in this universe.

So you're very technological, then. Your people have a very good craft, then.

I don't think of us as technological when I think of some other species who are vastly more technological. Rather, I would say that we have the means.

The means to . . . ?

Travel.

To travel. But you created them yourself?

Not always. We have exchanged—not traded, but exchanged—some with other cultures, no other beings you are discussing. Zeta Reticulans, but it is not in their nature to handle the machinery as you might call it. They don't think of it that way. So we have made such exchanges with some other cultures; we have some technology from the Pleiades, other places. But some also we create.

So the craft you're in—do you run it or fly it? Or do you have like a group?

No, a pilot. They do not always wait around for me.

So they drop you off?

Yes, and go elsewhere. If I have an extended stay someplace and they don't need to be there, they drop me off and . . .

Pick you up when you're done. What about this capsule, then? That's something that comes out of the craft. It can go back in time?

Yes, the capsule is associated with time. It's not exactly what you would call a physical capsule but something in between. It's hard to describe in your terminology. It protects me as long as I don't move around too much.

How far back have you been?

This is as far back as I've come. My communication with Speaks of Many Truths is over time. Neither of us has seen the other, although I have some idea now based upon observing your time of what he might look like. And he has described himself, just as I have described myself.

Well, actually, we have books with paintings on the covers that don't really look like him, it's just a . . . [Shamanic Secrets series]

Ah yes, he has mentioned this. He says the pictures don't look like him but he appreciates the intention.

Well, we didn't really want it to look like him because he didn't want people to know what tribe he was from.

Ah, that is a good thing, then.

You Have a Good Feeling about Harmony

What about family structure? Do you have wives, children, husbands?

We do not have that. We do not have male/female. One only.

One only, but you can give birth?

No.

You clone?

Yes.

So do you live in extended groups or families?

Weren't you going to ask more about the future time after feeling it?

Yeah, it just felt so good—blissful."

Oh, all right then. There is limit to what I can tell you about my people, partly because the Explorer Race must have the capacity to discover for the first time my people the way they are. My people will be the Explorer Race's first contact with beings who look significantly different than them. So a certain level of surprise is desirable.

Okay, we'll just leave it then, unless there's anything else you could say that would not interfere with that.

For example, to the degree that Zeta Reticulan beings look different than you, we would be several degrees past that. So we are not what I would call humanoid.

But, I mean, it doesn't really matter. You have the same soul, you know. You could have been humanoid or not humanoid.

Exactly. All beings have the same soul structure, which allows a basic form of communion between all beings—at least, this is my understanding. It is time to stop now.

All right, thank you so much.

I would like to say greetings to you Earth people and to encourage you. You are doing very well considering not only what you have to do to achieve harmony in the future, but considering that you do have a good feeling about harmony. I am impressed. So may you all have a happy life.

Thank you very much.

I'll give you a name. Let's see if I can draw it in your script. Spelled out, it's T-u-w-a-s-s.

Tuwass. Oh, how beautiful. Thank you, thank you very much. Good night.

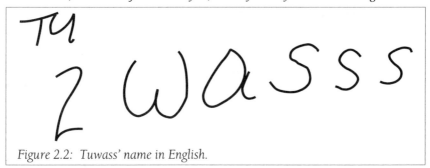

Figure 2.2: *Tuwass' name in English.*

❋　　　　　❋　　　　　❋

This is Speaks of Many Truths. I thought perhaps you might be interested to hear from my friend.

Oh, extremely. Thank you very much.

My friend and I have communicated for a long time now, and it occurred to me that this is a . . .

A very important thing, yes. And for me it was interesting.

I think that's all for now. Good night.

Oh, thank you very much.

※　　　　　※　　　　　※

[Robert]: Most of them whom I could see had one or two walls that just weren't there. The structure was built so that it would be completely open to the surroundings. And it's very attractive and there's plenty of room. It's not like a tropical jungle or anything like that; there's plenty of room and lots of space and no real big trees overhanging or anything like that.

I know where they went! Of course! The pyramid and all the buildings are in 3.0-, 3.5-dimension Earth, and in this future time we're in 4.7. I couldn't figure out what happened to all the buildings! It's a different dimension—that explains it. Of course. I was thinking, "Well, 500 years ago we had churches and they're still here. What happened to the buildings? What happened to the pyramids?"

[Robert]: Where's McDonald's?

Did you see him?

[Robert]: Yeah. I don't think he really wants me to describe him, but I've channeled someone before who doesn't look exactly like him but is similar in appearance, maybe a little smaller, when I was training in the early days, before I went public. But that being was very difficult for me to channel. Of course, in the early days it was different.

It wasn't this guy—he said he's never been back in time this far before.

[Robert]: Oh, yeah.

He sounded delightful. He had an exoskeleton and a tail, but he couldn't say very much about himself because his planet is the first nonhumanoid planet that the Explorer Race is going to visit. That explains it. Of course—their future time is in a different dimension.

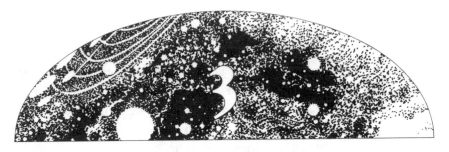

ETs Create an
Alternate Path to Earth

Xzhetah, Zeta Hybrid
September 10, 2001

My name is Xzhetah. I am a being who is of Zeta influence but not only that. I'm a hybrid—I don't like that word, it makes me feel like an ear of corn. But I am a cross between a Zeta Reticulan being and a human being.

Oh, how interesting.

My people have a particular interest in the development of your people. Therefore, we stay close to your planet almost always; there are two, three ships here all the time. I'm assigned to one of those ships, and I can brief you on anything you need to know in regards to the ET, as you say, or UFO contact in recent years and currently.

ETs Have Found a Means to Create an Alternate Path

I'd like to talk to you a little bit about you and your culture. I had heard—and obviously it was an error—that three, four, five years ago with the High Frequency Active Auroral Research Program [HAARP], no craft could get in and they had to move the motherships back way out, almost to the edge of the solar system. Evidently, that's not correct. Who is coming and for what?

That was true for a time, but there was a means to create an alternate path. If your planet was not in transition from one dimension to another, it would have been more difficult. But because you are in that transition, it is possible to travel in what I would call alternative pathways to your time, and that works. What we do is, instead of focusing on your planet, we focus on certain individuals on your planet and your time. That way we do not make a direct physical connection, at least with navigation, between your planet and our systems for travel. In that way, we are able to avoid excessive interference.

What about when you get here? I thought they were shooting you down. It's safe when you get here?

It is safe—we cannot be touched because of the way we arrive. Also, they have not figured out yet how to locate us, because the tools and techniques they have at their disposal do not have enough spiritual qualities or love centers to be able to access us. Of course, only beings who have benevolent interest toward the human race can use this system. Therefore, until your technology becomes heart-centered, which some people are working on, you will not be able to regularly detect or easily communicate with us other than by methods such as we are using here, or in the case of other individuals, some form of heart telepathy. By "heart telepathy," I mean it is possible to bring through words and so forth, but there needs to be a heart connection also.

How many years in our time did it take, and who figured this out?

Our teachers were quick to suggest that we use this method, but it took time to fine-tune the means. So it didn't take that long to be resolved, but the application took longer.

So did each civilization figure it out independently, or did you share it?

We shared it, of course. We are not greedy.

No, but it was your cross-cultural group, your native people who figured it out, right?

No, I could not say that we were first or only. When we found out about it, we shared it. We didn't ask if anybody else was working on that too.

So who now is coming into the planet? Andromedans?

Sometimes.

Pleiadians?

Yes.

Sirians?

Rarely.

Zetas?

Occasionally.

Arcturians?

Not very often.

I don't know who else comes here. Do the Alpha Centauri come here?

Not very often.

So who else comes who I'm not tuning in on?

A lot of beings come from far away who have longtime traveling expeditions. None of the names would make much sense to you. But, you know, it is not at all unusual for civilizations to send out ships to travel just to engage with other populations in a friendly way or to find out more about life in other places, not unlike your own ambitions with your cosmonauts and astronauts. Such things are of long standing in other places. So there is a steady stream of beings and ships from these distant places, sometimes not even in this universe. But to travel from one universe to another takes a highly tuned spiritual civilization. Technology cannot do it. It can only be done if there is very well focused love energy, and it has to be very broad. It can't just be . . . let me say, it is well-focused but it has to be applied in a very broad way, meaning that, generally speaking, whatever universe you are coming from, you have to in some way represent in love energy every variable in that universe.

You also have to be able to equalize by essentially touching the other universe. You obviously can't know what's in that other universe, but you have to equalize all that you are, all that you represent in those variables with which you are passing into, so that nothing in the universe you are coming from will in any way offend or harm the universe you are going into. This means that you might have to leave some energy behind, since it might not be compatible with another universe, and that as you go in, you have to have a great deal of receptivity. So you move in very slowly to make sure that whatever is in that new universe you are going into does not harm you and (this is almost as important if not more so) that it will not travel through your vehicle into the universe from which you are coming from, in case it is not compatible with that universe. So it is almost like an open switch passing through circuits, which has a great many checks and balances so that both circuits will be safe.

Our Culture Is Considered by Others to Be Eccentric

Do you travel, do you know about this? Or have you traveled in other universes?

We have heard from travelers about this, but we have not done so. Our interests are more homey. We are interested in the Zeta culture, but we're also interested in the Earth culture.

What percentage are you?

We are about 51 percent Zeta Reticulan and about 49 percent human.

Describe yourself a little bit, if you would.

We are taller than the average Zeta Reticulan being—perhaps four and a half, five feet tall is typical. Our eyes are not so big. They are a little bigger than yours, but not so very big. Our skin color runs from brown to dark brown. We have been described by others as being stylish. But this means that we are interested in our appearance. So we do not appear only one way. We might have different garments that we wear, often of bright colors, but sometimes something subdued. We have a particular skintight garment that we wear, and we often wear it when in the actual act of traveling because it feels comforting. It is a dark garment, but then, to use your body as an example, right around the chest to slightly above where the legs start, there is a weave in the pattern that represents stars. We find this most comforting as a means to travel. We tend to be artistic and often personable. We are sometimes described [laughs] by other cultures as eccentric—but not destructive or self-destructive.

Just creative, yes.

They sometimes describe us as eccentric because of the combination of the Zeta intellect with the broad variety of personality associated with the human being.

You sound wonderful. Do you have your own planet somewhere?

Yes. We have a planet in the Zeta Reticulan cultural influence, but it is almost nothing like what one might see where Zeta specifically—I prefer to call them the parent race—where they live. There it is much more modern, you would call it . . . modern art, new things. We like to express ourselves in visual and musical ways. Our culture is very up-to-date.

What do you do here on Earth? Do you monitor us in some way? Do you monitor our development? Do you monitor the planet? What specifically do you do?

We do not take human beings on board much, because we are not involved scientifically in any way. We don't do science. We're more a kindred spirit with art, music and culture. So if we bring anybody on board, it is to exchange things like that. We haven't had too many human beings on board, but we've had a few. Also, we will sometimes make connections in dreams with people. People can accept us in their dreams more easily.

Than in real interaction, you're saying?

No, I wouldn't say that. It's just that we don't want to become overly influenced during your time of transition from extreme discomfort, from our perspective, to one of more benevolence. I don't think we can easily accommodate your extreme discomfort, because you have to remember, as basically artistic people, we are highly receptive.

Oh, I see. How, particularly, was this receptivity gained? Was it genetically? Are you cloned, or do you undergo regular birth?

We were initially cloned and given the opportunity to choose that birth method. We haven't had to choose yet because there's no need. It's a long way off before anybody is likely to die. So we haven't had to choose how to reproduce ourselves. We have a stable population. What else did you ask? You've got to ask one question at a time because I won't be able to answer more than one.

About how many of you are there?

About 40,000. So there's lots of space.

[Laughs.] But you're here observing. So are you interested in what you can learn from us, or are you interested in teaching us?

We're interested in what we learn. We do not feel in any way that we have much to teach you yet, but someday, when you are ready to interact with us more and even interact with the Zeta beings more, we will probably be there as an intermediary, because we are, you know, so much like you. You will be able to identify with us, certainly your younger people.

What are the other groups coming in to do? Do you watch them? Can you observe them? For what purposes are they coming?

Mostly they're coming to see the children, which is typical, because the children are less likely to be nervous around beings who look different. Occasionally, they are checking in with people they have connected with before—that is the case with the Orions and Zetas and Pleiadians to a great extent. It's not that they're not meeting new people, but that's what they're doing. And they like that. They like to establish a relationship with some individuals and make it a lifelong experience. Whereas with us, we tend to observe the general culture and cull out of the general cultural things we either would like to imitate or things we think we can expand on, putting our own cultural stamp on it, of course.

The Future of Your Weaponization of Space

For how many years have you been coming now? When did you first come after HAARP?

It's hard to say, but we've been coming for a long time. What is it you want to ask? How long we've been coming or . . . ?

I'm sorry, I'll ask it two different ways. How long is this second, this new coming now? Is it the past one, two, three years, after you figured out how to come in on this heart basis?

About two years.

Two years. So when was the first time you came here, then, back before this, originally?

If you remember, we can travel in time.

Oh, you can too!

Almost everybody who travels from planet to planet and place to place, all the ships that come here, travel in time, with very few exceptions. If you don't travel in time, you're not going to get home, most likely.

Hopefully none of your people were involved in any crashes or shootdowns or anything on this planet, true?

That's true.

Good, okay. So with this method, can they still densify into the third dimension so that we can see the craft?

The only way that can be done safely is to leave what I would call a trail—meaning pass very quickly through the dimension you are in and leave an image of one's self, even though you've already moved on to somewhere else. In that way, what you see is something not like this, but something . . . as an analogy, akin to a photograph. That way, you can be seen and be very difficult, if at all possible, to detect, and even if detected, completely safe.

That's because if somebody shoots, there's nobody there.

There's nothing there, just what I would call a latent image, not unlike a wake kicked up by a boat on a lake. You can't hurt the boat much by poking a hole in the wake.

[Laughs.] So the whole weaponization of space that they're talking about is ludicrous. They'd never be able to shoot at anybody.

They will try, but they're actually less interested in shooting at extraterrestrials than they are in carrying their cultural competitiveness with other nations out into space. They're fearful that one nation, for instance, might say, "This Moon is ours and we're going to mine it, and if you try to mess with our mines, we're going to get you." But think about it: Why is that any different than what you have on your planet right now? If you're a mining company and you suddenly experienced an invasion by another country or their mining company, don't you know that your government or the companies themselves would fight, they'd resist? So it is not at all surprising that such plans are in place to extend that to Mars and the Moon and places that seem reachable.

Whether it will actually come to pass in the long run is dubious. But in the short run, it is possible.

But as a matter of course, doesn't somebody from some other planet, some civilization or other planet, disarm the nuclear weapons if they try to shoot them in space?

Oh, I think nuclear weapons are very unlikely to be used in space as a weapon system. What a nuclear weapon needs to explode in space is largely unavailable there. No, the weapon systems will be different.

Lasers?

Perhaps, or some kind of attempt to focus energy. There have been a lot of attempts there but not much success. That's why the laser program has been able to produce so much, because it has shown results.

So for a time you'll see mostly development in those areas. Though once sound compression becomes viable and able to last without losing its vibrancy resolution over distance, then that will replace lasers because it will take significantly less energy to produce and be a lot cheaper to produce, I might add, and have an effect that is much more useful than a laser. You can hit something with a laser, but it doesn't necessarily immediately have impact, even with a powerful one. But with something that uses sound, it almost immediately creates problems. When you have a compressed and condensed sound, if something you are shooting at passes through that beam or the beam passes through the object, depending upon the intersection point, you will have a disruption of all of the mechanics, either computer or even particle-based, that will just simply make the object be pretty much useless. It will go out of control. It will perhaps crash someplace other than what was intended, or many other options.

The reason I'm mentioning that is, the countries that don't have the money to develop lasers will put their money into developing compressed sound mechanisms like this. Also, these compressed sound mechanisms are less likely to do greater damage. See, a laser can go way out into space and cause problems. You might miss what you're aiming at. The chances of missing are pretty good. But with a sound, it will only go so far and then disintegrate and become essentially benign.

So that is actually good. You don't want your weapons going wild in all directions or you will attract beings who might not be so patient. They will come and say, "These things are creating problems for us and others in travel lanes," and simply eliminate all weapons. Without saying hello or goodbye, they'll just come eliminate them all and then leave. It will happen so fast you won't even know what hit you.

Can't we invite them? [Laughs.]

I think the way to invite them you would not want to do. It's better not to get them mad at you. If they're not mad, they won't come and obliterate your civilization, they'll simply come and obliterate the offending weapons and leave.

Who would that be? Anybody we've ever heard of?

Many civilizations are like that.

Not negative, but just sort of . . .

Not negative.

But not as benevolent as some of you guys?

Well, less patient.

Less patient, okay. I think the United States and Russia were told to stay off the Moon, so would we be fighting over Mars, then?

Oh, I think the U.S. and Russia will go to the Moon, just the way they've been doing it, slowly, and they'll tend to stay on the light side. There's not much action on the other side of the Moon.

There are other bases of other beings on the other side of the Moon?

Yes.

So by staying on . . .

They will have to be discreet. And they will probably have to cooperate with each other. Russian and U.S. cooperation is already happening. What is really necessary is to include China more. I think that's known and understood and in the works.

ETs Are Here to Support Humans in Their Spiritual Growth

You understand the Explorer Race, right?

Yes.

Is it your feeling now that all of the civilizations from other planets coming here understand that now?

I wouldn't say all, but I would say the ones who come here with regularity. But passing cultures, from long distances, don't usually . . . with time, they will assimilate that information to the degree they can. If they don't have the time, they just . . . won't.

What I was getting at was that in the seventies and the early eighties, all cultures were coming here and trying to tell us all the terrible things that were going to hap-

we didn't change, giving us information that maybe we shouldn't have had. Is there a difference now in the information being brought to the contactees?

I think the main point of the information from enlightened beings is to train and support human beings in their spiritual growth. I believe that is the main focus, with possible exceptions in the case of long-term contactees where there might be that but also follow-ups to anything else that had happened between the parties mentioned insofar as their previous encounters.

In the case of Billy Meier and the Pleiadians, it would be more like that, right?

Yes, but they would still be wanting to teach him spiritual practices if he is open to it, which he most likely is.

So there are not so many attempts to bring new science now?

No, because it is not a good time for that, wouldn't you say?

Well, we never get it, you know. It goes to the secret government.

That is right. There's not much point in that, eh?

Right, right.

We Have Created a Library of Wisdom

You can't be very old in terms of our years, right?

None of us are very old.

Fifty years? Forty?

Something like that, yes, with a lifespan of at least 1,200 years, perhaps more—which is why we haven't had to decide yet how we will reproduce [laughs].

That's exciting. So were you all born . . . how do I say this? You became aware when you were an adult?

We became aware when we were . . . yes, whatever size. We didn't have a childhood and grow up and all of that. At least speaking for myself, I didn't. I think some early conceptions of individuals in our society did have a form of childhood, but I'm not one of them.

So in forty years you formed a civilization, colonized a planet, created modern art, all of that?

No. We didn't colonize the planet. The planet had no beings, no humanoid beings on it. And it was prepared, meaning it was welcoming of such colonization. The planet was colonized for us by the parent race, and they made certain provisions for us so that we wouldn't have to immediately erect dwellings and create habitable places and all of that. But they didn't do too much so that we could make it our own place.

Is your intelligence as much as the Zetas? More? Less?

I don't really think about that. It doesn't measure like that, because intelligence is a measure of the capacity to learn, whereas mental capacity is a measure of the quantity that you can learn. So I would say that our capacity is similar, but our interests are so different, I don't think I can . . .

Right, it doesn't compute because you're able to feel; you have a human feeling nature.

We have a nature to feel and a lot of the same feelings you have, though not all. So therefore we have other interests, rather than simply the expansion of the mind and its acquisition of knowledge.

Right, right. So it wasn't a good question, I understand.

It was a good question because it pointed out the difference between us. I just couldn't answer it in the way you phrased it.

So when you choose, you can come down to land on the planet?

If we chose we could do that, but we never have. I don't think we will until you move through the greater portion of the discomfort that you are experiencing. I don't think I would want to.

So the parent race couldn't handle our emotion, but because you're so receptive, you could handle our negative emotions even less?

Yes. We would feel a more kindred spirit with you, but our compassion level is so developed that even a minor problem for any one of you would cause us great grief. So we couldn't be around an average human being.

But you have technology from the parent race, right?

Yes.

And you have monitors where you can watch pretty much anything you want? Anybody? Anything? Events? Places?

We are not nosy.

No, but I mean you have this available?

It's not like monitors. It's more like your friend Speaks of Many Truths says; it's more like long vision. We can see. We don't have to use machines, though they are available to us in the vehicles—we can see. And that is what we prefer to do, because when using that technique, one naturally filters out all of the discomfort. One does not see everything as you see on a monitor, as you call it; with that you would see everything, and that would be upsetting. So we would rather use the technique to see.

The long vision, right. So what are you interested in? I mean, do you look at cultural events or art galleries or architecture? What kinds of things do you look at?

Yes, we are interested in your art and music and methods of creativity. We are also interested in the way different cultures represent themselves. We are particularly interested in families and how children are raised and nurtured. We are also interested in the aged and how they are treated and cared for.

We are a little baffled as to why the aged, who are repositories of wisdom, are not . . . how can we say? There are not people talking to them to extract their wisdom for permanent filing in some library—not "extract" wisdom, but you understand, to talk and get their life experience and learn what they did about a problem and how they eventually solved it, how that worked and so on. We are at a loss to understand why you don't do this. So very much wisdom that you could use at any time has been lost this way, and now you have the technology to store and classify this. Oh, it is done with some cultures and civilizations, but for the vast majority of individuals, when they get older, their wisdom is only left in bits and pieces to family members but not to the community at large. We hope you will do that soon.

This is because not only the wisdom would be valuable but the sense of value of the older person would be accentuated?

Yes, that enhancement would be very helpful to the feeling one has about oneself. Often craftspeople want to have apprentices and don't. But even for the average person, many things are not titled "crafts" but they are—like childrearing or grandfathering or grandmothering, for example. There are so many skills and wisdoms to be offered, and when one doesn't have someone to pass this on to for one reason or another, it is very sad.

Oh, I agree with you. Maybe that will come as we move to a more benevolent time.

I believe that will come as we speak, in these times, and I am speaking of it because it is happening and I want to encourage it.

Ah, very good, very good.

It won't be difficult in this day and age of international communication that you have to be able to translate and at least roughly apply solutions on a cross-cultural basis. It will not directly apply, but it might roughly apply, to give suggestions. For instance, a highly intellectual or technological culture will still have the same problems with childrearing as a more agrarian culture. And the agrarian culture might have solutions for childrearing that the technological society might not think of. Likewise, in other ways, perhaps with the education of children, the agrarian society won't have the full depth of application of intellectual tools that the technological society can provide. That is just a simple example, but it is one that would work, perhaps, in some form.

Absolutely. I mean, the first thing a woman does when she has a baby is try to find somebody who's already had one, to find out what to do.

That's always a good idea.

How did you get to be the spokesman here? How did that happen?

I think perhaps because I was welcoming the job. I was doing what they're doing, but I thought I would welcome this as an opportunity.

You are so knowledgeable at forty years of age. Are you . . . . there's a word I like, "inculcated." Is there some method with this or is your mind open to what we do? How do you know so much in such a short time?

We have created a library of wisdom—not only from the parent race, but from the human beings we've connected with and from the human beings the parent race has connected with. And when any of us were created, that library of wisdom was passed on either to us, once we became fully engaged in our personalities and could assimilate other information, or it was passed on to someone within our immediate group whom we could ask. So we have that information available.

I don't think of it as "inculcation." Inculcation goes into your subconscious and is not readily and immediately available in your mind. Whereas this kind of wisdom education takes awhile to assimilate, but it is more enjoyable to hear people in their voices. You enjoy them talking about their cultures, and in some cases, you see pictures or music or other stimulations that we find attractive. Of course, we do not have to worry about making a living and so on. We have time.

You also have that device. I've talked at length to some of the Zetas for another book, and you have the device you can put your hand on, right? I forget the name of it.

We have more than one like that—what are you referring to?

Well, there's something that sort of holds the wisdom of the Zetas that they always have a copy of on a ship or they can refer back to the home base when they want to know something.

We do not have that. They have that for their own purposes, but we prefer to acquire wisdom more directly from individuals on a more personal basis in the manner I suggested.

HAARP Research Will Yield New Technologies

I'd like to ask you, what is your perception of HAARP? What is it doing right now? I had heard someplace that it took 30 percent of the electricity on the planet to run the thing—I don't know if that's accurate or not.

That's not accurate from my experience. I don't know too much about this thing, but it's largely intended to experiment with broadcast signals to see what can be done. It is basic research for the most part; it is not really intended to knock down extraterrestrial vehicles or so much like that. But it does basic research, and because a wide variety of signals can be broadcast in greater or lesser amplitude, it is essentially a research mechanism, which is why it is so isolated, because they do not know what the impact will be. They're trying to—you understand, on Earth, communications and so on—do this research in someplace where they can have a minimal impact on Earth.

I do not think that the intention is for it to be used as a weapon. But, you know, if something is being done such as basic research like that, you might unintentionally create a problem without really meaning to. It could be a big problem, a small problem or no problem, but because you don't really know what you're doing—you learn what you're doing after the fact rather then while you're doing it—it can create certain hazards. So that's my understanding of what's going on there—not so much that there is some intention to create destruction.

But what's the point of broadcasting the signals?

What's the point of doing chemical basic research? The point is to see what happens and if you can use it for anything. You know, most corporations have basic research going on all the time. Lots of things have been developed that way. Usually you don't know what you've developed until long after you've done the experiment.

Do you see anything potentially positive that could come out of that?

Yes, because in time they will discover several things. One, they will discover a means to instantaneously communicate with Earth vehicles at vast distances. Right now it is still somewhat problematic, long-distance communication from Earth to, say, Earth vehicles—meaning if you send an unmanned craft out to the outer planets, communication can take place, but not instantaneously. Many times you would want to be able to communicate instantaneously to avoid a greater problem, but you can't. That is something that will come out of this that is positive.

Excellent. But we're not there yet, they're not there yet?

Far from there. But things like that are the reason the device and the experiment have been funded. Oh, granted there might be military applications, but that is not all that is going on there. Those applications are what gets the funding, but as basic research, that means just that anything that seems like it might be worth doing is done. Initially, for instance, you scan your research on the basis of who's funding you, yes? So they might scan the research and developments—meaning not how they develop it but what has been learned from the research—or scan it on the basis of who funded it, perhaps military uses.

But others will go back and scan it for other purposes, because you might stumble across something like a wave induced with a certain pulse and a potential frequency that might, for example, cure certain diseases. That is also likely to be developed in time—not that this has not already been developed to a lesser degree by certain individuals on Earth, but when you have a much greater budget (and this is more in the long-term)—but you might, for example, be able to develop a electronic inoculation whereby you could inoculate all of the Earth inhabitants on the entire planet by simply broadcasting a certain pulse or frequency or tone or wave for a given amount of time, and no one gets that disease anymore. Won't that be wonderful?

That would be divine.

This will come about as the result of utilizing this device or other devices like it. There'll be one out in space, and there might be a smaller version on the space station at some point, and other countries will develop variations of their own. There's a lot of interest in this area, because as you know, vaccines are often hard to get and frequently hard to get when you need them and where. If you could do it electronically in some way, it might be very helpful. And "electronic vaccines" work less by what they do—what the pulse does, for instance—than what it prompts in the physical bodies in the individuals it touches.

Essentially, it would prompt an amplified reaction of your own immune system to produce the body chemicals. That's why it works so well, because each person's body is different, so the dosage per person would be different, you see, because your own body will produce it. That will generate protection for a given disease or group of diseases. Ultimately such electronic medicine will be chosen over chemical medicine because of its wider availability and broader application.

Ah, that's brilliant. Of course, it could also be used to control people.

There's that. But, of course, the spiritual side of people's nature will accept that only insofar as they cooperate. If they do not wish to cooperate, then it will not work so well, that kind of control. But there will be a desire to cooperate. You might find that hard to believe, but there will be a desire to cooperate as such signals produce more and more benefits.

That is likely to take place and will have to do with some of the initial states of a world order. This is not so much to control the citizens, but you have to understand, your natural tendency is to bristle at the idea of being controlled. But think about this: What if people were controlled from being violent or self-destructive?

Well, that's interesting, but like you say, the very word "control" makes one bristle.

What about if you, as an individual, were restricted from being violent or self-destructive? You don't think of yourself as self-destructive, but have you ever had an accident—stubbed your toe, bumped your arm, bumped your shoulder, like that? It would prevent you from having that also.

Well, right now I think that part of the Explorer Race school is to deal with the consequences, so I don't think we can just cut it off like that.

Well, I'm mentioning it to you because you will have to face these issues. It is typical on other planets to have such broadcast energies that keep civilizations calm, benevolent and cultural. We have it, and almost every other civilization I know has it, though it does not take form as you are experimenting with it now—such as radiated energies, like that. It is more spiritual in its nature, but it does involve radiated spiritual energies. You're just experimenting now with using electromagnetic radiations, but in time, as it includes spiritual and loving energies, then as it applies to each individual, it will be more benevolent rather than forceful. But one step at a time, yes?

We Have Interest in Our Roots

So you've been to lots of other planets?

No, but I'm aware of these cultures.

So this is the only one you've been to?

As I've said, we do not have much interest in anything other than Zeta influence or human influence. Our roots—we have interest in our roots, yes? There's so much to learn about our roots, and we are a young civilization. We have so much to learn that we are not yet that interested in learning about other places, other people, other things of which we are not direct descendants.

Right, I understand. You said that, but then your parent race is so eager to go look and see and learn everything that I forgot for a minute that you have different motives. What about other civilizations that have been formed in roughly the same way yours was—the only words I know are "hybrid" or "cross-race"—have you interacted with any of them?

Not too much, no. We tend to stay within our own culture. The parent race has indicated that when we are older—maybe 500, 600 years old—we might start to do more with other cultures, but they completely understand our desire to explore our roots. Many of our people are doing that in the Zeta culture right now. It's just that our group, who are here around Earth, are exploring your culture.

How many are in your group?

Oh, on our ship we have about nine, and it ranges from nine to fifteen on the other ships. There are just three of us, three ships. We were all interested in Earth culture, music—not all forms, but melodic music and rhythmic music, we're interested in that.

Do you sing or create music or play instruments yourself?

We don't seem to have very good voices, so our songs don't hold anything remotely to your standard. But we are very intrigued by tympanic instruments—drums, cymbals, things like that—and rhythms. We explore that. We have on occasion been gifted with certain instruments on Earth that we have used. There's a rattle, a thing where you rub a stick across it and it creates a scraping sound—I don't know how to describe it; it's sort of an instrument—and a piece of hollow wood that makes sort of a drum sound. We are very interested in that, and it's popular to play.

Is a piano a tympanic instrument?

No.

Okay. Let's see, there are 40,000 people on your planet. Are very few of them out and about? Are a lot of them on the home planet?

Most are on the home planet, yes. There are just perhaps maybe eighty to a hundred on other Zeta cultural planets and then a few on the Earth expedition here. But everybody else is at home.

But they learn what you learn. How does that work?

We pass it on through empathy, because we have well-developed feelings. We don't send them to space; we send some of our members home. There are people on our expedition, for instance, who are here for the long term. Then there are people who are here for a short term, say for a couple of years, and they learn all there is to be learned that we have accumulated up to that point, and they have their feelings about it. Then they travel home and speak of these things and radiate these feelings, and everybody else can assimilate it to the degree that they are comfortable with those feelings and of course have the knowledge.

Are you a long-term one?

I am. [Loud buzzing sound.]

Are you there?

Yeah, what happened?

Some strange jamming. I will use the headset, yes?

Some strange jamming?

Some strange jamming. I do not know why. Perhaps it has nothing to do with the communication we are having, but it is affecting the talk phone. However, it does not appear to be affecting the headset.

The headset, how interesting.

I do not recall what we were speaking of.

I asked if you were a long-term one.

I am long-term, yes.

So even though some were born and then you were cloned from that, you still have individual unique personalities because of the soul that inhabits . . .

Nobody was born. Everybody was cloned. But some had childhoods.

Oh, I misunderstood. Some were cloned as children. But because of the nature of each soul that comes in, you all have unique personalities, right?

Certainly, just like on Zeta. We all have unique personalities in my experience. Beings I've come across all have unique personalities; I don't know any beings who don't.

Well, still though, they're more of a unified field I think than some of [laughs] . . . I mean they seem more alike than not alike.

The Zeta parent race?

Yes.

Perhaps because they don't know you very well. Once they get to know you and feel more at ease with your energy, then they demonstrate more of their personality—not unlike you do, eh?

Yes, yes. There's one being—I wish I could think of his name—who talked for a month, I think, about the Zeta, about everything in the Zeta's home world and what they do and how they think and everything. [Zetas, Hybrids and Human Contacts]

So you have soaked up sort of how the planet runs, the politics, the animosities of the unions, the friendship—you sort of soaked up how the Earth works, right?

Yes, to a degree, but not to the depth that you other Earth people might know, because I am not experiencing it in a polarized way—meaning I do not experience the knowledge that we have of your culture based upon both comfort and discomfort, but only based upon comfort. So given that, there are large gaps and spaces necessarily missing.

Learn the Love-Heat Exercise as a Greeting for ETs

Well, you certainly know an awful lot. Is there something you think you could share with us that you think we need to know?

We are looking forward to meeting you all on a more friendly basis. I encourage you to develop astronauts and cosmonauts as you have been doing, not just in science and military, but also spiritual people, people with love and calm and focus, like that. That is essential if you wish to have benevolent meetings with extraterrestrials who can give you great gifts, if you want them. I do not expect your governments to promote this right now, but some of your companies, your businesses might. If you wish to acquire such contacts as can support and nurture you, and give you education and perhaps little gifts if you want them that could benefit your society, start using more educators or people of wisdom who are heart-centered.

It's very important to be heart-centered. It would be extremely helpful for them to know how to do the heart self-love exercise, because this is a form of universal greeting that is safe to all parties. That is most important. You can feel it with a being from anyplace else and feel safe. If there is anything about their countenance, meaning energetically, that is a little unsettling to you, this will tend to calm you and nurture you so that you will feel safe with that. It will also tend to deflect anything in their feelings, for instance, that might feel odd to you, and equally the same for them. Therefore, such a universal greeting, even if your initial meeting does not go beyond that greeting—which is very likely in many cultures, just to have that initial exposure and feel safe—then I feel that this could be very useful.

Safety is the most important part. If you don't feel safe with some being, even if they have a great deal to offer you but you as an individual did not feel safe for some reason, you will probably miss out on lots of good things.

That's wonderful. I didn't realize that could be used as a greeting.

The Love-Heat Exercise

I am giving what we're calling the love-heat exercise in a way that Speaks of Many Truths taught me how to do it. Take your thumb and rub it very gently across your fingertips for about half a minute or a minute. And while you do that, don't do anything else. Just put your attention on your fingertips. Close your eyes and feel your thumb rubbing slowly across your fingertips. Notice that when you do that, it brings your physical attention into that part of your body. Now you can relax and bring that same physical attention anywhere inside your chest—not just where your heart is, but anywhere across your chest, your solar plexus area or abdomen—and either generate or look for a physical warmth that you can actually feel.

Take a minute or two or as long as you need to find that warmth. When you find it, go into that feeling of warmth and feel it more, just stay with it. Stay with that feeling of warmth. Feel it for a few minutes so you can memorize the method, and most importantly, so your body can create a recollection, a physical recollection of how it feels and how it needs to feel for you. The heat might come up in different parts of your body—maybe one time in the left of your chest, maybe another time in the right of your abdomen or other places around there. Wherever you feel it, just let it be there. Don't try and move it around—that's where it's showing up in that moment. Always when it comes up and you feel the warmth, go into it and feel it more.

Make sure you do this when you are alone and quiet, not when you are driving a car or doing anything that requires your full attention. After you do the warmth for five minutes or so if you can, or as long as you can do it, then relax. And afterward, think about this: The warmth is the physical evidence of loving yourself. Many of you have read for years about how we need to love ourselves, but in fact, the method is not just saying, "I love myself," or doing other mental exercises that are helpful to give you permission to love yourself. Rather, the actual physical experience of loving yourself is in this manner, and there are things you can do that are supportive of it. But in my experience, and the way I was taught, this is the method you can most easily do.

The heat will tend to push everything out of you that is not of you or that is not supporting you, because the heat, as the physical experience of loving yourself, also unites you with Creator. It unites you with the harmony of all beings, and it will tend to create a greater harmony with all things. You might notice as you get better at can do it longer that should you be around your friends or other people, they might feel more relaxed around you, or situations might become more harmonious. Things that used to bother or upset you don't bother you very much, because the heat creates an energy, not only of self-love, but of harmony. Remember that the harmony part is so important. You might also notice that animals will react differently to you—maybe they'll be more friendly, perhaps they'll be more relaxed, maybe they'll look at you in a different way. Sometimes you'll be surprised at what animals, even the smallest—such as a grasshopper, a beetle, a butterfly, a bird—might do because you're feeling this heat.

Because it is love energy, it naturally radiates just as light comes out of a light bulb. Remember, you don't throw the heat out, even with the best of intentions. You don't send it to people. If other people are interested in what you are doing or why they feel better around you, you can teach them how to do this love-heat exercise in the way you learned or the way that works best for you. And the most important thing to remember is that this method of loving yourself and generating harmony for yourself creates harmony for others, because you are in harmony. Remember that this works well and will provide you with a greater sense of ease and comfort in your life no matter who you are, where you are, what you are doing or how you're living your life. It can only improve your experience. The love-heat exercise is something that is intended to benefit all life, and in my experience, it does benefit my life.

—Robert Shapiro

It is often used as a greeting between people all over and, even on your own planet, between plants and animals and some humans who have learned this.

Which do you think will come first, that you get to land and talk to us or that we go out and see you on your home planet?

Probably we will meet in space, a different thing. It is more likely that what comes first is that we meet in space, as this has already occurred. But the reason I am suggesting that you learn this form of universal greeting is so that the meetings do not feel awkward, as they often have in the past. Perhaps people—either my people or, more likely, others—will look unusual to you and you might feel unsettled. Perhaps they will demonstrate skills or abilities that are unlike your own. If you have this form of greeting, it will put everyone at ease.

What do you mean "as we have met in the past"?

Astronauts or cosmonauts have had encounters already with extraterrestrials, either in ships or occasionally more personally outside the Earth ship. I won't say too much about that because your governments would prefer that these things are not discussed openly, but . . .

But they have to be, they have to be. People have to discuss them.

No, we don't have to. I can be polite.

No, no, but I mean, there's a movement on Earth now to bring this information out, the disclosure of these facts. They don't need to keep it secret anymore; there's no reason for it.

Well, sometimes there is.

Was your group one of the ones that encountered our astronauts or cosmonauts?

No, but there have been others who have, and if they had, if your cosmonauts or astronauts had had this form of greeting, it would have been much better. Hand signals and words often mean different things to other cultures. But feelings are universal.

Oh, we'll send this to NASA. [Laughs.]

You can send it; they may not . . .

They may not pay any attention.

Perhaps they will send you a polite response saying, "Thank you so much."

[Laughs.] Oh, you're great, you're great!

I have had enough exposure to your culture to appreciate some of your humor.

Yes. [Laughs.] That's wonderful, though, to have the feeling qualities and the capacity of mind that you have. What a gift!

It is a pretty good life. I'm not complaining.

[Laughs.] Well, listen, if you ever think of anything else interesting, I talk to beings through Robert all the time, so just kind of tap Zoosh on the shoulder and say, "I'd like to say something."

All right. Have fun, and maybe we'll see you around.

That would be great. Thank you so much.

※   ※   ※

Greetings, Zoosh here.

Hey Zoosh, what was that jamming? What was that noise?

It could be a problem with the phone, but it is also possible that it is some Navy thing. You understand, the speaker phone is not only a communication device from person to person but it's also a mini-transmitter. Therefore, even such a minor level of transmitting could create feedback and might create a problem for the Navy, who is in fact very active around these areas [Hawaii] as one might expect near a naval base. It could also create a very potential feedback with the broadcast antenna nearby, but I doubt it very much. There are different frequencies involved, you know. More likely it has to do with sort of a Navy jamming, which is by way of saying, "Don't do that right now, please. Thank you very much."

You noticed that the conversation on the headset was not a problem because the transmission is much, much reduced, not enough to create a problem. Other people who were transmitting, for instance people on HAM radio sets and so on, also probably experienced a brief burst of interference. Of course, the location of Hawaii sometimes has problems there, but most of the problems that occur like that are because of various naval transmissions and so on. There are other military services here, but the Navy is the branch of the service most involved and most sensitive to broadcasts because of the surface and subsurface transmissions that take place. You see, other surface military networks are perhaps taking place in the air and on the ground but are not subsurface for the most part, whereas the Navy has subsurface things going on all the time.

You told me years ago that when HAARP was activated, no ET ships could get in, and I never thought to say, "What's the current status?" So there are plenty of off-planet people out there to ask to talk, right?

Yes. They got over it, they got past it. It took awhile, but they figured a way around it. I think it was eloquently explained by your ET.

Oh yes, he was wonderful!

Well, that is really how they got around it. It took awhile. It was clever, when you think about it, not to engage the planet but to engage individuals on the planet. That was pretty clever.

It sure was. Thank you very much.

Good night.

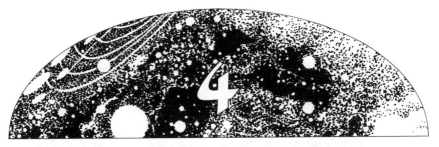

A Being from the Planet Odin Visits the Iroquois Nation in the Thirteenth Century

Ahsan Gadan

January 2, 2002

y name is Ahsan—A-h-s-a-n G-a-d-a-n. I am not the Ahsan you have heard from before. [Ahsan is also the name of a warrior teacher in Speaks of Many Truths' tribe in the 1600s.] I lived with my adopted brothers and sisters in the Iroquois nation about 780 years ago from your time. My ship, which was carrying just me, crashed (but was not destroyed) not too far from where the Iroquois hunt. They saw the ship come down, and two of their brave people came over. I first determined the planet was safe for me to breathe and touch, but when I got out, because I wasn't used to the gravity, I was staggering around and falling down. The two young men spoke to me in their language. At first I did not understand, but I was able to activate a small device we long-distance explorers have with us, and very quickly I was able to communicate with them. They would hear my voice in their language—but I would speak my language. They speak their language in their voice, I hear their voice, but I hear it speaking my language. That's exactly how it works. They asked me if I was all right, if I needed help. I told them honestly where I was from, a star system called Odin, which is, I believe, a term used here by some people in the north.

It is a name that people in the north countries use for their god, their creator.

Yes. But this is the name of our star system, Odin. It would suggest, would it not, that some of our people have been to visit people in the north? I have been told that Odin is about 400,000 light-years beyond Betelgeuse. Beyond meaning from Earth to that, and then on, but not in a straight line. I can draw a map.

Now, I told them that our people traveled sometimes great distances to explore where other generations had traveled, and that I had come to visit the Iroquois nation because they were originally from not our star, but a nearby star. And they were interested; they asked me if my ship could be repaired, and they said it was safe to leave it where it was, so I did. I set certain controls in the ship so that it would repair itself, but the repairs would take about two weeks of Earth time. I asked the people if I might stay with them for two weeks and they said that I could come back and talk to the elders, and it would be up to them.

I traveled with the hunting party for another three or four days, until they gathered what they needed; then we went back to where their tribe was. And the elders said that as long as I would tell stories of where I was from, and not try to have sex contact with any of the women, that

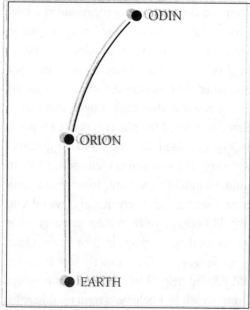

I would be welcome to stay. So I stayed, then, for the rest of the time until the ship was repaired. But by that time the elders had grown fond of my stories, because I knew some stories about their ancestors, which I told them. Some of the information they knew, which I can't talk about since it's a tribal secret. And some of it they did not know, which I really can't talk about either. But they were very interested to hear about their history and to meet someone who was not a direct relation, but a cousin. I wound up staying for three

Figure 4.1: A map of the line made by travel from Odin to Earth.

months instead of a couple of weeks, and I did not, as you might say in your time, fraternize with the women, but I did have opportunities to see them when I told stories. First it was to the elders, and then to larger groups of people.

I think they were particularly pleased with the fact that they could hear me speak in my voice, but in their language, so that communication could proceed, including innuendo. It is the innuendo part of communication in translation that is so often lost, and usually the most important; wouldn't you say?

Yes, the nuances.

One Iroquois Travels to His Ancestor's Home Planet with Visitor

Yes, nuances. So after three months I went to my ship, and the people told me that I was welcome to return sometime. I asked them if they would like a trip. The ship I came in has a comfortable room for one guest, so would someone like to go into space with me for a time? They thought about that; they said they hadn't considered it. Of course there were several young men who wanted to try it,

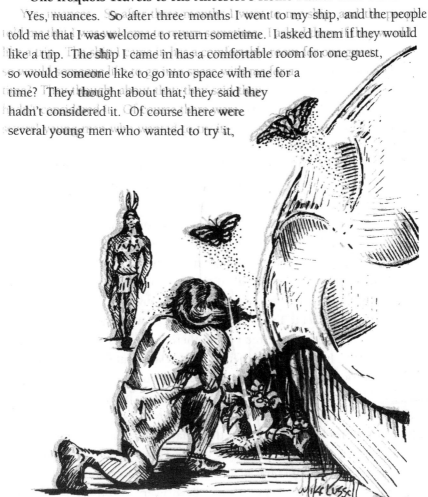

and even one young woman. But it was decided that one of the elders would go, as he had a lot of knowledge about their people and some knowledge about the stars. He was not the person assigned or talented in that direction, the star person, but he had some knowledge and would perhaps like to acquire more. I told them that it would be possible to have a lengthy voyage, to see many things and do many things, and then to return without having been away for much Earth time; the people could wait near the ship if they liked. And they did not understand, but I explained that the ship had the capacity to move through space, yes, but also could displace (that's how I put it) time. And so they were interested, particularly because the elder would not lose any time from his life on Earth.

The elder chose to accompany me, even though we were gone for only about five minutes of Earth time. I decided to make sure he was gone for a few minutes, to make it seem like a real trip, instead of coming back before we left, which would confuse everybody. But in experiential time we were actually gone for three and a half months, during which time I was able to take him to Odin and show him my world, and also to the planet where the Iroquois people were from.

We were there for three months while he studied and learned more about his people. He was given a special object that was placed very gently under the skin of the back of his head, with his permission, and this allowed him to communicate freely with the people on his home planet. This way he could pass on all the stories that had been lost through the years and create a welcoming path for their people when they would choose to pass back to their home planet. And he liked that. Also, certain gifts were given; he left something there, and several gifts were given that could be safely taken from that planet to Earth, and he took those with gratitude, of course. He also offered stories, and the people there loved them and appreciated them so much. It was like a gathering of the clans, but from a distance; he wished, the elder said, that he could have had more people there, but that they would all meet again someday. When he came back, he looked a little different because they cured certain things in his body; they fixed his teeth, which was a problem for people in those days; they also fixed his body so that he would live about another 150 years. Therefore, he could guide his people that long. If you know anything about Iroquois culture and history, you know that some people in their past lived a very long time. He was one of these people. I'm couching that in certain terms to honor their culture and to not speak their secrets.

Now, this visit, then, was very good, and he returned, as I say, with gifts the tribe could use. One was an object that could find water and bring it to the surface if they needed it in their travels; another was an object they could use to see things in space clearly. Another gift was a pair of objects by which they could see and hear a person who was at a distance, and that would make a connection not unlike some devices you have today. So that was the journey. He returned; the people completely accepted him as he was. He told them that he would live a long time. Some of their people had lived a long time before, so it was almost, for those days, like being immortal, living for another hundred and fifty years after about thirty-eight years of life at that time. That was perhaps a worthy gift.

What a wonderful thing you did for them!

It was the least I could do, because they were so helpful and welcoming to me when I arrived. I am still in the same body that I was in then, so I'm a little older.

Still traveling?

Not traveling any more; that is a young man's occupation. Or a young woman, too; we have men and women, like you. We look like you, pretty much.

What is your normal lifespan?

About 35,000 of your years.

So you were here only 780 years ago?

Yes, but our people do not voyage like that for more than 1,500 years. It is a long time to be alone and away from one's family.

Oh, yes! Were the Iroquois from your star system, or from a different one?

Not from ours, but nearby.

Well, can you tell us about your life on your home system? What dimension? What kind of life do you have, or how is it like ours?

We do not experience fixed dimension; we have access to more than thirty-two, so depending upon how we are feeling and what we are doing, we are in a different, as you call it, dimension. This is not so dissimilar from what you do; your range of feelings is focused into a very narrow range compared to your usual access to feelings. But the narrow range is intended, I understand, so that you will stay in a given dimension and change dimensions only when you purposely expand your feelings. That's how you change dimensions, and all the people have to do it at once for it to happen. That's the mechanics; I thought it might interest you.

Visitor's Form Changes with Change of Feelings

Can you say a little bit about how you live? Are you in form all the time? In those very high dimensions you wouldn't have form, would you?

We have a form of substance, our personality. Higher dimensions do not mean that you do not have a body, just that you have a choice of form. If you were able to observe it with physical eyes, you would see that the form changes constantly based upon the feelings of the moment. But there is a form that can be perceived. It might be large, even vast; it might be small. But there is a form that is perceptible given the ability to see in that stratus, which you call a dimension.

So when you travel, does your ship have the ability to expand and contract also?

The ship that I traveled in can travel to any, as you say, dimension, but I'm going to call it stratus if that's okay. It can travel to any stratus that is known. You understand, it's not my property. The ship has been to the second dimension, as you say, the second stratus, and all the way to the ninety-eighth. I have not been to all those places, but the ship has that capacity.

I don't think we've heard of anything higher than thirty-three before.

Ninety-eighth—according to the records on the ship, because I was interested, too. The ninety-eighth stratus seems to be composed largely of tympanic sound and fragrance, and also some very fast-moving somethings. Substance, I'd call it.

Well, probably some kind of being.

Oh, yes, certainly that, or the ship would not go there. The ship is, as you say, programmed to go only to places where there are beings that can be interacted with in some way. It will not go someplace where there is nothing. We have that capacity to be vast, and also the capacity to be a man or a woman, individual. It is a pleasant flexibility.

Well, when you are man or woman and in a form that we would recognize, do you have family life? Do you have communities?

If we choose. I've known several individuals who chose to live as a family for a time, but then you need to have volunteers to be children for a while, although maybe whoever is father and mother might choose to change places with the children sometimes, so that everybody understands what it is like to be in these different roles. A healthy thing. I believe that you have a therapy on this world where people try to experience other people's lives so there is some sensitivity for others.

A moment. Water. [Drinks water.] I have had water before, of different viscosities—ice, of course, but I've also had very thick water that you have to spoon, that feels kind of viscous between your fingers. An Earth person could take a spoonful and it would last you two, two and a half weeks. It is concentrated water.

So does the water you just drank taste similar to what you drank 780 years ago?

No, that water in those days was much sweeter. It was sweet in the mouth, sweeter when you swallowed it, and it left a sweet aftertaste.

Because it was so pure?

Yes, but I think also because of the minerals in it. It might be possible to find water that sweet, still, in that part of the country, from the northeast United States into Canada. It might be possible to find that sweet water, yet, in parts of Canada.

Where there were not many people then.

That's right. If you found it, it would have to be a spring. Water recoils when it is dug for, because it's not intended to be on the surface. When it recoils, it has a bitter flavor; that's why sometimes when people dig for water, they find bitter water—that is water that is recoiling.

The Higher-Dimensional Creation of Personality

On your planet, if you live 35,000 years, there must be births at some time, then. Or do you materialize some other way?

There are births, yes, for those who wish to experience it—giving birth or experiencing birth. But the other, most commonly experienced way is higher-dimensional creation of personality. It happens around the seventy-eighth stratus; that is where most of our personalities emerge. When that occurs, then the personality will usually stay in the higher stratus for a time or different higher strati, but will not choose to come to the ones you would recognize as physical life, usually, for a few thousand years. But if they choose to have birth—not dissimilar to yours, but without discomfort—then they will do the opposite: They will experience life in the realms of what you would call physical for a few thousand years before they experience the other strati.

So the ones who emerge into the seventy-eighth stratus, and then come down to where there was form . . . they would create their own body?

Yes. It's the same thing going the other way. It's not a willful creation; it just happens. There's a difference. One of the difficulties in understanding how to create a different body is that there's a belief that you have to do something. But it's not like that; it's that your range of feelings changes. You become responsive to things you don't normally respond to, a broader response; it creates a different vibration or what could be called a harmony (actually, tonal) and that is what causes the change in body.

That is how a shaman might choose to experience—not by creation, but by occupation. By this I mean that a shaman might visit to run with the lions or the deer or the elk for a time, just to acquire the skills, abilities and sensitivities of those creatures—not to do warlike actions or sorcery, but to experience and accommodate, to adapt and learn new ways to honor those beings. That's why that is done. And it has everything to do with what you feel; it's not a willful act of what you do. Those who attempt to do these things and change their form by what they do injure their own bodies and can injure the bodies of those around them, even if it is not obvious at the time. And I would call that sorcery.

My understanding of sorcery is that it is magic done without the permission of others, which might or might not harm them. Magic is done with the permission of others around you and does not harm; it only helps with the cooperation of all beings who are involved in any way with the magical creation.

How to Expand to a Higher Dimension

Yes, that's what our teachers are explaining. We're in one frequency now, and we need to expand to a more harmonious, loving frequency. And, as you said earlier, to make the whole human population move to a higher dimension, we need to do it all at once; but as different people do it, that helps anchor it, right?

I will tell you how it can be done.

Please.

First, you learn how to do the warmth, which you would feel in some part of your body. After you've learned how to do the warmth, you go someplace where there are flowers—any kind, even a weed; it makes no difference. There are no weeds; there are only plants. And you go to the flower and try to get your heart at the same level as the flower without lying down on others of its kind, see? So it might be near a path. You don't have to be right on top of it, but you lie down so your heart is at the same level as the flower—the plant has to be standing up a bit, you see? Then you go into that warmth. The plant will probably respond in some way, or if there's more than one, there will be a response. You do not go out of your body, but because the plants are responding, and maybe other plants around, as well, you will experience yourself not only as yourself physically, but also as the plant. Then you will be able to experience the emotions or range of feeling the plant has, which is greater than the range of feeling the human has.

In this way you can expand your own range of feelings. The plant's feelings will be only benevolent; the plant does not have any uncomfortable feelings that you have access to. So you will only feel and notice pleasant ones. Sometimes they will increase the warmth; other times it will feel warm and cool at the same time. There will be a physical feeling inside, and sometimes both inside and on the surface of your body.

That's how you begin, with different plants, different flowers; then you can try it with wild water. But the water has to be as pure and clear as possible, like a mountain spring near its beginning, not polluted by humans any more than you can avoid. You also can try it with sky or rain or sunshine. Don't look at the Sun, just be near it and make the connection; then the Sun will have only benevolent feelings. If you look at the Sun it does not work well; you have to just put your attention near the Sun. It's okay to close your eyes. You can locate it, then move your head to one side so that the sunlight is something you are connecting with, you understand, the same way you connect with the flowers. The foundation, though, is the heart/warmth, which you might also feel in your stomach; it depends where it comes up.

Ashan's Fascination with Butterflies

In the beginning, regardless of what stratus you choose to emerge in, you are allowed to acquire it on your own. You do not have any teachers until you choose to ask for them; then teachers are made available to you only as long as you want them. It is not a rigid course; it lasts as long as you want them, and then when you no longer want them, they depart or go elsewhere or resume their lives. That is how the acquisition of knowledge and wisdom takes place.

And what was your area of interest?

My area, when I was young, was how things emerge from one form to another, like your caterpillar becomes a butterfly. When I was on Earth, oh, I loved that. I was able to see that more than once; it was marvelous.

But what examples did you have on your home planet that stimulated that interest?

Of course, anyone emerging was an example.

Oh! Either by birth or into the seventy-eighth stratus.

Anyway, I was fascinated by transformation from one form to another. And then when I was young I asked several teachers how this happens in other places, and they showed me all the different types of birth that they could find. I asked if there was any other kind of transformation from one form to another, and one of the things they showed me was the caterpillar becoming a butterfly. When I saw that, I knew I had to come to Earth.

Do you find them only on Earth?

Only on Earth do you find them with that kind of variety. In those days there were thousands of different kinds of butterflies; there are not so many in your time. But think of it—every butterfly with a different pattern of color on their wings, and every one flying in a slightly different pattern. It is almost infinite. So the change from one form to another has its own form of infinity. And then, of course, the caterpillar itself is so amazing—all those little legs? Think about it. How is it possible that a being with, say, thirty or forty legs should transform so completely so that when it comes out, it has just a few long legs?

And then it flies!

And then it flies! That is not an accident, that butterflies should choose to come to Earth and demonstrate that such transformation is possible.

It's supposed to be a lesson for us.

All the beings on Earth that are not human are here to teach you or to offer something you can assimilate or consume. This is intended to teach you from the inside out, physically or physiologically. It might teach your cells by transforming them in some way. Even now, what you call cancer cells are teaching the rest of your body the impact, not only of pollution (fully 90 percent of cancer is caused by pollution), but also that the misuse of something intended to be interacting with something else will always create something self-destructive in one way or another. And a cancer cell kills its host, so it is self-destruction personified.

So how else were you taught? Is your planet technologically advanced, at the same time as you're very spiritually advanced?

Odin's Technology Is Organic

We have no technology that I can point to and say, "There is a machine." We have nothing with moving parts.

So you're beyond that.

The ship itself has no moving parts whatsoever. Remember, I said I activated some of the controls so that the ship would heal itself? These are like places you push on the ship, but they are not buttons. You know, when you have someone who does the acupuncture or acupressure on your body, he or she presses certain spots on your body, but there are not buttons there. It's the same thing; the ship is alive. You press certain places on the ship, and it repairs itself, much the way your body repairs itself with acupressure. And when I would step out of the ship, it's not that a door opens; I just step through a certain part of the wall, you might say, or the skin of the ship, and there I am able to step through.

Because it allows you to.

It allows me to, yes. And stepping back? I step back in through a different part, because that first part allowed me to step out, but one way, only. Then I step back in through a part that allows me to step in. One way only. Just like your physical bodies—some things go in one way only. And some things go out one way only. It's exactly the same.

Our scientists would have a lot of fun trying to figure that out.

But you see, that is what you could refer to as organic technology, because it is technology of a form, but all done with the permission and cooperation of every tiny portion and every major portion of everything around you. Then everyone is happy doing what they are doing. The ship is a ship because all the particles of itself wish to do exactly what it's doing; the ship celebrates its existence just by being—to say nothing of traveling from place to place, which all the portions of itself that make up its whole self are happy to do. So the ship is fulfilled by its existence. This is the same as a baby being born; all the particles in the baby's body are happy to be part of the baby's body, so when the baby is born, it is being fulfilled just to be. Of course, birth can be improved, but that will happen in your time.

So those gadgets the people from the Iroquois' home planet gave the elder were also organic, then?

Yes. Only portions that wanted to be part of what would appear to be an object were engaged in that; and they would do only that, and be happy. If the object were to fall into the hands of someone who did not know what it was for or how to use it, it would simply dissipate, and the particles would travel into space and return to their original place by untraceable pathways.

I thought each being could only eat of the planet that he came from. When you came here, were you able to consume Earth food?

Yes.

Was the elder able to consume food on that planet, the home of his ancestors?

He did not have to eat. It was possible to make that arrangement. I remember him saying how strange it felt not to eat, but we did have a liquid that he could take, concentrated water, and something that was like a concentrated nutrient. He said each time he ate the nutrient, it reminded him of a different food—even though it was the same substance all the time. That's because whatever food you're longing for, in that moment, even if it's a combination of foods, it will taste like that. So he did not have to eat and drink.

What Ashan Looked Like on Earth

What did you look like when you stepped off the ship? What did they see?

They saw someone who looked rather like them, but the color of my skin would have been closer to that of polished copper—darker, a little darker than they were. I was not wearing a shirt, so in that way I looked a little like them. It was a warm time of year. And I was wearing a loincloth, plus something else. It covered me in the front and the back, but only about halfway down my hips, so the garment ended about the length of a hand above my knees. And nothing on my feet.

And was this a form that you transformed to, knowing what they looked like?

No.

Or is that the way you looked?

This was something I traveled in, a comfortable garment.

So that was the normal way you looked when you were traveling, then?

Yes. The body was a comfortable garment for travel.

Well, how many places did you go to?

In number? When I was traveling? Thousands.

How many places did you land?

Oh, you mean, like, mingle?

Mingle, interact with, yes.

Mingle or interact? Oh, maybe fifteen, sixteen, seventeen.

And did the population in those places have different forms and different shapes . . .

Oh, yes. If the shape was significantly different—and this is important, as the people might be uncomfortable with someone who didn't look at least similar to them—then I would change my shape to look similar, but not exactly the same. It would be obvious that I was from someplace else; I would transform myself just enough that they would be at ease.

Give me some examples of what some of these shapes were. I mean, we're going to go out there, someday.

Well, I would tell you about places where you would see beings. I did go to the planet where there were the hybrid beings, something that would be spelled . . . it sounds like "fawn," but the word would be spelled f-a-u-u-g-h-n, something like that. It's a long u, it's [phonetic] faaaooohnn, something like that.

Oh, yes! We know of that place.

In any event, that's one of the places I went, and I went there first to assimilate some form of human energy, and I interacted with the people. They did not require that I looked like them; they are very artistic and appreciate different shapes, forms and feelings. So they were a lot of fun to be around. Artistic people often are, because they are flexible and spontaneous and often cheerful, which these people were. So I stayed with them about three and a half years in terms of Earth time. They were a pleasure to be with. They didn't need to go for a ride in my ship; they had their own. But they got a lot of pleasure out of the way I would get in and out of the ship, and they used to ask me every day [laughs] sometimes more than once, to get in and out of the ship. It would make them laugh; they never got enough of it, that I would get in one way and out another way. For some reason it struck them as very funny.

They had standard technology that had doors?

They have fixed technology, yes. You open a door, you get out and you go back in the same way. They had never seen a door that you step through while it's closed and you step back through a different place. I would step through slowly, sometimes, so that my body would gradually disappear. It's like going through a membrane, and you feel it physically as you go through. One of them was brave enough to stick a hand through when invited, and I could see him kind of shuddering, and then he pulled his hand back out. Afterward, he did something that human beings can identify with: He shook himself a little bit, like a shudder, and then he laughed. He said, "It felt funny!" You would say "creepy," but it's a feeling they don't have in their culture.

That's great. No matter where you go, you don't have to eat?

No. But I can.

And assimilate it and process it and . . .

Yes, in the way that is acceptable to, if not exactly the same as, the people with whom I am living.

That's amazing. What are some of the other places you visited?

A Journey to the Pleiades

I went to the Pleiades. They are your first cousins, but they do not like to think of themselves as being that close a relative. But I assured them that the similarity was so striking it might make them nervous. They have a good sense of humor, so we laughed about that every time someone (not everybody) would occasionally make a joking reference to Earth people. I'd say, "You're talking about your brothers and sisters! It could be you!" And then they would laugh and apologize.

We've been told that when we go there, we will activate them a little bit. And they don't like it, but they're getting ready.

Yes. You will have to be very gentle with them, because they are vulnerable. On the one hand, yes, you could harm them if you are too enthusiastic or spontaneous, but there is another side to that. If they feel threatened, they will find a way to keep you away; they will not harm you, but if they feel threatened, they have the capacity to keep you away indefinitely. So you have to train your people to travel very carefully; they will get thorough training in diplomacy, but the kind of diplomacy that an anthropologist would have to have—not just whether you should bow or shake hands or hug, but what you might encounter, to be prepared for anything.

Yes, sensitivities to the life . . . .

Yes, highly sensitive training so that in the first interactions, your people will feel very—how can we say—not stultified, but like you're afraid to be yourselves. And it's probably good not to be yourselves immediately, because the first encounters will require very polite interactions without any physical contact whatsoever—no shaking hands. And then, when these contacts are ongoing, it will have to be the same people meeting every time, time after time. Eventually, different things will happen every time, until someday there will be a touching of one fingertip to another, to see if that feels okay. And waiting, and so on. It will be a long, drawn-out, highly sensitive interaction on both sides.

Until there's open communication?

It will take quite a few years to make a regular physical interaction, as if you were talking to one of your own people. But you would still have to be very broad-minded, not argumentative in the slightest.

Well, that's the next generation's joy, I guess.

The next generations will be happy to do that. You have to remember that you can't just blunder into somebody else's culture and hope that they will accept you as is. [Laughs.] I can assure you that out of the cultures I've seen, there are some that you could blunder about in, and people would say, "What strange animals! Let's put them in the zoo for all to observe." You have to be careful so that you're not classified as barbarians.

You headed in our direction, but you could have gone anywhere.

I came this way on purpose.

Because?

Butterflies.

Oh! Because you wanted to come to Earth, for the variety of butterflies. All right. Are there others you interacted with that we might meet?

You will meet the beings from Andromeda. I've met a few of them. Different ones from different planets look quite different, but there are some who look like human beings, who could almost pass for human beings.

But they're a little tall.

A little taller—heads are a little bigger, brain capacity, more significant. And I don't know what to say; it was an interesting encounter. I didn't stay much more than a day and a half, Earth time. They were very smart, very intellectual. That was their interest. But that is not mine too much, so it was more of a diplomatic call. But your people, the people who will travel in space, will also be smart and intellectual and will probably want to talk to them for longer.

Do you personally recall other lifetimes?

No, I don't.

All Part of Love's Creation

Does your culture, your history, say you were from this creation, or did you come from someplace else?

They say, in terms of your historical understanding, we are from Love's Creation.

Ah! So you understand the Explorer Race.

We understand the purpose the Explorer Race has.

Were your ancestors, your progenitors or whatever, invited to come to this creation?

We are part of Love's Creation.

No, but I mean, this particular creator's creation.

This particular creator's creation is part of Love's Creation.

Right, but it's much bigger than this creation, so I didn't know if you began here or had been invited to come here from someplace else.

I do not know how to answer your question.

Okay. Love's Creation has billions of creations, like our creation?

Yes.

So I just wondered if your people had started in one of the other ones, and then been invited . . .

Ah, I see! No, I think we have been here.

Ah, came from this one. [The questioner's question and Ahsan's answer are explained more clearly in Chapter 5, when another being from Odin speaks and clarifies this issue.] What is the interest and purpose of your culture besides traveling and transforming form? I mean, what are the interests of the other people?

As is so well said, for the pleasure of being. No, we do not have a purpose that we must fulfill; we can be or do whatever is compatible with all life around us, and within us.

Do other people or cultures or entities or beings visit your planet, your star . . . is it a planet?

Yes.

Do they visit your planet?

We have had visitors to Odin from time to time, yes. Not too many, because . . . I think it is because our people are not living in fixed stratus. So the visitors we have tend to be either creators or creators-in-training who are comfortable with sudden and potentially constant change of stratus.

That implies that your planet is awesomely advanced, if all of these strati are on your planet, in your planet.

It is all part of the planet, yes.

That's highly unusual, isn't it?

From my travels, I would say you are correct, that it is unusual.

So you have a very special being ensouling your planet?

Yes. I would say someone who is probably a full-time creator who also has part of its existence focused as a planet. Maybe that's why the name Odin is part of it. I grant that there are other names there, but that's the name that seems to be the one that comes through for Earth.

Would the being like to talk to us? And could we possibly find out how the mythology of Odin began? What their interaction was with the Scandinavians?

Yes, I think it is possible, though the transmission would probably be short, because the energy is very powerful, and you might or might not feel it. It depends . . .

How many beings on your planet? Millions, or ten, or . . . ?

It's a little hard, but I can give you a count. Just a moment. [Pause.] Roughly, as you say, about 18,000.

Oh, that's all! And so how many of them have you personally interacted with?

Every one.

Every one! At different times?

Yes, and sometimes at the same time, but that's the nature of living in different strata. There are some strata where you are in touch with everyone at the same time. So in such a place, when one feels a great sense of the universality of life, and also after a compatibility with such a place, the feeling of compatibility with all life in other places is then very easily assimilated. It then feels completely natural and normal, if it hadn't before, you understand.

It's like union.

Yes, it is. It is union.

I wonder if immortal personalities go there as a training. It must be an incredible opportunity to experience all those levels.

I do not think that it is used in that way. I agree that such an experience would be good for a training, but I think such things happen elsewhere.

So you have almost half of your life left. What will you do when you're not traveling anymore?

What am I going to be when I grow up? [Laughs.] Well, on the basis of what some of my fellows are doing, I'd have to say, more of the same. But I do not expect to travel anymore, as I once did in my ship. I'm available for teaching. I would teach, though, only what I know about, meaning not all our people know about many things, but I would teach only my specialty—the emergence from one form into another. That's my specialty; that's my hobby. I could talk for years on butterflies alone.

A Place of Liquid Light

Is there a planet where the butterflies come from?

Oh, certainly.

Have you been there?

No, but they have told me. It is a place that is predominantly color, and after my visit with the Pleiadeans, I would call it a place that reminds me of . . . not exactly, but it reminds me of liquid light. There, they have a greater sense of individual personalities.

You didn't want to go there? Or you didn't have an opportunity, or . . . ?

I just happened not to go there. Remember my specialty, the emergence of one form of life to another? Their home planet isn't about that. They only do that on Earth; on their home planet, they don't look like butterflies.

Oh, I see! Did they tell you what they look like?

They didn't have to; they showed me.

What did you see?

That's why I compared it to liquid light.

Ah. A flowing . . .

A flowing, changing . . . . but with a sense of individuality and corporeal identity.

Teaching on Odin

Oh, how exciting! Well, back to your planet. If there is a union, is what you feel transmitted to the other inhabitants when you share, or only when you're asked?

Only when they desire to feel it. One does not have the feelings of others thrust upon one; if I wish to feel the feelings of the beings around me, it is available without secret, in that sense. But I do not have to acquire it.

You do not have to, right. So how do you know what's available, and which ones you might want to experience?

It is not unlike the way you would sniff the soup to know whether you wanted to taste it. There is an outer sensation before one experiences the more intimate impact. You might smell the soup; it smells good. Stick the spoon in, bring some up by your nose for a closer smell, then touch the tip of your tongue to the soup—tastes pretty good. Then you might take a mouthful, and it's pretty good. It is similar. Similar, although without consumption. I do not take it in; it's more like a merge. That way there is no taking. There's no loss on the other person's part.

So when you asked for teaching, is that how the teaching was done?

No. It would be a form of communion, but it would be, like you would say, mixed media. It would be perhaps simultaneously sound, color, light, feeling, touch plus smell, all the senses you have, plus about thirteen or fourteen others that are not fully translatable into your language, but one of them would be multifaceted reflection.

Part of why you're so interesting is that you represent all this incredible potential of what's out there for us to experience after we get through with our duty here on Earth as the Explorer Race.

Well, that is exactly the purpose of these *ET Visitors Speak* conversations, because once you have completed your school here, you will rejoin the rest of your personality who wanted to come here in the first place and be reminded of why you came here, something one often forgets during life, I believe. Then you will appreciate your experience here, because you will have accomplished your purpose, and you will have a place to put that experience. You see, it is not just experience that doesn't seem to have any purpose; you'll be able to put it into something else, and as a result, that something else will become much more complete, or possibly totally complete. Then, if it's totally complete, you will go on and live some other way, some other place, for example.

But if it isn't, you might choose to continue your completion process either on Earth or someplace else where you can have that completion. The main thing is that once you leave Earth, your Earth experience will certainly become crystal clear to you, and you will understand why you had it. What you experience on Earth is never a punishment or a reward; it is always and only a continuing acquisition of something you are attempting to complete. Sometimes you must acquire different facets of the experience, perhaps, for one example only, to expand your compassion. Or, for another, to stimulate your creativity. Other examples you can imagine yourself.

Explorer Race to Create a Benevolent Expanded Potential for All Beings

Well, one of the things we're supposed to be doing here (when we get the entire thing put together), one of the purposes of the Explorer Race, is to expand the potential of everything, everywhere, everywhen.

Yes, that's a good word, expansion—but it's not like with a balloon. It's like, everything that you can do, all right, you can still do. You will not have new foreign things that you can do; you will simply be able to do more with what you now have. It would be as if you could play music in only one octave; suddenly you would have an octave on either side that you could use. It will be like that for everyone. But it will not be so foreign that you wouldn't know where to begin to use it, much less its impact or any consequences that would be invasive.

You see how it's all planned carefully with ultimate respect and honoring of all beings? To be able to do more and be more of what you are now would feel good to almost every being that I can think of, maybe all beings. But to suddenly have thrust upon you something that is completely foreign, something that you not only wouldn't know what to do with but with which you might very easily do something chaotic or harmful without any intention of doing so, simply because you have no familiarity with it? If, for example, you had always walked on ice, the lake was always frozen. Then someday you are climbing out on a rope ladder over the frozen lake, as you think, and you drop down to find the lake is liquid, not frozen. What happens?

You have to learn to swim.

No. That's not what happens. You drown.

I understand. That's an example of how it's not going to work.

Yes. That's how it's not going to work. Better, in this case, you go to the lake, and it is maybe frozen solid except in the very center. Maybe you can access the rope ladder, but not at the very center. You can walk up to the part that is liquid water, but you can't really approach it; it becomes something fascinating. You study or honor it, you understand? It becomes something that people can interact with, slowly, slowly, exactly; but you are not suddenly thrust into it, like into bubbling water. The carrot does not consider it an expansion of its life form to be boiled.

Right. So you have always known about the Explorer Race?

No.

When did you learn?

Only when it was clear that I was coming here. The instructions came through in the ship. I heard a voice that said, "Now that you are intending to go to Earth, you will encounter a race of beings who will look very much like others you have seen other places, but this race of beings has a specific purpose. They are the Explorer Race, and here is their purpose." And then it talked about you—a brief overview of where you have been, what you are doing, where you are going, but more to the points that I would understand— that you, as the Explorer Race, have an underlying agenda. And that regardless of what each individual might say or do, you are driven by that agenda, even if it flies in the face of your personal desire.

That's a great explanation. But look at that; you learned that 780 years ago—the Andromedans only learned it four or five years ago.

Well, I was coming here; I needed to know, didn't I?

But the Andromedans came here and didn't have any clue until just a few years ago.

I can't speak for their teachers but I have pretty good ones, myself. I wouldn't care to have blundered in and stumbled around and made trouble.

That's the only place you touched down on Earth?

Only within the Iroquois nation, even though they did not stake out claims and say, "This is our land." I mean places they would go.

With the quality of your home planet and the planet the Iroquois came from—the Iroquois inspired our government. That starts to make sense.

They were great beings when I met them. Perhaps it improved their lore, their knowledge, their wisdom a bit to encounter me and my people, but they had already established those principles that your government, that people who came to be members of your government, admired.

Oh, I didn't make myself clear. I didn't attribute it to your particular visit; I just meant the quality of who they were in their immortal personalities.

Oh, from their home planet and so on.

Yes.

But because they were nearby, I wanted to see them. I thought, "Wouldn't it be nice not only to see butterflies but also to visit my cousins?"

But the cousins are closer to normal 3D life forms, not . . .

Well, they are humans.

Well, I mean they're nothing with ninety-eight dimensions.

You are not aware of their other dimensions because of your range of feelings. Remember, what you are here is only temporary; you have a limited range of feelings here, which keeps you focused in the stratus you are in. That's how you're kept in.

Yes, I understand—like a matrix. But the beings who became the Iroquois from the planet that's close to you, that planet is not even similar to the planet that you're from, even though it's close in space?

I would say that the planet is similar. That is part of the reason I felt that they were first cousins. It doesn't have the same quantity of stratus, but almost—seventy-nine.

And they also do the transformation and the emergence of beings and other things similar to your planet?

No. I think they have their own culture.

Well, still, that's extraordinary. Seventy-nine dimensions. I was just saying that the quality of the beings probably had something to do with the marvelous civilization they built here. That's what I was trying to get at.

I see.

The quality of where they came from, you know, who they were before they came.

I think that is the case for all beings here. Who you were before you came, even as an individual born in an individual culture, always impacts what you become and those you contact.

What we were in our lives before we came to Earth impacts our lives on Earth?

Certainly.

Even though we don't know why we act that way, or why we have those feelings or those radiations or whatever?

That is why very often when you explore past lives, those you explore primarily focus in very specific planetary groups: Zeta, Orion, Pleiades, Andromeda, Arcturus, Sirius and others. Certain types of individuals with certain ranges of feelings would be attracted to the Explorer Race based upon their range of feelings. The range of feelings is everything; that's why your teachers have recently been focusing you in feelings, trying to expand your feelings and so on. That's how you will shift, not only dimensions, but shift form.

Your Feelings Enable You to Shift Form

You can shift form and not look any different from the outside, but on the inside it can be radically different. You might change or transform certain body organs to become more efficient. Say, for instance, a space traveler could travel to a certain place with only a certain amount of oxygen and the way to do it would be to have larger, more efficient lungs. You might, with such techniques, be able to improve the quality of your breathing apparatus to use, say, one-quarter the amount of air but with full and complete efficiency. Right now, when you breathe, you acquire just a little bit of what you need from the atmosphere before you have to blow it out. But with a different type of lung shape, form and biology and microbiology, your lung might become more efficient. Maybe one lung instead of two.

You might also do something else—for instance, you might wish to increase your heart's capacity to pump; you might increase the size of your blood vessels for more physical efficiency. You might, in the case of a space traveler, wish to do the opposite: temporarily shrink the size of your heart so that it might pump either faster or slower, depending upon what is the efficient necessity. The variables are wide-ranging.

You have such an ability to teach and such wisdom! What was the process? The call went out, and you heard it? How did you . . .

What process?

That we got connected to you.

Butterflies.

No, tonight.

Oh, yes. It is not exactly a calling; it is more like a receptivity with an editorial subprogram. The editorial subprogram is what you want, what would also be compatible with the channel, what is of interest to you as a person, what would be of interest to the readers. That's the subtext, so to speak. But the rest of it is all receptivity, and then individuals just volunteer. I happened to be the one that felt the best.

The Origin of the Legends of Odin

Would it be possible to talk to whoever came to Earth before and started the Odin god legend?

You mean beings from my culture who might have come to visit the people in the north?

Yes.

Oh, I think that might be interesting, don't you?

I think it would be very interesting, yes.

It would build nicely on this, like a companion piece.

But I would try to read a little bit, sometime before tomorrow night, just what is written here about Odin.

I think that's a good idea.

That's great.

You don't have to do too much, because it might not relate, after all. What has been spoken, you understand—it wasn't written so much, but what has been spoken was passed down through generations and generations before anybody thought about writing anything down. That is what has been a bit mischievous with a lot of your history here. Someday when you have access to the original stories, your history will suddenly take on a whole new look; your history will look more like a drama that does not really have a great deal of relevance. Of course, in recent times, your history has become more accurate as writing has become more widespread.

But one of the things we're trying to do is make our history more accurate.

Yes.

What else would you like to say that interests you, that you think would interest the reader?

The worlds of life in their infinite variety are reflected here on your planet. Look around and appreciate the variety of life in your own backyard, in your neighborhood—not only your neighbors, your friends, your family, but the different forms of life. Those little ones that fly, little creatures, birds, snakes, fish, deer, elk, dogs, cats, flowers, trees, plants—every one is an individual. Every blade of grass, every ant [laughs], every bird, every human . . . every one owes its origin to some other planet somewhere. You can look at a dandelion, the next time you see one, and you can think to yourself, "I wonder what planet you came from?" And even though you might not hear the answer, the dandelion knows. Good night.

Thank you very much. I really enjoyed it.

DISENTANGLEMENT: A GIFT FROM
THE EXPLORER RACE MENTORS

THE DISENTANGLEMENT BASIC PROCESS

SSJOOOO THROUGH ROBERT SHAPIRO

Lie on a flat surface on your back, hands by your side, palms down and slightly away from your body—preferably three hours after eating and before you go to sleep, but it works anywhere, anytime. Remove any metal buckles and take coins or metal keys out of your pockets. Do not cross your legs or feet. This position allows you to get used to being open in your most receptive area.

Say out loud (if possible), "I am asking gold lightbeings, Earth gold lightbeings, lightbeings who can work through gold lightbeings and lightbeings who can radiate or emanate to gold lightbeings, to disentangle me from my discomforts and their causes."

Squeeze your eyelids shut and then focus on the light patterns—don't think. If you catch yourself thinking, gently bring your attention back to the light patterns and continue.

Do this for twenty or thirty minutes or for as long as you feel you need to do it or until you fall asleep. This can be done twice a day.

After a few weeks, make a list of every person and event in your life that makes you feel uncomfortable. Say the above statement and add, "I am asking to be disentangled from the discomfort and pain of _____," reading one or two names or events from the list. Do each name for two–three days or until you feel clear with the person.

SPEAKS OF MANY TRUTHS ADDS:

"You may notice that if you say those specific words or names during the course of your day, after you've done disentanglement on them three to five times, that you no longer feel physically as uncomfortable about them as you once did.

"This means the disentanglement is working. The objective is to feel physically calm. Keep saying those specific words or names in your disentanglement process until you feel physically calm. When you do, move on to other words or names, never more than one or two at a time."

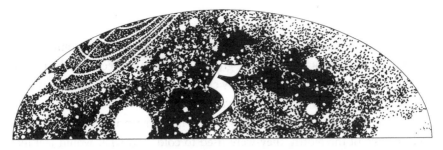

Odin, the Norse God:
How the Myth Began

ET Visitor from Planet Odin
January 3, 2002

Greetings. I am one of the beings who came to visit the people of the North. I am from the planet Odin, but the visit was so long ago, I have since returned to spirit form in the sixty-seventh stratus. I can speak for a time about our visit to your Earth. We came in a vehicle that held the three of us: two females and one male. I was one of the females. We generated the form of the people we came to see. They, in their root souls, had come originally from Odin and could trace their spirit line there, though they had forgotten. We came to remind them who they were and to support their existence with stories. They were established in their culture and traditions and did not require any further assistance, but they needed a sense of self, a sense of purpose and direction and a foundation of moral values beyond that which they had established traveling.

So we came and we recognized that our arrival would cause alarm and possibly fear, so we made certain that we would look as much like them as possible, only taller. People in those days were not so very tall, anyway; so we were each about six-and-a-half feet tall, which by your standards today would not be that tall, but by the standards in those days would be very tall, indeed. So we dressed like them, we looked like them; we had capacities that would allow us to win in any contest, should they choose to set us to a competition, but they did not. As it was, we were greeted after about three days; the people kept away, though we had landed very close to where their encampment was. The people kept away because they were frightened.

One of the reasons they were frightened might surprise you. Since they were people of the North, they were used to cold, and what would feel like cold to people in the South, to them, would feel like warmth—meaning that bitter cold was cold to them and that mildly cold, temperatures in the thirties, would be what they would consider to be warm. So they were frightened by the warmth that the ship had. The ship landed and was warm, and it melted the snow and ice underneath it. And fortunately it was early enough in the winter season so there was not that much snow and ice in that spot. You know, the snow does melt off before the spring. So the warmth plus perhaps the surprise of it all kept people away for three days. But then the braver ones approached, and we opened the door. They ran back, then they approached again. Then a ramp came out, and it was like that, back and forth and back and forth, until finally we were ready to emerge. We emerged all at once, the three of us. The people were afraid of many things, but when they came to the ship, they saw us; we were looking like them, though instead of blond hair, we had hair that was a platinum blond color.

Other than that, our appearance was similar to theirs, with some extra decorations thrown in so that we would appear to be special. This was all done theatrically, I grant, but it was done with the intention of catching their eye and generating respect and admiration—not for us as individuals, but rather so that they would feel, initially, the kindred spirit. After we were able to tell our stories with this connection, they would then feel a more natural kindred spirit. But the initial dramatics and theatrics of it were necessary so that they would not run away.

So we were invited into the village and asked to eat. It was not in our nature to eat, but we were able to do so. And then, of course, they wanted to know where we were from—the first question, naturally, yes? "Where are you from?" And then, of course, "How did you get here?" But first, where you are from was our opening, and we told them that we were from Odin, and that they were from Odin also. Now, if you think about the way we said it, in hindsight we might have said it differently; but by saying we were from Odin and they were from Odin as well, I think this might have been what unintentionally created the idea that they were like children of Odin—that Odin was something, rather than a planet where people lived, you see?

You could be from the Creator, you understand, or you could be from a planet, and there's a distinct difference, yes? So if we had it to do over again, perhaps we would say that we were from the planet Odin, and this is what it looks like and this is what it is like, and after describing it completely, and our culture there, then we would say, "And your ancestors are from there, too; that's why we came to visit you." See? But we didn't say that.

But they may not even have had a concept of what a planet was.

We were able to give them that by showing them pictures. We educated them. We were with them for years; we did not rush them through it. But because we began with that statement, "We are from Odin," you could say we were from the king; we did not make that connection of language until much, much later, and then it was too late. Anyway, that was our error. But even so, it is not a colossal mistake; it is just something that I'm hoping to correct with this talk.

What year did you come? In our time, as close as you can.

Year of your calendar? The people of the North have been living there much longer than people acknowledge, but it was about two generations into

Figure 5.1: A meeting between beings.

the Viking culture, what is called Vikings. But they do not call themselves that; they just refer to themselves as the people of the North. That's why I have called them that. So about two generations into their culture.

You have to remember that the initial people who came from Odin did establish a culture on Earth, but it was very otherworldly, meaning the culture that was established was more like Odin culture. Odin is a place that expresses many different types of potential.

You can have snow if you want it, or ice; you can have tropics; you can have anything, up to a point, perhaps. But the initial culture on Earth, while the people lived there for thousands of years, did not spawn or attract a culture that would live outside the bubble.

Original People from Odin Created a
Miniature Odin in a Dome/Bubble

Oh, I didn't say that: When the original culture from Odin arrived on Earth, they created something like a culture inside a bubble—you would say like a city, but a city is too vague. So it was many different spheres, many different stratus inside the bubble. A stratus would be a level within the universe. So they created several different spheres within the bubble so that it would have a great deal of potential flexibility and as full a range of experiences like Odin as possible, but within a smaller volume of Earth space. Nevertheless, such an exotic culture did not catch on on Earth, meaning there were no imitators.

So what was done, after a time, is that outposts were built. Some individuals from the original landing party conditioned themselves to the environment and walked about on the land. And they would meet travelers who would come through, sometimes partly from the Siberian area, where there are people of the North, still. Also there were a few travelers from space, but they did not stay. So the bulk of the population of the people of the North originally came from the colder places in Russia and in what is now Siberia. You think to yourself, "Well, they don't look like the same thing," but if you were to explore the peoples of Russia and Siberia, you would discover that what is called the Scandinavian look is actually there and has been for some time.

Where specifically did they build the bubble? In what now country?

Let me look closely at that. It would have been the extreme northern part of Norway.

And roughly, how long ago?

The initial settlement took place about 30,000 years ago. It lasted for quite some time. Now, people from Odin do not make quick decisions; we assimilate all the potentials. Once it was fully understood and agreed on by everyone that the culture of Odin in its natural form could exist here, but not in a way that could support the people of Earth, then only the individuals who wished to stay, who had become conditioned and liked the environment, chose to do so. And everyone else, including everything in the bubble, simply left and returned to Odin. It was about 7,000 years ago when most of the people and the bubble returned to Odin.

How many of the original people stayed here?

About eighteen.

The Eighteen Odin Set Up a Culture in Russia/Siberia

Did they intermarry with the Russians and Siberian people of the North? I mean, is their DNA still here?

They had the capacity to travel using portals and dimensions, as you say, so essentially they did travel. They went to the Russian place, the Siberian place; they invited people who were interested to come to Norway. But most people did not want to go to Norway, they wanted to stay where they were. So the initial culture was set up in what is now Siberia, but very close to what is now the border of Russia. So that's where the culture started. As time went on, there was a desire to move the culture back to Norway, because the conditions were more benevolent. There would be more likelihood of interacting with the rest of the population that would begin to form up in various places, in what is now Europe. And understanding that if they stayed in what was the Russian/Siberian area, that isolation would remain quite significant, and their whole point was not isolation, but the spreading of their culture of Odin.

That was the purpose for which they came in the first place?

Yes. They wanted to tell the people who they were; they wanted to spread the culture, morals, values and principles of Odin, which they felt were of value to people. Unfortunately, when the original people finally left, about 800 years ago, then some of the culture got confused. But during that time there was a lot of religion that was competitive, and the whole Odin culture got caught up in that feeling on Earth. And then there was a lot of attempt to coerce people to believe in the values of Odin, and Odin began to be projected as being a superior being. That did not work out well. But there are still some cultural remnants of the original idea of Odin and the values of Odin, and I feel that it overall was a worthy effort. But I'm not satisfied with the results.

Okay, 7,000 years ago they went to Russia/Siberia, but you said 800 years ago the original inhabitants left. Were those the eighteen who stayed on Earth?

Yes.

But in the meantime they had families and children?

Oh, yes.

They were immortal, compared to the life span on Earth.

They would have appeared to be immortal, but of course, as time went on, they had to return to Odin to change forms.

But how did they explain that to their families? They lived for thousands and thousands of years.

They just said that it was because they were from Odin; that's how they put it. Looking back on it, it would have been better to have said, "Because we are from the culture and planet of Odin," but they didn't say that. They said, "Because we are from Odin, we can live this long." So they came to be revered a little bit as superior beings. And the curiosity is that because they were not linguists, they were not social scientists, they never understood why they were being revered as superior beings, and it was actually frustrating to them.

Seven thousand years ago they went to Russia/Siberia. When did they get back to Norway?

The Odin People Return from Russia/Siberia to Norway

Once they had enough people who would wish to participate in the civilization, they were led through a doorway. They thought they were going to Odin, and for a while no one bothered to correct them. They were told after a time that this was Odin on Earth.

Back to Norway?

Yes. So they went through a doorway/portal and were able to simply be in Norway.

Okay. So the eighteen beings are the basis of the religion and the mythology and the religious doctrine of the ancient Scandinavians?

Yes, the eighteen who spoke of their culture and values of Odin, much of which has survived today in terms of values.

Some of the myths are interesting, though. Odin is called the Norse god of wisdom, war, art, culture and the dead, the supreme deity and creator of the cosmos and humans.

Yes. Some of that is because of competition with the Christian god. You understand that in your world competition is in everything. You'd be surprised—if you examine anything in your culture, in almost 90 percent of it you'll see competition as an underpinning. Even going to a restaurant, a restaurant says, "Come and experience our wonderful Mexican food," and another one says, "Come and experience our wonderful Thai food," you see? It seems to be an option, but the underpinning is competition—even something as innocuous as that.

This is why the god of war was never part of it but was adapted to that when there were battles between the Christian warriors and the Odins who called themselves the people of the North. And they had to transform their culture and their gods and deities to warriors, in order to convince the people to fight. Because there were some parts of Christianity that were appealing— it's just not appealing when someone says, "You will become a Christian, or we'll kill you." That kind of convincing does not make for permanent beliefs. The Christians are still battling, but maybe not in the same way, to convince people that their god is the best.

You said the eighteen only left Norway about 800 years ago, and you said that you and your two other friends came 800 years ago, to tell the remnants who had forgotten who they were, where they came from. So had the eighteen just left, then? Or was it a couple of generations later that you came?

They had just left about thirty years before. We came because the people weren't able to maintain the culture in the way that it was hoped without the eighteen. The eighteen who came back to Odin said they were concerned, so volunteers stepped forward to say, "We will go and remind the people," which we did.

So did you have any special training or anything?

No, the training we had was from the ones who had returned to Odin, the eighteen. They spoke to us and it's not like speaking as you understand it—they communicated their full range of experience to us. Then we could go with an understanding of who the ancestors were, of those who were living there, so we could talk to them about their physical ancestors, as well as who we were in order to establish our, well, you say bona fides.

The Eye of Odin on the U.S. Seal

Yes. Ahsan [in the previous chapter] explained that the communication would have been in full-color, sound and about thirteen more senses than we have. I would like to ask about a couple of the things that are in all the Norse mythology books. The god Odin wanted to drink from the well of wisdom, so he gave one eye. That's in all the books. Where do you think that came from?

Look at the back of the one-dollar bill. Do you have one on you?

I can go get one. Oh, the eye above the pyramid!

So the story goes, that he gave one eye. Do you know which eye it was? The eye in the center of his forehead. That is the eye on the back of the one-dollar bill. The people who designed the Great Seal of the United States knew about Odin. The Seal is mystical, primarily; one sees the Seal with the bird, the phoenix bird on the front of the Seal of the United States. It has the phoenix (it's not an eagle) on the front, with the choices. This means the front of the Seal represents the choices that people have to make, whether they will choose peace or war. Once they have made the proper choice, then they are able to pursue the mystical goals of the United States, which are on the other side. That is the whole point of the Seal of the United States; it is intended to be a journey by the people of the United States to enlightenment, as laid out by the founders of your country, who knew all about Odin.

That's why you see the eye. And the eye is also part of the culture of Egypt. It is assumed by people that the eye on the back of the one-dollar bill has to do with Egypt, and people have assumed that it has to do with Coptic, but it actually has to do with Odin. If you think about the people who designed the Great Seal, they were all light-skinned, so they are not going to do too much about Coptic, even though Coptic, you understand, has some roots in Egypt. They are going to, however, use Coptic, because Coptic is a good form of Odinism. There is a relationship between Odinism and Coptic and Egyptian stories.

So the eye that Odin gave is the eye of transcendence. It wasn't that he gave his third eye so that he could have wisdom; it's that he gave his third eye as a gift to the people of Earth, so that they could achieve soulful wisdom and therefore achieve their greater purpose.

Fascinating. Was one of the eighteen more or less a leader?

All the same.

Odin Culture Introduced Runes

Another thing that the myths of the people of the North all talk about are the runes. Would that be because they brought a knowledge of writing?

Yes. This has to do with writing. It was realized that the reason that the stories were not lasting from generation to generation was that the people were creative, and they were adding their own parts to the story to make the story more interesting each time it was told. And while that was considered to be amusing and typical of storytellers, it was felt that it would be better to have a long-lasting principle and value system that could be represented symbolically. And therefore the designs and patterns were drawn on stones, actual stones, and those stones still exist today in the hands of people of Earth. They are not together as a set anymore, but they are held by certain individuals who are protecting the culture of Odin. These are relics, you might say. They have an energy of their own.

There are also some of these original pieces that are in different forms and have been passed out to different cultures, some of them in pure metals, others simply in stones—it just depended on what the culture valued, or what the culture might consider significant. But if they were not in the shape of actual stones—river stones, creek stones, smooth and oval—if they were not originally like that, with the shapes cut into them, then, if they were in metal, for instance, some pure metal, they would be angular. The angularity was not just to represent a piece of a puzzle, but also to represent stone or a crystal facet under a microscope.

When the eighteen were there, they had the runes with them?

They took them with them.

What's here now, then?

We brought them back.

And you handed them out and told people to safeguard them?

To guard them, and we told stories about each one and then we fitted them together in certain ways so that if you were to stand back six to eight feet, they would look more like a page with writing on it.

I've seen them used as fortune-telling devices.

It is not unusual in other cultures; other cultures might use stones or pieces of wood or even shells as a similar device to decide what the future could bring. If used by a trained practitioner it can be accurate at least half the time, sometimes more. And it depends how long they've been doing it, and whether they took the time to study the effects after the fact and made sure that things were read correctly. If not, then they would continue to practice until they got it as good as they could.

There are many legends that discuss Odin's wife, Freya; a son, Baldur; Loki, who causes Baldur to be killed; Valhalla. Do you want to talk about any of these?

Most of those stories have to do with additions that were placed by the people of the North, in order to make Odin seem like part of the people. They were encouraged to consider Odin to be part of their daily life, and when they would bring up stories like this, or the storytellers would add these things, we did not correct them because it was a way of making Odin and Odin culture part of their daily life. If Odin does not have a wife and children, then Odin is something separate from the culture of human beings. We allowed that.

Vikings Are from Odin Culture

We have legends of the Vikings; they are the adventurers and explorers extraordinaire. Was a lot of this exploring done while the eighteen were still here? They colonized Greenland; they went to Newfoundland, to New England. They went all the way to Russia.

It is not good for you to think of colonization as a good thing. Do you know what most colonization amounts to? The United States was colonized; what happened?

A lot of the original inhabitants were killed and/or their lands were taken.

That is a form of colonization that the eighteen would never have allowed. They would go to places and visit. When the eighteen were here, you have to remember that doorways were available, and people were allowed to come and see other cultures, to tell their stories, to share stories with those cultures, but never to battle and kill. All that came later.

It's only after the eighteen left, then, that the people of the North built the ships and went out and did what we have in our history?

That's right. But almost all of that, from my understanding, was in response to the invasion of the Christians. The Christians came to invade, you understand, in ships, so the people fought back and captured a ship. And then they built boats, but they built them in their own style and, as warriors in your time say, took the fight to the enemy, so that the enemy wouldn't be able to invade them any more. They went to invade the enemy, and that's how all those battles got going, unfortunately. But the people originally did not start the battle; they were invaded. And there's another term for that, invasion; the Christians were attempting to colonize.

I see, and convert them.

You must remember that true adventure does not require a broadsword or an axe. It only requires a story, a warm heart and acceptance of the differences in culture of others.

NASA should put that on our spaceships when we go out to explore.

I think that that is a good way to define adventure, and if the militaries of the world used that to define adventure, there would be much more happiness in the world. That is part of the culture of Odin, what I have stated.

Right. In another Explorer Race book, Zoosh (a being who also speaks through this channel that you're speaking through) said that there was a time when some beings came from Orion to the North, and there were some beings there from Polynesia, and the melding of those two was the basis of the people in the northland, in the Scandinavian countries.

This is also possible, because you have to remember that the original eighteen, when they went out to get recruits, went to various places to get those recruits. But that did not stop other people from coming and emigrating there. It depends what you consider as the root culture. Remember, when the eighteen came there, they were not the root culture; they were from Odin. It isn't as if there weren't other people there already.

Oh, I thought they were the first ones there.

No, they were not. The eighteen simply went out and attempted to interest the people who were there. The people were not interested, so the eighteen went other places to find people who were interested, and they brought those people back. But there were already people there, though not in the immediate area where the settlements were created, so that there would be no competition for resources and so on.

So were what we call the Vikings the descendants of the Odin?

Yes. But they were not from that part of the world; they were from Russia and Siberia. They were just brought there when they volunteered to participate in the culture of Odin.

So the Vikings were not everybody in Scandinavia; it was just that one group?

No. The Vikings came later. The Vikings were warriors, you understand, but they came later, out of necessity, after having been invaded. Those who came to be called the Vikings did not call themselves that.

But during all this time the DNA of the original eighteen was transmitted to these people they gathered together?

Yes.

Did they have special qualities and abilities as a result of being sired in part by the eighteen from Odin?

Well, no different than any other peoples on Earth, because all the peoples on Earth were generated from visitors from the stars.

But not all of them came from such a very special place.

But you understand what you are saying now; you're competing.

Yes, "these are better than those."

So you can see how insidious competition is.

Well, it's because I think Vikings are special.

But in order to be special . . .

Somebody else has to be less . . .

What's another name for special?

Better?

That's it. Go no further. You're in competition, better. Thai food's better than Mexican food. No! Mexican food's better than Thai food. It is important to understand how insidious the culture of competition is. It is not typical. Do you know, I have looked around other planets; I have not seen competition anywhere. I have seen teamwork. That is the natural culture. You have teamwork on your planet, in your culture now, but it has been channeled into competition—one team against that team. But there are sports that exist that are only based on teamwork—nobody against anybody else, a goal to be accomplished. The individuals come together to form a team; they have different tasks, and the goal is to accomplish the task. Once the task is accomplished, then the team has won. That is more rooted in culture that fosters a society of people who appreciate the value of one another, because they each contribute their own unique skill to the team. Much better than the good guys and the bad guys. Would you mind leaving that part in so people can see how competition has distorted your society, even though you are all very attached to it?

Cultural and Moral Values of Odin

I want to ask you some questions that I didn't ask Ahsan last night. Then we'll go to the cultural, moral values.

May I speak to the cultural and moral values first? The cultural and moral values are represented in other places, in other cultures, in other philosophies that have come to be appreciated on Earth already. Different cultures from different planets came to seed those ideas, so that the people of Earth would have some general guidelines to follow, meaning: Be kind to each other, as you would desire others to be kind to you. Such a foundational principle is important. It is obvious, but the obvious needs to be stated as a moral principle, so that people feel it is not simply a cultural tradition within the social group, but a principle from wise beings. Then other simple truths emerge, such as honesty and heart-centeredness, for example. There is the love of romance, the love of friendship, the love of companionship, the love of appreciation . . . all of these loves are true and equal, and all are different. That is something that might have been stated by one of the eighteen to the people of the North, things that you know to be true, nothing so very startling. Think of the basic tenets of religion and culture, but take out the deity parts.

You will find that the reason most religions have been successful has nothing to do with the deity they are promoting, but rather to do with the common ground of cultural and specific moral principles. If the religion does not promote those moral principles, then it does not survive. If it says, "We are better, and the others are no good," then it is like Nazism, which was a religion even though it wasn't identified as a religion in the Christian world. But it was a religion; the leader was considered a god in his own time and was honored as a living god would be. But the culture didn't last, because it didn't have the moral principles that unify the peoples of Earth. That's an example of a religion that you all know about that didn't last. Oh, there are still some followers today, but they treat it as if it were a political system. But it was never intended to be political; it was always intended to be a religion, and it was promoted that way—not in the beginning, but after a time it was promoted that way so that it would last. But it didn't have the common values and moral principles that people cherish.

Even if you look at Christianity or Buddhism or other religions, as they are called (Buddhism being more of a philosophy, but even so), you will find that the values and moral principles are similar. That's why they've lasted. Buddhism is perhaps a bit more successful in that it is not a competitive philosophy, whereas Christianity is. It is rooted in competition, even though it has values and moral principles that are of the common culture, which is why it is still here. But as time goes on and people become clear, through their communications getting better and better around the world, then Christianity will have to change. If it changes, it will last; if it doesn't, it won't. I think it will change; I have seen signs.

So when you came to remind the people of the North that they came from Odin, you told stories of their homeland, but you also told stories that embodied these moral values, right?

All the stories embodied moral values and all the stories that were told were of a cultural and traditional manner, so that the homeland was represented as something that sounded like Earth, meaning we would talk about culture of the homeland, but as it relates to Earth. We didn't talk about tropics; the people of the North didn't know anything about that. We talked about snow and ice and how you live in snow and ice. The people there would fish or hunt; we talked about fishing and hunting as principles, as values. We talked about speaking to the deities of the fish, so that the fish who would offer themselves to be caught would be caught easily and that other fish who were not meant to be caught would be allowed to return to their people. This way people could just go down to the sea, and the fish who would offer themselves would swim to them, and they would not capture the fish, but simply retrieve them. And then they would thank the spirit of the fish for making this great sacrifice, that they might eat. Such things were done; such things were taught. That is why the people of the North have a sacred relationship to the sea, and they know this. If they are happy there, they know this.

Other cultures have been taught this, in tropical areas, how to welcome the fish that offer themselves for consumption. And it was taught to the people of the North also. But in your time, it has been forgotten or is told only as a story. But the fish would still make this offer. The problem in your time is that many, many fish who need to be in their culture—their philosophers, their teachers, their mothers, their babies—have also been caught for food, so there is resentment from the world of the sea toward humans. And now the fish would not offer themselves willingly; they would fight. And it would take a long time to heal the wounds between creatures of the water and the creatures of the land. It could be done, but it would require a great deal of song, praise, appreciation and sacrifice by the people of the land, meaning to not fish in the sea for a thousand years, during which time there would have to be songs and praises and stories and gifts.

One might offer a gift to you that might be a sacrifice; perhaps you would have a crop in some part of the country, and you raise some of it and you would offer some to the sea. Maybe the beings of the sea do not need that crop, but they would recognize that it was a sacrifice. And the sacrifice cannot be in the blood of unwilling victims; it can only be something that is an actual sacrifice by those who are offering it. But it has to be something from the heart; that's why I say part of your crop. A small part, perhaps, but enough that would fit, say, in the scoop of both hands held together. Take some to the sea, out in a boat. Go out a ways so that you can still see the land, with two or three people, and you say to the people of the sea, just talking right to the water, "We offer this, our crop, as we have grown it, and as we have pounded it and made it right for us. We offer this from our own hands, with the love from our hearts to our friends of the sea, to apologize for misdeeds of the past and to request your friendship in the future." Drop it in the water, and then go home. This will take about a thousand years, and then the fish population will rebuild and the philosophy would be that it would be all right to offer themselves. And then it could start over again, where true fishing takes place.

That's beautiful. These stories were also told by the original eighteen, right?

Yes. And the people did learn to fish that way, and they only would receive the fish who offered themselves. And it was done that way and there was always plenty to eat. And the same with the animals and hunting, sacred hunters of your time. Some of these stories have lived on, sometimes presented by other cultures from other planets. Sometimes the culture of Odin stories has lived on in peoples that have either been from the North and moved to the South or, when people of the North went to the South, they told the stories, and if the stories were appreciated by the people of the South, then they took them in as their own.

So there are people still in your time who know how to do spiritual hunting. You make an offering; you ask for the spirit of the animal to come. You go to the same spot every year; you don't tramp about the forest and look for whatever animal reveals itself or is chased by other hunters into your path. You ask, and then you wait. You might have to wait two, three days, so you have to camp out. You leave no trash there, and you apologize to the plants you may have stepped on; you bring gifts for the forest, food, enough for yourself, enough for the forest. You do not put the offerings near your camp; you put them at least a quarter of a mile away. Whatever is personal sacrifice—perhaps some fish, or some crops or something you've grown is best, but at least something that is food for you and that the people of the forest, the animals, could eat. Then you wait, and you ask the animal to come. When the animal comes, you either use whatever you're using, your gun or your bow, and you kill it quickly so it does not suffer—that is, the animal that presents itself to you. When it comes to present itself, it will not dash out of the woods, look around and dash on; that is not the way it will come. It will walk out of the woods, and it will stand and wait for you to shoot. It will not move. That's how you know. And it will usually be the male of the species, say, a buck. You must wait; it is never good to shoot the females or the young ones. That is always a transgression in sacred hunting.

So you told these stories to the descendants, and do you feel that they followed the teaching and they then repeated them to each generation that followed?

They made the effort. But of course, you have to understand that during that time there were battles going on, so sometimes the best storytellers, the ones who had the stories memorized and could tell the best variations of the stories so that people could be involved, sometimes they were killed or injured, and an injury in those days usually meant death. You could have a simple injury in those days, some broken fingers, and they could kill you.

Earlier you said that you were talking to straighten out the record. Other than saying, "from Odin," what would you have done differently?

We would have made it clear that we were from the planet Odin. By saying, "We are from Odin," the people, after a time—through generations of telling stories, you understand—said that, "Emissaries arrived from the god Odin. They were from Odin." Not "Emissaries arrived from the planet Odin to remind us of our culture and that we were from there." Big difference. It was a mistake on our part; we are taking credit for it. [Laughs.]

Why did the original beings from Odin, who created the dome/bubble, choose the far North of the Earth? Why would they go to someplace where survival was so difficult?

Oh, the reason is very simple, simpler than you might imagine. And that is that other cultures were in other places and nobody was up there. So they went there because there was nobody there, and no one was serving the people there and offering them values and principles that were of enduring worth.

The Iroquois Live Their Teachings

Now, Ahsan said that the Iroquois are not from Odin itself, but from a planet very close. How close are they to you? They just happened to be from a planet in the same proximity? Or there's some relationship amongst the peoples?

Nearby. There is some relationship, yes. They are, what, first cousins, eh?

Because the Iroquois left an incredibly beautiful legacy to people on Earth today.

Yes. They were very good at assimilating and applying. The difference with the Iroquois people is that they didn't just take it in as a story; they applied the enduring values to their culture, and when they would interact with other cultures in some benevolent way, they would speak not only of the stories that were important to them, but they would give examples of how they had used the stories in their culture, and then demonstrate what they were talking about.

So they would teach. It is in their nature to teach, at least it was in the old days, and I think it still is, but because they were mistreated they do not feel as if their teaching is still appreciated. So sometimes, if you know people from that culture, and they do not teach right away, you will have to wait until you become friends, and then ask them if they will teach you anything from their culture that they feel would be of value to you as a person. They will say yes or no, and if they are good friends, maybe they will. If they are not knowing you well enough yet, you will have to wait. But, as in the old days, it was always their way; if it felt good to them, if they could see how to apply it in a way that was worthy for them, they would do so, and they would share it with others. They were not greedy with the information, of course.

But more to the point, they assimilated it so well into their culture that they lived it. It was a day-to-day experience; more like that than simply a separate story to be told around a fire to remind you of the value of yourself, so that you do not simply think that life is about suffering. These stories, they keep people going in the most difficult circumstances. Sometimes you think of them as religion or philosophy, but the root of all religion and philosophy is stories. Humans are adept at storytelling. To survive your conscious disconnection with your true nature and your true abilities, you need to have stories that can be repeated and give you a sense of continuity, because your natural sense of continuity is not with you.

As a Spirit, All of Life Is One Incarnation

You're in spirit now. Do you get to plan your next incarnation? Are you resting? How does that work?

Being in spirit is an incarnation. Because you are physical, you think of a physical life as an incarnation, for example. But when you are in spirit, that is also an incarnation.

How does that work? You came to the end of your 35,000-year life, and then you chose this next step you're in now? Or it happens?

The end of the life, a life in which you accomplish your purposes, your intentions . . . you could go on past 35,000 years if you cared to, but most beings say, "Well, I have done what I wished to do in this form, and now I will continue my life, but in a different form." That is what Earth people do. You accomplish your purpose in the form you're in, and then you continue; you let go of your physical form but you continue. There are no separate incarnations; it is only one incarnation. You just change forms. For example, if you want to be able to expand your means of understanding or creating, you might come to Earth, as the Explorer Race has. And you forget who you are so that you can expand what your potential is, out of necessity. But you do not die; you shed your Earth body when you have accomplished that purpose, and then you move on. But your incarnation is the same. There are no individual lives, just the forms change.

Right, but you do it consciously, deliberately, whereas we are unconscious in the leaving of it.

No, you are mistaken. All people who, as you say, die . . . all death takes place consciously. Everyone—even if it is sudden, in the moment of exit of the body—is conscious, completely. You're completely conscious.

But you choose when you want to leave your body, right?

We know (let's say, in terms of linear time, for your sake) well before we are going to leave our body, and we say, "Okay, we are going to leave our body," at a certain point—not in terms of time, not a calendar point, but when we have accomplished what we came here to do. Then we are going to change form. We're still going to exist and be ourselves. Whereas with you, since you do not have your normal connection to yourself in your conscious, mental self, your death usually just happens. That's why people struggle against death, because they don't realize that they, themselves in their personality, just go on. When they do realize that, you understand—not after they die but just before they die—then they release the body easily and they go on. But that is a conscious choice.

In the time that you spent on the planet Odin, during that period of experience, what was it that you feel you went there to do, and are you happy with your experience there? Did you feel you really grew from it, learned from it?

It's not defined, because in terms of your calendar, we're talking about billions of years. Where do you want me to start?

Ah! So you are conscious of your life before the time that was on Odin?

There isn't any life before; all is one life. The form changes. It's not that you wish to change the form; it's that you wish to accomplish something that you are unable to accomplish in the form in which you exist. So you change your form so that you can accomplish that which you are attempting to accomplish. If that form exists on some other planet, it does not matter; if it exists in some other culture, that does not matter. The whole point is that you are attempting, as a . . . let's call it a soul, for your understanding, though I do not think of it that way . . . you are attempting to accomplish something as an immortal personality that can only be accomplished if you are in a different form.

Why She Chose a Life on Odin

During the 35,000 years that you focused your energies in the form on Odin, includ-ing the time you came to Earth and went back, what was it that you enjoyed the most? What did you learn the most from?

The reason I took that form was so that I could experience the multiple faces that one expresses to other cultures, other than Odin, and experience the reflection from those cultures and peoples to remind myself not only of who I am, but to remind myself of who I am to others. Therefore the fact that I would voyage to Earth for this project makes complete sense, because it was an opportunity to see myself and the value of what I was contributing (or not) in the faces and the eyes and the personalities of those on Earth who were not unlike the personalities on Odin, but distant from such personalities. This allowed me to understand the value of my own contribution.

I see. So you made many voyages, then.

And in this way I was able to modify the way I presented myself on dif-ferent trips, because the three of us went to other places as well. By the time we got to the third or fourth place to speak of the value of Odin, we were no longer saying, "We're from Odin." [Laughs.] We started saying that, "We are from the planet and culture of Odin," and so on; we didn't make that mistake too many times, but I am embarrassed to admit that we made the mistake two more times after we left Earth. Fortunately those cultures were not impacted the way the people of Earth were. They were able to understand when we said, "We are from Odin," that Odin was a place, not a person.

What cultures were those?

One was in a very remote desert planet, in the outer boundaries of this uni-verse. I'd be hard pressed to give you a name; it's more of a sound. It was a cul-ture of the people of the desert, and they had lived there a very long time. We stopped to see if we could be of any assistance. We thought perhaps they might need water or water in a concentrated form. But as it turned out they did not require water, and therefore we just visited for a time and exchanged stories and wisdom. And when we said we were from Odin, they had had other visitors, so they knew when people said, "We are from . . ." a place, that it was a place, not a person. They were perhaps a little more advanced than we were.

What attracted you there?

We were always interested in visiting places that were outposts, where people were living remotely, and these people were. The planet was largely unpeopled, except for this small group living in the desert. There was a more tropical climate on the planet where there was water and so on, food, but these people did not require water or food, so they preferred to live someplace that was warm. The desert was warm even at night, and because they did not have the capacity to generate body heat for themselves, they lived out in this climate, and so we just spoke to them. And they were able, one of the rare times, to accept us in our multisphered presentation. First, we didn't know that; they told us they were insightful. I'm paraphrasing it in your words, but they said, "Please relax and be yourselves; we can accept you as you are." And we were quite surprised; and we did that, including the ship, and they said, "Now, there; that's better, isn't it?"

Okay, so describe what I would see if I was watching you at that time.

If you were able to be there, you would see parts of us disappear and parts reappear, because you would probably not be able to see all of the different spheres.

The Odin People Exist in Multiple Universes

Ah, by spheres you mean dimensions or stratus. So you would be in many, many different stratus at one time.

Different spheres, different universes, all right?

Different universes? Okay, this is a new thing.

My predecessor did not tell you that we could be in different universes as well as different stratus. That is why it is not typical for people of Odin to travel, because it is unnecessary to travel. We travel only if there is a purpose.

You can consciously be in many universes at one time?

Yes. This is why I believe that my predecessor who spoke to you yesterday referred to being part of Love's Creation.

I didn't realize that; I thought you had to be in one creation.

No. We can be anywhere in Love's Creation. There is no limit, but it's where we choose to be. There are other creations of other forms of love, but they do not resonate, all right? We do not feel at home there. We have tried, but we do not feel at home there, so we stay in what you've come to recognize as Love's Creation.

Oh! That's awesome. So you can experience . . . you can feel, see, hear, touch, taste, experience other people and fourteen other senses more, all at the same time?

Yes. It is efficient. I have had the opportunity to experience life as in the form of a human being, where one has things slower, and I can see the value of that, as well. You can have a thorough experience of seeing or touching slowly, and that has great value, especially when you are learning about physical creation. We do not, in our native state, do that. It is more a multiple experience all the time, or at least as it is appropriate.

Did you have a life on Earth, or are you referring to the length of time that you spent 800 years ago talking to the people in the North?

The latter.

So you have always experienced this multiuniversal experience, since you've been aware of who you were?

I have always been aware, and yes.

So this ability has nothing to do with the planet Odin?

Let me put it to you this way. Before there were Love's Creations, I was aware, and so were the others from Odin. I do not think that that is unusual; I've met many beings who were.

Love's Creation. I thought that was created just so we could end up with the Explorer Race.

Explorer Race Focused in Love's Creation

Love's Creation, I think, was generated so that all of the different possible variables could be played out at least once. Then if anything was missing or might perhaps be improved in some way, the Explorer Race would be launched to accomplish that.

Since the time that the Creator of this particular creation launched the seeds and roots that became the Explorer Race, have most of their experiences, then, been within Love's Creation? Not out in the rest of the totality but within Love's Creation, so that we could accomplish this, doing everything at least once?

You're asking about you now, not about me, right?

That is correct.

Love's Creation, the one you are in, was created so that all the variables that are possible within Love's Creation could be played out at least once—not just talking about the Explorer Race, but talking about all the variables of all the beings in the entirety of Love's Creation, that the whole thing could be played out at least once, which has been done. Everything has been done at least once. And then Love took note whether anything might be missing, or whether anything might be expanded in some benevolent way, and when she noted that, then she launched the strands which eventually became attractive to the Creator of your universe, who then went on and established the values, foundations and principles of the Explorer Race, and invited the entities who became the founding seeds of the Explorer Race. That's how it went.

What was the purpose of experiencing everything once before the Explorer Race was launched?

You think in terms of purpose, because your life is consciously disconnected from your total being, but the purpose is for life, for the purpose of life. Life is its own purpose; it does not require justification, accomplishment, goal or achievement.

But pure Love's Creation is just one of the thirty-seven Love creations in a small part of the totality, right?

It is the part that you're in. [Laughs.] It's enough.

Beings of Odin Created the Planet of Odin

All right. Were you aware of yourself within the totality before there was Love's Creation, as all the other 18,000 of the beings on Odin were?

As far as I know, yes.

So then, why was the planet Odin created as a place for you to reside?

Because when you have physical creation—not when you have nonphysical, okay?—when you have physical creation, there needs to be a physical place to anchor it. That's why. Physical creation is part of the universe you are in, and we needed, then, to anchor our place within a universe that has place, with physicality. So that's why Odin exists; it is much more vast than the physical location in which it exists now, much more vast because the beings of Odin are the planet, but the planet itself is not separate from the beings. The beings and the planet are one, but the anchor—just as if you were to throw an anchor out of a boat, the anchor into physical reality—is in the form of the planet.

So there is no separate being creating and embodying the planet Odin, as there is, for instance, in terms of the Earth? It's all of you?

But if the planet Odin spoke to you, it would be the mutual shared voice of all the beings who live there.

Oh! How incredible! So you all created this incredible playground.

We created a place whereby we would have access to physical reality, all right, and still have the capacity to be and exist anywhere.

What was the prior experience before the planet of these 18,000? How did you come together to begin with? You've always been together?

We have always been together.

Do you have a name or sound that we can use as an identity for you?

The difficulty is in your language. The language is the problem. The best explanation for me to give you of who I am is a feeling. When you come next time, you will have the opportunity to speak to Odin—the whole culture, all beings. During that time you will experience a feeling. The feeling will not define itself in mental terminology, but it will be a feeling you recognize and enjoy, and the feeling will be the answer of who we are, where we're from, why we exist and what life is. But it will not define itself in mental concept. Mental concept is what I would call . . . Say you go to a canyon, and you shout out your name, and then you hear the quick echo, yes? But then there are fading echoes. The echo that is the most distant, fading echo—that is the analogy of what mentality is to consciousness. But it is a faded echo, not because it is unworthy, but because it can bridge the gap of continuity and stillness.

Stillness is not actually still, but it is a fixed point that experiences motion all around it. That's where you're living now; you're living in a fixed point. Your life is completely and totally fixed, and so is everybody else's, but you're living in a world of motion. You might move, go out to the vehicle, go out to the car, yes? Go here, go there—you would seem to be moving, but wherever you are in motion, you are still there. You are conscious; you are aware. You are inside yourself. Even as you are moving around, you are conscious, aware and inside yourself—ergo, a fixed point. This is not that dissimilar from what I am. I might be able to spread out over many spheres, if I choose, but I am still a fixed point—even though the point is, perhaps, broader.

Much, much, much, much broader! So each of you 18,000 have an individual perspective?

Yes, an individual personality. Now I must go. Good night.

Good night.

Good night, good life.

Good life.

Sirian Researches
Earth Life Forms and Their
Harmonious Interactions

Bithan'galan'cachun'fatun'sa'taskakaduts'ta and Zoosh

January 9, 2002

reetings. I am Bithan'galan'cachun'fatun'sa'taska-kaduts'ta. Or if you like you can just call me B. [Laughs.] The letter B. Now, if you don't mind, I know you requested someone who is here on Earth now, but it is not safe to discuss such matters. But if you do not mind, I was on Earth until just a few hours ago. I have left now and am at a significant distance, so I am safe and my people who are on the ship with me are safe. Would that be adequate? I have been there for quite a few years, until just a few hours ago.

Well, how exciting. Tell me about yourself.

Research for a New Planet

I came to Earth—and I was there for quite a while, as I said—from a planet that has some similarities . . . not in discomfort range, but similarities to Earth, and that is why I came. I came to study the capacity of different types of life to get along with one another in a harmonious way. Earth is famous for such a thing, even with human beings being an exception—although not a total exception, you understand, because human beings have the capacity to get along with most other forms of life on Earth, and even some forms of life that they do not see themselves as getting along with, because there has been a way to adapt to those forms of life, such as what you call germs and viruses. You adapt to their presence, even though you'd just as soon they were not there. [Laughs.] But I came to study this because it is my job as a researcher to report my findings to those who are carefully putting an environment into action, you might say, on this planet in a star system in what you call galaxy of Sirius.

New Life Forms on the New Planet

So you can see why it makes complete sense to study your Earth, which has had years and years of time and interaction between life forms. The planet that is being . . . not created so much as re-created in Sirius will not be occupied by any life form that is like a human being. It will be occupied, however, by life forms that are very similar—if not exactly the same, since it won't be necessary for them to have immune systems, for example—to life forms on Earth. There will be, for example—not exactly the same but similar—dolphins, whales, turtles (land and sea), a form of life very similar to the gorilla, beings of the cat family . . .

I will start to give you some differences so you will have a feeling for the similarities and the differences. The cats, for instance, will not have claws, because none of the beings on the planet will have to eat. And they will only occasionally take in something like water, but the water will be very . . . not thick like tar, but just a little thicker than water. It will have the consistency of a thin syrup. And they will take it in only on occasion, to supplement their oxygen—or at least their air supply, let's say, because there is some oxygen involved. There will not be anything like dogs, as in house pets, you know, but there will be similar beings. For instance, there will be something like wolves, but again, nobody has to eat, so it's all very peaceful. But the difference in the wolves is that they will have a silvery kind of fur, and their tails will be much more bushy.

Generally speaking, these forms of life—and many others, if you'd like to explore it—will have tails that are much more significant. For example, the gorillas will have tails. And beings you do not normally think of as having tails will have them. Because the tails of what you call animals on Earth contain a vast amount of nerves and truly the capacity to have what in animals is called the sixth sense. The sixth sense is highly developed, past the physiological capacity of the human being, in beings who have tails, because it essentially extends the brain/spine and extends it into the tail. The brain/spine—the whole nervous system that can conduct and process information, physical feelings, sensations, instincts and so on—is compounded in capacity because of the tail.

I have studied, in the course of my work, on a planet that is also in Sirius . . . Oh, hold on. I am using that wet cloth; it's very comfortable. I have known human beings who look very similar to you but who have tails. And because of their tails . . . the tails are not . . . Oh, you can't lean on them [laughs], but they are significant tails. These tails allow for a much greater capacity mentally and instinctually and so on. But I'm only mentioning this to suggest that tails are common, not something that is a curiosity.

As a Scientific Research Team, They Didn't Encourage Interaction with Humans

So there was a great deal of study by myself and my crew—which has varied from three to five and occasionally more—over the past eighteen years on Earth. We studied environments in the sea, in the mountains, in deserts, in the tropics . . . generally speaking, wherever there were as few people as possible so that we would not disturb your civilization or become—how can we say?—noticed too much. I wouldn't say that what we did was clandestine so much as it was intended to appear innocuous. If the casual observer happened to see us, we would appear to be a scientific research team from a university, for example, and that's pretty much how we passed ourselves off at different times, saying we were from this university or from that university, sometimes universities in the United States and sometimes in Europe, but, generally speaking, like that. Generally speaking also, if the person or persons commented to us, we would always make an effort to have a native tongue of some other language. [Laughs]. This would tend to discourage communication, even though we did not wish to be standoffish. We did want to be able to conduct our research with a minimum of interaction with the human beings on the planet, so that we did not cause any problems for you.

So you look like us?

When we were there we did, but we do not look anything like you.

You have the ability to shift your shape, then?

I wouldn't say that we have that as a function of our being, but the vehicle in which we traveled could create something like that. So it is more like a mechanism that does it; we do not do it ourselves.

Did it change your body or did it just create a costume for you to inhabit? Did it actually change the cells of your body?

I think the way you describe it, like a costume. It was more like a mannequin that we occupied. But we could not have stood up to a medical exam.

We would simply have had to leave on an emergency basis. But as it turned out, we were fortunate enough to never have to encounter such interactions. I think that our disguise of being a university research team was very useful on numerous occasions. Occasionally, when we would meet people who were—how can we say?—not trying to figure out who we were, who were just simple, either simple country people or friendly people, then we would be all right with them watching what we were doing and so on. But, generally speaking, we didn't encourage interaction with the population.

What do you look like in your natural state?

If you were to see me now? You could make a distance between your fingers, or your thumb and finger, of about an inch and a half, maybe a little more than that. And I would just look like a point of not exactly bright light, but a point of light. Not the kind of light that would illuminate a book, for instance. [Laughs.]

Introducing New Life Forms to a Planet

So you're from a high dimension, then?

I am from the ninth dimension.

In Sirius someplace. And you're doing what we would call terraforming this planet? You're changing its ecology or something?

I wouldn't say that so much. There was a planet that . . . you will find that when you start doing more planetary research, when you go out and have other planets available to research—Mars, for instance; you will consider that on Mars, but I don't think it will work very well for you, because it's too soon to really have success in that area—you will find that some planets are more receptive to change than others. Planets that have had complex civilizations or organisms on them but no longer do and are perhaps becoming more desert and so on, they will not be very receptive. But planets that are more tropical in nature or that give off other signs that they are highly receptive to life, they might be receptive to influence.

We don't change things so much as we attempt to influence. Influencing, for example, might be to go to, say, a tropical planet and introduce—in a very fixed way, so that there is no contamination of the planet—a form of life in a fixed, enclosed environment, to see if the form of life can be happy there and thrive there for perhaps a few years but without really allowing any direct contact.

Nevertheless, during that time, the planet itself will have an opportunity to react with its feelings, to see whether the life form is something that it would welcome. So it has to be both ways: The planet has to welcome it, and the life form itself has to want to do it. If both are compatible, then the barrier is removed and the life form is allowed to interact with the planet and other life forms there, as it would choose to do so.

And so the purpose of introducing these life forms to this planet is that you have extra life forms? What is the purpose of it? Do they need a place to go?

It is not like that. It is not so different from your universities; we just wanted to see what would happen.

Oh, it's an experiment!

It is an experiment; that's right. We want to see if we can reproduce, on a smaller scale, something that you have on Earth, in a way that does not naturally evolve. But it involves . . . well, for lack of a better term, interference on our part. It's not offensive interference, because the planet and the life forms themselves must be fully embracing it on their own. So we do not just drop things in together and see if they can survive.

You're moving these beings from another planet in Sirius?

Say again?

Are you moving the beings you're putting on the planet from another planet in Sirius?

Not all, no; some of them are from other places, but the ones from other places are all volunteers.

Oh! And some from Earth perhaps?

No. No, that would not be appropriate, because Earth is already an experiment.

[Laughs.] Yes, yes. So if it's a successful experiment, then what? Will they set up a civilization there? Or will you move them back to where they came from?

No. No, if it is successful and everyone is happy there, we will allow them to be there; we will not interfere with it. But we will reveal the information in detail. Right now, it's not a secret in Sirius what we're doing, but we will report our findings if it works out the way we would like. Even if it doesn't work out, we will report our findings. It is just a form of education and research, not that much different from things you do on your planet, only perhaps done with more respect and gentleness.

So it's not like a PhD project; you're not completing a course of study or something.

No. It is something more along the lines of research and application, just to make it available to others should they wish to produce something similar.

It is research, not unlike what goes on on your planet, only perhaps more respectfully done in some ways.

To Look Human, They Had to Be inside a Mechanism

So you've always known about our planet?

For myself, I cannot say always, but once I became interested in these kinds of studies and applications, then I researched and discovered not only that your planet was a potential place to study such interactions between various species but also that there was a connection to Sirius. And even if there wasn't, we still could have come, but because there was, it told us that our ability to survive or even thrive, even in a disguised form, was more likely to work, which is why we could come and be on the planet for such a long time and not be impacted in any negative way by the experience.

That's interesting. But because of your original form, then . . . most people come here and find the vibration to be so low and so negative . . .

Well, we could not have done our research in our natural form. If we would not have had the mechanism to create a form that would cause us to look like a human being and then be inside that mechanism, we . . . [Laughs.]

So whenever you went out of the ship, then, you were in that mechanism?

Yes.

Oh, I see.

No one left the ship even for a moment without looking, for all intents and purposes, like a human being. And of course, if a human being had come up and touched us and so on, we would have seemed to be a human being. But we couldn't have stood up to a medical examination; it would have been quite obvious that the tissues and even the sweat and everything like that was artificial.

Well, that's very unusual. So during the eighteen years you were here, what percentage of that time did you actually spend inside those mechanisms on the planet, then?

Oh, the whole purpose of a research project is to research, so I should think at least 70 to 76 percent, something like that, of the time that we were actually involved on the planet. Day and night didn't make any difference to us; we don't need to sleep or eat.

You don't sleep or eat! All right. But on your home planet, then, you still have this shape as a light? You don't have a form there either?

That's right. The former, as I described to you, is the way we look.

So I can imagine how you would be very interested in these environments, then, because it's so different from the way you live in your natural state.

Yes. And part of the reason we are doing this research is because we have the technology, the capacity and the desire to be of service in this way. It is not something that we are motivated to do for our own ends; it is rather a research project that has always been intended to be of service to communities and planets and cultures who may wish to apply it, or even some portion of it, themselves. But it is not something that we personally need to know.

I see. So what is your personal life like? On your home planet?

[Laughs.] I don't know how to describe it to you, but it is like this: It is a constant; there is almost no comparison between our culture and yours. If we wish to have a communion between one and another or many, we might come together physically, and our size would spherically become larger. But that would be the only outward difference that an observer might note, and we would feel a stronger sense of communion. But there's no marriage or eating rituals or anything like that; there are almost no similarities. I mentioned the communion because that is as close an example of a ritual or a social activity that you could identify with. We do not have to breathe; we do nothing that you do.

I'm sure it probably is hard to do, but in terms of our years, what would your lifespan be?

There is a lifespan; let me try to interpret it in years. Of course, it doesn't relate directly, because of the different levels involved, but if I . . . Understand that if I stay at my level, for instance, or if an average one of us stays at our level, the lifespan is almost what you would call immortal. But going to other places, such as I have done, being a researcher and all that, tends to shorten my lifespan to something around a quarter of a million years.

Why is it shortened?

Because of the impact, the personal impact of being exposed to other forms of life, other types of places, the mechanized adaptation to the human, to the apparent human, and being exposed to discomfort—in short, exposure to experimental conditions.

Beings Look the Most like Their Natural Selves on Their Home Planets

Have you ever been to Earth before?

I had not before this; I didn't even know about Earth before starting this experimental program.

But others on your planet had been here?

I really do not know that.

Well, have you gone to other planets, then?

Oh yes; quite a few.

In this area?

No, not in this area.

In this creation?

I went to other planets that would fit into the scope of the experiment, planets that had a variety of beings or planets where beings similar to the ones whom I might encounter on Earth were living in different circumstances, meaning, for instance, in some cases, the native planets of some of the beings you have on Earth.

Yes, the home planets.

The home planets are the places where they are the most at ease and look the most like their natural selves—sometimes looking surprisingly the way they look on Earth and other times having no resemblance whatsoever.

Give me an example of one with no resemblance whatsoever.

I suppose the one that struck me the strongest was the polio virus. The polio virus—I think it is a virus, or it is classified that way on Earth—is actually a living being about four to six inches long on another planet, and it has a mouth and something that it uses . . . not a visual apparatus like the eyes but something similar to that. They have a personality; they are amusing [laughs]. It is radically different from how they appear on Earth. They do not in any way cause people to become sick [laughs]. This was just something that they were volunteered for to do.

Are all the places you've visited in this creation?

Explain?

There's a creator who creates a creation, and then beyond that there's another creator who creates another creation. So is everything that you've visited in this creation?

Apparently I do not know this other information.

Well, we've been exploring for years, and it's really big out there. I mean, you know . . .

There are other places?

There are other creations, oh God, yes.

Wait.

✳   ✳   ✳

All right, Zoosh here.

Zoosh?

You must be very careful how you talk. You have now created a problem. You cannot tell just everybody willy-nilly, okay? This was unknown on their planet before. We are going to have to take that being and do a little something, which we're doing right now, their people are doing right now. There will be a gap in time; when you resume communication with him, do not tell him anything about other places, all right? Do not automatically assume that when ETs come to visit Earth, they are great and powerful mystical beings; this would be a person just like anybody else. Such beings can talk about other places they've been, things they've seen, experiences they've had, but they are not in any way what you would call the great and powerful Wizard of Oz.

Oh, I'm sorry.

You did not know; there is no reason for you to be sorry. But it is good for you to have this experience and for it to be printed, so that future astronauts or cosmonauts or whatever you want to call yourself will recognize that you cannot just simply blurt things out, assuming that all beings have the depth and breadth of your own capacity for information. So now I will say good night, and the being will be back in a moment.

Okay, I see.

❋   ❋   ❋

A Cultural Exchange Program

Greetings. I seem to have fallen asleep for a moment.

Ah, that's okay. So this is exciting! When you go back to report, do you have peers who are doing similar things? Is it your own people you report to, or do you make this available to other planets?

We put it into a system that you could consider like a central library. We have no idea who will ever use it, if anyone. But it will be available as information and with the full range of visuals and other sensory capacities, many of which we do not use or have any purpose for, but we know that other beings might. For instance, there will be a full range of smells and all of that, and that is meaningless to us, but for other beings it might be very helpful. So it will be available for them should they wish to use it. It's not unlike a research library in your country or in any part of the world where you might find a research library—in, say, a university or some other place of higher learning.

And do you have such a place on your planet? Is that where you go to study when you first become conscious?

No. I don't know about becoming conscious; we are always conscious, but this was a project that I was recruited for, and I was taken aboard a vehicle, or welcomed aboard a vehicle, with others of my type of being, and we were asked if we wished to participate. And I thought it seemed like it would be a worthy thing to do, and as a result, the vehicle itself and those upon the vehicle had the information. But we do not have libraries and all that kind of business there; we were simply told that it would be a project that would be worth doing, that others might find it valuable, and did we wish to participate? If we did, then ships and other things would be provided for us.

So the ships are not of our own making, you understand, because we do not have any need to travel. All this was provided by the people who came and asked if we wished to participate. And because it was something different and we are interested in doing things that are different from time to time, and because we had recently joined a cultural exchange program between planets . . . Perhaps one of the members, who were the people who came by, felt that we might wish to participate in some role of service. So this is really one of the first things—I can't say it was the first thing, but as far as I know, it was one of the first things that came about as a result of this cultural exchange.

Adaptability and New Medical Technology

The other planet, though, was from our galaxy. They had the ships; they had all of this stuff, but we did not have it. I think that the reason they asked us to participate is that we can so easily assimilate a physical body—an adaptive body that they use, like a human body—without any impact, without any deleterious impact on us whatsoever or, for that matter, without any radiation coming from our physical body into the environment that we might occupy while disguised as a human being, so as not to create any problem for the population in the area.

So I believe we were chosen by these individuals to participate in this experiment because we were so ideally suited to do this, whereas they could not have done so, even though they had the technology. The technology they demonstrated . . . I remember, in the original demonstration, they showed me how the technology could be used for them. The actual technology was designed initially to be a medical aid. For instance, they showed an example where one of them had (now, these beings were humanoids, but they didn't look like humans) an injury to the hand, and this being had lost a portion of the hand and was suffering. The being was taken aboard, and this medical device rebuilt the hand, using, I think, some kind of genetic mapping. But it also desensitized the body, not only in such a way that the procedure would not be painful, but also in such a way as to remove the memory of the pain so that there would not be an unconscious connection between whatever it was the person had been doing that caused the injury and the pain itself. Even though the instruction would go out—for instance, don't put your hand in this being's mouth [laughs]—and become part of the person's wisdom, the person would not be permanently scarred on an unconscious basis.

But they discovered in the course of the use of this medical device over years that certain beings could . . . that it could be used to generate a full and complete body. For instance, when we first went on the ship, one of the other volunteers from our culture was able to occupy a body that looked like one of these beings. A body was generated, all right, and they said, "Well, it will only last for, in Earth time, a few minutes, but we want to see if you can adapt to that." So our being immediately went inside the body and could walk around and look, for all intents and purposes, like one of them, even though he wouldn't have known how to act. He didn't act like them, and everybody thought it was very funny. They thought it was very amusing. And then my countryman, if I can put it that way, stepped out of the body and that body was re-formed into whatever it is that the technology does. It just basically . . . it was like it melted, but it wasn't, like, turned into liquid or anything; it just sort of gradually dissipated. But they did that to show us that they believe we could adapt to this kind of research comfortably without any impact on ourselves or any uncomfortable impact on the others, even though in the case of this example, we all had a good laugh, you might say.

How did you become known as an adaptive people? Have you adapted to other bodies?

No. Apparently, other cultures have studied us for some time. And we have only really had visitors to our culture; this might be because many of the cultures who have studied us are humanoids, and it may not have been quite clear in their culture whether it was acceptable to, say, land and interact with our culture, because our culture had not made any attempt to reach out and join cultural exchange programs, you understand? But because we have joined the cultural exchange program, I believe that's why this ship and these people approached us, because they felt that it must be all right to do so.

Yes. Because you made the first move.

Exactly.

Re-creation instead of Death

So what do you do on your planet? Are there ten beings or ten billion beings on your planet? How many beings are like you?

I do not know; I would guess there are several hundred thousand. But as I described before . . . I gave you an example of something that we do that was as close to something as I could find to what you do. But other than that, I'd be hard-pressed to describe our culture to you in terms that you could understand or, more to the point, that you would find interesting or appealing. It's not a secret, and it is probably why humanoid cultures have not approached our planet in the past, because we probably would not appear to be anything that would in any way attract them. Maybe they observe us for a while and say, "Well, that's enough of that!" and fly off, you understand?

[Laughs.] Right. But there have to be some differences and similarities.

It's not that there are no differences; it's that the differences are so great that a humanoid culture could not identify with our culture in any way.

Right. But how do you learn? Do you study with one another? Do you have some type of cultural repository of your wisdom?

No, none of that. We are born . . . we come into existence; born is not the right term. We come into existence knowing what we need to know. And if there's ever anything else we need to know, someone in our culture touches us, and then we know it.

But there is an ending of life? I mean, it's a very, very long lifespan, but there is, then . . . what? The light goes out or something at some point?

No. What happens is that if there is ever a desire by, say, an individual to become something that the soul who occupies that individual did not originally create itself to be, something that the soul cannot easily adapt to, then there is a re-creation. The re-creation is as close as I can get to what might be like a birth. But the re-creation happens—for all intents and purposes, within the scope of your time—instantaneously.

With the same soul?

Oh yes.

So the souls there stay there; they don't go anyplace else?

Yes.

On Sharing Earth Information

Interesting, interesting. So when you go back now, you will go back to your planet, and these beings who recruited you will take the ship and go off, and then you're the ones who will make the information known, right?

Say again? I'm the one who will make . . .

Let's say, when you get home . . . How long will it take you to get home?

A little while.

Days? Weeks? Months?

We'll be there any moment.

Oh, any moment! Oh my goodness. All right, so you will go . . .

All of the information we acquired we will leave onboard the ship.

Then these other beings will disseminate it? Will put it in the library or something? Yes. But then as far as communicating with your fellow beings once you get home, do you have to touch them all to share the knowledge?

Oh no. We volunteered for the project because we were interested; nobody else volunteered, so I'm assuming they're not interested. I have no reason to assume they are interested. I will not pass on any information whatsoever unless others indicate that they want to know, and then I will pass on only what they want to know and nothing else.

I understand. So all the other planets that you went to, that you told me about, have been on this mission, then, on this ship?

All the other planets we went to?

You said you went to some of the planets that were the home of some of the beings who were on Earth.

Yes, and we did our research there.

But has that all been part of this mission that you volunteered for? Or were those other trips you took unrelated to this one?

No, no, it was all part of the mission.

So all the things you're telling me, then . . . This is kind of like your first trip away from home, then?

It was my first trip away, yes.

Do you look forward to others?

No, that was plenty. [Laughs.] That's enough; I've been away long enough.

That's an honest answer. [Laughs.]

Yes. And I think that it was . . . I do not know what cultural exchange programs may have occurred since I left, so I do not know if other members of our culture are out doing other things. But if anybody asks me, would I do it over again if I had the choice? I would probably say no. It was a bit too long.

Okay, and what—in words that I can understand—have you missed? The interaction with your fellow beings?

Just being at home with my fellow beings, yes. I had no idea that it would take this long. I don't think that the people who recruited us knew it would take this long either.

Well, you were, in our terms, here for eighteen years. How many years have you actually been away from your home planet?

In terms of your years? Hundreds.

Oh! I didn't realize that.

Yes, it was a very long time, much longer than I would have cared to be away. But we had to see it through once we had started.

So going to all of those other planets, you spent some time at each one?

Oh yes. Years. And you see, unlike your planet, where even in your travels, you can travel someplace and make a phone call, we are unable to communicate with our fellow beings on our home planet unless we are right there. Remember, communication from one to another happens through touch; so we've been completely out of touch for the entire time we've been gone.

Oh, I see! And there's more than touch; there's communion, sharing, everything.

Communion and so on, but the main thing is that there was no way to have any communication whatsoever. I do not think the people who recruited us fully understood that; I'm not sure if they understand it now. But I think when they do understand it, they will probably be profusely apologetic and will probably . . . I have a feeling that they may not ask us to participate in such missions again. Just putting myself in their place, I would certainly be apologetic. No, we are not expecting or demanding an apology, none of that. Obviously, if we wanted to say, "Well, that's enough of that," we could have requested a return voyage home. But we decided that we had made the commitment and that the whole project might never be done properly or at least would have to be started all over again from the beginning if we did not complete it. So we decided to complete it. But we have been desperately lonely for our fellow beings. And pretty soon I will be there, and I will have to terminate our conversation.

Earth Beings Should Work on Interspecies Communication

Well, I am so grateful that you shared your life with us, because we're so interested in who's out there! What do you do? What do you look like? How do you live? You know, what's it all about?

There are so many varieties. I would say that the personal gain, perhaps, that I achieved, if I had to state one, would be my awareness, now, of the varieties of life that there are, and how some get along only by being in contact with others, and how some thrive in contact with other beings, even though the other beings do not always thrive. Sometimes they do, but not always. For instance, what you call germs or viruses on your planet, they might thrive by interaction with you, but they might not, and you might not thrive by interaction with them [laughs]. And from my interaction with them, from studying life forms on your planet, I would say that a great many of them, because of the impact they have had on you . . . which, I might add, is not why they came to Earth to volunteer; they came to Earth to interact with Mother Earth, as you call her, with Earth herself. They didn't come to interact with you as human beings, and the interaction with you as human beings appears to largely be either a secondary capacity that they have or something that was unintended in the first place.

Really? I didn't know that.

So I would say that they do not like the interaction that they have with you that causes disease. Apparently the reason they came to Earth was to support Earth herself, as a planet. They did not realize that this support might take the form of causing pain and suffering to any life form. I think they felt upset about this; my impression from them, in feeling their feelings, was that they felt very upset about it and, not unlike our people, if they had to do it over again, they would never have volunteered.

Oh. And maybe like you, they just weren't told the whole story, you know?

My feeling is that the whole story wasn't available to be told to us. Remember, the people who recruited us didn't know much about us. And my feeling is that a similar situation may have occurred with these other beings. Perhaps not much was known about them and how they would act or react; perhaps it was known . . . The problem with communication that I've noticed on your planet and others is that there are entirely too many assumptions being made that the other person or being knows what you're talking about, which I've discovered from interacting with human beings even just during my short visit on your planet. I would have to say that most of the time, the other person doesn't know what you're talking about, and even if you take the time to explain as many points as you can think of, you will still have many pieces that you didn't explain about. So I'd say that [laughs] one of the biggest challenges on your planet for all species appears to be communication, especially interspecies communication. This appears to be a huge problem.

We Are Almost Home

Yes. Now, what about you, on your planet? Are there any other species on your planet besides you?

No. We're it.

You're it.

That's part of the reason the project was appealing to us—because we'd never experienced variety of any sort.

Well, this planet supposedly has more variety than any other place.

Yes, it was almost overwhelming at first. I remember when we first got there . . . Oh, I see my planet coming up now; we have to stop in a few minutes. But I remember when we first got to your planet, the . . . [Pause.] My fellow beings on the ship are excited.

And so are you!

I must admit. When we first got to your planet, no one, even in the adaptive-human-being costume, no one could go out and be engaged in your planet, wherever we were, for more than a few minutes of Earth time, because we were overwhelmed by the different species. You have to understand that even if we're in the atmosphere, there are life forms in the atmosphere, and we'd never been exposed to anything other than ourselves and those who recruited us. That was our sum total of exposure to other life forms at all. So it took us—I would, speaking for the members of my crew who were with me and for myself—at least a year and a half to be able to be in the costume of a human being and say, for example, walk around on the surface or swim in the ocean or just be in contact for periods of time up to an hour and a half, or perhaps closer to an hour and three-quarters or two hours . . . It took us about a year and a half to actually be able to do that, a year of gradual adaptation to the overwhelming impact of the stimulation that occurs consciously and unconsciously.

In your natural being, you're aware energetically of everything that's here?

Yes. But you understand, we're aware consciously and unconsciously, like you. Now, we are alert to the fact that you, for the most part, are aware; most citizens on Earth are aware only unconsciously or subconsciously.

Yes.

But there are some people on Earth who have been trained, mystical people and so on, who are aware almost all the time, even consciously. That's why these people are so sensitive and sometimes get overwhelmed by interactions with human beings, because it's just one thing too many. That's why I think these shamanic practitioners or mystical people have to go out into the countryside sometimes and just relax, because human being interaction is just one too many complexities added to their lives. Now I'm going to have to say good night; we're approaching our planet's atmosphere.

Welcome home!

Everyone is excited and bouncing around the ship. So it has been a pleasure to speak to you.

Thank you for sharing.

And as one of your friends says, good life.

Yes, good life. Thank you.

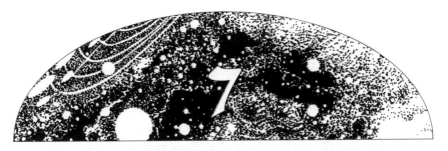

An ET Visitor from the Twelfth Planet Looks for His Planet in the Future

Chedan
May 23, 2002

reetings. I am Chedan, an ET visitor. I will give a short talk. I'm from a planet that used to be in this solar system, out around the twelfth orbit . . . but not there anymore that I see in your time. I'm just passing through, will probably return to my past, my time, yes, soon, because I've kept coming forward to see if my planet might miraculously return. But apparently not, so I will have to look elsewhere. I move forward from my time on my planet standing in this special booth, and the booth itself is connected in many ways to the planet. I've checked all of the futures that are substantial; they can be felt by the booth and by myself. But now I'm checking directions where there's some vague sense of feeling . . . but it's not, there's no continuity. So I happen to be in your area and thought I would say hello.

Well, wonderful. What planet? Did it have a name that we would recognize?

I don't know if you would recognize it.

Well, what did you call it?

We do call it, and I am living in that time. We call it . . . [bumps the microphone]. What's that?

It's the microphone.

I will get closer. We call it Ceetsee. How would you spell that? C-E-E-T-S-S-S. That's not quite right. C-E-E-, what is that? This is one word. It might look like two. [Writing something down.] I have to . . . this is a punctuation you don't have yet, but I'm sorry, I have to add it. There's no other way to do it. This is a sound that sounds like a flying creature you have . . . but does not alter the fact that that's what they sound like. That punctuation, that's one word. That punctuation—oh, I'm sorry I'm not talking [into the microphone]—doesn't mean a period. It means . . . it has to do with the pronunciation of that word. Ceetseect. It's almost at the end a "t" or a "c" sound. So that punctuation means to repeat the beginning sound at the beginning of the word without actually repeating the sound. There's a feeling of the sound, meaning Ceetsee-C, almost as if you were going to say the "c" again but not doing it. That's the punctuation.

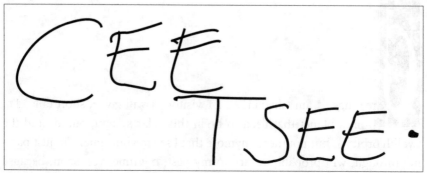

Figure 7.1: Ceetsee's name in written form.

Fascinating. In our time, how can we understand when you were on the planet? You're on the planet, but I mean . . . in our past, when was that?

Oh, you mean the memory. You mean years.

Years, eons, a thousand years, something.

I have to give you a measurement other than years, because it doesn't interpret, but about the time—no, if you can get this estimate from your astrophysicists, it is about the time of 10 percent into the living life cycle of your Sun.

Ten percent, okay. Was there an Earth here? Was this Earth here then?

No.

But there was another Earth in this orbit?

I can't talk about your planet very much.

What kind of orbit did you have? A wildly varying one, or did it change every year or something?

No, it was a fixed orbit.

Around our Sun?

Yes, in the twelfth position. But our planet is not there. Perhaps it is just your time. Or maybe it is because of who you are and what you are doing. But it is vastly different. I might add that the other planets all had cultures on them. I notice in your time that I don't see any obvious, fixed, well-established cultures on the other planets—but all the other planets had them in my time, although the planet at the closest orbit to the Sun had an unusual life. But they were able to live just under the surface—not on the surface; nothing could live on the surface easily.

Were you in the same dimension then that we are now?

No, not that pulse. But close enough to investigate.

When you looked out from your planet or when you traveled from your planet, the lights you saw on the other planets . . . was it like in the third dimension, the fourth dimension or . . . ?

I can only say what we were, what we are in my time. We're at dimension 3.75—as it compares to your scale, granted.

Oh. You would be seeing the same thing we do, then.

No, I don't think you're at 3.75.

No, but I mean, not on the fourth dimension yet.

There's no progression. There's no "yet." It's just what is, and I'm using that terminology because I think you can have at least some grasp of it. We are physical.

The Sun's Life Cycle

The Sun's current age is approximately 4.57 billion years, and it is at a midpoint on the main sequence. When a forming star stabilizes, burning fuel at a predictable rate, it enters what is known as the "main sequence." A star's age is determined by its location in the main sequence, which measures star brightness against star color to arrive at the star's mass. The mass of a star can tell us how much fuel it has to burn, from which we learn the rate at which it must consume fuel to maintain equilibrium.

The Sun converts 4 million metric tons of matter into energy every second. Given the Sun's mass, this rate of conversion tells us that the Sun will spend a total of 10 billion years of its life as a main sequence star—meaning that it has burned fuel at this rate and will do so continuously for a total of 10 billion years.

The luminosity of the sun increases around 10 percent every billion years as it approaches the end of its main sequence phase. In around 5 billion years as the Sun begins to run out of hydrogen fuel, it will expand into a red giant. After a few billion more years, it will shed its outer layers to form a nebula. At the center will remain a white dwarf—essentially a dead star—which will radiate its leftover energy over many billions of years until nothing but an inert rocky core remains.

Life on the Twelfth Planet: Physical Appearance,
Environment, Population and Technology

Do you look like us? Are you humanoid?

Well, we are "humanoid." We don't . . . humanoid is of course a self-congratulating description.

[Laughs.] I know.

But we have a body, two arms, two legs and a head. I certainly wouldn't call us humanoid, but I do understand why you call it that.

What would you call it?

In our language some other word that is acculturated to this general appearance by ourselves and other beings, meaning a classification. You're asking what word would we have as a classification to mean that type of being, yes?

Yes.

[Makes choppy, guttural sounds.] Chaktchatakptk.

[Laughs.] All right that's not going to work. Thank you for that.

I do not think you can spell that easily, because it has sounds as well as apparent tonal qualities.

If I were to look at you, what would I see?

You want me to describe my appearance?

Please.

We don't have hair. That's really something, hair. I've never seen anything like it. We have eyes, about your size of eye, perhaps a little smaller. We do not really have a large nose like you all have. Smaller, one opening for the nose's purpose. We have a mouth, smaller. Head is about two thirds your size. Average height in terms of your measurement may be about 4 foot 6. Body in general is about two thirds your size, but arms are a little longer than the average human being. Four digits, not five on the hands. Same on the feet.

And what else is on the planet? You, and what other type of beings?

Plants. Only a few other beings. We don't consider other species to be "animals," as you say—a generic term for what you would consider lesser beings (not you personally, but your culture). But there are a couple of other species that have their own culture, live by themselves and occasionally mingle with us. But generally they keep to themselves, and that's fine.

What size is your planet, in comparison with ours?

About one and a half times the size of your planet. Not as much water as you have, and that more in the form of ice, under the surface as well as on the surface. We live under the surface, where the environment can be made more comfortable. We like a similar temperature range as you do, though not as cold and not as warm. Using your number system in your culture, we might be comfortable in the range of temperatures of say, oh, 50 to 80 degrees [Fahrenheit]. We will sometimes expose ourselves to the icy surface, but we have something that keeps us warm. Not a garment, though. More like a mechanism.

Like a force field or something?

Nothing quite as fictionally fantastic as that, but it is something that heats up our bodily fluid. If our bodily fluids are warm enough, then the heat keeps our body comfortable.

What about your culture? What interests you? What do you make? How do you live?

One question.

How many of you are there?

What is the population? At any given point the population is . . . I'll give you a range: from 40,000 to 60,000.

Is that all?

Yes, no more than that. The planet is vast, but it has limited resources, like your planet. Your planet is not vast; it has more abundant resources, but nowhere near enough for everyone on it—although I've been led to understand that you are all trainees to learn how to create and re-create the resources on your planet so everyone has everything they need. So I would, from my culture's point of view, say that you are all magicians in training. Though I can see that some of you are more aware of this than others.

What is your level of technology? Do you have spacecraft?

We do not require the use of vehicles, extra-physical vehicles such as you call spacecraft. We can travel in . . . the usual term as you would call it is "condensed light," but we would call it "travel in condensed purpose." We have a purpose, and then we travel in a condensed version of our personality. Right now, I am here. If you were to see me as I looked, I would look like a tiny little dot of slightly illuminated light, because my purpose is so strong you cannot see how I look, because I am quite fully engaged with my purpose. So you would see my purpose before you saw me. For my people, that allows others who know and understand us, including my own people, to know whether or not to engage with us. Because if, in reacting to the interpretation of my purpose and its energy, it is compatible with someone or something exterior to me, if they are aware of my purpose then they are more or less likely to engage with me. If they can offer nothing, they are not just going to stop me and say hello. If they can offer something, they might make themselves known to me in some benevolent way for us both and offer what they have available.

Exploring the Past, Exploring the Future, Exploring Interdimensionally

Right now your purpose is looking to see if your planet is in this solar system. Well, if you're on your planet now, then how could your planet get lost?

Who said it did? I'm exploring other . . . I explored all of the futures of my planet—all of the futures, all of the potential futures. I am now exploring all of the vaguely possible futures, meaning that there is some signature of my planet here. Maybe not because my planet is here—obviously, quite obviously—but because perhaps there is some other reason for the signature. It isn't a very prominent signature. It's quite latent, but at this point in my research I am exploring such latent possibilities just to see what may or may not be . . . more to see what may be present that has to do with my purpose.

All right. You're on your planet in your past, and you're exploring all of these realities within this solar system. Within what range?

Within, as you say, this star system, but with particular attention to this solar system, since it is our own. I've done some looking, you understand, at the solid potentials for futures that range out past our solar system but are within this star system. I am putting my attention right now in this stage of my research to vague possibilities within the solar system, as I indicated.

So that must mean your orbit has changed and your planet is in some new orbit going someplace else, right?

That's one possible explanation.

What are others?

It doesn't exist anymore, or at least it doesn't exist in this place. One cannot rule out the possibility that it simply does not exist. You have to remember that I'm exploring a place, not a time. I'm using time to explain it to you. But that may not be the only means by which . . . I'm looking for resonance.

Well, what if it just went into the fourth dimension and you can't see it anymore?

You are assuming, because that is the progression of your culture, that it is a natural progression for others. Or are you not assuming that?

I am.

It certainly isn't a natural progression for others. I think it is only a progression that is engaged with you all at this time because you find that place . . . you identify with those words; they are attractive and so produce a signal that you are attracted to. So [the idea of dimensions] doesn't pull you, but you pull on it to get there. Rather, you don't pull it to you; you pull, and you are attracted to it. In short, it has attracting and attractive qualities that help you get to where you want to be—not so much in your case exclusively, because it is a nice place, but because the process of getting from where you are now to this attractive place is what you need to do in order to learn, grow, engage . . . in short, to accomplish your specific task. With you, everything is about process rather than being about the arrival.

That's correct. So on your planet, then, you would expect it to stay in the same dimensional plane.

Of course.

Ah, but obviously you can range beyond that. You couldn't travel around as a dot of light if you couldn't participate in other dimensions.

But there's no reason to do so. I will, however—because of your suggestion—consider looking for my planet in that other dimension. I'll do that right now. [Pause.] No, it's not there. That's all right. We have firm futures. I've explored all of those. Now I'm exploring vague possibilities. Not to change anything, just to see.

Did this work on your planet too, where, if you're in your purpose, you condense to a dot of light? Or is that only when you go out to travel?

Only for travel.

A Future Researcher, Traveling with a Purpose

Okay. So on your planet, what do you do? Do you have interests? Studies? Responsibilities? Jobs? Cultures? Do you have a job, or something that you are interested in, or something that you do on your planet?

I am a future researcher. But I do not get paid to do this. This is something that I find personally interesting. And when I have something to report, I report it to any and all who are interested. I notice you have developed some tools of doing this—your methods of communication, computers and radio and images, broadcasts and so on—that allow people to choose what they might be interested in to study or read or so on and so forth, yes? It is similar. We have things like that too. Those who are interested in future studies might be interested in what I have to talk about in terms of my explorations.

So is this what you do, then? Or do you have . . .

This is what I do. You are asking like a job, yes? As a vocation, this is my vocation.

I'm just trying to get a feeling for the life you have there.

I understand.

Do you live in families, communally or alone?

I am currently living alone. My wife moved on some time ago and I have not—even with my social interactions, and I have those extensively—met someone yet that I would care to, um . . .

Share.

Share life with, thank you. Share life with. Although that could happen.

What is your lifespan?

Again, we don't have years. It is, well . . .

Twice as long as ours? Half as long?

Lots longer than yours. [Laughs.] That doesn't help you very much.

A hundred times as long?

It is not fixed. It is fixed according to our purpose. When we are born, we have a purpose, meaning something that we are interested in doing. We stay alive as long as that holds our interest. Then we have the option to become engaged in something else that's interesting, yes. You all find different things interesting from time to time. But if we become engaged, engaged means to take it on as a vocation.

Have you ever done anything like this before? Talked to other people or other beings?

Yes.

In what situations?

Like this, for people like yourself doing research. Remember, our culture is structured to purpose. It is not only when I travel that others engage me on the basis of my purpose. If I happen to notice others with a purpose with whom I can contribute, who are open to it in that moment, then I will also make an offering of what I may have to provide for your interests. Our culture is engaged in serving such purposes.

So you consciously choose birth on this planet to accomplish a purpose? Can we say that?

We are really no different from what I have observed of your culture. You souls or spirits are born to accomplish some lesson or purpose. It seems to be very much the same. Perhaps we are more focused because we are not distracted with having to keep life and everything else organized, nor are we being overwhelmed by the complications you find in your culture. Things are more fixed and calm.

So you're aware consciously of your purpose as you grow up, then?

Yes. It is much more efficient, but efficient for our purposes. I can see that for your purpose, it is fixed in the way that is right for you.

Well, this is the Explorer Race, so it's a whole different ball game. So do you train, do you study, do you have schools or something that you attend or people you interact with on the way to doing your purpose?

Our teachers, guides and instructors support us—not only with what is known about our purpose, but also giving us tools to accomplish research in a manner and means that might prove to be beneficial for accomplishing our research to serve our purpose. That is all they have to offer. Once we have acquired all that is known, then we use the tools to pursue that which is either not known or has simply not been pursued by others. But with the proper tools, one can pursue it.

This booth that you're in . . . is it a tool that's provided to you for your studies? Is that an example?

Yes, and [this tool is provided to] anyone who studies . . . who wishes to explore past the planet in such a way that taking one's body would be impractical or unnecessary.

So many of your people go off to study something on other planets and other solar systems and other galaxies?

If their purpose takes them there.

So if their purpose takes them there, then that's perfectly all right?

Yes, as long as their presence there, as in my presence here, does not create any possible problem for the cultures present. It does not create any possible problem according to my experience, and the technology of the device does not disturb you or the plants or animals or the planet as far as I can tell. If I did not notice, the mechanism would let me know if it noticed. It would let me know by immediately taking me out of where I was. I might suddenly discover that I'm someplace else, which has happened once or twice, and then I would know that something I was doing or my presence was creating either a problem or a potential one. So the whole purpose of the mechanism and the method of exploring like this is to prevent problems from happening, not just having problems happen and then fixing them. It's much better to prevent problems in the first place.

Communication, Food Supply and
Reproduction on the Twelfth Planet

Can you share a little bit about your life? How do you interact with people? Do you talk verbally?

We can. We have a mouth and we can speak. We do that sometimes. Sometimes there is simply a shared feeling. I believe you do that, too. You might have people you know for whom, when you are with them—simply being present with them and the sharing of feelings—quiet is adequate. We are like that too.

When you breathe, what is it that you breathe on your planet?

It is not oxygen. It is other gases, but that is not my field. Something. I think methane is one of them.

Do you eat food? Do you eat solid food or liquid or . . .

We have a sometimes solid, sometimes syrupy substance we assimilate, yes. Food is not of the same importance to us as it is to you. To us it is nourishment but not—what is that word?—not cuisine.

Is it easily grown, so you don't have to spend a lot of time preparing food or searching for or growing it?

We have people whose purpose is to create such things, plus we also have mechanisms that do a lot of it. But we are self-sustaining as far as our food coming from our planet. Is that what you want to know?

Would you call the food plants?

The food? I could not say. I am not a chemist.

It's something that grows naturally, not something that's synthesized or created?

I really couldn't say. As you can see, our culture is created in such a way that if one has an interest, a purpose, you have points of contact with your culture. But I do not need to know about the food; others are good at it. They do it right and well. I do not need to know much about it, and I don't.

Is the food supplied to you in your dwelling place, or do you go to a community center?

Our dwelling is much the same as yours, though you apparently have to go and acquire food—for us, there is a distribution system. It comes from someplace to our homes, and then we can utilize it when we need it.

Do you have a reproduction system similar to ours?

It is similar, but we do not often reproduce that way anymore. We found that when reproducing that way, there is a tendency to overproduce, to create more beings than you might want for a stable society. This is because the act itself is attractive, and—I do not wish to make it sound clinical, but—previous generations discovered that on a planet such as ours, population fixed in the range I mentioned previously was ideal, not only for our culture but also for the planet's resources. Therefore, over time, external body reproduction was supported. We do not clone, but a lot of what would take place in normal sexual intercourse happens externally. The egg and the . . .

What we call in vitro *fertilization?*

Yes, something like that, and then like a cocoon. What do you call it? An incubator, but with lots of contact when needed, and good energy and support and love. Nothing set up to be dry or cold or scientific, as you sometimes call science in your time, because science has yet to embrace the feminine. When it does, of course, then it will be called something else, and will still have the provable effects of science.

So even though you're what we would consider way, way in the past, your technology is beyond ours?

Well, yes, but that is because your cultures on this planet have . . . because of not having the usual balances and checks on certain things, you have tended to destroy yourselves multiple times, and sometimes the most peaceful and advanced cultures are the first ones to be destroyed because they do not have adequate defense systems. In other cases, some of these cultures simply went underground and, in one or two cases, created impenetrable barriers so they would simply not be seen or, if they were detected, would not be harmed. A few years ago—in your time, as I understand your time—one of these cultures decided to leave, to emigrate, because it had been detected and was perceived to be a threat. Even though harm could not befall these individuals, attempts to penetrate the barrier created some slight nervousness for the occupants, so they emigrated to another planet.

Can you say which planet they immigrated to?

It was not in this solar system.

Can you say where?

Was not in this star system.

Are there any other beings still underground now?

Yes, at least one prominent culture. They have chosen to remain in such a way as to not be perceived by your current technology and, even if perceived, they would appear to be something else, something benign. They are remaining in this way until your cultures come to a certain level, and then they may send, may send, emissaries to the surface to offer advice, guidance and support for your culture's sustenance, to help you to thrive in a way that of course requires a great deal of feminine and nurturing energy for each of you to one another. That's why they are waiting, because you have not yet let go of being enamored of the masculine approach. This is not a bad thing but, when fully polarized as only the masculine, it is prone to self-destructiveness.

Can you say where they were on the surface before they went underground?

No.

Thank you. I didn't know there was anybody still there. But this is supposed to be about you! So you have the ability to look into the past and future of our planet?

Yes, if it is relevant to my purpose.

A Lifetime of Searching

So while you're looking for your planet, you've learned an incredible amount about everything in this area, right?

Yes, but I do not retain it. It has to be relevant to my purpose, for my purpose, for me to retain any of it. If you ask questions, for instance, about something that isn't relevant to my purpose, I may or may not be able to provide that information, because retention, if not present, will simply disseminate it to its own proper place, and my mechanism of the function of my being will simply exclude it. It's already been proven to not be relevant to my purpose; therefore it has been excluded from accessibility as compared to something you might ask about that has not been excluded, in which case I may be able to provide you information as I have done, or maybe not.

I see. So how long have you been on this adventure? You don't do time. What portion of your life?

My whole life has been associated with my purpose, without exception. In terms of this particular exploration that is taking me through this time of your culture and civilization . . . this time of your culture and civilization that I was passing through—just through that, if I might isolate to that, although I don't measure time the same way—but I was in your culture and civilization for as long as it takes me to do this [claps hands four times]. I felt the opening, and therefore I paid a call. Is that one of your things you say?

What I meant was, how much—as a percentage of your life—have you spent search-ing all the futures for your planet?

Oh, yes. Most of my life. You are asking how far am I along in my life. That is really what you are asking. Most of my life. I am no longer having just begun life.

So would you say you're halfway through, or a quarter through?

Our life is not measured in years. It is measured in the completion of our purpose. When our purpose is completed or I have acquired all there is to be acquired that is available to me associated with my purpose, my life will either come to an end or, if I've acquired another purpose along the way as something that I might wish to pursue when I'm done with this purpose, then I may gain—meaning do that purpose, like that. Or if that hasn't been the case, as it has not been with me so far, then my life simply comes to an end. But that's fine, because my purpose has been entirely fulfilled.

Do you see a long journey ahead of you, a long duration regarding . . . you've searched almost every place. Do you have a lot of places left to look? I know there's no time, so I'm trying to find some other way to phrase it. Are you close to the end of getting all your knowledge about this purpose?

I couldn't say, but the fact that I'm exploring that which is only vague feel-ings might suggest to you how far along I am in this exploration.

Right. Almost running out of things to explore. That's a strange purpose—looking for your planet in the future. Isn't that an unusual purpose?

I should think not, since your people seem to be fully engaged in an attempt to know and explore and understand your future to the best of your abilities. Actually, perhaps that's one of the reasons I may have stopped or been attracted here, since our lives are so much alike.

Hidden Abilities of the Human Being

I see. We just don't have the wonderful abilities you have. We have to send out probes and take pictures and speculate.

You have other abilities.

We have spiritual abilities.

You have a wide range of abilities; you just do not use them all. You use them when you need them. It is like you have this vast potential because you have all these abilities—but one might have many abilities and only use the ones you need in the moment, simply because that's where your energy is focused according to your purpose. That purpose might—in your case, since you are so engaged with each other—be culturally purposeful, or it might be individually your purpose. You will use only that which serves those purposes, but you may have vast abilities you don't use, either because you don't know how—you haven't received the training—or because you don't need them so they are simply dormant. They are active, meaning they can be activated easily, but they are simply dormant.

Name some of those abilities.

It would be better if you asked, such as "What about this? What about that?" It would be better for me to comment than for me to name them, because I do not know what might interfere with your pursuit of your purposes. I might say something that might make a distraction.

Well, everyone on the planet has the potential to be clairaudient and clairvoyant and see at a distance and travel in time, but truly we don't do that. Is that the kind of thing you are thinking about?

That is one small facet of the things you can do. Any other things you can imagine doing that your people don't necessarily do or that you don't do?

Well, we can get out of our body and travel anywhere, any time, any when, but we don't do that consciously.

All right. What else? Ask about physical things.

Well, we should be capable of . . .

No, no. Ask about things . . . don't say "should." May I say that to you?

Yes, shoulds are limitations.

Yes. It would be better to say, "Can we do this? Can we do that?"

Oh. Can we? All right. Can we travel to other star systems?

Ask about physical things. Ask about things about your body. I'm trying to help you. I can go only so far.

About our body?

Well, doesn't that come first? How could you be here without one?

Can we ask our body for answers to some of these questions and your response? I don't know what you're saying. Just say something. Give me a clue.

No permission.

Our body has all this knowledge. How can we access it?

Yes, you can do that. Ask about what you can do. That's what I'm saying. I won't tell you how. Just ask what you can do—things that are dormant that you aren't doing (most of you, although perhaps some of you are), or that you may do in the future, perhaps, depending on which future you choose.

We're going to choose the best future. Can we . . .

You always do that.

We need to get these things out there so people know they're possibilities. I don't even know what to ask about.

What do you think would . . .

They won't let you say anything? Who's talking to you?

My teachers. Remember, if I say or do anything, I'll be gone and that will be that.

Can we use our imagination to a much greater extent than we're doing?

Physical! They're allowing me to say that.

Can we ask questions of the body and get answers?

Yes, we already covered that.

Can we turn the body into light and travel and know everything and go everywhere?

Not that way. Ask about physical things. I did not say potentials. That's your word. Ask about what you can do that's physical.

I can't even think of anything that's physical that will allow us to know about the future.

Why are you limiting yourself to that just because I do? I'm not limiting myself. That's my specialty. Ask about what your bodies can do. Ask about the physical. I have to be specific. "Can I do this? Can I do that?" Let's go on to something else. I don't want to create a problem for you. What else would you like to talk about? Maybe you'll think about something later.

But you're offering me an incredible opportunity, and I can't even imagine what the body can do to expand . . .

Because you're limiting your question, your whole concept. You're stuck!

Well, unstick me.

No.

You keep saying the physical.

I am. You've got that part right. We're talking about untapped potentials . . .

Of the physical body.

Yes, but you're saying can we use the physical body. I'm saying different. I didn't say that. What did I say?

You said, "Can we, in the physical . . . "

Ask Zoosh later. He'll tell you. Let's go on.

Well, I want to know more about you. Do you remember your past lives? Do you remember choosing the planet you're on?

There are those who explore such things. That is not my field of specialty. I don't put my attention in past lives. There is no need to because, if one is interested, one can simply inquire of the teachers who know about such things. I have never been interested in that, but there are those among my people who are interested in that. I don't think there's anyone specializing in that at the moment, meaning . . . there's no one who has a purpose to explore that at the moment. I believe it has been explored purposefully in the past, and much is known about the individuals in my culture and their past lives.

My purpose in asking was . . . I should have phrased it like this: "You know that you existed before this life and that you will exist after."

Certainly.

Okay, that was really my question. So do you have a chance to plan your next life before you leave this planet, or do you just trust that you will do that in spirit, between lives?

Say again. Someone else is talking to me.

When you come to the end of your life, when you've completed your purpose and you're going to leave your body, do you work with your teachers to plan the next life consciously, or do you just trust that that will be done in spirit?

We can trust. We don't plan the next life consciously. Do you think you're capable of planning your next life consciously?

Not at the moment.

I agree with you. I do not believe I am capable of that either.

We have all these legends here that the twelfth planet is the planet Niburu, which helped create humanity, but that doesn't fit in with anything you know about it.

That is not our planet.

Follow Your Purpose and Ease the Way for Fellow Humans

May I give a parting statement? Don't feel bad. Your friend will tell you, and you will say, "Oh!" It will be something you'll just laugh about. I want to suggest to the people of Earth in your cultures now that it is good to have a purpose. You may have many purposes in your life. Please do not become engaged too much with somebody else's purpose. Find out in your life, or just notice, what you are interested in. What intrigues you? Don't assume that if it seems to be slight or insignificant in your culture that it is insignificant. After all, people who made great inventions that are very beneficial to your society and culture were interested in something in their time that nobody else was particularly interested in at all. So just because it may seem to be insignificant to your culture does not mean that it has no value. Give purpose its due.

If you like it, especially if it's beneficial to you and it's not harmful to others, as you learn and explore and grow and find out more about it, it may even have benefits for you and others. Give it your attention even while you do the other things that you have to do in order to get along and be a good citizen. It might just be that you will be one of the people who contributes something about this supposedly insignificant thing to your society and culture, and if you're not the one who provides the ultimate product from this thing, perhaps you will create stepping stones for those who will follow to provide that product or service. And, at the end of your life, when you talk to your teachers and angels and Creator, they won't have to ask you what you've done with your life. You won't have to be shy. They will know that you helped others who would follow after you to ease the way of your fellow beings, or that you produced something yourself that could ease their way. They will just look at you and smile and say, "Well done." Good night.

✳   ✳   ✳

Greetings! Zoosh here. Well, let me put it to you like this. Can my body repair itself? Can I grow new teeth? Can I grow new arms? Can I grow new legs? Can I grow wings?

I see. I was trying to use it to expand out into the universe and check things out.

Yes. That is a residual from the previous tenant. "How far out can I go? What? Stay here? What's here?" Lots and lots! Just because you don't see it doesn't mean it isn't here.

I see. He was a sweet man. Thank you. Did you kind of catch him going by or something?

He came to call and contributed to yes and no about what he can talk about. I didn't want to complicate his life. There's no "him" there—no "he or she," not like that. They are a little more complicated than that.

Can I ask . . . is he listening?

No.

What happened to his planet?

It's not here.

It's not here. Where'd it go?

No. I don't want to pursue it. Now that he's met me, you understand, he will be able to . . . and since he knows I have something to offer toward his purpose, he's open to me. I don't want to discuss it. Otherwise I'll interfere in his purpose.

That's fascinating, that some beings have a purpose like that.

He is right. So do human beings. They just have a little more to do. Good night. We'll talk again soon.

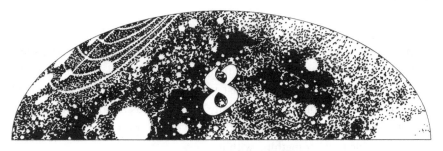

Individual-Specific Communion among Human Beings

The Sound of Breath and Speaks of Many Truths
May 25, 2002

will give my name eventually. My visit here has less to do with the human population than it has to do with the particle beings who make up the energy that transfers from being to being. Because of recent technological devices being largely disseminated here by humans, there has been some interference in energy transference, not only from one type of species to another, but more specifically there has been a breakdown in the subtle communication from one human being to another.

An Adaptation to Improve Communion

I might not be able to do anything about this, but I can provide a detailed report to those who may. Whether they will do it or not is up to them, and of course, you and others who might read this can attempt to do something yourselves. This energy is particularly having to do with the way human beings complement each other—not in your conversation type of complimenting, but rather in the way people might go together, might be attracted to someone else as a friend or a lover. This has been disrupted—not completely, but to put a percentage on it, perhaps to the extent of 30 percent, which is significant.

I believe this has something to do with why your human-to-human relationships have been in some difficulty. Of course, it also allows that friendships and relationships can evolve. So on the one hand, it has created some difficulty in communion, which is perhaps a better word here, but on the other hand, because you—and what you are doing here—are involved in problems and their solutions . . . usually the conscious mind is involved, but sometimes it is the subconscious or the body or the spirit. Nevertheless, you have been able to do something with it.

You have been able to find different ways to communicate, and you have had to use . . . let's call it a circuit, even though it is not obviously wired or even electronic, but let's call it a spiritual circuit that unites you all as one being. Granted, this is not complete, but you can see that with the communion avenue being disrupted, you had to have some means. It is not as individual-specific, but it is that which allows you to at least make contact with groups. This might be why in the past thirty years or so—perhaps forty even—that this grouping idea has become attractive, more so than in the past. In the past, I think that individuals in small groups, families, were more attractive, and now larger groups seem to be more attractive. This, I think, is largely due to a compensation for the breakdown in individual communion.

I also see an adaptation, an attempt by your spirit and physical body to utilize the gold light that can operate in a more restricted environment and actually improve communion. This is partially adapted to beings consciously doing things; intentionally attempting to incorporate the gold light works better. But even for beings who are not—how can we say?—able to function or are not interested in the spiritual realm that much, even so they are incorporating some gold light because of the adaptation to communion taking place as one being.

This adaptation happens through the top of the head, physiologically speaking, and this has been happening more and more for people, which you are doing intentionally because your normal individual-specific communion isn't working. So that has allowed individuals who were not engaged in intended spiritual or emotional or feeling growth or who are on their spiritual path in some form to also grow and achieve greater clarity of purpose. I speak to those people specifically now: That often begins for you with a questioning process. You question what has been, what you've been doing and that which is going on around you because it is as if a veil has been lifted. The first thing you notice is what's wrong. The next thing is that you begin to process what's wrong and attempt to correct it so that these established things work better and perhaps more smoothly or comfortably for all individuals and are ultimately humanized with more heart. Some of your institutions need that, and you're working on it. After you begin that work—not after it's accomplished, but after you begin and make such motions with intent and follow-up—then another veil is often lifted and further progress takes place.

The main thing, the interesting thing to me, is that here you had a problem in individual-specific communion, and your spirit and feeling self almost immediately in spirit terms—meaning a time in a longer volume—turned this around to something that would actually be good for all beings, all human beings in any event. That is often ultimately good, if not immediately, for other types of beings around you, because it engages more of your natural insightful consciousness. So you can see that although I am not here for you, I have had to observe you and understand what's going on for you somewhat in order to assist the particles that are involved in individual-specific communion between human beings. These particles are not part of human life, but because they have volunteered to engage in this function, then it is necessary for me to study and appreciate their applied techniques of living so as to observe the difficulties in an attempt to assist by passing on this observation to those who might choose to come and help these particles.

The Soul Personality of Particles

Now, I come from a place where there is no planet, no substance that you understand as physical. But could you visit that place? If you were visiting that place, if you were to move your hand quickly through what would be like the air, the difference would be as compared to moving your hand through what feels like space or the air now. Go ahead, move your hand quickly. Now, you see, after you do that, there is a distinct feeling, one that you have felt many times before. Were you in the place where I come from, the resistance—if you can call it that—or the feeling of the air would be about a third to a half more. It would be noticeable, but it might not dawn on you if you were just passing through. It might not be until after you passed through that you realized there was something distinctly different about that place and that's what it was. It would make an impression, but if you were not looking for it or considering it, you might not notice it right away. So that's where I come from, which tells you that where I come from is a place that is densely occupied with particles. That, of course, tells you that I am a particle.

To give you some idea, since you are involved in a highly physical place . . . I'm obviously not a particle of your dimension, but if it were possible to measure my size, about 8 trillion particles of my size could fit comfortably into an object the size of a molecule of water. I mention this and I'm speaking to you today because it's important for you to realize that when some of your teachers will talk about how everything around you is alive, this doesn't simply mean some kind of vague biological life, but life that actually has a soul personality—yes, an immortal personality.

But you ought not to then become nervous about damaging such life. After all, if a particle—if I can call it that since that's how I identify life—of oxygen is breathed in by a human and incorporated in your function, and then either transforms in part and leaves a residual portion of itself after it is exhaled, or is engaged in full in your body and traverses through your body in its usual cycle, it will at some point, in some way, exit. What I mean to say is that the personality is not lost; it's simply transformed into another particle of something else, not unlike your chameleon who changes color. Of course, you don't have something you can readily see with your eyes that changes distinct shape, but you sometimes see things that change their shape, such as the porcupine whose quills form a different pattern when it becomes alarmed. It doesn't actually change shape, but it changes the volume of its apparent mass. You see that sometimes with other forms of life.

For me and for other particles, you would find that you might get a transformation into something that appears to be entirely different, but even though it is entirely different in measured substance . . . you understand, we are not of your dimension. But speaking of particles in the example, the oxygen particle in your dimension, that oxygen particle's personality is not lost, even though it may find itself either incorporated into some other type of particle to perform a function in your body, or transformed into something else entirely. Still, its personality remains. At some point, when discharged from the body through your body's many means of discharge, the particle will go on. It will tend to return, if not immediately, to what it was before it entered your body, if that was its natural state of being. It might take awhile for it to return, and it is not uncomfortable being something else while it gradually reassimilates into what it was. After all, unlike yourselves, the particle is fully aware of its immortality. You might have uncounted numbers of particles within you, all who are aware of their immortality while you, as a human being—at least in the average human being—are not at all conscious of being immortal. That's an interesting irony there.

Particles Assist in Individual-Specific Communion
What was the technology that caused this change in the particles?

I believe it has something to do with satellites—not the natural ones like the Moon, but the satellites you put up in the sky—and their means of broadcasting or communicating their signals back to the surface of the planet. Certainly this was not intended by those who are using those satellites, and in one way or another, now almost everybody on Earth is using those satellites in some way, so it is not something you would care to give up. But you are here in this school, and the school's primary function is lessons and consequences that require adaptation on your part. So you have managed to make the best of it, but nevertheless, these particles are somewhat impinged.

I will explain what I mean by "impinged." The volume they might normally take up, even in their dimension, has been restricted, so they are impinged. As a result, the function they are able to provide has been impinged. They cannot do what they do for you as well as they once did, and in time, perhaps their service in this way of individual-specific communion will no longer be necessary because you will engage more fully through the top of your head on a broader scale. This I do not know. Or you might find other means of communion in your function of adapting to the consequences, which is part of the school you are in. So you are constantly putting that into practice. Should you accommodate such a change, not only through the top of your head but in other ways, then it is possible that the ultimate resolution here will be that this form of individual-specific communion will cease to exist and these particles will simply resume their former lives doing whatever they were doing or just resume their lives wherever they wish.

The particles themselves do not feel uncomfortable, but their request for an observer, which is what I am, was based upon their desire to assist you in your need for such communion, and of course, they want to do the best job they can. They do not do this because this work they do for you is their purpose or personally fulfilling; they do it out of kindness. They know you need help and they are perfectly happy to help you while you need it, but you can tell, on the basis of my observations and the particular direction my conversation is taking, that from my observations up to this point, it appears you are finding other ways to make this communion. Therefore, if not immediately, they will ultimately not be required to assist you in this manner.

Does this affect any other species within its own members or between that species and humans?

No. Just human to human.

Universal Communion Connects All Humans to the Gold Light

What percent of the people are going to pull in gold light through their heads?

I didn't say they were doing that.

I understood that they were asking the gold light to help through the top of their heads.

They might simply be working with gold light in some way or with gold lightbeings in some way, and the fact that they are interacting with gold light in some way has helped to bring this about. But they did not ask for gold light to come through their heads in order to support communion. It was not mentally conscious at all. And it was not subconscious in some cases, although in other cases, it was. It has more to do with simply getting used to the gold light and working with and interacting with the gold light so that the idea that the gold light is present becomes part of the natural process of their spiritual life or growth—or their religious growth, for that matter, since some religions and philosophies recognize the value of gold light.

So what percentage of the people have, on whatever level, begun to compensate? Most of them?

All people, to one degree or another—greater or lesser—are connecting in this manner, which is what I said. But some people who are purposefully engaging with gold light or gold lightbeings are doing it more. For other humans who are not in any way consciously involved with gold light or gold lightbeings, because you have had to adapt because of a problem—since individual communion is not working as well as it once did and, in some cases, is creating some difficulties or challenges, which I indicated—it has created a solution on more than one front.

The problem was that individual communion was being challenged or restricted. So the adapted solution was, "Let's connect on a more global scale through the top of the heads of all human beings." That was one solution, but the secondary that comes along with it—because there are consequences to solutions as well, and it's a good consequence—is that as a result of these individuals initiating this . . . this is more of an initiator, just as a spark in an engine might initiate the engine going. The initiators of this got it going, yes, but all humans now as a result have more communion on a mass level, are aware on a mass level of things that need to be corrected. All this I talked about.

If you saw it mapped out in front of you—this connects to this and this connects to that, dot to dot—you would see clearly how one thing necessarily leads to another and how its impacts, consequences and ramifications create other good things and sometimes (as always, because of your process) just create consequences that you need to resolve and/or adapt to. But one of the pleasant resolutions that was not part of the initiator was that other human beings who were not engaged with the gold light or gold lightbeings in any way have become exposed to that through the network of more universal communion—universal in this case meaning planetwide communion of human beings.

Churches Need to Respect the Physical Body

Let me ask, is there any difference in the quality of the communion with this new way of doing it?

Yes, and it still makes for some challenges and upheavals in small groups or institutionalized groups of humans. For example, right now some of your churches are going through challenges and it's very difficult for the participants—who are dedicated for the most part but who are also human—so the churches simply need to adapt. The participants or the church personnel need to be able to live their lives as human beings as well as being dedicated to their particular service. These are rocky times right now—bumps up and down, difficult challenges—but, in time, if the churches are going to survive and thrive, which of course they want to do, they will have to simply change. It will be difficult, and for some of them, it will be slow, but in the past, other churches have accommodated these changes, and these churches can do it too.

Maybe the church will change its face a bit as it appears, but it will become more honest to itself and ultimately to those it serves, which is not going to be a fun process. But this is a needed process so that things that don't have to be corrupt or discomfort or painful . . . none of those things have to take place and certain honest facts of the way the human body was created by Creator can be acknowledged, recognized and appreciated—the fact that Creator created your body this way intentionally can be acknowledged as being valuable in all of its respects. Once the church acknowledges that way, which will largely come about through this bumpy road, then things will smooth out.

Now, I'm not interested in becoming involved in or commenting on your religions or philosophies, but I use this as an example because it is something that is dramatic and to some degree is globally affecting your world cultures—

but to a greater degree of consciousness, perhaps the United States. The U.S. is a country that has been slow to mature, if I might say that, to the needs of human beings as they are created by Creator. Sometimes your European brothers and sisters will seem to patronize you in their attitudes and opinions, but that is because their cultures have been going on for longer and they recognize that the human-being body is what it is, not a philosophically disciplined scientific object.

Becoming More Aware

Would it be fair to say that the gold light is helping to expose things, not just in religions and the church, but in businesses and governments and associations, bringing to light that which needs to be altered?

No. It can only trigger a greater sense of perception on all levels for the human being. And it is that greater sense of perception . . . it is like looking through many veils and having at least one veil removed. You can't see as crystal clearly, the way you'd like to, but you can see better. Some things that you see or feel, feel good, and other things that you weren't aware of as being a source of pain or discomfort, suddenly you become aware of them. Then, because of your greater lesson—which is problems, challenges, solutions, adaptations, consequences and so on—you immediately set out to correct what is wrong in what you are observing so that it will work smoothly for the betterment of itself and all people. So the gold light does not cause it, but it allows you as a human being to simply be more aware.

We have to become aware of all that needs to be changed so we can change it, right?

Well, that is part of your training. In order to be a good creator . . . even parents know this, because parents are often forced into situations not unlike what creators might find themselves in. Sometimes the best of your intentions do not produce what you intended to produce because the beings you created—in this case, the parents created the children, or working with Creator they created the children—even though you attempted to bring up mannerly, quiet, obedient, wonderful, stimulating, joyous, happy children, Creator has programmed into your physiological bodies . . . Creator's most important point of view is individuality, each individual becoming who and what he or she came here to become and adding to the variety of different expressions that Creator finds so appealing. Therefore, as you know, no matter how good a parent you might be or how wonderful your children might be, physiologically, when their hormones change, even the child who sits up straight to chew his or her food, many times will suddenly want to play rock 'n' roll and dance in the street. This might be alarming to the parents, but similar things happen for creators.

Creators will set something up to work in a very specific way, paying attention to anything and everything, but sometimes things happen. This tells you obviously that creators—not unlike yourselves—are growing, changing beings, which is the nature of life itself: to grow, to change, to adapt, to achieve and to continue often in the same way so that more is achievable in the most benevolent way. You have to have a fixed system established so that growth and change and adaptation and solution and all of this can be accomplished, and creators must be masters of this. Parents, granted, are not masters of this, but they are clearly interested in engaging that process. Sometimes it is not a conscious act on their part to become parents, but spiritually speaking, it is always a potential, even for those of you who do not have children of your own. Sometimes you might find yourself raising them for a time.

We Have Been Welcomed by Creator

Can you say how long in our time you've been observing us? You evidently know a lot about what's going on.

But you see, I'm not observing you. I've had to learn about you. I understand your question: How long have I studied you in order to understand what I need to understand so that I can observe what I came here to observe? I have assimilated what I know about you in about—you understand, I'm not from your dimension, but I'm trying to put this into some sequence you can understand—in about three or four microseconds.

What dimension are you from?

We do not number dimensions; it is all on feeling. That's why I described where I was from on the basis of what you might be able to feel were you able to visit such a place. But to put a number on it creates a value in your conscious or subconscious, so I think I will not say. Just know that we value you as beings of Creator enough to offer services that have nothing to do with our lives but would be of benefit to you simply because we feel that what you are doing is of value to you and, more to the point, because you requested help and we were happy to accommodate you in that way.

Are you from our creation or from somewhere else in the totality?

We are from elsewhere, but we have enough familiarity and comfort with the Creator of this universe that we have been welcomed by this Creator to perform the tasks that we perform for your benefit and, obviously, with the whole-hearted embracing of your Creator. Otherwise, we would not presume to offer a service for which your Creator did not welcome us.

Have you performed other services for the Explorer Race in the past?

This is the first time we have been requested to directly participate, though on a previous occasion, numbers of our individual personalities were asked to observe and comment. This makes sense if you think about it, because we would be asked at a later time—which is now and for some time in your ongoing—to be engaged in this support of your communion with each other. As a result, we were then able to pull on our previous (in your time sequence) experience of you to our benefit so we could adapt, take the form that is most comfortable for you as well as for us, in order to perform the task that you asked to be helped with, the means that would support individual communion.

It sounds like you took a form to work with us—a literal form.

It is a shape. It's still the size of a particle, but it's a shape like a dot.

The Immortal Personality Is a Constant

Do you have a life cycle, or are you basically immortal?

Like you, we are immortal. You are immortal. You simply take on different shapes, but there is no gap in your immortality; when you have finished with the body you are in for your purposes, you move on. But there isn't even a microsecond gap. You remain alive in your own personality. You simply move on and perhaps take on or inhabit another shape at some other point in time. But you move on; you are immortal. That is my understanding of immortality, that the personality is a constant. It might change, adapt, grow and so on, but the immortal personality is its unique self.

Based on that, do you change shapes, or do you keep the same shape forever?

We maintain the same shape unless those we serve could be better served by our changing shape to something that is perhaps more comfortable in their world. For example, you have seen many pictures of molecules and mitochondria—things like that as your words go to describe shapes and forms and cells and so on. Most often these things have rounded shapes in some way. So that is something we knew would fit into your system in a way that would be most welcome, understood and comfortably interactive within the system of your existence here.

So what shapes do you have in your natural existence at home?

I am not going to reveal that at this time.

Is the purpose of the beings of your civilization to give aid to other beings when asked?

No more or less than your own. All life has that purpose, including your own. It is temporary that you find yourselves in a situation where you do not remember who you are. But outside the boundaries of this situation, you and your immortal personalities are always doing that—all life does that.

Are you called on frequently to give service to other worlds, other planets or creators?

No more than anyone else does. Just as often as you yourselves do. In other words, all the time. All life assists all other life all the time with joy, not because we are programmed to, but because when we assist some other life, it invariably might bring some quality of our own to the surface that we never knew we had; it is an assistance that provides self-discovery. We discover new things about ourselves. You do this; you can identify with it. Very often someone might ask you to do something, and at first, since you don't remember who you are temporarily while you're in this school, you might feel, "Oh, I don't want to do that," or "No, I don't want it." Then you go and do it anyway, and you find in the course of doing it that maybe you have a talent for this or there is some part of this that is really fun; you really like it, and you never would have guessed.

For you it sometimes unfolds in that bulky way because you temporarily don't remember who you are, but for us it is simply natural. Sometimes we discover something about ourselves that we didn't know we could do, and that's wonderful; it's fun. Even if we don't discover some new thing, in assisting others, it's not a strain. We wouldn't be attracted to assist them if that assistance was a strain for us. We're attracted to provide that assistance because providing it is completely natural to us and is part of our natural harmony. We're doing something that is harmonious to us.

Our Cultures Do Not Relate

Are you in your home place speaking at a distance, or are you here on this planet?

Here. As I said, I was requested as an observer. I am here alone.

Do you have what we would understand as a culture?

All immortal personalities have a culture. It would not be anything you could identify as a culture, with the exception of the fact that you could identify with the feelings.

Can you give me an example of some interesting service you provided by going to some other planet or civilization?

No, because it is so different, so remote, so not like yourselves. You might be able to mentally understand it, but it wouldn't benefit you to know. Based upon what I've learned about what you are doing here, I have to take into consideration that it is not good to provide you with too many details about things you may find fascinating or interesting, but which, under no circumstances, would benefit you in any way to know. Not that it would be dangerous; it would just potentially create a trail of interest for you that would lead you to no advantage for yourselves or your culture. So, generally speaking, tales that beings give you because of their experience, what they are, who they are . . . they give you these long stories because you might get something out of it. You might be able to apply it or adapt it. It might enrich your civilization. But there are things we've done on other worlds that you might find interesting, but they wouldn't provide you with anything that would support, sustain or nurture your growth.

Is it fair to say that you and the other beings in your civilization do this a lot? Do you go out to other worlds a lot?

No. It's uncommon. I've never been asked to do this.

Did you just happen to be available, or do you have some specific training or interest that led you to be the one who came here?

I was available.

Can you tell us anything about your culture: what you do, how you behave, what you're interested in?

The only thing you could identify with are the feelings. We have experiences of love and joy and happiness as you do—those kinds of feelings. But other than that, you couldn't identify in any way and I wouldn't even know how to describe it.

What interests you most about observing humans?

Please do not take offense by my response. Nothing. But I have to do it in order to understand my purpose for being here. My purpose for being here is not to observe you and tell you about yourself; this is just something I can do because I'm available. I am here, but that's not why I'm here. I'm here to do the task as I explained it. This is not to say that I do not consider you to be a valuable and beautiful species as I indicated before, as we all do, but I did not come here to study your culture. So perhaps my saying that nothing about you is interesting is not the actual way I feel but a response to your question as phrased.

Do you have a system of learning? Do you bring this information back and deposit it somewhere? Would anyone else be interested?

No. My report will be given strictly on the basis of my observations of what is going on. I don't make recommendations; I am an observer. An observer's job is to observe and then relate what has been observed using the multileveled means of communication that we use. You understand, the problem we are now running into is not that I am withholding information from you; it's just that your questions do not relate, nor is there any way I can really talk about it. So we're really at the point now that we're running into those areas where I'm going to be coming up with answers like this, one after another, because your natural questions do not relate to our culture.

Transformation Does Not Destroy Personality

Your lives here in this school are often something that appears to be overwhelmingly individualistic. Your Creator supports and nurtures that, wants you to be an individual as well as to be able to accommodate interacting in groups of other individuals. Know, however, that you are constantly surrounded in every moment—when you breathe, eat, just simply exist—with other forms of life that in their natural existence are happy to assist you. If you know this, you will grow in time to appreciate how you constantly live with the living and how the transformation of life you call death, which is sometimes traumatic and sometimes terrible . . . that even such a transformation does not destroy personality. It only changes form. Personality, your own, in the most unique and beautiful and wonderful sense, is absolutely immortal.

Don't be afraid of death. It is truly just a change of form. You, your personality, the things you like about yourself—not your pain, not your suffering, but you, who you are in ways you would recognize yourself to be—go on, and what goes on from here you would want to be. Pain, suffering, all of that, is left here. You would not want to take that anyway. You have just grown and learned how to adapt to it. But you, right now, are immortal—not in the shape, not in the body, but in your personality. You come here to grow, to learn, to change, to adapt. When you move on and go through your process of reviewing your life to see what you learned, you are still yourself. Don't be afraid to be yourself. Do try to be kind to each other. It is the natural way of life. If you cannot be kind or if others cannot receive your kindness, just know that all life is united. Things will get better—if not in your lifetime, then in the generations to come.

✸   ✸   ✸

This is Speaks of Many Truths. I'm here briefly because the being wanted to give you a name and wanted to pass that on. It is not so much a name as a description. The being said, that which would accommodate or invite that being and other beings of its type is the sound of breath: as you breathe in, as you breathe out. That's as good a name as any for that being. The particle said it would say later, but asked me to give you the message.

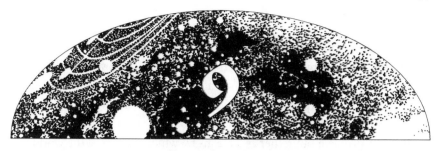

Predictions for the Past-Anchored Timeline and the Future-Anchored Timeline

ET Visitor from Orion
August 30, 2002

reetings. I will make some comment. I have been here for a while exploring your potentials. I am from the galaxy Orion. I have interest in your past and future potential. I will give two sets of predictions for your next time period by your calendar. The difference in my predictions from others is that I will give past-anchored timeline predictions first.

The Future of the Past-Anchored Timeline Isn't as Bad as You Think

For those of you reading this, this means for the first time that if you continue to build on the time you have been living, then this might be a possibility for the future. I would expect continued vigilance and security to be applied in English-speaking countries or even, generally speaking, westernized countries. I would expect the Middle-Eastern countries that are typically referred to as Arab nations to becoming increasingly hostile toward the West for their lack of interference and support of the general state of what you call honoring of state borders and honoring national interests. I would expect that the reaction one might expect from oil-producing countries is to use their product to influence, but that may not happen.

Another possibility could take place: A truly united Arab league has long been desired. This has been tried before and has not been as successful as many people would like. If there is not honoring of borders and governments, however much they might seem objectionable to the West, I would expect that toward the end of 2003 perhaps to see a real step toward a genuinely united body that would incorporate the Arab countries, as well as to have outreach to people of the predominant religion in those countries to other places. I do not see this as a problem but rather as a means by which the rest of the world can communicate perhaps more effectively back and forth. Still, the West might consider it a threat. I do not think the West will act on it, but I'm liking to put out this prediction now because I am asking westernized countries and other countries that have influence to discourage rebellious westernized countries from acting too aggressively in order to, can we say, get their way.

It is fine to strive toward what you want, but it will always take longer, so don't expect to get what you want without waiting and moving slowly. The other countries of the world know this—and of course, I'm speaking to the United States government in its temporary stages, and when I say "temporary stages," I mean those who are elected to office and serve fixed terms. Of course, the government remains in its fixed, long-term status. I feel it is very likely that next year we will see some significant increase in the vision that is involved in the political world, and that vision will be for something that incorporates something along the lines of a global influence but not quite a global government. I feel many other countries will begin to talk about that.

In the past, the general vision has been around the form of government of the West, since it appears to have greater freedom of expression and other things. But I feel there might be some other government that becomes the vision—not the United States, not England, not France, like that, but some other government that is a smaller country, perhaps in a cooler climate, that has a broader vision of how to apply democratic principles to its citizens. I feel that following that past-anchored timeline, there is a distinct possibility that there will be new ways of expressing oneself, perhaps not just through technical means that interpret language, but that the arts will flow more into day-to-day communications. This will allow freedom of expression heretofore unknown for many people.

I feel that there is a blossoming of a sense of right and wrong, as well as another sense—that which is transitional between the two. There will be a motion toward trying to legitimize things that have in the past been considered in some way taboo or perhaps even illegal, and there will be less likelihood of illegitimizing things. So, you see, the past-anchored timeline is not just a bad thing. I feel that there will be in some communities more and more of a desire for finding ways to come together, not just as political rhetoric but actually in simple, practical ways—neighborhood parties that involve the whole neighborhood, not just certain parts of it, and things like that. This has been done successfully in some cultures and in some cities. I would expect to see more of that in this coming year.

Do you have any questions about that part of the prediction, meaning the past-anchored timeline? The questions are to be along the lines of, "What will happen with this, what will happen with that?" They are not to interpret anything about timelines. This is meant for the general public.

The surprising thing, as you said, is that it doesn't sound that bad.

Ask about other things if you like.

Education Will Be More of the Same

Do you see anything new in education? Education needs a new direction—do you feel that coming in under the timeline?

What's wrong with the old one?

The children aren't taught to read properly, the schools are falling apart—everything's wrong with it.

If anything happens in education in this coming year, it will be more of the same. The situation hasn't gotten to the point yet where people in the community begin to do what is traditional. The traditional thing in the past was always for the community to come in and, if the school needed fixing up, to fix it up. If there needed to be different teachers, then teachers were either found or solicited, and an offer was made to encourage them to come. Maybe you have to give the teacher housing as in the old days—that was typical. In short, there needs to be not just community activity in the sense of the board of education or the parent/teacher group; there needs to be actual involvement and allowance for that.

I do not expect anything like that to happen in this coming year, because people will still be wanting government institutions to take care of it and they'll be complaining about it. The issue won't come to a head until it makes one news program after another about scandalous situations in the schools. Quite obviously, there have been problems in the past in the schools. Their situation is in serious imbalance. You cannot abandon one segment of the community and say, "Well, these children are going to have to make it the best way they can." They're going to grow up, you know. Then what will you do with them? But that is my opinion; nothing to do with prediction.

The Economy Will Shift to More Service-Oriented Products

What about the economy? It's still very sluggish. How do you see it next year all over the world?

Globally speaking, I see that the economy picks up in many places. But the economy has been built on products to make other products and then products that are desirable to individuals. The economy begins to make a shift in this coming year, where it's not just about the latest thing people can purchase. People are becoming overwhelmed with things that require too much action and interaction and complication in their lives. They are going to want more services. I would expect to see something like a renaissance in services offered to people, not just that simplify their lives in some desirable way, but where the service itself becomes something that is desirable. For example, it will probably be a pretty good year for caterers. This is becoming increasingly a desire by people who have parties or even have the family over. It is becoming complicated: this person can eat this, this person can eat that. It's not like the old days where you put out a bowl of chips.

So I think it is a very good time for caterers. People who want to start restaurants but haven't got the capital—don't feel bad about that. It might be just as fulfilling with perhaps less overhead to do catering. Pick out what you do best. Maybe it's desserts or entrees, and you might have more than one. What I mean by "more than one" is, for instance, you might have an umbrella company, and in the company there are people who specialize in desserts and those who specialize in main dishes and those who specialize in salads or appetizers or what-have-you, and they can all function under the umbrella of one company. Therefore, a catering business could be very versatile, plus it could also be providing a great deal of employment for many people.

I pick out this service in particular because, even if the economy is tight, people will want to eat and enjoy what they are eating and experience adventures in eating. In recent years, the idea of the restaurant with unique or unusual cuisine—maybe of a certain country that has not gone out very much to the general population—has become very popular. Now it is time to take this food directly into the home and allow the homeowners or the residents in the home to relax and enjoy the party themselves. Why shouldn't they have a good time too? Many of you will think about the effort and struggle to provide a good time for others by doing all the cooking and so forth, and others will say, "Well, if I count my labor and stress, the caterer is almost the same if not cheaper."

Thus I recommend this as one form of service that will begin to really take off now. I think there are other ways of performing that job too, but the general thing I'm saying is that I expect services to become much more the factor—not that caterers do not provide products, but ultimately they provide a service. Think of all the things you would like in your life that you don't have time to do. Then ask your friends about all the things they would like in their life but don't have time to do. So we're not talking about a new car or a new house but things that you don't have time to do but need to do or want to do.

What about starting a service business where you go into somebody's house and for a few dollars you do their laundry in their house? If you have maybe college students or someone like that who is trustworthy—it's a job, it's a service. The whole idea of domestic help is something that is so desirable by many people, and many more people can afford it than are utilizing it because a lot of people don't want to do the job or there is a stigma on it. But if you think about domestic help as being something that is a specialized service, there is a vast reservoir of demand for domestic service. I'm not just talking about maids—someone could be trained to be a special assistant. You could be not only something like a butler, but you could also do certain chores that might otherwise take up the time of the employer.

So I feel that, generally speaking, you need to look over the field of service and recognize that most services that are desired and can be afforded are not being provided right now that have to do with services coming from the outside into the home. There is tremendous growth potential available globally for this. Some places are already doing it, but in places like the United States and others, the demand far exceeds the supply. Still, if you are a creator, an entrepreneur, you will be able to find people who will be happy to do this on a part-time basis. The problem in the approach to domestic service help in the past has been that people have wanted full-time help, but maybe two people doing twenty hours a week would be fine. That way you'd employ two people. It can be done, various things can be done, and there is, as I say, much more demand at the moment and even more so next year.

War Is a Possibility

This is suggestive, and what I'm suggesting is that the business climate is likely to improve next year as people start to grow in confidence that things are going to be all right, as you say, most of the time and that even if something happens that is a serious situation, it is extremely unlikely that anything like your airplanes into the building will happen again, at least not intentionally. People will come to accept that there might be situations where there are so-called terrorist acts, but there is a global climate to alter this. Ultimately most—not all terrorism, but most—can be resolved in places like the United Nations because most terrorists have a cause. And with the ones who are simply criminal, trying to get money, in the next three to five years there will be cooperation—intensely, like people have never seen—to make such acts almost impossible to do. There are certain security procedures coming up and things that will happen. Some people will find them objectionable, but with the almost sure-fire guarantee that they will eliminate terrorism, most people will say, "Well, I can put up with it."

You mean like universal ID cards?

Some kind of universal ID that will make it possible to keep track of people and their motions. As I say, you won't like it, but once you accept that it has a practical purpose and that it's not being misused, that will be good. Governments will make mistakes for a while and misuse it, meaning they will allow personal information to travel outside the government circle. When they get control of that, then it will work well and the public will feel a sense of faith in it. But it will take awhile for the government to remember that its job is to govern, not to be part of the business community. The business community has, in recent years, become increasingly annoyed with the government for forgetting that fact.

You don't see a war next year along this timeline?

There are little wars going on right now.

I mean middle-sized wars.

What are middle-sized wars? Be specific.

You don't see the United States invading Iraq or any other countries, do you?

It is a possibility. I do not think there will be any support for it, certainly not globally. I think that if the United States wants to find out how much credit they have in the world, not only economically but politically, just even making the initial gestures toward that—I'm not talking about ongoing skirmishes, but actually bringing it into something like a warlike state—you as a country will be surprised at the reactions of the global community, politically speaking. Since you are a debtor nation and you owe more than you produce in terms of money, other countries, regardless of their military power, do ultimately have great influence over you. I wouldn't be surprised to see them use it.

So I would recommend that you take the slow path. I realize you have perfectly legitimate objections with various countries and their policies, but the direct path will very rarely be accepted in the global community now, and more so in the future. Although that might be annoying to parts of the government of the United States at this time, the long-run picture will find that politicians running for election will be supported much more if they promise to work within the global community to produce values, conditions, opportunities—in general, situations that most people in the world want.

In short, the days of just taking action are really behind you. It is uncomfortable for you, I know, since you were attacked. But you were not attacked (in the case of the airplanes into the buildings) by a country; you were attacked by a small group, and that is a fact. And the nations of the world have gritted their teeth while you have attacked a country regardless of how legitimate you made that seem. Nevertheless, as legitimate as it seemed to you, the nations of the world did not see it your way, even though they seemed to back you up. I assure you, in the long run there will be very little tolerance for you sticking around in that country and an expectancy that you will make your presence there scarce.

This does not mean that the nations of the world will bring pressure to bear about that country, but should you move into an oil-producing country, there will be a great deal of pressure brought to bear in a legal manner—don't worry about anything military or drastic or dramatic. But pressure is possible to bring to bear on the United States, as well as pressure being brought to bear by the United States. Although I do not feel this would create any significant problem for anybody in the U.S., it might create the threat of one. For instance, what if certain economic things happened? A lot of support happens globally for your currency. I'm not trying to make suggestions; I'm just saying that people in other countries have talked it up: "Well, if they do this, then we'll do that."

I'm not going to be any more specific about that, but those of you who understand these matters know what I'm talking about. I'm not trying to influence your decisions politically, but I want to make it clear that as admired as the United States is, generally speaking, by citizens of the world, it is considered at this time by most governments of the world and many business people in those countries to be the loose cannon—which is ironic from the position of United States elected officials, since they feel that other countries are the loose cannon, but this is often the case in a minority point of view. You wouldn't want—would you, elected officials of the U.S.?—the rest of the countries of the world to think of you as terrorists, would you? That is their point of view sometimes. I think it's much better that they look toward the United States as being something that is a good thing rather than being the loose cannon.

Barriers Will Continue to Fall

You're going to give the same predictions for the future-anchored timeline, right?
 Not as specific.

Before we do that, can you tell us something about yourself?
 No, because there's more you need to ask about. I covered politics and economics—anything else? What else is there? What else to people do?

They work and they have entertainment.
 I will just say this. I do not want the questioner to have to rack her brain too much given the demands of the day, so I will simply say that the current evolution in relationships is going to prompt circumstances globally to find a broadening of what constitutes a relationship. By "relationship," I mean a loving relationship that often involves a sexual interaction. The barriers about same-sex relationships are likely to continue to fall. No matter how conservative you think the government is and no matter how conservative a conservative government thinks of itself, it invariably miscalculates what the population's point of view is—and one finds the same for a liberal government or liberal politicians. The tendency is, when operating in those atmospheres, to miscalculate what the public thinks.

 I feel that the barriers will continue to fall, and you will find that same-sex relationships become not only increasingly tolerated but promoted. By "promoted," I mean not only from person to person, but commercially. One will find that there will be not only special programs on television for people in relationships like that but also in the music world, in the arts and, more importantly, in the commercial functioning. There will be products catered to them advertised on TV; there will be maybe even whole networks on television and radio that cater strictly to such relationships and tend to prompt and encourage such relationships.

How about religion? Anything that is trying to be controlling and secretive seems to be falling apart.

That's a good point you are making there. I believe we will see a continued progression along those lines. The religions that are more inclusive . . . meaning that just because somebody is from another faith, if he or she happens into the church that day for the ceremony, that's considered a good thing. By inclusive, let me give you an example: If people of different religions happen to marry, then neither religion makes a demand that the other person convert. This has been the situation in the past, and I do not see that changing in the near future, but religions that are more broad-minded and broad-hearted will thrive. Those that remain narrow will fall by the wayside, even including some that people cannot imagine your world being without.

What about movies and entertainment—movies specifically? Will they ever turn around to be simple movies of drama and emotional interaction without the wild special effects?

There are movies like that now. The advantage of movies like that, of course, is that they are cheaper to produce and will look more attractive, and I think you'll see more of those in the short run. But the problematic situation for actors is that technology is not quite but almost at the point of being able to produce artificial actors. When that happens in a way that looks real, then I think actors will have something to seriously worry about—of course, not stage actors. I do not think that most people for the next forty to fifty years will find that particularly desirable, but some will, and it will grow slowly but not precipitously.

Our Societies Are Distantly Connected

Can I ask about you now?

Not very much. I will just say that I am from the constellation Orion. The name I use does not translate into your language.

What is your experience? You're looking into our potentials?

I'm a historian associated with both the past and the future of civilizations, and my specialties are civilizations for which our culture or any civilizations in our culture have some distant connection to.

What is our connection to you?

I believe some of our genetic material has worked its way into yours and is still in there. I can see it.

Are you from our now time or our future time?

Roughly, given the variances in living vibration, from this time.

How long do you live?

Well, according to your measurement of time, our life cycle is anywhere from 1,300 to 1,700 years.

And where are you in that cycle?

I'm young. I'm about in the 600 range.

Are you aware of the special nature of the civilization on Earth?

Yes. In order to perform my duties here, it is necessary for me to remain encapsulated—meaning that the vehicle I travel in has a smaller version of itself that can be occasionally close to human populations without being detected.

Do you scan them? How do you come to know us?

I will say no more. If I say any more, what will happen, do you think?

They'll find you.

Yes, and more to the point, I do not wish to be seen. If I am seen, I will change the evolution of your history. I will speed it up, and I do not wish to do that. You need to travel at your pace. Now I will move on. I will say no more about myself.

Okay, thank you.

There Will Be a Sense of Vagueness on the Future-Anchored Timeline

Now I will give some . . . not predictions of your next year based on the future-anchored timeline, because you're not on that yet. But what I will do is talk about influences of the future-anchored timeline that would not be present in your lives were it not for the fact that it exists.

I appreciate this. I didn't know that you would list it as a future timeline.

So one of the influences that some of you sensitives will feel—this is why I'm giving this, so sensitives will notice it—will be a sense of (and this is how you'll identify it) vagueness that is more specifically noticeable by sensitive people in this coming year and which some of you have already begun to notice. By "vagueness," I mean that there will be times when you are not only unable to recall something that you can normally recall, but there will be times that are gaps of time. You will notice in the past, when you had spare time, that you could do your spare-time activities, whether it be a hobby or even watching entertainment on the television. But you will notice now that such entertainments might be less appealing. This is because they generally present somebody else's opinion.

You will find that there will be times when you are just resting when you will need something as simple as possible. By "simple," I mean, for instance, music that is comfortable melodiously—and by "comfortable," I mean it is either calming or it is even containing something that could be referred to as a monotone or several singular tones that you find pleasing. I'm not saying that this music is better; what I'm saying is that it is relaxing. There will be more times when you will simply need to just sit.

You will have a feeling at some point as you're coming out of it, so to speak (or maybe the phone rings and life goes on), that you have been doing nothing. But, in fact, there will be a synchronous change happening on the mental, physical and feeling levels that is allowing you to feel more in tune with the present. In the present, one is very clear how your entertainments or anything else like that actually cause you to feel, and if your feeling is not relaxed in these moments of desiring to relax, or it is not nurturing or comforting—not a substitute for the comfort and nurturing you're not getting, but is not in its own right nurturing or comforting—it is not going to be appealing. So these times of that which you'll refer to as having a vague time—or a "no-thought time" some of you will call it—will be more frequent.

Some of you who are sensitive will even notice this in others. If you do, don't say anything to them. Just be tolerant and say, "That's all right. I understand. It's relaxing. It's okay." Lean back and put your feet up if you want, but you don't have to tell people how to sit. Don't try and save them. The whole point is, this is allowing people to become more genuinely aware of how they are actually feeling as compared to what they have thought in the past would entertain them—which in the past has not always been but has frequently been for many people (certainly the majority of people in western-ized cultures) something of a substitute for what you're missing.

So this time, this feeling coming up that you'll experience (in this coming year more so, and that more people will experience) is associated with what has been called the future-anchored timeline—which is not dependent upon what's happened in the past but is in fact responsive to life as it exists in the future in a slightly quicker vibration of Earth and broadcast back to you as something that is available. It's not making any effort to influence you or to bring about your compliance, but it is broadcast back to be offered as an option for those who wish to connect with that vibration, be influenced by it and in time come to identify with it, feel nurtured by it and even become a part of it. But this will take quite awhile. For now, this particular influence is something you can know, identify and, with the markers I've given you, be able to delineate from other experiences.

That's beautiful. So people who have never even heard that there is such a thing as a future-anchored, benevolent timeline are going to feel the calling from it?

They're going to have moments like this. Not everyone, but sensitive people will notice it significantly. But even people who do not consider themselves to be sensitive or who consider themselves to apply their sensitivity only to specific moments in their life, these people will also have these experiences. Even people who do not appear to be particularly sensitive, though they might consider themselves so, might have these experiences as well.

I'm talking about it here because I want you to know about it so it won't upset you. You're not going to have these moments when you're driving—that's unlikely. But if you should feel one coming on, pull over. You won't be able to drive very well, though most of you will be able to drive by rote—is that what you call it?—or instinct, but I do not consider that particularly safe. So if you feel that feeling coming on, pull over or ask someone else to drive or what-have-you.

This Vibration Isn't Mental

What is the mechanism of the energy coming back? Is someone directing it, or is it just that we're close enough and the veils are separating and it's coming through? How would you say that?

Those individuals who live in your time who have lives in that future benevolent vibration of Earth are responding to the individuals in your times and need to generate or at least offer an option to improve the quality of life here on Earth, as it develops year to year, that is not continuing to reproduce your past history of violence.

That's wonderful. So it's not interfering.

The one way you can avoid reproducing past history is to disconnect from the past as you've known it. This does not mean that families and friendships and relationships don't exist in the future. It just means that if you project the past into the future, old resentments will continue, whereas if you project the future at a quick vibration into the present, those resentments aren't there anymore and you get along with everyone just fine. You still see the same kind of faces and so on, but instead of them being foreigners or from the other side or "them," all that's gone. They are just friends, new people to meet, new things to talk about, fun.

That's all I will say for the prediction for the future, because I wanted to give you something for that future timeline that was practical, measurable and could be experienced, rather than something that "might be"—because you are at the stage of your experience right now of life (past, present and future) that is in flux.

Can you sit and ask for that vibration?

It's not mental. You feel it or you won't. Don't expect to always feel it; don't try to meditate to find it. When it happens, generally you will know after the fact—meaning that you will notice that the past few minutes will seem to be difficult to measure. You might look at a clock and say, "Gosh, what have I been doing for the past ten minutes?" But you will feel relaxed.

I might have missed something. Is it specific from future people to their past lives, or is it anyone who has the ability to tune in to the energy?

As I said, the response from the future is generated by past lives in your present, if I'm answering your question correctly. But it's for everyone; it's not exclusive to past life and future life, and only those people.

So it's for everyone who can tune in to it.

No. It's for everyone who might experience it. You don't tune in to it. You experience it—it happens. The reason I say you don't tune in to it is that when you think of tuning in to something, it is a process. This is not a process; you just notice it's happened. Once you've had the experience one, two, three times, then you might be able to relax into the feeling whether it's there or not because you have a sense of physical identification with the feeling. You know that it is there. This doesn't mean that if you relax into the feeling as your body recollects feeling it in your unique way, you will automatically be connecting with that future time vibration. But it will at least be a nice way to relax, and it will create the potential to be more receptive to such vibrations should you feel them again in the future. And at the very least, it will give you another way to feel better about your life.

So they're random?

Not exactly random, but let's not pick it apart too much. I want people to be able to have the experience without having to say, "It's this; it's that. It's not this; it's not that." Let's let it be what it is. Good night.

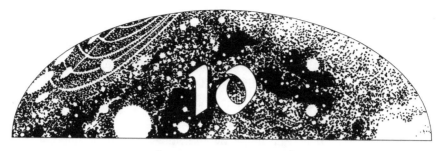

The Key to Life

ET Visitor from the Orb of Interconnectivity and Zoosh
December 3, 2002

ow, I must tell you that I don't look anything like you, nothing at all. I'm not humanoid; I'm not human. If you were to see me, I would look at any point in time like a line or a long thin tall open door. My visitation here is more to provide you with support for what you are doing these days, because all personalities radiate their personality. What my personality is radiating for you is the capacity to create doorways that connect you with future times and that allow such doorway openings, if you will, and to ease your connection to these future times—in short, to help you to bring about spiritual change, benevolent change and, yes, timely change, because it will be synchronized not only with future time but with the future time synchronized to the souls in your time who will have future lives where I am from.

"Where am I from?" you might reasonably ask. I am from an outer orb beyond this creation of orbs that is focused entirely in the interconnectivity and capacity for interconnectivity of all beings. In my place of existence, we do not have many individuals, so to function in a world where there are so many individuals is unique. In my world, there are only two other clearly divined personalities. As a result, these divined personalities do provide a distinct capacity to connect. Now, you understand that I did not say defined personalities. That is because we in our place have been asked by creators everywhere to bring about support and energy to help beings wherever they may be to make connections to times and places that can support them and others to bring about benevolent change for the good, for the heart and for the love of all beings. Such a request can only be divine.

I am not saying that I and my fellow individuals—we don't think of ourselves that way, but I will refer to us as individuals for your sake—are divine beings any more than you are, but our role is such that the word divine is associated with our service to creators. You might reasonably ask, "What in the world"—or in this case worlds—"are you doing here?" I am here because you all need support to make the connections you need to make that would help you to bring about benevolent change beyond your own capacity to picture or to imagine on the felt level what true and total benevolence is felt like and experienced. Some of you might have this experience in your lifetime, but you are the exception. Others need to have the means, the linkage to bring it about. My job is not to provide you with that means or linkage, but simply to move about on your planet and to be myself. By being myself—as it is the case with you being yourself, no different—there is a natural radiation of my personality, and simply doing that supports these capacities for linkage for you.

How long have you been here?

Oh, perhaps 947 of your years, but my personality has become more expressed in the past sixty years. I think this is because, to the best of my observing skill, there are more of you here now.

Do you know how long you will be here?

Time is not much of a factor for me, but we will be here—sometimes the others come—for a while yet. I cannot say. It could have deleterious effects.

How do you live your life or express yourself while you're here? You go around observing and radiating?

No, I don't go around observing. I do not need to observe. The observation just happens, but I don't go around to observe—I'm not watching. Yet one simply exists in a place as a visitor. You might reasonably go some place, perhaps for a task, and you notice things, but that is not why you are there. So the radiation that happens simply happens because I am in existence, but I do not go around heaving out radiation for myself.

If I looked at you . . . you said a door. Was it the expression of verticality, or was it the expression of height? Would I see you as six or eight feet tall?

I Respond to the Needs of the Creators

So what are your joys? What is your experience?

As I've described myself. This is what I am—no more, no less. That is my joy; that is my reason for being.

The radiation?

No, to be as per the creators' requests—just to be.

Many, many creators?

All that I have ever felt.

So you've responded to the needs of many creators during your time of being.

Yes.

Is your orb in this realm, the same realm we're in?

No.

So you feel a call and then you go there? Do you spend a comparable time at these other places with what you spent here?

I am in a place as long as I am needed. Of course, many of these places do not even have time as you know it—simply experience. One could make an intellectual argument that you do not have time either, but you have experience measured in the formula of time. If you remove time from your place of being, you still have experience, but if you remove experience, you do not have time. If you think about that, you will understand the nature of time itself. It is a formula to understand and work with time, and I grant it as a formula to those who are doing so.

Well, right now we're stuck in time. So do the other two beings come here sometimes also now that it's getting toward the end here?

That really doesn't have much to do with it. They might come just to support what I am doing or to allow me go somewhere else to do what we do and then return. So there is no . . . how can we say? Working in combination does not increase or decrease the energy radiation.

I see. So then even during this 900 years, you have been called some other places and then come back?

Yes. Or even during the experience.

Are there times when the three of you are in your place of origin and you don't go anywhere else?

Be aware that our place of origin is not so much a singular place but rather the place of need. Therefore, where we are needed is just as much our place of origin as anywhere. But for the sake of clarity, you could say our point of emergence into worlds of experience—that is the place I discussed before, though we have always existed. There are places where there is no experience, but such places are not relevant to anything you are involved with here as a race or anything you are connected to on any level.

I understand. Different beings have told us that in the past.

I Am Giving You the Formula

This is a time of tumultuous negative energy on the planet right now. Do you feel that? Does that affect you in anyway?

No, because I am not receptive to what is going on here. I am exclusively projective—that is my job. As a being who is radiating, you radiate, yes, but you also receive. In the larger sense, I am receptive to who and what I am, but in terms of being receptive to who and what you are—no. That would interfere with my job description.

In all the many places that you've gone and all the many things that you've done . . . this has been going on long before there was . . .

Long before there was "before."

In the books we put out, we refer to everything we've ever heard all the way up to the pre-creation as the Totality. Are you from beyond that?

We are from beyond the Totality.

That's going to be the final chapter of a book we're putting out [The Totality and Beyond, due in 2010 from Light Technology]. We have to get somebody to talk about that.

Perhaps this could be the final chapter as an appendix [in *Totality and Beyond*). After all, what I'm speaking of here is simply to allude to something that does not have any personal connection to you here but does exist. Remember, we have to come back to the formula for time and experience. There's not one. It is an equation, a philosophy, a release, a key, a capacity, a transformation, a liberation, a connector, a Creator, a means. It is the way to find what you "think" you have lost and a way to feel ultimately all that you need.

All of you who read this know that I am here to speak to you now in this one time only to have given you that formula. Many of you who are working non-time or with time will pursue it in your own way. Many of you who will simply think about it will be reminded on the basis of what you feel of the immortality of this formula. Many of you will know that this formula and the nature of the origin of love and the food love provides is most easily attained and, yes, achieved by a complete felt understanding of this formula. You will not "get it" as you say immediately—nor is it intended that any one person get all parts of it. But working as a global society, you can use that formula to achieve. This person has this, that person has that, and yet you are all one. If many of you get different parts of it, then on the felt level you will all have what you need to move forward—the key to life. Good night.

✹   ✹   ✹

All right, Zoosh here, for a short time only.

All I wanted to say is that I understand the loop of time because we have to have time to get the value of love according to what he just said, right?

Yes. One thing leads to another, and I'm not the least bit surprised that you, as that being said, "got it."

That's why the loop of time. Good night and thank you.

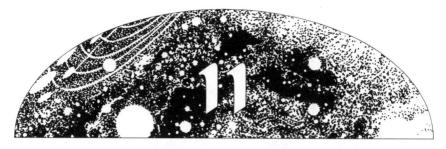

Orion's Visitors Are Still Here on Earth

ET Visitor from Orion
March 12, 2004

am available to speak this evening. My job has involved me in your planet's human culture, but not in ways that have prompted my direct contact with human beings. Still, my exposure might be of interest to you. Some time ago, in your calendar measurement, there were beings who came to influence your governments for the primary purpose of keeping your governments in the perceived (at that time) progress to keep them safe for us. And then once infiltration took place—speaking of something historical in that context—then other ideas came to be goals, one of which was not just control but influence. "Influence" in this sense means, how we could influence your population to not only be safe for us but also to be working with us toward our goals. I am speaking as one who looks back in time on my people's past. So sometimes I will use the present tense to describe something that is past-oriented, from my point of view, if that is clear.

Now, my people—or in this case, my ancestors—wanted to influence different levels of your governments, and in order to do so, they promised certain tools, techniques, and held out the promise of more to come in the future if you did just that (you, meaning Earth governments). Not every government responded. Of course, we were most interested in those governments that were most influential or the ones we could see would become most influential. Based upon the gauging of these governments in the light of our own development in our past, we could make the best guess of who might do what. We were not what you might call visionaries; we had only extremely limited abilities to take a look at future possibilities. But even those limited possibilities were very impressive to people who did not have that capacity in a technological way.

During the time of our initial contact, technology was still the most wonderful, the best, the answer to all problems, in terms of your then-culture. You're changing now, you're now trying, but at that time it looked like the answer to everything. Looking at your culture now with my instruments, I believe you are moving beyond that on a global level, as well as in societies that practice technology as a way of life. I've seen in some places that it has become almost a substitute for religion. When you think about what religion is intended to do, you can see how that might happen.

So that passes because there's nothing more beneath it. It is what it is, but there's no good feeling behind it, something greater than one's self that you can aspire to. I ought to be clear about the culture I'm speaking of. I'm not clear yet, you do not know, but perhaps you have made guesses. I'm talking about beings who have been influential in the past and still have some influences in your present that you're still dealing with.

Ah, the Orion thing.

Yes. My culture does not practice that.

Some Beings Have Assimilated and Remained Among You

Even in your contemporary time this is considered something that my ancestors . . . I am in the future, okay? My ancestors are trying everything they can to extract, actually not your people, but agents who are from that place and have been so infiltrated into your societies that they are very difficult to detect for your culture, but we can see them. They are there, and in your time they have greatly assimilated your manners and values and are no longer striving to project the old values of my culture onto your people, nor to control, manipulate or even influence—meaning that they have transformed, as happens, as we discovered in the past, simply by being on your planet. Your planet has influences even for those who were not born there, sparked by Creator's support with the planetary substance.

The planetary substance was not recognized early on as heavy in influence. It just seemed like any other planet. We had no reason to believe that it would have an influence, but it had an influence on our people. So we've got people there who are not just able to adapt to being Earth people, but who are able to adapt to your cultures, to your languages, to embrace them. But there was something else we didn't see. Not unlike your own people, even within what you might call the generic spectrum of the human race on Earth, some people have this biological and other people have that— meaning some people you could put in a room with lots of people with a communicable disease and they wouldn't get it. Some people just are less likely to get that, whereas you could put them in a room in other circumstances and they might assimilate something.

So we had a few that we didn't know simply would not break down, would not get sick, would not die, would not have a lesser duration of their life cycle. This happens often in my understanding in the study of these matters, of cultures coming from afar, even when they have trained and conditioned their people to live in another place, often with technical apparatus to support them but occasionally not. In our case, we had some apparatus to support, but we did not know that there were two or three individuals who had the capacity to adapt, to essentially become Earth citizens and be amongst you.

These are the ones where there has been this ongoing effort to extract them. This is not because they present any danger to you. But for the culture of your time from my people's point of view in the past, which represents a very diminutive influence in that galaxy from which we speak about and are concerned in your time—not that there will be any action on their part to create difficulty, but it is like something I think you can still identify with, some of you—that if they are detected, such detection might result in anger and, understanding the body chemistry of the individuals, could result potentially in not an immediate but a long-term threat.

To humans?

No.

To you?

Yes, to my people in that time. So the perception from my people of that time, your time—I'm about 2,500 years into the future of that—is that there's a threat. It's kind of like if you had a spy who is captured by another government.

They might trade secrets.

Yes, but in this case we're not worried about secrets.

Oh, the biology.

Yes, the biology. It is sufficiently different from your own to represent a threat should that information fall into the hands of those who might wish to use it destructively against my people of that time. It certainly would not be unreasonable that if this information came out in a wider context—a few people on Earth know it now who are in positions of influence—I would expect there to be some anger and even trying to prompt your representatives and your militaries to do something.

You have the capacity in your weapons technology even now to do something at a distance. It might be ineffective, but it would give you something to work on, revenge, that would not only represent a fairly minor threat to us but would probably, from my perception now, throw you off, get you sidetracked. I have seen people in your culture propose the idea that a threat from afar might unite the peoples of the Earth, but my feeling is that although that might look enticing, in terms of your spiritual progress it would be a side road.

We Are Trying to Extract Them without Attracting Attention

How many people are you talking about?

Where there is that desire to extract them? Three.

If I saw one today, he would be working at a job someplace on the planet and I would take him to be a human?

There is no apparent difference between them and human beings, but there are biological differences. If you looked at them at the beach wearing swimming trunks or something, you wouldn't notice. You would assume that they were fellow human beings.

But inside they've got different organs or different arrangements?

Well, I will simply say that inside they are different. I won't elaborate how. So it could be hazardous for them. That's why they require certain contacts, which we have not withheld from them, to support the means by which they are able to synthesize your atmospheres.

Why don't you just pick them up and take them?

That would require doing exactly what you just said: sending a ship, picking them up and taking them. Don't you think that might just [laughs] get some attention? That's just what we do not want. Our ships are not that exotic. We cannot land a ship in those times that would not be immediately detected by the means you have now. Even if it could land without being fired upon, which is a possibility but could create problems, it would then just simply aggravate that which we're trying to avoid in the first place. So the whole point is to extract them with as little notice as possible, which requires them to go to one, maybe two locations on the Earth, where they could be extracted with the least amount of notice.

How do they feel about this? Do they want to leave?

They do not want to leave because extraction would mean their death.

Why?

If the ship was detected, say, landing in the borders of your Nebraska, the same detection equipment is working anywhere on Earth. It might be at a heightened state of notification within your own borders, but especially in your now contemporary culture, it would be almost perceived as dangerous if it landed anywhere on the planet. So the only way to extract them is to get them off into a remote location and to use something that would eliminate them from being on Earth and would leave almost no residue. It is unfortunate, and in times gone by, they might have been able to get on board a vehicle and return home. You can see now why they are . . . they have assimilated Earth culture. They are able to survive any exposures. They are changed because of Earth, you understand.

These Three Beings Are Fascinated with Earth

So they're benevolent.

They're benevolent, yes, completely benevolent, but they are fascinated. Here they are, astronauts from another place, and life is a constant exploration to them. They have capabilities, meaning they can maneuver in your societies reasonably well, without much restriction. They have a command of languages. They are fairly well trained, I believe, from my point of view—even from my time looking back—to assimilate well into many different cultures if necessary. And they are enjoying the experience.

Say you went to some place entirely foreign that you were well trained for and, at least according to your own beliefs, your mission changed. At one time, they would have been considered, not traitors to the mission that was sent, but as they began to change, as everyone did in exposure to your planet's process of working with you . . . essentially converting whoever comes here to being like yourselves in terms of you being born to something, born to an agenda. Then at that time, some years ago, they weren't immediately detected because everyone was fascinated that they weren't likely to catch Earth diseases amongst humans or animal diseases (which is a possibility you're all experiencing now), and that was considered fascinating.

So they were considered valuable individuals, even though they had already lost their initial agenda for their mission and had assimilated in terms of adapting to your Earth culture—not exactly becoming members of the Explorer Race, but becoming benign to your cultures. And yet because they were so resistant to Earth diseases or being drawn into any dramas and so on . . . others had become drawn into Earth dramas, picked sides and became almost zealots for one side or another in your Earth cultures, and in the process they sort of lost the purpose of their mission. It kind of went like that, which created some problems for you on Earth, but eventually they just turned into—how can we say it?—partisans for one cause or another. Those beings were all easily extracted.

But these people weren't extracted right away because they were resistant to all of that. Once they lost their mission agenda and adapted to Earth energies and the influences of planet Earth, they were immune to other things and they became benign, not only to the mission at that time, but benign to Earth culture. So they were considered very valuable, someone who could be studied: If they can survive, how can the other people survive? In short, they became . . . not exactly objects of study, but fluid samples and tissue samples would be taken from time to time.

By our government?

No, no. By our people—certainly not your government.

I'm trying to get it clear.

Yes, of course. So the study was ongoing: How can we change our other people to be like those three. But it was not possible at the time, looking back, because of the nature of the instruments. The technology was not up to it, meaning that the fluid samples and the tissue samples looked identical to everybody else. So they didn't understand it, but they figured that this was a gift.

So the mission tended to go away from them, and then those in command at a distance realized that this was a failure, because of the unforeseen physical adaptation of our people sent to your planet's purpose with you individuals, the Explorer Race, as you have been told you are called. And so they started pulling everybody out. These three would have been amongst the last to go. But by that time, they were so fascinated with your cultures and they realized they could go anywhere, up to a point, and literally be travelers: study, interact, enjoy your cultures and be safe, and no longer have any allegiance to our government, which sent them.

It was not fun to be a citizen then. For them it was like they were escaping some horrible thing and were like prisoners released from some terrible thing. So their whole desire was to just live on Earth as quietly as possible—you know, not making any big fuss or becoming famous—to have fun and to occasionally be in each other's company and be with those from back home, but mostly to settle down and have a pleasant Earth life and just enjoy Earth life as much as possible.

Will they live the same earthly time here that they would have at home?

I will not reveal details. I do not wish to threaten their existence. From my point of view, I feel that—in your calendar time—they represent no threat to my people in the past, in your time. They're not a threat to anyone. They have assimilated and ought to be just left alone and allowed to live out their natural life cycle as an Earth person, having as much fun as possible and staying out of the public eye as much as possible, which they do. Essentially, leave 'em alone, they won't hurt anybody—that's my whole point of view, using your colloquial saying. That's about it for them.

As They Became More Earthlike, Their Mission Desires Fell Away

So my whole point is, I want to reveal the fact to you that they exist, because it's important for you to understand that even in these times, in your time, the government that originally sent them no longer exists and the culture has become completely benign. The desire to extract them is kind of like a feeling of fear rather than a desire to extract them for the purposes of gaining information about you—a fear of being threatened, of retaliation.

If retaliation came, it could create problems—and not only for our people to a minor degree. It's not that the weapons would affect them, but the people there in my culture, on my planet, in your time are just moving in that planet past that old government, and the idea is to nurture them to move past, not to feel anger and hate from another planet directed toward them. And since they are very vulnerable in their feelings right now, they might—some of them, not all—pick up those feelings and it could affect them, and progress could be slowed toward establishing a more benign, benevolent culture.

On your home planet. Can you think what year they came in our time?

According to my studies from where I am, the initial contacts and influence began around 1937 and then accelerated to its greatest degree in terms of contact and infiltrating the greatest numbers around 1945—it was easier to do that infiltration during your war time. The influence peaked around the early to mid 1950s, and from that point on the influence began to fall off as everyone, even more recent arrivals, began to assimilate to the Earth influences on their bodies.

So their mission desires fell away, and some of them got caught up in causes on Earth. And of course, the more they got caught up in causes on Earth—meaning polarized causes; this faction, that faction—the less they were able to utilize the technology, tools and even strategies that they arrived with. So the more Earthlike they became, the less support they were given to carry out the original and then the continued applications of the mission.

What was their mission?

To control and then to influence—meaning to control your governments so that they wouldn't become a threat to our planet and the ships and the travels we made. And then after a while, it was perceived that, now that there was this control to a degree, what could we do with it? So then we tried to influence you in ways that would serve the purpose of the original mission, you see. And then things changed.

How many came?

Altogether? Including those who returned and so on, there were, I think, at the height of it—counting individuals all over the Earth in this or that place, and I'm going to count those who were even below ground in bases that were secured—no more than . . . well, I'm going to give you a general number rounded off to the nearest thousand. About 37,000.

You're kidding me! There were 37,000 Orions?

That's a lot or that's a little—I don't know.

That's a lot!

Yes, you have to remember that the duration of their capability to maintain their training for their original mission began to break down right around the five-year mark. But it wasn't really noticeable, meaning it wasn't detected right away, until they got to about the seven-year mark. And so with those early arrivals, we thought—or my people in the past thought—that they were just experiencing something like overwork or stress. It was assumed to be like that . . . you have words for that? When people work so hard they . . .

They have like a breakdown?

Yes, it's a colloquial term. I almost have it: burnout. So it was perceived that this was what was going on for them, because it wasn't understood what was really going on. So, of course, the most recent arrivals would be the most devoted to the mission, even though the arrivals who had come before them were their commanders. Those were the ones who were in charge; they were there the longest. They weren't the ones who were higher up, so to speak—the ones who were directing the thing.

But those who had come first and knew the most, as is typically the case, would become those who would direct the ones who followed. But after the five-to-seven-year thing started, it became gradually clearer to those who weren't on the planet that the most recent arrivals were the ones who were most devoted to the mission. It was the beginning of awareness of the problem, which was misdiagnosed in the beginning as being what you call burnout.

So when did the last ones come, then? When did the last ones actually land?

The last arrivals who actually came were, in your time, around 1949. The amount coming then had slowed to very few. The last arrivals, I think, were five, six, seven individuals—I'm not sure which. Very shortly after that time—meaning within that year but after that last arrival—it was understood that the mission was a failure because of the unforeseen influence on your planet, your planet's influence on the bodies of those who are here to the intention of your planet, working with Creator of course to support and sustain the purpose of the human race on Earth.

There was some vague understanding about that, that there was a human Earth mission going on here. But it never occurred to my people at the time that that would affect people from other planets. There wasn't an awareness of that until it was too late, and then it was, "Oh," and we had these people here, and it was a really, really, really big job getting them off. These three didn't go, and they're still there, but I think it's okay.

Did they forget the mission, or what was the process? What happened to them? Did they forget, or did they remember but it became unimportant? How would you describe what happened to them?

I have to be careful here, because I do not wish to share too much of their assimilation method. I will simply say that the original mission purpose became less and less important, and the joy of discovery of what they could do as Earth citizens became more and more important. It was almost like the birth of an Earth child, with the joy of discovery of one's physical body and then surroundings, except that they weren't children. But they went through a process very similar, and for years and years they were just . . . well, I have to be careful now. But they were discovering and just having fun. The fun didn't harm any Earth people, nor themselves, so it was just like children discovering a new playground they had never been exposed to before.

Earth Humans Were Considered a Threat

Now, when you extracted them, did you bring them back home or were they killed or what?

No, they were not killed, but they were brought back. You understand, they hadn't adapted as much as these three who have been here for a long time. So they were taken back to a larger ship, and they were on that ship for, in terms of your time, two to three years, depending on different variables within their constitution. And when they were returned to their home planet to continue their lives, they weren't exactly isolated, but they weren't allowed full contact with the rest of the population for another ten years, during which time they weren't in prison, but they were being . . .

Conditioned?

No, no. They were discussing and studying their mission, their experience, what it was all about, their individual perceptions based upon their individual experience. That's how we gradually understood more of what your planet was doing. It was understood that this was an influence of your planet somewhere, I'd say, within that ten-year span, where everyone's shared, common experience was involved and certain things were noted to be more influential and other things less influential.

I will say that one of them is Earth food. What you eat—plants, animals and so on—of course, have all assimilated Earth. Therefore, our people who had been trained to be able to eat Earth food were assimilating Earth every time they ate. This is the one common denominator that was noticed, and that's how the people who studied those matters began to realize, about the third year into that ten-year time back on the planet, what it was that caused the change.

Did they feel like they were back in prison? What was the attitude?

No, no! It was very open. It wasn't . . . just because it was a more militaristic society . . . you have a militaristic society in a similar way. It was just that we had at that time the capability to travel beyond our planet, and naturally we didn't leave our culture at home.

You must have sent somebody here?

Your society's perhaps not quite as militaristic as that society on my planet then, but it is approaching that at the moment. I don't think it will become a totally authoritarian global government, but there are those in your time who are attempting to bring that about.

But how did you . . . when your people first had this idea to send people here to control the planet and eventually possibly come in and then take it over or something . . . ?

No, no—never that. We didn't need to do that. We had plenty of room in our own part of the . . .

Why did they want to control humans, then?

Because humans—Earth, as I said—were considered a threat.

Oh, to keep them from being a threat. All right, but you must have had some spies come ahead or some observers—how did you get the information to use to train the people you sent?

In close observation by ships, which at that time were undetectable by your culture. The ships could come very close, could hover within ten feet off the ground, as long as they weren't bumping into anything or birds weren't going to fly into them. If a bird suddenly hit something in clear space and fell on the ground, you would say, "What's that?"

So they were cloaked. They were from a higher dimension?

They were not viewable.

Okay, invisible.

As you might say. But they still had mass, and if a bird was flying along, it might hit it, not unlike your bird might fly into a window and hit it and fall down. So the ships could come close, but we always tried to do so in a way that would not disturb the population of birds. And we didn't go to a park where children were flying kites or something like that. But we could make very close observations of your culture. It is not uncommon for other planets to do that. Cultures that are more advanced might just send an individual to observe in the most benign way, or in some cultures people can look and study without even leaving their planet. Our people weren't like that; they couldn't do that, but we did have vehicles with which we could make observations.

It was perceived that some of the societies at that time on Earth were developing in a manner that might represent a threat—*might*, that's all—to our ships traveling near your planet in some future time. And the best way to head off a threat like that is not to wait until it happens but to come in well before and do what you need to do, hopefully with the least amount of impact so that you're not noticed, and be able to first control that to the best of your ability, and if you can't, then at least influence—or from the point of view of our culture in the past, to manipulate.

Manipulation can be done in ways that are not necessarily harmful. I can give you an example. Zoosh is here helping me to make this communication, and Zoosh says that, for example, in contemporary Earth culture a mother might say to her youngster, "Don't do that because . . ." and give the youngster a reason that might never happen in any circumstance, but the child is essentially manipulated, even for the child's own good. The child is manipulated to believe that if he or she does something that the mother perceives as harmful or that is in fact harmful . . . depending on the cultural conditioning, you understand, or simple observation. So a parent might say, "Don't stick your hand in the fire," something like that, meaning an obvious danger or a cultural conditioning—meaning a perceived danger, according to that culture. He or she might say, "Don't do that because this will happen or that will happen."

Terrorism Is Self-Defeating

So what's an example of what your people did to our government? What's an example of one of their manipulations?

You cannot say that without creating extreme rage and anger. You have plenty of material that you can bring up from your books in the past, if you want to bring up an example. You could create a brief side story, could you not?

Yes, yes.

I will ask you do one thing: Make sure it is our culture and not some other culture as an example. [See *Shining the Light 1–8*.]

Was it some of your people who became part of the sinister secret government's inner circle? Because they were Orions?

That has nothing to do with the three individuals who are on your planet now.

No, but were some of the 37,000 who landed . . . were any of those the ones who . . . ?

Yes. But they're not there anymore.

How many died in partisan causes?

See, that was the real problem—some did. I cannot tell you the intrigue involved in making certain that their bodies were not autopsied or noticed. It had to be done with extreme finesse. Sometimes a fire was encouraged after the death of the individual, and in a situation where others had died around there, very suddenly a fire would be encouraged that might burn up the surrounding area, including the bodies of other people already dead. Nobody who was injured or was still alive was hurt—that would be considered an outrage. We weren't trying to destroy your civilization.

Just the evidence.

Yes, just the evidence. So there was a lot of intrigue involved in bringing that about. It wasn't easy. And it was detected on the battlefield more than once. Due to of the grievous nature of battlefield injuries, both times that I have been able to pick up, every individual human who noticed or asked "What's that?" either went on to be injured in the course of battle and didn't remember what he had seen, or in one case, the individual died in battle later that day himself. So there were a few human beings in battle who saw it and said, "What is that? That's not human," but they received head injuries later in battle themselves and no longer could recall who they were, much less what they had seen. I believe there's only one of those individuals still alive, but he's in a comatose state and will probably die before this is published, which is why I am speaking to you now.

Oh, because if anybody knew . . .

If there was any threat at all . . . think about it. Considering the heightened state of your people right now, which to some degree, from my perception, includes attempting to create a global authoritarian government . . .

Oh yeah, absolutely.

Some, however, are genuine political attempts to say, "Hey, we've got a problem. Change it or we're going to make trouble for you," which of course tends to defeat itself—it's self-defeating. Many in the past have realized that terroristic things, blowing up, hurting, maiming people . . . this is not a battle where one side fights the other for domination. This is just something that everyone is outraged by, and ultimately, whatever your cause is, it's self-defeating. There's no way it can be anything but self-defeating. All evidence and logic points to that as well. If there becomes a reaction of authoritarianism, whatever it is that you are trying to accomplish for your people will get caught up in that and you will not get what you want. There's no question about that.

So all individuals working toward these things will in the next five, six, seven years realize that. And then the only thing that will be necessary by your governments is essentially to keep dangerous weapons out of their hands—they may not be able to keep knives out of their hands, because you use them to eat food, but bombs and chemicals that can be used to make dangerous things—

meaning out of the hands of . . . you understand. I'm not trying to say people can't go around with flintlock guns and have fun shooting at paper targets, but the people who want to obtain things . . . you will have to become authoritarian on a global level about the distribution of bombs, weapons and stuff like that. But once you have controlled the distribution of products that could be used by terrorists, then in five to seven years, the terrorist threat will be over.

If you were striving for a cause and the government became authoritarian, no matter what your cause was, there would be absolutely no chance of achieving it because the authoritarianism would crush all causes, including your own. So that is going to become quite obvious to everybody. I'm just mentioning it to remind people that regardless of how true your cause is, how valid your proof is, how dedicated and patriotic you are to your cause, if the means you use to achieve your cause—not political means—is harmful to others, you will (especially in your now times) perpetuate a guarantee of self-defeat for your cause by harming others, especially those who are just people going about their lives.

I am just putting this out there, not to stage a campaign, but as one who has studied my own people in the past, has seen horrible mistakes made and has studied widely other civilizations who have attempted this for, in their eyes, the best of reasons and the best of causes. Ultimately in societies where conflict is allowed, it takes place, and it all leads to the same thing—and that's that no matter how valid and worthy the cause is, it leads not only to self-destruction but to self-defeat. You don't have to take my word for it; just look at your own situation.

We Were Active in Earth Battles up until 1956

How many of your people died in battle?

About eighteen.

So all the other 37,000, except those eighteen and the three, were returned home alive?

That's right.

That's good.

Yes. Believe me [laughs], I have to laugh when I think of how I have studied the incredible intrigue involved to eliminate the remains of the bodies who died. And it wasn't easy.

It was done by beings in ships, not other Orions on the planet, right?

I won't say. I will just say that, if I can use a term from your time, it was a miracle that they weren't detected. I think it might really have been a miracle.

If they had been detected, it could have made a horrible mess. Hostilities, one side blaming the other—it just could have been terrible. I think I am very thankful—to Creator that they were not detected, and to all who helped to bring it about.

Whose side were they on?

I won't say. The more you know about it, the more likely you can find out, explore, document and literally defeat the whole purpose of why I am discussing this. I am discussing it because it's safe for you to know at this time. But I don't want to bring up details that you can use so you can go backward and run back down that path that would lead ultimately to your own misery. What's the point, eh? [Laughs.]

Right, right. Did they fight in other battles besides the second world war?

No comment. Well, all right. There was some activity in the second world war, and there was some activity in conflicts—I will give you dates, not places—up to your calendar date of 1956. By that time, it was quite obvious that the mission was a hopeless failure. Then the whole objective was just to get everybody out as quickly and as discreetly as possible.

What if they weren't willing to go? Did any of them express a desire not to return?

Yes. Some of them said that they'd like to stay longer, that they enjoyed it here and wanted to stay. But we were convinced that it would represent a danger not only to themselves but to the cultures on the planet here. And because many of them felt warmly, felt good toward your cultures, it was possible to convince them that their staying here might actually create a problem for your cultures, and ultimately that's what convinced those who felt warmly about it—with the exception of the three essentially assimilated.

Did they have skills and abilities, natural abilities beyond ours that they were able to use? You can't talk about that either?

I will say yes, to a minor degree—nothing like a magician on a stage producing some effect, all right? But to a minor degree, yes.

The Technology of Personal Identifiers Is Coming

Can you say which governments cooperated with them? I know the United States did and Russia, but can you say which ones?

No, I will not say because there will be points in time in your Earth cultures when you will all be making . . . this is a sad time that comes. It hasn't come yet. Oh, you can see what's come in the past, you can point to historical examples, but a time is coming when, sadly, there will be like a hunt for blaming former politicals, even some military and others who did this, did that—blaming.

Blaming is a big problem in many of your cultures: "You did that," or "Your father or your mother did that, and you're their child, so I'm going to blame you," like that. That's unfortunate and, of course, not logical either, but there's a time coming when many of your political people globally—and you can see it now at times—are going to be blamed and mistreated. So I'm not going to say. I do not want to add to that fervor.

It's a sad time, but it passes quickly. Everyone realizes, "Wait, wait, wait a minute. They've changed, they're not like this anymore, and if they ever do anything . . ." That's what people will decide to stop. By that time, you'll have a means to keep track of people pretty well, and you'll say, "If they ever do anything that is harmful to others, then they'll be in jail for . . ." so on and so forth—some kind of punishment that even if any of them have any . . . you know, just being caught up in human society, things that happen, you get mad. They are going to be more likely to be holding themselves back from doing anything sudden that they would feel sorry about later.

So at some point in the not-too-distant future, your people will have what other cultures might call an identifier, meaning something attached or even possibly subcutaneous, that is a means to know individual citizens. There will be resistance to this in some areas, but I feel right now, from looking back at your cultures and societies, that the resistance will not be as great as some fear. And all of the dramas and also the stressing of dramas and also some analysis of certain things—saying, "The terrorists did this," when it might have been something else entirely—all of this sort of manipulation and forming of public opinion and so on is not necessary to bring about a large degree of cooperation to accept that personal identifier right now, or as soon as it is readily available.

The main thing I suggest you do, those who are promoting the personal identifier, is to make it as accurate as possible—to put in multiple layers of checking on the product once it's in a person to make certain that all the information is actually correct—not just based on your own records, but based upon personal consultation with the individuals themselves. There also needs to be something that you build in, even if it's another layer of the device itself, that can adapt new information. By adapting, I don't mean simply adding things, but also adapting, say, attitudinal changes, because you're going to want to do that at some point. They have an attitude this way, they have an attitude that way, but people grow and change, and once their attitude has fully adapted, you need to be able to put that in there so that you can predict or have an idea of how they will behave in certain circumstances so they can be supported, nurtured, helped to grow and so on. This is particularly important for youngsters in order to support and nurture their growth and change and excitement and all of this educationally and in other circumstances as well.

Now, I am not talking with a purpose of trying to influence you as a culture, but rather I am suggesting that having these personal identifiers is actually going to be a vast, wonderful thing, that older people will say, "Well, I wish I'd had this when *I* was a youngster," because it will have unexpected benefits. Zoosh gave me an example of this. Say you go to school, and you have no idea who you're going to be friends with. In this situation, you would know, based upon your personal identifiers, who are the people you're most likely to be friends with because you'll have things in common. It will prevent a lot of fights and problems and so on. It will be a great calming and nurturing support for people globally.

So don't worry about it. It's typical to all other planets that I've studied, and for the most part, it's a benevolent thing. Granted, there will be some minor misuses in the beginning and the occasional mistakes. The main thing for those of you involved in the program to develop these things is to watch out for mistakes, meaning false information planted in people's identifiers that might cause harm to them. That kind of harm might make them angry and could create a scandal and make a bad name for your program. So you want to make as sure as possible, multiple levels of checking to see that the information is correct—not only within your own organization, but within the people themselves. That's critically important and is the area most likely to be overlooked by you.

My Ancestors Made a Mistake

Okay, let me ask again about the Orions who were part of the inner core of the sinister secret government. It's my understanding that they had special powers. Were they a little different from the common run of those who were part of your project, part of the 37,000?

They had technical devices. The way you're asking the question, see . . . you're saying it as if they themselves . . . no. But they had technical devices—very highly exotic according to your technology of the time—

that allowed them to do different things. And of course, it would dazzle
your people at the time, because . . . well, you know, you can see now in
your culture that technologically is determined toward miniaturization.
But our culture at that time had really gone much further than you are
now in miniaturization, so a technical device in great complexity could be
almost imperceptible to the naked eye but could still produce quite startling things.

So our nanotechnology is still way behind where your people were in 1937?

Yes, but there's a certain amount of resistance to nanotechnology in your
time, because philosophically speaking and religiously speaking, it is not
going to appear immediately, and those who are developing it do know this.
That's why they're trying to be sensitive to this, that there's going to appear
some religious and philosophical resistance to the uses of nanotechnology,
especially in biomechanics. So these are probably the areas that will embrace
nontechnology: more will be in the technical manufacturing and aerospace
industries. But insofar as there are biomechanical uses, there will probably be
some resistance to that.

Can you say what technology your people gave our government?

No, I won't, because that would just be another reason to get angry at our
people. We don't want that. The whole point, from my point of view looking
back, is to say that my people, my ancestors, made a mistake. They perceived
a threat where . . . granted, I honor the fact that they perceived the threat.
From their point of view, it certainly looked like a threat. But from my now
point of view, looking back, it wasn't. They made a mistake. Now, I think
your cultures in your time can identify with that. How many times might you
perceive another person or another culture as a threat when in fact there isn't
one? It was like that.

*But why do you think we'd get angry at your people for giving us technology that
we now use?*

Think of the whole spectrum of technology that you now use.

It all came from ETs.

No, I'm not going to say that; I'm not going to agree with that. You're rul-
ing out your own people's creativeness and inventiveness. I would not rule
that out.

Okay, a lot of it came from off-planet, then.

No, I will not even agree with that. I will say that some things came from
off-planet, including suggestions, ideas and stimulations. But your people

also have inspirations, and they are creative and inventive and adaptive. So I do not agree with you on your blanket statement.

Okay, I welcome that, but I don't understand why we'd get angry, then, since you gave us, um . . . I don't know what.

Well, why don't you think about it. Stop for a moment. I will say that what was shared with various governments . . . they were not *things* so much as they were *ideas*—"Why don't you try this; why don't you try that?" you know, for research. And then with the knowledge of how creative and inventive your people were, we could be reasonably sure that you would want to try this or that in your researches. That's what was done.

So Orion at that time, which is only sixty-five years ago, sounds like the empire of old.

Oh, I wouldn't call it that.

Tell me how it was and how it changed.

Well, that's a lot for tonight. I will just say that it . . . think about it in terms of a given sphere of influence. Your people now are caught up in a battle in a foreign country, and your strategists look at the situation as being almost tribal—that there are groups of individuals who would be perceived of as spheres of influence. In the time past on my planet, there were also spheres of influence. So my planet and one other were engaged in a very small sphere of influence that was allowed to exist by the rest of the planets and cultures in that galaxy, and was allowed to pursue avenues of expression up to a point. And always, even during that time, we had teachers from other points of view—more benevolent, as you would say, more benign—who were suggesting (not unlike the suggestions I referred to a moment ago), "Why don't you try this? Why don't you try that?" to encourage more benevolence, and eventually that took hold. That's why our cultures became more benevolent.

But in those early days, our sphere of influence was comparable to the way your now government is interacting, as I described in that example—it was a minor degree. It wasn't a vast . . . the term you used, like an empire. I don't consider it an empire in terms of planetary levels. You might have been able to say that this would be the case for a single planet and the other planet that was only partially engaged in that, but not in terms of many, many planets being . . . you know, it's not like your stories (in this sense, meaning your fictional popular stories).

Life on My Planet Now Is Benign

Can you say something about your life and your planet now?

I will say a little bit. Now my planet is involved and engaged in the study of cultures in a benign way. I personally am particularly interested in the uses of sound to support and nurture new life. By "new life" I mean that which is ... in your culture, new life would be the sperm and the egg coming together at that moment. I am particularly interested in the uses of very benevolent sound and even temperatures, like in mother.

There is this warmth, and there is the distant sound and vibration of the heart and the breathing and the circulation—sort of a rushing sound of fluids. All of these sounds are actually sounds that I believe you sometimes use to support ... later in life, I believe that sometimes when you have distracting sounds around, you will sometimes use something that generates these body sounds that a child might hear growing inside of mother. It's things like this that I'm particularly interested in personally.

But generally speaking, my planet is involved in the study of cultures beyond our planet in order to coordinate and to create groups of similar influences with the ultimate purpose of making that knowledge widely available so that people from all over in different cultures can see that they have certain striking similarities. They might wish to explore that further, perhaps to see if these other cultures on these other planets are related in some way.

How interesting. And then you're also interested in the past of your own planet?

Only slightly. I am consulting the records to pass on the information just for the purpose of this talk.

Oh, this isn't a topic of study that you focus on? You're just doing that to talk to us now!

Yes. That's why I said that I was only indirectly associated with your people. I'm indirectly associated now by looking at these things, but I've had no contact with your people.

I see. So you are effeminate in nature, yes?

Yes, and if you were to see me, you would say, "Hah! Woman!"

[Laughs.] How long do you live?

In my time, according to your calendar, something approaching—I won't be specific, but roughly ... I'm not going to give you too many details at this time—I will say in the neighborhood of 1,200 to 1,500 years.

Okay. Is that because Zoosh said not to?

No, it's just a certain reticence I have owing to the past of our culture's contact with you. I want to honor that past. They didn't feel it was safe to give you too much information about them then, so it is not for me to question their decision in their time.

Oh, I understand, I understand. Do you give birth the way that we do it here on your planet now?

I will simply say that it is pain-free.

But it's the sperm and the egg creating the baby?

I didn't say that. I gave an example that you can identify with in your culture.

So reproduction is different.

I didn't say that; I said it was pain-free. I'm sorry, didn't we just cover why I'm not giving you that information?

You said because in the past your people thought we were a threat, but I don't see how we could be a threat to you in the future.

You're not.

Okay.

Times Have Changed in Your World

Think! [Laughs.] What comes to mind? I need to honor my ancestors' decisions according to your time. How are we now, in 2,500 years difference, different from my people in the past? How are your people different in your now time from your people in the past? Not very much different. The culture's different, but not very much different. There's very little different; I don't see any difference at all.

Except for technology.

That's right.

Okay, I understand. This whole new thing of no details . . . I recall spending fifteen years getting explicit details about beings all over the cosmos.

Times in your world have changed. You said something important there: "I recall," using that. I understand why you use that vernacular, but the times for your culture, your global culture, have changed. Do you know anyone who is past being a child in your times now, in your country, who says, "Things today are exactly like they used to be." Do you know anybody?

No.

Everybody says that everything seems to be different now. Do you not agree that times have changed?

Yes.

So that is why you are not told the same thing. But you are told a lot about other things. Those other things help you and your society to grow, to change, to improve the quality of your life—in short, to do things. This is not just information about how others are doing things, but rather about who you are, what you can do, and how you can do it in the most gentle, benevolent and nurturing way for yourselves and others.

That's definitely Zoosh.

It is a quote—he's right here. And he reminds you that this is what you need now. Things are not now the way they were in your society. I think that's a consensus of agreement, yes? So that's why you can't have that anymore. Maybe it will change in your lifetime and you'll be able to have that again, but if it doesn't, after your lifetime you will have it anyway, so what do you care? [Laughs.]

The Study of History Can Be Enlightening

Now perhaps we are to come to a close. Can I make some closing remarks?

Please.

I'm speaking as I have been to your cultures and societies from my time in the future of our time. I have made a point to suggest certain things to different groups in your time who are involved in very influential projects, some of which will be very beneficial and, in some cases, some of which will not be beneficial. But I felt I could make a contribution to their understanding through the venue of this communication and its continued printing and broadcast that would support different groups of you working on different things.

Equally, for those of you interested in history, tactics and strategies, I suggest that you read up on the matters referred to in this talk [see *Shining the Light 1–8*]. I recommend that you read about it because it will draw to your attention how even on other planets there have been similarities to your own struggles to know and understand yourselves and to achieve a desire to create benevolence for one's self and one's family, and to understand that as everyone experience benevolence, so it becomes guaranteed for yourself and your family in perpetuity.

You are working and striving along similar lines. Therefore, sometimes the study of history can be enlightening, if not always pleasant. But for those who choose to study it, you can very often when applying the lessons of history predict the outcome of current situations with a high degree of accuracy.

My understanding of those who read this is that there might be an interest in predicting or even knowing the outcome of possibilities so that you can make clear and perhaps benevolent choices for yourselves and others. I bid you benevolent and happy experiences in your lives, and provide my personal blessing in form and substance that you might experience the best your life has to offer.

Thank you very much.

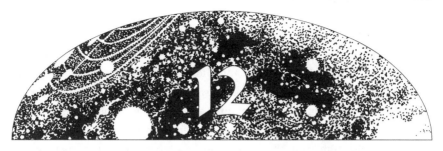

Earth Children Have It
All Worked Out for You

Tsong Ti from the Pleiades
March 13, 2004

am Tsong Ti, in my language. I am visiting your planet at the moment. I've been here, in terms of your calendar time, about twenty-one days and am observing the way you raise your youngest children, especially having to do with manners of earliest schooling taking place at home and sometimes taking place away from home but often nearby. I am from the Pleiades, and I cannot say how, but I have been welcomed to the Pleiades in one generation previous to me. I'm not native in culture to that star group, but I am native in line of appearance on Earth as you describe people, an Earth person. I look, perhaps, most like people in cultural succession from China.

I have a job in the Pleiades observing and guiding parents in the preparation of children's education to prepare them for a successful assimilation into society and to help parents nurture, bond and relate to children in the language most accessible to children themselves. One similarity in the young from both places—from the Pleiades, whom I work with, and here on your Earth—is that very often young children with themselves and with others like them do not always speak in words. Children are very quick to note that on your planet they do not speak the same language. They very often speak in sounds, grunts—sort of "eh, eh," stuff like this that is filled with meaning.

Children do not hold back on their feelings, you see. Those sounds are universal in your Earth meaning, and they are literally universal—because speaking as one who works with youngsters, the children of Pleiades, even though there's a common language, often use the same sounds when they are very young. And think about perhaps the babies and very young (two, even three years old, sometimes five, six, seven years old) on your planet, who if they don't have the right words or if they are in a situation where people do not understand them, as happens sometimes in your society, will often use sounds like this: "Uh, uh," meaning, "I want something," or "Eh, eh," meaning urgency. This is sound universal, and I have observed that with interest on your planet.

I Am Living among You on Your Planet

I am a female being and am able to speak to you now because I will be leaving your planet in approximately fourteen days and the publication will come out after my departure.

Why here? Your people come here . . . ?

Yes, we come here occasionally. It is still possible to come occasionally, especially if our mission is very family-oriented, meaning no intrigue involved and running, hiding—able to be open, so not working in any political way, which is not our way anyway. I can still come for these gentle-type purposes.

Meaning you can come and talk to somebody on the planet?

Yes, I've been given permission by teachers and those who protect your planet that it is all right to come for the type of thing I am doing. But it is not all right to come and make a formal presentation to governments or representatives of people or your United Nations or something like that. That kind of political interaction is not allowed. But to come and do the kind of thing I am doing is still acceptable because it does not interfere with your cultures, and anybody who would see me would immediately assume that I am an Earth person. I look exactly like an Earth person.

Oh, you're observing from on the planet?

Yes, I was not clear about that. I am on the surface. I am able with our current mechanisms to be on the planet and in complete comfort for a very fixed amount of time, not past that time. I must admit, I'm using that time almost completely, but that is the amount that the mechanism is set for. It was perceived by those who allow such passage that this amount of time would be safe and would not disturb anyone, that no one would become too attached to me and miss me and all of that. So my nature is friendly, but I have found a way to present my appearance so that people do not become overly attached to me.

I appear to be an older lady who cleans up. That's all I'm allowed to say. I'm an older lady who cleans up. And I do clean. I go to some houses, I go to some centers where children are often playing or the parents are there. I wish to see parents' interactions with children. I am also able to be at playgrounds. Sometimes I sit on a bench and observe parents and children interacting together. This is how I've been able to make that correlation I mentioned about the sounds that children make, which might not be new to your educators, but it's interesting considering that the same sounds are made on the Pleiades by children for exactly the same purposes. It is an interesting continuity.

Are you in one place, or do you have something that lets you bop all over the Earth?

I have been able to move about a little bit using some conventional means. I'm sorry, I cannot say where I am, but I am in a culture that is particularly . . . perhaps I'm not enough of an Earth sophisticate to say this, but my impression is that the culture in the places I have been . . . let me say that, to me, I have noticed that parents are very warm toward their children; their children are happy and very expressive, and everyone communicates with enthusiasm. It's very nice.

Talking to other people who appear as in my age group (as people of different age groups tend to congregate), I have found that parenting skills do not wear off just because one gets older. Very often I think on your planet older people are underutilized who might not have the stamina to interact with youngsters all the time but who are not only invigorated and refreshed working with the youngsters, but the youngsters can get something from them that they are unable to get from their parents.

So if a grandfather or grandmother is not readily available, then perhaps you might find at your nearby elder hostel . . . that is not the term, is it? In my experience on your planet sometimes, there might very well be a place where elderly people gather, and often as a young parent, you might be able to go in there, speak to the director and say, "Are there any people here who have volunteered or would like to look after children whom you feel might be good for my youngsters?" Round yourself up a good grandfather or grandmother substitute, if a related grandfather or grandmother is not available.

There is much talk about that amongst older people on the planet who would like to be able to help. An older gentleman said to me the other day that he would like to help out his family more and even be available for other families as long as he could have help from other elderly people and could, to use an interesting term, "tag-team." He said if he could tag-team—which I took to mean working with more than one—then the whole thing would not only be fun for him and his group of friends but the durability factor of an elderly guardian would not wear out. He said, "I've got a whole group of pals here, and we could grandfather. Between the six or seven of us who could show up at any given time, we could grandfather two or three youngsters and not get too tired. We could 'tag-team' it." [Laughs.]

On Earth I'm Finding Ideas for Pleiadian Parents

You said you weren't from the Pleiades—can you say where you're from?

I was born and raised there, but my parents were from another planet far from the Pleiades, having some relation to the elemental, as you would call it (perhaps not all of you call it that way), planets of the galaxy my parents know as Neer Vah. We would say galaxy, as my parents refer to it—that is their term for it. There are a lot of planets there that have beings who are associated with different plants and sometimes associated with different animals, what I would call elemental planets. And you have such beings here—"elementals," I think, is the term you use. Elementals . . . that is how we trace our roots.

You don't look like the Pleiadian people, then?

My parents and myself as well look a little bit shorter than the average Pleiadian, perhaps four inches shorter, but acceptable for an old lady on your planet. Sometimes old ladies are short, yes? Our appearance is very similar to people of Chinese descent. So my appearance is assumed to be of that culture on your planet.

So that's what you really look like?

Yes, I did not go about any alterations. This is what I really look like, with very, very minor alterations so that I'm more Earthlike. But you know that Pleiadian people and Earth people are . . . I'm not a doctor, but they look alike to me.

I think we're related. How did you get the chance to come here? Did you request it?

I work in a program that allows me to travel to different planets in our home galaxy and a few galaxies beyond to compare methods of parenting, child raising and early education that support our own on our home planet—

to gather information to see if there are any ideas we could apply to our own culture to nurture our children more and to encourage them to use their energy. In my experience, children are energetic all over in ways that do not suppress their enthusiasm and happiness. So the outgoing of as much energy as children have, while at the same time supporting them to use that energy in ways that are completely constructive . . . as all parents know, this is an ongoing challenge on your planet. On our planet, it's not as much of a challenge, but it's still there to a degree, and I'm allowed to travel about and make these observations and notice things.

What are some of the things you've come up with?

I noticed in a cultural event that there's an animal-shaped figure (of course, it could be shaped like anything) and it has candies and maybe little treats or games inside. The child is blindfolded and is led to a certain area, and they strike the object, that's the intention. The other children stand far away with the parents, and everybody laughs because the person is blindfolded, they can't see, so of course they're striking out in all directions. And then the game proceeds where someone gives them directions, "To your left, to your right, reach up . . ." this kind of thing, until by striking the object it breaks and candy or other little toys fall on the ground. In the event I saw, the person who does the striking gets a separate little treat, because by the time they get their blindfold off, everything that fell on the ground is gone. So they get a special little treat for being the one who does that. Often this is done, as I've noticed at birthday parties or special events, to amuse children.

I don't think we could use this exact thing on the Pleiades, but I can think of things we can do that will keep children amused for hours and be not violent. But there are ways this can be adapted to our culture that will keep children happy for a long time. Right now it's right around the top of my list for things I'm going to recommend.

Oh, that's great!

Where I'm From, People Just Feel

How did you get into this planet? Mostly no one can.

I would prefer not saying. But it was completely benign and did not disrupt anybody's manner, did not cause any stir in those of you who observe the skies. It is only allowed if it does not create any stir or upset. The whole point is to come and do this kind of work and not create any upset and go, so that it is done very calmly.

Do you have children?

Personally? I do not have children yet. I am not married yet. I am not with a mate yet. I'm still too young, you see, to have a mate and have children. But I am . . . how can you say? On your planet, it would be like I am . . . it's not the same, but you have people I've noticed in your classrooms who are often called student teachers.

So you changed your appearance to look like a little old lady here, but you're young on the Pleiades?

Yes, but it is not done by some exotic method; it is not difficult. I think you have similar methods available. It's just a little bit more difficult to detect and more comfortable to appear this way for longer periods of time—not like the actors who have to put on heavy, cumbersome equipment and feel very uncomfortable and use temporarily self-sacrificing methods to portray dramatic or fictional characters.

Do you eat our food?

I can eat it up to a point. I have found that the food most comfortable to me now . . . no comments or judgments on your foods, but the foods I can most easily assimilate are rice, vegetables and small quantities of fruit. But it all has to be from a health-food store, organic. I am able to assimilate small quantities and I can get through. I will lose a little weight being here, but it won't be so much that I cannot enjoy putting it back on, on my home planet.

So when you get this information, then you go home and consult with educators on your planet?

Yes, I will consult with my teachers and I will consult with those with whom I work. I will often report to something not unlike the school board that you have here, but it is more made up of parents and elders whom you might call grandparents or great-grandparents. We discuss these matters and I talk about my experiences of my travels, as do you when you're on your travels, and I say what I've observed. Then I give my suggestions on how they might be used, and the others discuss amongst themselves how they might be used with their knowledge. It is purely a cultural experience.

It sounds wonderful. Are there others like you who do this?

There are a few others. I do not know them all, but I know some of them. We like to talk about our adventures. We don't show slides [laughs], but we talk about our adventures. Sometimes we're allowed to go to the same general places; other times we are specialized according to our personalities and our scope of education. Then I do not have to make these decisions to assign people, so they must have their own methods of choosing.

How did you find out about it? Were you tested for it?

It is not like on your planet. People just feel. Perhaps it is a compliment to my parents, the way I was raised. They felt that my parents had a quality about them—sometimes people say they have a childlike quality about them, even though they are very wise. And they said I am like that, and people in our society recognized that I get along well with children and children get along well with me, and I get along well with parents and parents get along well with me. They said, "Well, it is clear how you could complement society with your personality and how society could be complemented equally with your personality, so maybe you would like this job?" And I like it very much.

Is the planet you live on bigger than Earth or smaller?

It's a little bigger—not a lot, just a little bigger. I'm not a scientist—it's a little bigger. That's the best I can do.

Okay. People are interested in knowing about other worlds, but I'll just ask Zoosh.

Understanding "Dimension" as Non-Hierarchical

Are you from a different frequency or dimension?

Focus. I'm not a scientist, but if you take a magnifying glass, any glass that magnifies, and you put a light through it, you can see the light condense and sometimes you can even see the light expand again. The point at which the light condenses to the small point might be considered the focal length. You see, if you're looking through your eyes through that lens, the focal length would have to do with your eyes, but if you're just shining a light through, then you might consider that the focal length, the condensed wave. See, it is more like a picture. You can see a picture that is a much better explanation of my experience of how different whole groups of societies can live in the same space. They each have the capacity not only to see a certain focal length but experience it as well. If your focal length is different, you simply do not see, observe or experience people who have other focal lengths. Is that helpful?

Is ours shorter or longer than yours?

There is no such thing. I am not a scientist. I am trying to explain something that is not helping—I beg your pardon. You see, what I'm saying is that to classify dimensions . . . I was given a certain amount of education coming here, and I think this has created a confusion in some circles here. You have the scientists who study physical dimensions and parameters, and so they use the word "dimension." Then you have other people interested in matters like this that you explore, and they use the word "dimension" to mean different levels of existence. The problem with this is that your culture perceives different levels as ranks.

Higher and lower, yes.

Higher and lower. And this has put that connotation on the word "dimension." I would prefer to use "focal length," because you would not say that the light as it condenses through a lens . . . this focal length or this focal length [moves left hand out], different focal lengths, you would not say that one is better than another. Do you understand?

Well, can you say that the longer one is more expansive?

You are trying to put a rank on it.

Well, yes.

What you said does not reflect on you, but it does reflect on the nature of your planetary cultures—not all of which are competitive, but many of which are—which rank things in some sequential order. Do you understand? Say you're at this level and then you work hard and you get to this next level—it's a ranking, you understand?

A hierarchy, yes.

My feeling is that the classification of the occupation of space by different beings is best utilized without the application of any form of cultural ranking and hierarchical ranking, because then you will necessarily say that one is better than the other or you will get in your mind that one is better than the other. There's no "better." In my experience of travel from place to place, I cannot say that there's one better than the other. When you are in one type of place, the applications of existence apply to that place. When you are in another type of place, it is the same—the applications of existence apply to that place. There are often differences, but the differences exist solely in order that that place can live and everything in that place can be harmonious to that place without any danger of such applications accidentally going through to the other place and creating a combination, when the whole point is to utilize the same space to the greatest degree possible and allow as much as possible to be present in the same space without it interfering in any way with the other.

Is one more expansive than the other? Does it vibrate faster? What keeps it separate?

That's the best I can do. I am not a scientist.

Okay. But you have the ability to interact with different existences, or whatever you want to call it, then?

Within a certain range where my physical body is comfortable. I can pass through certain ones. I can pause and observe, given certain safety mechanisms, perhaps in a ship. I know you want to know the scientific, the mental, but that is not my training. My training is love and nurturing children, parents—that's my training. I've shared with you what I can. If it is not something that feels good to you, then please do not use it.

Oh no, we'll use it here; there's no problem with that.

If you had pictures in front of you of the focal length of light . . . perhaps I'm using the wrong term. You wear spectacles, yes? There is a focal length through which you can hold the object out in front of you and you can see

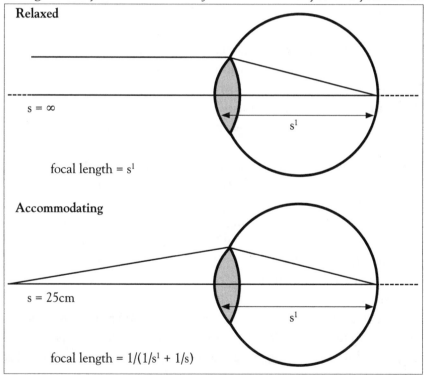

Figure 12.1: The simplest model of the human eye is a single lens with an adjustable focal length that forms an image on the retina, or the light-sensitive bed of nerves which lines the back of the eyeball. The eye is either relaxed (in its normal state in which rays from infinity are focused on the retina), or it is accommodating (adjusting the focal length by flexing the eye muscles to image closer objects).

detail, yes? And then, if you move the object around, at some point you cannot see the detail. That is focal length.

So if you had a drawing of that or pictures of that, it would be quite obvious that different people might have different focal lengths. I am told that this is actually causing confusion in your mind, because you're thinking that the people see only to a certain distance and then that creates the separation, but that's not it at all. I am trying to create an analogy, not a physical description. Let us move on.

Yes, we will put a picture in and those who get it will get it.

So Much Common Ground Can Be
Found amongst Parents and Children

Say whatever you can that would interest us.

I could make some closing remarks.

Sure.

[Laughs.] I was drinking the water and when I leveled the cup off, a drop came up and hit me right exactly in the forehead in the center. It felt very good. It was fun.

Have you ever done this before? Talked through a human?

No, this is a new experience for me. It's not something I need to do in my profession.

How did you get to know that we were looking for someone to talk?

From another one of your friends who speaks through this channel.

Ah, they talked to you.

Yes, she asked would I care to make comments about my specialty and what I'm doing. She felt that it would be of interest to some of your readers.

Oh, absolutely. It's wonderful.

May I make closing remarks?

Yes, if you like.

I would like to let you know how very similar children and parents are on your planet and on my home planet. They really are. If your children were not exposed to so much drama and fearsome things—not because of what you do as parents, but because of your culture that you cannot get away from, you see—then everybody could get together in the same room and make each other happy.

I think that someday the needs of children and the needs of parents and the needs of parenting (also including uncles and aunties and grandparents and great-grandparents) . . . that this is the most important thing, the children, the way the children are raised, so they someday become the parents, the good parents. I feel, in my capacity, that this is the most important thing on your planet. And it is, I believe, at this time being taken for granted by those who are not doing it and sometimes even by those who have children at home. I think if you all looked at how children and parents are all over your planet, you will find very much similarity. And when you see family life, you will find so much similarity that you won't understand why you are fighting about anything with each other.

I know that some parents and children study these matters, and I know it is of great interest to you. I want to encourage you to continue your studies and to talk about it with other parents and to try to be influential to suggest that more attention is paid to children, to children's needs, to family and friends and educators working with children. That is the best way to create a union of common agreement—not an authoritarian union, but a union where all parents agree that certain things work in raising children and certain things don't. This isn't cultural differences, just certain things parents know and children know—that certain things work in parenting and certain things don't. All children know this.

There's so much common ground. I think if more of your attention is directed to how you are so alike, you will be able to find in that unofficial way a lot more reason to be friends, to like each other, and perhaps how to get to know each other in ways you can communicate freely, which is very important in your times and cultures. A big challenge in your time is different languages and even different nuances of meanings in the same language. But there are coming now ways to do this communication. It will start technically, and then there will be some people who can do spiritual things and teach about feelings and other things. And for those of you who do not have the technical available, you can simply observe the children.

Say you are of one culture, and the people down the street are of another culture. The children get together. The parents might not be able to communicate, but the children get along just fine. Parents, you have seen that time and time again. This is because the children have a universal language: "Eh, eh, eh," or "Uh, uh." All these little sounds filled with feeling, without words, are a universal language that children use. Adults—those in positions of influence and grownups in general—pay attention. Children really have it all worked out for you now. Have a good experience on your planet.

Wow! Have a good experience on all the planets you go to. Thank you.

Plant Researcher and His Brother Visit Ancient Earth Peoples

ET Visitor from Ganymede
May 7, 2004

am not from your planet, but many years ago (of your time), I visited your planet and worked with many of your planet's mystical people already working, doing their work, and shaman people and medicine people—all of these names. Some were in what is now Africa, some were in what is now North or South America, some were in what is now Scandinavia and some were in what is now Europe. I did not, but my brother went to other places: Australia, as you now call it (I think it had a different name then); Malaysia (as you say); and Zealand, New Zealand.

We Were Looking for Sustenance for the Peoples of Ganymede

This was years ago, when there weren't as many people on your planet but your planet was very vital, with many flowers and trees and trees that flowered and bore fruit. That's why I came—my brother and I were interested in the fruit-bearing trees of what are called, I think, by your people native species, meaning trees that had been in those locations for some time or were well-established. The focus of our investigation started, then, with the natural.

At that time, we were looking to see if it might be possible to acquire some fruit and maybe even cuttings of the various trees to see if they could be transplanted, would do well in the soil of a planet we were working with in order to help the people on the planet to have a broader diet of food that might nurture and enrich them. We were particularly looking for what you call seeded fruits, fruits with many seeds inside—apples perhaps, though there are not a great many seeds. But there are other fruits you have—I think papaya is one—that you know have many seeds.

Kiwi? Some oranges?

Yes, things like that with many seeds, so that the people could not only enjoy the fruit, but they could also have the opportunity to nurture the growth of other trees that would support and sustain them and allow them to be able to multiply and have more children with the sustainable diet. They already had a good quantity of material that they made into something similar to bread, but it was not baked and remained somewhat of a soft consistency. They had strong digestive systems, and they could consume such a product. I think your people, if you consumed too much doughlike substance, would not feel too good [laughs], but they could do it. Their planetary system was in what you now call Ganymede. You've heard of Ganymede?

We had someone here from there in the past.

We Communicated with Mystical and Medicine People on Earth

My brother and I were particularly interested. Our ship was well equipped, we were alone on the vehicle and we had been looking around. Others had told us that your planet was one that had many, many species of plants and might be ideal for our expedition. So we came here for that reason, and we did acquire many samples. But in the course of doing that, naturally, because they were fruit-bearing trees, we would very often meet peoples who were living on the Earth and coming to gather the fruits or, even in some cases, encouraging the trees to grow—not planting them so much, but supporting them in some way, learning about them, learning about their qualities, how they could feed but also nurture and even medicate. There had been much research that way handed down over the years in various places.

Although your peoples did not share greatly with me their customs and abilities, they did ask from time to time . . . they were open to us. We weren't frightening to look at; we looked not quite like them. At first we wore equipment because we weren't sure if we could assimilate your atmosphere, and then after a time, we discovered that with a slight alteration of our chemistry, which small inhaling of certain, ah . . .

Gases?

No, it was more like plant fumes—not unlike fragrances from flowers, but the substance was actually living. If you looked at it, it would look very much to you like moss, and it has a fragrance. It is in a dish, and you pick it up and you breathe it in when you are in atmospheres that might be difficult. So that's what we did. And the breathing of that—at least once every cycle of eight to twelve hours, as you call it—would allow us to travel on the surface of the planet without any breathing apparatus.

After we found that there was no danger to our skin and other organs on the planet, we were able to strip off bit by bit almost all of our survival equipment. And we never strayed too far from the ship. But we met people. And this was the one thing people were willing to discuss, especially since they saw we were gathering the fruits—we didn't take too much, just samples—and we were inquiring about those fruits. We had this device; it was about here.

On the left shoulder.

Yes. It was in our survival equipment and would allow us to communicate in our natural way, but the people would hear us in their own language. And the opposite was also true. They could speak in their own language, though some of them did not speak that much, but we could assimilate their desires, interests, conversation and, to some degree, pictures (if they were holding pictures in their mind for the purpose of communication). This was not to eavesdrop on their private thoughts, but for the purpose of communication we could acquire the photo so we would know what they were trying to speak. That would be available to us so communication could take place.

They would help us sometimes and, once they knew what we were looking for, say, "Go here, go there; we heard this, we saw that." Over time, we developed a rapport with some of these individuals. Very often, because we were investigating plant life, we found ourselves talking to medicine people and sometimes mystical people—but not people who were ceremonial in nature, meaning people who were creating or helping others to go through ceremonies, that wasn't it. Even though that is perfectly valid, it was something that was not part of our research, so those were not the people we would usually meet.

As a result, we found ourselves very often meeting these mystical and spiritual individuals. Therefore, I felt that perhaps a little discussion about our context—who we met and where we went, preserving their dignity and private lives but sharing some of their wisdom—might be of interest. Now,

I will at some point give a name for myself, but our names do not directly or even concentrically translate into your language system. Our name would come closer to being a mathematical pulse in our actual language, and we don't consider ourselves pulse beings—please do not call us that. So if you are attached to a name, I will try to come up with something. But if you're not, then I will continue.

Continue, that's fine.

Physically We Were Not That Different from You

Do you have any particular areas of interest that you would like to ask about before I simply proceed?

How did you look? In what way were you different from humans?

The people in those times were not as tall as I observe your people in this age. It was quite unusual to see anyone even five feet tall. Occasionally we did run across some peoples in Africa who were quite tall, but they were the exception. Other than those individuals and the occasional person you'd meet who was tall unexpectedly, for the most part the peoples were five feet tall, five foot one, four foot nine, four foot eight, sometimes shorter. That's simply the way it was, perhaps having something to do with the diet.

But that is how it was during those times. So, therefore, our height, which would not seem excessively tall to you these days, was quite startling to most peoples then. We were, by your measurement, maybe six foot three, six foot four, something like that—which if you were five feet tall would be quite significant.

Our skin color varies, not unlike your own skin color varies a little bit from parts of your body to other parts. But it would vary roughly from a light green to some reddish tones—something like that around parts of our body. We were humanoids, you would say, and our bodies were fairly strong—a little thick perhaps, meaning wide through the physical part of the body, but strong—and our arms and legs were proportionate.

The proportions are a little different than yours are, since your arms are quite a bit shorter than your legs. Our arms were a little bit in proportion, you understand—our arms were not as short as your arms are to your legs. The proportion would have been that our arms—arms and hands, you understand—would have been about four inches longer in proportion, if that makes sense to you.

The equipment that we wore . . . the apparel was more to keep us comfortable, but it was not an excessive amount of apparel, meaning our legs would be partly exposed. We had very little body hair as you know it, a few hairs though: some above the eyes, a few around the back of the head and occasional hairs on the top, not many. We had a slight ridge, not much, across the top of the skull. And the side of our head, of the skull, flared out a little bit.

Above the ear?

Yes, above where the top of the ear actually connects with the head, there would have been a bony ridge that comes out a little bit and tapers down to being not unlike the ridge on this face, and in back also tapers around toward the back of the skull, so that you cannot feel it back here. It was not too shocking, but it was different to peoples not used to seeing people who are different.

Our feet were different from yours. Oh, we had a similar shape, but the toenails were stronger, more firm. I am not inclined to call them claws, but they had the durability of the type of claw you might see with some of your animal species, where they would help us to stand. We had one more toe than you have, and whereas your toes are tapering, where you have a small toe and then you have a large toe, we would have one toe that was just a little bit bigger and the rest of the toes would be almost proportionate, meaning just slightly smaller. They were not unlike yours, but the . . . curving is not perhaps the right term for an illustrator, but they were shaped like that. Your toes, perhaps, are more flat on the ground, whereas ours were more . . . they would bend.

Oh, I see. Curving into the ground, yes.

Yes, so the idea of something more clawlike on the end would be appropriate. This allowed us to make sudden quick moves, because our feet and toes were springy and had sort of a flexible quality, and they allowed us to jump, if necessary, or to take long steps. Perhaps there would be a hazard on the ground—we could jump over it. Our legs were very strong, and our capacity to jump at a considerable distance exceeds your own.

What about your hands? More fingers?

I'm looking at your fingers now and the fingers of humans then. There seems to be about the same for you: your peoples now and your peoples at that time. We had, not another finger, but something you might call a stub of a finger, which we were able to use. It's hard to describe it, but we had, as you call it . . . you call it an opposable thumb?

Opposable thumbs, yes.

We had opposable thumbs. And we had something that, if you would see our hand, would look a lot like there's another finger, a sixth finger, but it doesn't come out much farther than, say, an inch at most. But I have found it to be useful sometimes for moving things and manipulating things. There is no nail on that, whereas the other ones have a form of fingernail, not unlike yourselves. A little different.

What about your response to our gravity? If you could jump, were you used to our lighter gravity?

That's an interesting question, but in terms of the mechanics of planetary experience, gravity here is perhaps a little more ponderous than most other planets. This may not be something your scientists are aware of, but I think the gravitational pull for your planet is a little more firm than other planets. So we were used to a little less gravity. You might suspect that being able to jump like that, we were used to more gravity, but it was not the case.

I am not a great traveler, but I have traveled a little. I have found the gravity on your planet to be a little more than I expected, which is why perhaps only the most ancient trees could grow tall. I have seen planets where a tree is very young by your standards, and it has already grown thirty or forty feet, to use your measurements.

Trees have to grow against the gravity—I didn't know that.

Well, think about it. Many trees you see grow out, not up. And growing up takes time. But on other planets, it's just as easy to grow up as out, so they grow up.

Interesting.

The Earth Was Very Different When We Came

Do you have any idea how long you were on this planet in terms of our time?

I'm going to try to examine that. Your time has changed a little bit recently. I think it might be easier to say, instead of putting a time on it . . . I'll try to put a time on it, but it might be easier to say that the population on the Earth then was numbered in millions, rather than any higher number.

And there was no technology?

Not as you know it in your time. But the people we met didn't really need it. They were getting along just fine without it.

And they were more spiritual?

They were more aware of the land and attuned to their own bodies. They were more involved in their capacities, what they could do. They were highly instinctual, and they were peoples who were very comfortable living on the land, though they often would have some natural shelter that they would create in case of rain.

There wasn't as much in those days, when I was here with my brother. There were very few areas that were cold or snowy. We went to visit the cold and snow, just to see what it was like. It's an extreme rarity, in terms of the places I've been—my planet doesn't have anything like it. Just to see snow falling from the sky was a marvel, to see it for the first time. We were both just . . . we were stunned. We had heard about it.

What you call the polar icecaps were very small—I don't recall the polar icecap at all in the southern part of your planet. There was some at the northern part, but what is now Scandinavia and Northern Europe had no permanent ice tracts. And they were not that cold. To put a temperature on it, using your conventional temperature scale, in a northern Scandinavian country, even in the coolest months of the year, the temperature during the daytime would never be less than sixty.

Really!

It was fairly temperate. At night it might drop down to, say, fifty, forty-eight at the coolest. And then, of course, the people were more mobile. When it would get to be that cold at night, they would of course have already walked or moved—in some cases, with water-going vessels—to a warmer climate. But generally, the climate on the Earth was much more temperate than you now have. Temperate—that's a word, yes?

Yes.

Warmer.

Much warmer.

Yes.

Did people live on what we call the South Pole now, in that area?

No, I think in the South Pole area there is mostly water and not much land. As I recall, vaguely, we didn't really go there. We flew over there, and I remember seeing something that looked like an island or something. In the North Pole area, we did see land, and there was still some icecap there, only not as big as you have today.

Were you trained scientists?

We didn't think of ourselves that way. The ship had some capacities along that line, in terms of analysis and so on, but I wouldn't refer to us as trained scientists, no. Perhaps if I had to compare our level of scientific capacity . . . which means we didn't have to retain a lot of knowledge, because the ship had its own capacities. You don't have memorize tables of numbers if the ship can do it. But in terms of scientific capacity, we might be equal to, say, a first-year medical student as you have now, or a first-year chemistry student in, say, the graduate degree program. So we had capacity, but we weren't professional, practicing scientists as you have.

We Wear a Garment That Covers Our Entire Body

So you came from Ganymede, and the plants you wanted to take were for some other system?

For some other planet than was our home planet, but it was in Ganymede.

Would you say Ganymede is a constellation or a galaxy?

I don't really use those words. It's a place where people live, if that's all right. You can look that up, perhaps.

Okay, so it wasn't the little moon in our system. It was a place from far away.

Oh, yes—far away.

If you can say anything about your life at home, such as how long you live or how you live, that would be interesting. I'd also like to learn what you learned from the mystical people.

It has been made open for me to come here because of the nature of the books you are working on, and how we live on our planet wouldn't have much bearing on what you do here, even today. But I will give you some of that later in brief detail.

Okay, but mostly I'd like to learn what you learned from the mystical people and perhaps taught them.

Very well. You might wonder why I'm holding a hand up here. The reason is twofold. One, my energy is difficult for the channel and holding the hand here is helpful, and two, when we are at home, my people naturally wear a garment that covers the lower part of our face. It's not quite transparent, but you can make out the general details of our lower face. It is part of the natural wear of our clothing. I have noticed that there are some people on your planet who do something similar.

Yes, in the Mideast.

But I have not seen that spread to your culture. I have to tell you, I think it is very comfortable. Of course, I cannot speak for your fashion people, but we wear fabrics that are very sheer, flowing—I think you may have such fabrics.

You wear this under your eyes, then? Over your nose?

The eyes would be able to see, yes. The ridge on the top of our head is exposed, but the fabric is over the top of our head otherwise, and then the fabric comes across here, across the nose, and the eyes can be seen, as well as the forehead. And so it is comforting to me to do this,.

That's interesting that you cover your face but your lower legs and your feet are bare.

Well, this is on my home planet. When we visit other planets, we do not dress like this. But I am speaking to you now from my home planet.

Oh, I see. So then do you also cover your legs and feet at home?

We wear a garment that covers our entire body, although in places you can see through it—not entirely, but . . . what is that word? It's not transparent, it is something . . .

Sheer?

Sheer—perhaps that is the word. But it is not entirely transparent; it lends color. We find it attractive.

Is it just for comfort, or is there some cultural or philosophical basis for the fact that you wear these covers?

It may have started out because our sun is very bright. It is not really uncomfortable; we don't consider it that warm. But it is very bright, so bright that it may have started out culturally, perhaps. I'm not a culture researcher.

There's something extraordinary. We published a book called Earth History and Lost Civilizations Explained, *and many of our cultures were started by beings from Ganymede who lived underground. Did you know that?*

I did not know that, no.

They were.

Well, if you say, I cannot doubt your word. But my brother and I are not cultural researchers.

It Is a Mistake to Determine Life Expectancy

So your ancestors were our ancestors.

When we visited your planet, I did not see anyone who looked like us.

It had to be before that happened; you must have visited before. So you must live very long lives.

We live very long lives, yes.

Thousands and thousands or millions of years?

We don't like to say how long our lives are, because then that sets a terminal date for them. I think this is a mistake in your culture—perhaps it is a judgment on my part; if it is, I accept that—to state scientifically how long people might expect to live.

Because that sets up an expectancy for them.

Yes, it does, and I think then for people, once that time is beginning to approach, it is a suggestibility, isn't it? It suggests that, well . . .

We're getting close to the end.

Yes, and I have found in my travels . . . occasionally we would visit some mountain peoples. I visited some peoples on a mountain there that my brother found a little too cool for himself. He doesn't like the cool temperatures, so I did most of the visiting. It was very high up there, and the temperature range during the day was perhaps what you call fifties, mid-fifties. But at night it didn't go down much—not where the people were, though in some places it did.

They had some openings in the mountain where warm air came out, so the people went near those. The air was breathable, but it was warm. They were like heated places that were in the side of the mountain—not caves, exactly. There might be a word for it, but I don't have your word. And they were very comfortable in there at night.

So what I was going to say is that many of the people kept track of their age, perhaps in a different way you do. But converting it mathematically, it was not unusual to find elders who were 170 years old. Of course, they didn't know; no one told them how long they were supposed to live.

[Laughs.] Of course. Was it Peru?

No, I believe it was in Europe. Your physical body, quite obviously, has the capacity in certain conditions to live to that age without you having to change it at all. These people looked very much like you do today. As I recall them, they were a little shorter than you are, and living high up in the mountains, they also had very strong legs and could leap—not quite as far as we could, but they could leap quite far—and had good strong fingers and hands. They were quite capable.

Would that be Tibet, then? The Urals?

Some mountain areas in Europe.

The Alps?

I believe it was someplace in northern Europe. Some of their ancestors today, I believe, can be found somewhere around central Europe in the mountains, northern central Europe. I am not certain. It might have even been in an area closer to what is now called China. But I am not too familiar. These continents . . . are they sufficient?

Yes.

Your demarcations—it's too complex.

Yes, it has probably changed.

In terms of the language, yes. In those days, people did not have such terminology. It was the land; that's where they lived. I am able to use, however, your continent terminology to a point.

Using Ancient Cave Designs to Heal and Call in the Rain

So tell us some of the things that you spoke with these beings about.

Once they realized we were looking for the types of fruits and trees that we were looking for, they were always very helpful. They would explain, as we would, where they were from, who they were to the best of their knowledge. And we would explain where we were from and who we were, matching their stories—sometimes with a little more detail, if we thought they would be interested, and sometimes with a little less, if it might seem to overshadow their own stories of their origin. One must be cautious when meeting new people so as not to unintentionally insult them or cause them to feel like less than the people they are facing. The whole point was to be friendly, to be visitors from afar, but not to in any way cause them to feel like anything other than equals. And that was the way my brother and I interacted with them.

Sometimes they would sing and make some motions—dance and so on. This was not all the time, but sometimes, and my brother and I were not shy about such things. We would participate in our own way. We, I think, were more of a source of amusement in that than anything else, but that was good. It sometimes makes for more conversation and laughter. That was fun. I recall that the people would sometimes point to ancient caves, to designs they had found in the caves that they had reproduced once they understood what the design meant and its purpose, at least to them in their time. There is a design . . . I'll see if I can produce it here. I don't know if I can, but I will try. [Draws. See Figure 13.1.] At first the people thought this design was a sacred symbol, but after a while they realized that it was a message, a direction, a purpose, a function. They realized that if they did this . . . do you see what I am doing? [Gestures.]

With his hand, he's going around in a concentric circle.

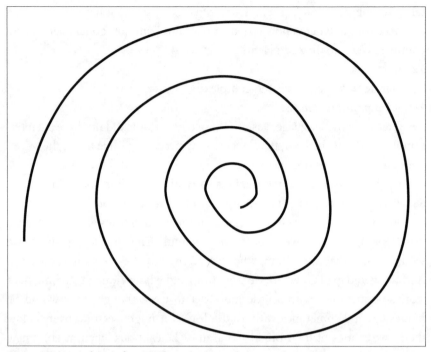

Figure 13.1: A design frequently seen in ancient cave drawings.

Yes, with the palm down. They discovered that if they made that motion over different parts of their physical bodies when they were not feeling well— perhaps they had eaten something that wasn't right—that their bodies might feel better.

From the outside in or the inside out?

Well, they just showed us this.

Oh, they just went around and around, okay.

It's a circular motion. So they used it that way, and then they also discovered that they could also do this pointing to the sky. They would make the motion. They would look up. Of course, they wouldn't have their face covered, but I must do that. And of course, they would be making motions in that same circular direction. They would use that to call in the rain if they needed it or the sun if there was too much rain. Occasionally, I have even met peoples who would call in a rainbow or other phenomenon of the skies. I think perhaps even in your now time the idea of pointing up might be some-what of a residual effect. [Gestures.]

With the index finger of the left hand?

Yes, but they did not use only the left hand; it's just that I am unable to use the right hand. So they would make those motions. Other peoples used them for other things. Other peoples noticed that radiated energies in certain shapes, including concentric shapes . . . you could begin in a circular place. Some peoples built circular places, walls or places where the stones rimmed, and created circles. They noticed that if the people in the center were feeling some energy and the people around the outside were not, that if you put three people in the center, then the energy would cycle around like this in that same direction and that the people around the outside—either standing on stones or in some cases being below ground in circular chambers—would feel the energy even stronger than those who were standing in the center feeling the energy.

So they discovered that this was all a message of how to do something left for people by previous individuals. They did not know who, but the longer they were around these types of symbols, the more they began to apply them to their lives in various ways to improve the quality of their lives and to improve their ability to be inspired and to do other things of value for their peoples. I believe what might have happened is that people came from the stars and left these messages, but my brother believes differently. My brother believes that many of the people who began doing these practices found that they made contact with people from the stars. And they then left the messages on the planet cut into stone (so that those messages would stay there longer), and then returned to their places in the stars. That is what my brother thinks. Perhaps he is right.

Sometimes there would be patterns cut into the rocks that looked to me not unlike a star chart or a route through the stars. The people did not always think of it that way, of course, because there were surface dwellers. And my experience was that they did not look at it that way, but there would always be at least one person—not necessarily the person practicing the spiritual methods, but sometimes one of their students (often an innocent, young child)—who would say, "That's about someplace else." Very often that would be assumed to be someplace else on their planet, but occasionally we did encounter (I think two or three times) where people made the connection between the youngster's statement, "That's about someplace else," or something like that, with the stars in the sky having similar shapes and patterns.

Therefore, they realized that this was a message that the stars above them might bring forth visitors. I believe they sometimes would add if they saw visitors, not unlike my brother and myself. Somewhere in my memories, in my records somewhere, I've heard that someone on your planet carved a big likeness of us near one of these carved star charts, but I can't say where. It might have been in South America, but I'm not certain. So unintentionally on our part, we apparently left a record of our visit.

I think perhaps what they would do, those who realized that these carvings were stars . . . they didn't know a star chart, that term, but I think what they would do is when they would meet people from other places, then they might attempt to keep some kind of a record of what they looked like, you see. But it was an addition; it wasn't right over the other thing. It would be off to one side or below, where there was room for such a thing.

That's fascinating. I love your stories.

A Healing by Earth People Living Near the Sea

I recall that once we were far from the ship, farther than usual, and my brother fractured (as you might call it) his toenail on his large toe of his right foot. To you this would be a broken toenail, painful, but to us it is more like a broken bone. It was terribly painful, and we were with some peoples who immediately detected my brother's great pain and could tell it wasn't a painful toenail, where one could walk and be uncomfortable. He immediately collapsed and could not walk, and I was supporting him. He could not put any weight on that foot. These peoples took him and carried him down to the water—what you would call the sea. And they took him a ways out into the water. My brother was a little unsettled being in the water.

Where we come from, water is rare, and the chance of . . . you noticed when I arrived, I immediately drank the water. Water is not common, and our reaction to your seas and massive lakes . . . it's like being exposed to something that is profoundly spiritual. So my brother felt nervous; he felt overwhelmed by the fact that such a vast amount of water was there, and for him to be carried out into it wasn't an experience he had ever had in his life—and as I said, we live a long time. So he was overwhelmed by the experience.

But they took him out and carried him. He was somewhat flat, and they held his foot out into where the waves were coming up. Someone found some sea plants—I think you still have those plants today—and they put something bulblike on the toe from the sea plant you have. You can find them sometimes on seashores, I think. I don't know if they have them on this island out here in the Pacific [in Hawaii]. The bulb of the plant was not cut but was split and placed over my brother's broken toenail. It was held there, and then someone sang. It was not a song with words. The tone was very high, and there was a vibration quality to it—not an energy vibration, but an actual shaking of the tone. That went on for some five to ten minutes of your time, and then two or three others started singing as well with the same high tone varying just a little bit, with the same shaking of the tone. (That's perhaps not the best description, but that's what I have.) That went on for another ten to fifteen minutes, during which time my brother fell asleep.

Then the person who had put the bulblike portion of the plant on my brother's toe went and took it off my brother's toe, and it was completely healed. They then carried my brother out of the surf, retracing their steps—not exactly, but they backed out of the water. They had walked in straight ahead and now they backed out very carefully, including the one who was directly behind my brother. I'm not certain whether it was to make sure that he was safe or rather to guide them, but that person was making little noises, not words. These people didn't have language as you understand it; they were more inclined to make sounds. So perhaps he was directing the individuals how to walk—I do not know. They carried him out and placed him onto the beach sand, and they brought over large tropical leaves and laid them over my brother, but his head was still visible. Then a woman sat near him, about two, three, two-and-a-half feet away from the right side of my brother's head, slightly in this direction. What do you call that—an oblique angle?
Yes.

She sat there for some time making a sound that sounded like humming—not a tune so much but a sound, but not the shaking sound. She made that sound for perhaps twenty-five minutes, something like that. Then she got up and stepped away. In about five minutes, my brother woke up. He was perfectly fine and more than that. He got out from under the fronds and stood up and said, "What happened?" He was largely unconscious for much of the experience. When he was taken into the water, he was awake, but he didn't remember being taken into the water. He didn't remember breaking his toenail. He didn't remember the pain. It was all gone. So not only was the toe cured, but all the pain and the memory of it were taken somewhere out of his body and he didn't remember it at all.

In my culture, we don't like to suggest things that are limiting or unpleasant, so I didn't tell him. But years and years later, when we were back home and he was surrounded by all his comforts, our people who know about healing and curing assured me that it was okay to tell him the story and then to share the story with others. But it must be done for our people under very careful circumstances so that no one imagines it and feels the pain.

The person who was consulting with me said he thought it was important to tell, so the wisdom was told and I remember my brother being totally startled, completely shocked. He didn't remember it at all. And under the circumstances, he didn't have to remember. I don't have to say . . . it's highly technical. So I thought to tell you that because such a ceremony once existed. I believe, from what I have looked over in scanning your peoples, that some of this high-pitched sound making, with the shaking of the voice, still exists in your time, but I'm not certain that most people know what it's for. It seems to be something that is best done by women.

That's right, the one who did the shaking sound was a woman.

Yes. They were all women, although it was women and men who carried him out into the water. I believe people in your time have the capacity to make this sound. This man I am speaking through has even been hearing about it from people, and I believe there are people in your time using sound to encourage healing. But apparently it involves more than sound. I do not know if they are achieving results from this in your time.

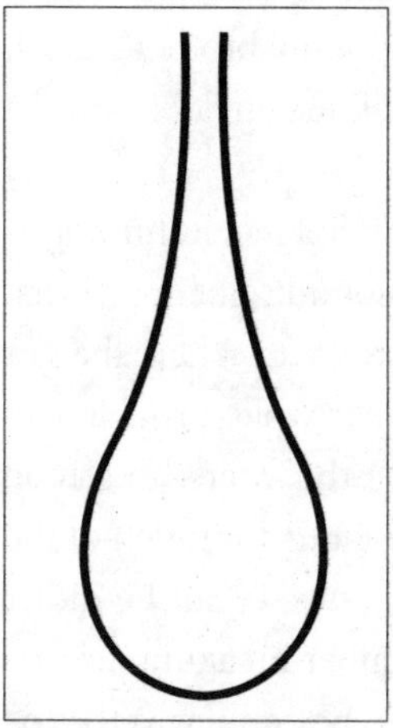

Figure 13.2:
A drawing of a bulb of seaweed.

But these people carried my brother out and they found the plant with the bulb. It looked like a bulb to me—I will try to reproduce the shape. It was green and the bulb was shaped like this. [Draws. See Figure 13.2.] It grew off the stem. This is not the best drawing, but it looked not unlike a drop of water. I will perhaps come up with a term. I'm hearing the term, but it is not the term they used. Apparently it's a common term in your time—the common term in your time is seaweed.

So that is how it was done. Of course, I didn't tell my brother this experience for a long time, but I was thrilled and profoundly grateful that these people would immediately stop everything they were doing to carry my brother down to the sea. When they saw me supporting him, they carried him all the way. I can see it to this day. It was a distance of a little more than fifteen miles.

Miles!

It was high up and the sea was in the distance, so they carried him down through the forest. When one would get tired, someone else would take over.

And they were little, tiny people too, right?

They were small people but very strong, and they carried him all the way. I walked that distance too, of course; I wanted to be with him. I have to tell you, I never walked so far on your planet in one direction and back. I had to summon all of my endurance. I had to move the ship—I could do so remotely—so that I could breathe the moss, as you're calling it.

Oh, that's right—you take so much time and then you needed to recharge, yes.

I had to hold it under my brother's nose so he could breathe it in too, and that didn't seem to bother them. They were going to carry him down there and do what was going to be done, and I didn't want to interfere, but they understood when they saw me breathing this outside of this curved dish. You can put the dish right up to the face. It wraps around here, you see; it's sort of curved. It has a crescent shape so that it can fit straight into the face and you can breathe in the fragrance. They saw me do it first and they knew this was something that needed to be done to support our life here. So when I held it up under my brother's nose, they paused and I didn't have to run along beside them. Then he would be breathing naturally. I had to do that several times.

It took awhile, as it might. Can you imagine walking slightly more than fifteen miles through dense forest? They apparently traversed this area all the time, and they went on this very clear pattern down through the forest. They were wonderful people. If they hadn't done that, I would have had to take my brother back to the ship and the ship would have had the means to create or repair and all that, but my brother would have remembered the pain and it might have shortened his life—because once he could remember it . . . people are sensitive. To remember pain, they feel it again.

Every time they remember it, they feel it?

Yes, so it could very well have shortened his life and made his life very uncomfortable. He might have even had to be isolated from people when he got home, because if he was remembering and feeling the pain, then others would too. So they literally saved his life, in terms of his happiness. They saved his happiness. So I'm eternally grateful to these peoples.

We Were Able to Share Information about Earth Plants

Did you in turn share information or technology or stories that would help them?

We told stories, but we were very careful when we found peoples who were happy and living well and comfortable and satisfied with their lives. We didn't interfere. If there was something we could share about Earth plants that were available locally to them—not something we would give them from the ship, how could that help?—Earth plants that we knew they could use to improve the quality of their lives, we would share that if we felt that it was something they wanted and needed to know.

Then we would say (we were always trying to be diplomatic) "we heard . . ." or "we studied . . ." or "we understood . . ." something like that, so that it didn't sound like we knew this thing. We wanted to make it clear that this was something we had heard about. It wasn't a lie—we had in fact heard about it, that the plant could be used in that way. We do not lie, but we said it in such a way that it was a suggestion of how the plant might be used.

We didn't tell them how to take leaves or needles or hairs off the plant; we didn't say how to do that with the plant. They would know what to take and how to take it and how to treat the plant according to their culture. But we would say, "It can be done this way, as a soup or a tea or a poultice, as you say, and it will have this effect. And then they would say, "We will look into that, we will try that," something along those lines.

That would be what we would share, but only if the plant was readily available to them in their immediate environment. It wouldn't do much good to tell them about a plant on another continent or to give them something from our world that would not survive here. Also, if we didn't know what the effect would be . . . we were not scientists. We had some knowledge and some capabilities, but it was our intention to leave nothing that could have effects we wouldn't know about. But this other was considered acceptable.

They seemed comfortable with the fact that you got out of the ship and seemed to just be there.

Well, they practically never saw us getting out of the ship. We would usually land someplace where the people weren't; we wouldn't land in the middle of a gathering of people. If they happen to come upon us, we would share. It was not unusual to meet people who were medicine people or mystical people that way, because sometimes they would go a ways from where the people lived. And sometimes they didn't live in one spot, but they would always be looking for plants and other things that grew, and mosses and so on. So to meet people like that first was not unusual, but we wouldn't purposely go to villages or to gatherings of people or to migrating peoples. We didn't seek them out; that's not why we came here.

So as far as they knew, you could have come from a village down the way.

No, no. They would see the ship. In our experience, we did not meet any people at any time who had not had at least one encounter—and most of them many, many encounters—seeing other vehicles land. So no one was startled or frightened by our vehicle. I think we were always outside of the ship when they saw us, but of course, sometimes they would see us go into the ship, especially if we had an extended stay, and they probably didn't know we were breathing that moss. But in the case of that one situation with my brother I explained, they saw that and they knew that it had something to do with our comfort.

Isn't that wonderful? I mean, people could just come and go.

Yes, they weren't surprised. They had seen other visitors come, so this was something they accepted. There were stories, I'm sure, in their culture, stories about others who had come, or perhaps it wasn't considered that important—visitors from here or from there, from somewhere else.

You Will Move Away from Invasive Healing Methods

I think I will finish. I have told you a little bit about our life, where we are from, and perhaps that is sufficient, is it not?

Yes, it's wonderful what you've shared with us.

I've been invited to come since you are studying the capacities and gifts and abilities and discoveries of ancient peoples. And you are fortunate to be exposed, I believe, but perhaps what is more important is that you are generous to share this with others who may be interested.

Someday, when your healing community is more together, with different practices coming together, it will be much quicker to heal someone who is injured because they won't have to go from this place to that place. Everyone will just come together doing what they do well, and there will not need to be any body invasion. That is a passing situation while people try to understand how to make things better. I understand that body invasion is something that is done now while your people are passing through this stage of understanding. But ancient techniques are available that do not require body invasion.

Such as what you described, right? Plants, songs?

Yes. I do not mean to sound in any way critical; I'm just suggesting that for those of you who are interested in body-invasion techniques—I think it's called surgical methods—this is something that is perhaps of great value in the times where you are, but someday this will evolve to being something that has to do with the external. Surgeons will still be trained, but they will not actually penetrate the physical body. They will make motions outside of your physical bodies, not unlike what they do inside your bodies now. They will make these very similar motions outside of your bodies and have the same benevolent effect without discomfort to the patient. This will require significant training, but it can be done even today. I mention this for those of you who are interested in such things, to consider experimenting, and perhaps you will have some good results. Take your time, plenty of time.

I am happy to speak through this person today to you. I wish you a benevolent and fruitful life, and may it be of great quality that you will share your story with your fellow humans to live the most happy life the best way you can. May you have the best of life experience.

Thank you.

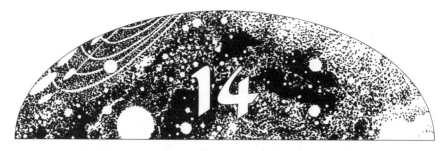

A Pleiadian Visit with the Ice People of Earth

Jemet from the Pleiades and Elder from Earth

September 23 and 27, 2004

am Jemet. I am from the Pleiades. My people came to Earth about 1,200 years ago in your time. We were particularly fascinated with your North and South Poles where the snow and ice is there all the time. This is not something common to our home. We had heard about it, and we wanted to see not only the place where the ice is but the people who had adapted to that environment. We came and landed carefully, because the last part of the passage does involve a little heating of the ship, and we hovered for a time to let the ship cool off so that we didn't impact the surface. In that time of hovering, two people came near to watch, and we were particularly careful; we didn't want to do anything sudden that would startle them. So we slowed down our procedure even more. It took, in terms of Earth time, maybe about twelve hours. Of course, the ship had cooled off much before that, but we wanted to make a very gradual descent to the surface.

Then this time about three more people showed up and they all stood together. We gradually set the ship down, and in this way there was no great impact to the surface. After a time, the people came up. One old one with white hair came up to the ship and did something that I do not recall. I am close to the end of my life now, so I'm thinking of other travels I have made and I do not recall anyone ever doing this before—not in a place that was what I would call unfamiliar with such vehicles. You understand, the outside of the ship does not show any seams as one of your vehicles would show a seam, suggesting a doorway. But the person came up to the ship and walked a little bit around the ship and stopped exactly in front of where the opening would be! I remember that we all in the ship looked at each other in total amazement.

No one had ever done that before, and we didn't know everything, but at the time we weren't aware of this ever happening before. Since then I've had the opportunity to find out that it had happened a few times before, but it's very rare. We looked at each other. We weren't sure what to do, but then we felt, "Well, this must be a welcome of some sort." So we opened the opening very slowly and we thought, we hoped . . . we didn't want to frighten him, but he wasn't frightened at all. He was right there and he waited. When it was opened all the way, we didn't know if he thought he was going to step in, but he waited. I didn't go out first; it was one of the others. They stepped out and he held his hand forward, the flat of the hand, like that.

Palm forward.

We had seen and studied that gesture before, and we knew that sometimes it means, "Come no farther." But we weren't sure, and because the other crew member stopped immediately when he did that, he shook his head and he moved his hand back a ways. Then we realized, because he moved his hand back, that that meant, "Do come out," and that this was some kind of a greeting.

Exchanging Gifts of Whale Dreams and Pleiadian Stories

So we came out and we stood in front of him, attempting to look as peaceful as possible since this was a unique experience on our part at that time. And he spoke. I did not hear his voice because of the instrument that functions to convert his words to our language. But even with the conversion, I felt this . . . it was like . . . how to describe it? It was like . . . I think you have a word called "true." Do you know that word, "true"?

It was like something went through my body and I felt this amazing . . . it reminded me of this instrument we have on the Pleiades. It is something not unlike what you would call a gong or a bell. It is struck very gently—not firmly, very gently—but because it is so massive, it vibrates and curves into many different directions, and it vibrates and it continues to vibrate. If you hold your head close to it, you can hear a tone. If you step back and don't touch it, you can feel your body vibrate. There are parts of it that are hollow, and you can stick your hand in and feel the vibration more. It's very interesting. It is a combination of music and other things, but the main thing is that the same feeling, almost identical, went through my body.

I was startled. I cannot speak for the other crew members, but my impression is that they were just as startled. Then I saw him speaking, and he said (these are not his exact words, but they're pretty close): "My people greet you, brothers and sisters who have come from so far. I had a vision that you were coming and consulted the other elders." And motioning to them with his other hand, they started moving toward him. These were apparently the other elders.

He continued to say, "We decided to come and greet you because we felt this would be a good experience. We have brought you some gifts." Then he produced this thing that our science personnel later confirmed was made out of whale bone. It was very intricately carved, and little colored stones had been placed into it in certain spots. He said, "This is a wonderful object that we use sometimes to invite the animals to offer one or more of their kind to provide us with food when the people are hungry. Sometimes it is a whale who comes; other times it is some smaller creature. They will swim very close to the shore so that we do not have to go out too far. They will allow themselves to be taken for food.

"This is something that has been with our people for many years, and we still use it. We know that you do not eat of the animal world. But in this object there are not only memories, there is wisdom. My people can hold this object and, before they touch it, simply say, 'I would like to have a whale dream as a whale would have it.' We would like you to use this object to have whale dreams while you are here, and then, before you go, to give it back to us so that we might continue to use it."

Well, I don't have to tell you that since we did not eat other creatures, there was some nervousness, and we discussed briefly amongst ourselves that we would reach toward it and see how it felt. The elder had it like this, out in front of him with two fingers holding it . . . it was about this long [gestures].

Two feet?

Something like that—a little less, maybe eighteen inches. And he held it with these fingers.

The thumb, index finger and second finger.

Yes, and then he supported it with the back of his other hand. It was very interesting. Then we came up to it and we put our hands near it. He didn't expect us to take it right away. He seemed to be familiar with this thing where we reached toward it. We were a little concerned, because we do not normally, as they say, expose ourselves to the consumption of that, plus we assumed that the animal had been hunted and there might be memories of suffering in that animal spirit that was in the bone. So we were concerned.

But we did not feel that. Apparently there had been many ceremonies with that piece of bone, and the ceremonies must have allowed the spirit of the animal to forgive and even love the people. As it turned out, when he spoke of the knowledge and wisdom later, it was in fact that. So it felt wonderful to us. We thanked the elder, and we did take it and put it very carefully on board the vehicle. Then feeling their diplomacy at the very least, to say nothing of their generosity, we wanted to offer a gift as well. In the past, we had sometimes made a display of some kind of art, but one of our people felt that clearly at least the loan of an actual object would be appreciated. So we quickly had a little discussion on this between ourselves that perhaps we could do something similar.

We happened to have on the vehicle a garment that was worn by the mother of one of the crew. The mother had died not too long before the voyage began, and the crew member took along this garment to remember the mother and to appreciate her value as a person and to sometimes touch the garment and then tell stories. The crew member felt that perhaps the garment could do a similar thing for the people. So the garment was brought out and the crew person, the child, said, "We would like to loan you this garment. It was worn by my mother who lived for many years and was a seer." It was said just like that [gestures].
With his right hand, the index finger and the little finger from the brow area out.

Yes, a gesture. "She was also a healer." [Gestures again.]
Right hand, palm up, above his abdomen, and the left hand level with his head, palm up.

So the elder took the dress and nodded and thanked us for this wonderful object. He said that if it was all right, if we were going to be here for a while, he would return to where the people lived and bring the dress, and they would touch it and ask to have dreams of the lady and her abilities while they slept and hopefully experience some healing, some seeing and some awareness of beings present who were welcome.

We said, "We will be here for three of your days," and that was it and they left. We thought they would say, "Welcome to the village," and so on, but we were completely startled by that. That is not typical. They left and we didn't know when they'd come back, but they didn't go too far. We noticed the phenomenon in the place of the snow and ice, and that is that while it appeared to be quite white off into the distance, the people walked, oh, maybe seven or eight hundred feet and then they turned to the left, and we realized that there was actually like a little hill there of ice and snow. It wasn't obvious, and we realized that our eyes had not adjusted. So we thought perhaps we were closer to the village than we had thought. So we thought, "Well, we will do that. We are here—we will go and get it if we need to, but probably they will be back." So that was the first day's contact with the Earth people.

Dreaming the Dreams of the Whale

We all went around, of course, and we experienced the snow and the ice, not unlike the way children would. We played and we rolled in the snow, and I must say that my favorite thing to do was, I would run as fast as possible and then fall down in the snow and just slide. Now, that was great fun! We had a wonderful time! We didn't acquire samples or anything like that; it wasn't a scientific research mission. So we went back into the ship and we realized it was time for our period that is like sleep, a meditation kind of period—it's a little of both. We looked at each other and we thought, "I wonder if we should touch the object before we do our sleep meditation?" Three of us did it. I did, the person whose mother's dress it was did and another crew member did, but the fourth member decided he wasn't sure what would happen. Since that crew member was involved in piloting the vehicle, we thought we'd wait and see what our experience was in case it had some horrific impact on us—a prudent decision.

I recall touching the object, and as smooth as it looked, it had more texture to it than had appeared. Of course, it had been extensively carved. I do not recall touching anything like that before or since. It was very unusual, just the texture. But also, when I touched it—because, you understand, we had reached for it before but not actually touched it—I felt a curious feeling that I can only describe as if I had been immersed in liquid. I was still standing, but here I was standing up in this very familiar vehicle that I had traveled in extensively and suddenly I felt as if I were standing in some kind of liquid. We're familiar with water, but it didn't feel like water. I didn't know what to make of it, and we had decided not to tell each other what we felt until after.

So the other people touched it and so on, and I went to lie down in my place—sometimes people would sit up and sometimes lie down, but I like to lie down. I did my meditation. Of course, we knew what whales look like; there had been other people here so we had an idea what the whale looked like. I remember falling asleep, and I had a dream unlike anything I'd ever had before or . . . well, I've had a couple of those dreams since. I think once you touch something like that, it doesn't go away. So I don't want to say before or since, but certainly nothing like it before.

The dream . . . I thought it would be like a whale swimming in the water. It was nothing like that, nothing like that at all. This is what I remember from the dream: I could see this planet. It was like I was in space and I could see the planet as I was getting closer. It looked like it was blue. It reminded me of the polar icecap, only it didn't look like ice, but there was white and there was light blue, and it covered the northern part of the planet. The southern part also had a similar thing, and then there was an uneven thin band, not completely even, around the center of the planet that was blue and had . . . oh, not unlike your planet, clouds and other things like that.

So in the dream, as I'm getting closer and closer to the planet, I'm suddenly feeling this liquid all around me and I'm able to breathe the liquid; it's perfectly comfortable. And in the process of breathing it, I'm also nourished by the liquid so that I don't have to eat. I breathe and everything good happens. The liquid is not watery. It's almost like it has contour to it, as if you were to feel small pebbles, but if you went to touch them, they were so ft and would be more pliable. So the liquid, it has liquid and form, but it is a fascinating experience. And I'm in that and I'm moving around. Occasionally, in the distance I get the feeling that someone else is there, and it feels wonderful. I can only describe that it feels like home. The warmth, the love—it's wonderful! And then I wake up. That's the dream.

I'm wondering if this is where those beings you know of here as whales are from. It must be where they go to when they are no longer on Earth in their bodies. I've never had an experience like that before in my life, and I've had this dream since, the same one and occasionally variations, several times. The interesting thing about having it since—when I'm on my own planet and so on—is that when I wake up, I feel nourished. I don't have to eat. I can go a day, maybe two days without eating, and I feel completely nourished. I don't get thinner, I don't get any bigger—I'm just nourished. But it isn't something I can reach for and do. It only happens in a dream now and then. It's fascinating, eh? So after having the dream the first time, I woke up and meditated on it a bit, and eventually we gathered in a spot where we all sat and talked. I found out much to my amazement that everybody else had the same dream exactly.

Well, everybody was touching a bone from the same whale.

I don't think logic comes into it. I think it is spirit; it is a message that had been delivered to us through a dream with intent. This is the way I see it—not as a matter of linear connections, because none of us were old friends. None of us had ever had the same dream before at any time, but since then every one of us has had this dream with some slight variations from time to time, and they're all exactly the same experience that I have. So we feel that, not only the whale, but the man, the people who gave us this, who had worked with this . . . we think that those people are from that planet too. This is what we think. We didn't say that to the people, but they almost said so.

The Villagers Share the Pleiadian Stories from the Dress

The next day here they come again, the five elders, and they bring the dress. We come out of the vehicle, not sure whether we should ask them to come in. They didn't ask us to go to their village, so we think that maybe this is what's appropriate. They have the dress, and I notice that the elder is carrying the dress the same way he carried the whale bone—the same way exactly. We noticed that, so one of the other crew members goes inside and brings out the whale bone, and to be honoring, holds it exactly the same way, and the objects are exchanged. Then the elder motions us, like this, with his hand here [gestures].

With his right hand, palm forward, toward his body, he makes motions as if to say, "Follow me."

So we make sure the ship is secure and we leave, and we walk with the elder down this seven hundred feet or so and turn to the left. Much to our amazement—we didn't notice it when we landed—there are all these people. We think initially that this is the village; then we think, "No, no, no, no, we would have seen that." So the people came from the village—wherever that was; we never did see it—and the elder said, "These are my people." From what I could tell, it was everybody—young, old, babies. They were all there, and the elder said, "The people know you do not have the time to hear all their dreams, so we have asked three of them to come and tell you their dreams of touching the dress."

The first one was a child (perhaps in terms of Earth years, my best guess would be maybe six or seven years old), a little girl. She said, coming through in our language, you understand, but having that personality . . . the thing that interprets does not remove the personality, so the inflections are there. We are not hearing something that is just like a recording; the personality comes through. If there is any extreme personality, we are screened from that, but that doesn't usually happen. So she described it in a child voice with enthusiasm and happiness. She said, "I touched the dress and then we went to our sleep place. And when I slept, I saw children, children everywhere. Some were a little bigger than me and some were smaller. And I saw . . . I think it was the lady," meaning the lady of the dress. "She was walking around the children, and she was touching them on their heads."

Then the child said, "I don't think the children were sick, but she was touching them on their heads so that they could understand and feel comfortable with meeting children from other planets." It wasn't that she was a healer—now, we knew this. You say, "Why would you need a healer on the Pleiades?" eh? It wasn't a healer as you understand it. A healer, in this sense, means to support ease and compatibility. So she would touch each of the children, you know, with these fingers [gestures].

Index and middle finger.

With both hands. She would touch them just on the sides of their head. She would reach and she would touch them on the sides of their heads, just a little bit in front of and above where the ears would be on your head. Then the children would be more relaxed—because they were very young, you see, and they were not yet used to meeting children from other planets who might look different and act different. So it helped them to be prepared for such things. So that's how the little girl described the dream, and then she went back to her mother, or perhaps an auntie or grandmother.

The elder then pointed to another person, a young man. We had the impression he might have been a hunter or fisherman. He looked strong and sturdy, even though they were wearing heavy clothing to be warm. He had something on his neck—I'm not sure what it was, but it was something made of bone or tooth or something, which is why we took it to be that perhaps he was a hunter, a fisherman or someone important to the people. He said he had touched the dress and he'd dreamt of holding a child, a male child, and of seeing a hand come and touch the child right in the center of the forehead, knowing that that child would grow up to be strong and a leader of people. Then he nodded to us with a smile. We smiled and nodded back, and he stepped back.

The third person stepped forward after being pointed to by the elder. This was an old lady. She had gray hair and a smile—there were a few teeth missing, but it was a charming smile. She said she had touched the dress and that she had gone home and slept, and she could see someone laying on a smooth surface and there were people all around. The people were filled with love, and she remembered that. She had the feeling that this had something to do with the passing of that person, perhaps a gentle death. She said that she would cherish that in hopes that she could have such a gentle death herself. Of course, we were all very moved by that because she literally saw the way that the wearer of the dress, the mother, had died—surrounded by friends and loved ones, and without pain. Of course, that would be very desirable on Earth. Then she stepped back.

We Felt a Profound Connection

The elder then said to us, "Did you dream as well?" We told the elder of our dreams. One of the other people spoke and said that we all dreamt the same thing. The words the other member of the crew said were very much what I would have said. And the elder nodded and said, "When we touch this, and we touch it like this, we hold it like so," just the way he'd held it initially [gestures].

With the thumb and two fingers of the right hand, and then holding it up with the left hand, palm down, from underneath.

Yes. He said, "Then we get visions and where to hunt and fish and so on." But he said that whoever touches it, they also dream, and he said, "I've had many, many dreams from touching it so many times, and it's the same dream that you have." And we were . . . I can only describe to you that that "true" went through my body again, and I checked with the other crew members and they had the same feeling. We felt a profound sense of unity and connection to these people, and I can tell you that the idea of staying there much longer occurred to us all at the same moment. But we had other places to go to.

I'll tell you that something occurred when we left a day or so later that never occurred to me upon meeting peoples. It had never occurred to me, and I don't think it occurred to me again. I had tears running out of my eyes. I had never met people like that before. They were so wise, and I felt like the wisdom of our crew was so enhanced. I've never felt such love and wisdom like that. It was the most wonderful experience I've ever had visiting another planet—fun and wisdom combined.

I have thanked many times, at a distance, those wonderful elders and the whale spirit as well. Of course, we passed on all of this to our people when we returned home. And my family, especially the children, never get tired of hearing the story. I'm very old now—as you would say, an old lady. And I will be passing some day—as you say, "passing over." I am here to tell you this story so that you will recognize and appreciate the natural beauty of the hearts of Earth people. Good night.

Thank you very, very much.

✷　　　✷　　　✷

I am an elder of our people.

Welcome.

I will go by the name of Elder, as I do not wish to say too much about the nature of my peoples. We have ancestors, descendants still living in your time.

We Knew the Pleiadians Were Coming

I will speak of the incident of the friends from space. Sometime before their arrival—in your measurement, maybe three months—a seer informed us that we would have friends visiting from the sky, a far-off star from which benevolent people have visited us before. These would not be the same people, but people from that place had visited us before. And while they could not say when, they could feel it. They said that on a certain day and time— they're using our system—they would be there and that it would be important to offer them something they could use during their stay here that would allow them to feel who we are and why we chose to live here and what we do to maintain our life. Much discussion took place for that, and we decided upon the talisman, you would call it, which we use to invite the animals who swim closer to us (so that we do not have to go out too far) to offer themselves to us for food and other sustenance.

This piece of bone has been handed down from generation to generation and is somewhat yellowed with age. But it has survived well and it works, not only because we believe in its value, but because we honor the memories of all the previous animals, all the current animals and all the animals to come, whether they have offered themselves to us for this life-sustaining energy or not. We do ceremonies daily to honor these beings, and this is why we feel that the talisman supports us in these ventures. It was, we felt, a worthy offering, and therefore, when they came we were waiting.

I think perhaps, looking back on it, that they were a little surprised. Normally, apparently—so they said in talks with us—when they land people usually run away, or are startled at the least. Not only did we not do that—we expected them—but we approached and offered them the use of this wonderful instrument of our culture and our planet. I have heard they got a great deal out of it and had wonderful dreams. This is part of its function, you know, because even though the animals when we use it come closer to shore, still the ocean is vast and we have to know which direction to paddle. Our hunters, when they touch this before they go out, all have dreams of the animals who are coming and we go to the exact spot to meet them. So it is not surprising that our visitors from the sky had dreams most appropriate to them and their people as compared to the dreams my people would have.

I recall when a friend from space offered the garment of the beloved one who had crossed over to the eternal land, that we were very touched that such a personal item would be made available to us. We treated it with the same respect and honor as we treat our special bone, our special instrument. We were very happy they came to visit us and talk about their place and tell stories, and we did the same. My people were enriched by the experience, and I believe that the people from the sky, the Pleiades, were also enriched. From what I understand about their culture, they speak of these matters openly, so their contact with us was made available to all the people on that planet. This feels very good to me, and I am happy.

Are you and the whale from the same planet?

We speak of Earth?

No, I'm sorry. The planet they had the dreams about, where they breathed this rich thick energy—is that where the whales are from?

Yes.

Are you from the same planet?

No.

Ah. They suspected you might have been.

You mean, where our people were from originally?
Yes.

No, no. I'll keep that to myself.

Your Future Is Moving Toward a Time of Less Solid Water

Can you tell me why you like to be where you are in that cold northern part of Earth?

I have always been there. That is where we live. I might ask the same question of you: Why do you wish to live where there is no blue air, where there is no clear, easy-to-breathe air? Why you wish to live in a time where there are machines that do personal things as well as group things? No, no, I was born to it. And I have seen its great beauty and appreciated its heart. I would never live anywhere else. Of course, I'm speaking at the moment from my overall spirit and from a current visit—I am in spirit there. Still, it is in my nature to go there to that time, to those people who are my own.

Those people are your own. So have you incarnated there since that life?

Yes.

Ah, and you will again?

No. It is not practical in your time. It might be possible in the distant future, but I don't think so. I feel your future is moving toward a more fluid time and less of a time of solid water.

Oh, I see. They will melt.

It is intended. If I may, it would probably be good for your cultures to learn how to live underwater, not that you will all have to, but if all the solid water melts, some people will have to move. Your people who experiment might learn how to live, if not underwater, then in boats on the surface. It might be possible to live in boats. I have visited in spirit places where people live in boats—it's possible.

Or maybe they need to move farther inland, away from the shore.

But you have so many people and you will have less land. Living on boats might not be so bad. Some people might like it.

It sounds great, as long as it's warm. But you like the cold. So how long have your people lived there? You said always.

Always.

Thousands and thousands and thousands of years?

I cannot say. I do not have the knowledge.

Is your interaction with the whales from Earth, or did you know them before they came here?

From Earth. I'm very happy to know that our friends from the sky enjoyed it. I heard some of what was said since they referred to me and our people—I was busy but I was able to hear some of it. I'm glad that the person I met still remembers the experience fondly and has passed on so many of the memories to fellow beings on that planet.

It wasn't just fondly. I mean there was so much love at the time, so much profound, deep, beyond love—you could just feel it.

Yes, I actually felt at the time that they almost wanted to stay here. But they knew that their place was far away. We told them that anytime they wanted to visit us, all they had to do was dream and ask to recall the experience with us and talk to us in their dreams. For them, dreams are something they can access beyond what you have in your culture at the moment. So it is another way of life, and they have many times come and visited and talked and asked for more stories about who we are. And we have shared, of course.

That's wonderful. So they have visited by interacting in the dream state?

Yes.

What about your descendants? Will they have to get used to living on water or what?

Those who are still there will adapt. But even though there will be water, it will be cold for quite a while yet and that will feel comfortable. They're used to that; it's not uncomfortable. If they were to go somewhere that was hot, it would be unbearable to them. The cold is their comfort; it's how they are comfortable. I don't know your word, but that's what they find comfortable.

A long time ago, years ago, some beings who lived in that area told us of their joy in finding that ice world, that they had come from another planet that was like that. I wonder if you are those people.

I do not know or, to a degree, cannot say. I'm not prepared to reveal our secrets too much here, because we have descendants.

Well, thank you, that was very beautiful.

May you have a good life and benevolent dreams.

Thank you very much.

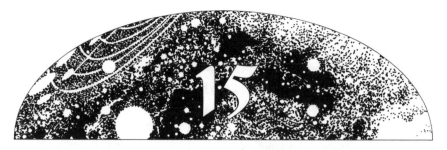

Time Loop Travel Is the Travel of Your Dreams

Time-Loop Traveler
February 18 and 25, 2005

I have been visiting your planet for about five months now, and I have donned a disguise. My people are small by the standards of your human race. In terms of our size, we would be . . . oh, let's see if I can get the measurement. We are about five-and-a-half inches tall, two or three inches wide, something like that. We are not humanoid. We do not travel in vehicles but through time loops. This allows us to arrive quickly and comfortably, and equally allows us to depart quickly if there is danger. This is not always the case; I have been told by those who have vehicles that they can easily be seen or at least tracked. But with a time loop, we can disappear so quickly that if someone saw something or we felt in danger, they might quite reasonably question what they had seen or if they had seen anything at all.

We are able to move about largely unseen, and when there are human beings present, we will usually stay close to the ground. This way, we might easily be mistaken for an animal. At times, we will be up on the limb of a tree where we might quite reasonably, if motion is noticed, be mistaken for a bird, especially where there are leaves or those other things on trees—needles, yes? We come from a galaxy . . . oh, I would say not much farther than 1,200 light-years from here. Due to the nature of the means by which we travel, time and distance—spatial reference, you understand—are not a problem.

We Are Interested in the Human Dream Cycle

You might reasonably ask, "Why are you here?" We are here because we are interested in the human dream cycle. It is our perception that when a human being dreams . . . I grant, your body does stay on Earth, but your soul travels in almost the same way as we travel in time loops. There is such a close comparison that my people thought it might be to our benefit to come and study the human being while dreaming.

We have the capacity to see your spirit leave your body—granted, not all of it, but the amount of it that travels when you sleep deeply and dream. There does appear to be some kind of tether, but we see it leave your body and very often we follow (at a respectful distance, of course, not to interfere) and watch you go. It is quite surprising. Almost everyone I have seen leaves the physical form almost immediately . . . it is as though a bird is just flying. The feeling is exultant happiness, and although you do not have a form like a bird, when you leave we see your souls as being, not large, but a version of light.

Many of the versions I have seen are quite angular in their appearance— not round, not rounder shapes—although I have seen some rounded angular shapes, yes. But they're very often flying straight off into space, as if desiring to return to the home planet—not going to stars or other planets, but clearly an attempt to get off the Earth. This is quite typical. But then what occurs almost immediately is a movement through time.

I have followed dreamers (if I could say that), followed their souls, and it's not at all unusual for them to go back in the past when Earth was quite lush and tropical even on the surface, with a very heavy, thick, oxygenated atmosphere—really at least 40 percent oxygen, quite significant. The other frequent occurrence is to go into the future on Earth, and these aspects of the dreamer would make up at least 16, maybe even 17 percent of dreams where I have followed the passage of the souls. The rest of it appears to largely be made up of going to visit one's teachers, which almost always involves a passage through time.

From what I can tell, other than that tether to one's physical body, the travel is apparently, to my perception, identical to our travel in time loops. So we are really enjoying the observation of your people this way. However, our mission is coming to an end as we have acquired enough observations. You might wonder why I'm saying "we." I'm not referring to myself in some regal fashion, but rather there are about nine or ten of us here scattered about on the planet—not in what you might call dangerous areas, because, of course, people do not dream very much there, at least not in the way that serves and nurtures them—unfortunately, the souls there have fitful sleep—but in areas where there is relative relaxation or the capacity to get deep sleep during the evening. Our mission will come to an end in about, in terms of your time, maybe nine days, when we will return to our home planet and share our results with our scientists and philosophers.

I want to be clear: Our scientists are philosophers and our philosophers are scientists. So these are not two separate groups of people. Many scientists on your planet also have a form of philosophy, but I think it is not quite to the same depth—not that you do not have the capacity to be deep, but science in your time, in your culture, appears to have a limit, a discouragement that the scientist does not get philosophical so much. This is unfortunate, because in my experience as a scientist, I have found that being philosophical, studying the ramifications of life itself, is profoundly helpful to allow me to interpret, at least through the eyes of my own culture, the experience of beings in entirely foreign cultures, to speak of your own culture as foreign. It is foreign to me, you see. It allows me to find a context within my own culture to place my perceptions and my interpretations of what I see in your culture.

Life on the Home Planet

Are you that same size on your home planet?

Yes. If you were to visit our planet, you would discover that it is about a third bigger than your planet. But we do not live on the surface of the planet—you have probably heard similar statements from other beings. This allows the surface of the planet to function as a living organism. We have plants, not unlike your own. There is a slightly different chemistry—not as much oxygen, but it is there, there is oxygen—and our plants are not as green as yours. They are a little bit bluer in tinge and not quite as lush. We don't have as much water as you have. But we have a lot of mineral content that supports the plants.

So yes, we are the same size. This is not changed. It does allow us, I feel, to travel in time loops a little more easily, because although we have complexities in our makeup (physically speaking), the simple reduction in the amount of matter decreases (on a ratio basis, of course) the complexity between us and larger beings such as yourself. For you to travel, in that sense, as a physical person in a time loop would be possible, but there would need to be some time—I believe several hours—for you to reconstitute your physical vitality afterward. But given our size, we do not require much more than, in your time, say, ninety seconds to reconstitute physical vitality once we emerge in your space.

Tell me about your society. How do you live? Is everything in relation to your size?

No, we have what you call trees. We have trees—they are quite big. From what I have seen, many of them are quite large, not unlike, I would speculate—having traveled into the past on your planet—what you call old growth on your planet. It's not unusual for us to have a tree (I'm going to use your measurements) where the diameter of the trunk might be thirty or forty feet and the height of the tree might easily be four hundred feet. You have had trees like this on your planet in the past—just not at the moment, but you have had them. I think you might even have some historical documentary on that. Perhaps there are still a few of them left.

There are a couple left, yes. So you live inside the planet, then?

Yes, we live below our planet, below the surface. It varies, but we live about seventeen to twenty miles below.

How many of you are on this planet? Hundreds? Billions?

On our native planet?

Yes.

About 800,000. It's pretty well balanced to that—about 800,000.

And you're the only beings on the planet?

No, no. Of course there are the plants on the surface, and of course there is the mineral spectrum of the planet. The planet is alive, yes? But you're talking about beings not unlike yourself.

I'm sorry, yes. Other beings like yourself, yes.

Yes, or what you say . . . not animals as you would understand them, but we consider them to be that. But they are molecular, and they are also on the surface. Some of them, if they choose to visit us in our dwelling space, are always welcome. They are very small, but because we are also quite small, we are able to detect their presence because of noticing another personality being present. That is more the case than actually being able to see them. But their personality is very distinct and they are very welcome. They have a unique perspective.

Tell me about your culture. You obviously have an active civilization.

Yes, quite active. There is not much wear and tear on our bodies; we live, in terms of your years, let's see, maybe 1,900 years, something like that. I'm about 530, so not young by your standards but young by our standards. Education is very important to us, and for the first 100, 150 years of life here, one learns about one's own culture, one's standards, science, philosophy, past, present, potential futures—in short, a well-rounded and thorough education.

Past that point, one can choose what one would like to study. Almost always, the studying involves passage from one place to another. Many of the people, the beings we trade with on other planets, are perfectly happy having us study their culture. They consider us to be a bit, not exactly naïve, but we are easily surprised and delighted by unusual attitudes.

I cannot tell you how many times I have been told by beings on other planets that they find us, let me say, cheerful, delightful, charming. I think it's mostly because we do not disguise when we are happily discovering something new to us that gives us a great deal of happiness. We do not disguise or attempt to control our happiness. This seems to prompt others' reaction to us to consider us to be appealing, which is good because then when we do visit our friends and neighbors and trading partners, they are almost always happy to see us. Unless, of course, they are involved in some major effort of their own, in which case we do not linger.

I don't have another word for dimension, but are you at a much higher dimension than us?

I understand your term "dimension." I would say, if I had to put it in such terminology, perhaps around eight. I don't consider that much higher, because that's just a matter of convenience, one's density. You might, as an Earth person, go to another life and be in any density. There's no progression in density, according to my travels. I have not seen that, nor do I perceive there being any progression. One just simply focuses in a given structure or state of being, plateau. One is there because that's where one's culture or planet or solar system or galaxy is.

If I were to look at you, what would I see?

If you were to see me, for one thing, on Earth and right now I am somewhat disguised. You would see, you would have a . . . how can I say? You are not here. I'd like to make a drawing, but it would be not unlike making a dark shaded area that is an oval. Near the top of the oval, if you have good vision, you might pick out a couple of eyes set the same way as your eyes, but no other features would be noticeable. But you could see how, with a quick glimpse into a tree, if you saw something shaded with two eyes, you would quite naturally assume that you are seeing a bird. And just the same way on the ground, if you were to see that, you might think that you are seeing a chipmunk or something like that.

But that's here. What about at home, if I could see you at your home?

Yes. I see now. If you were to see us there, you would see us as being somewhat tubular, but we have some considerable flexibility there. We do not have arms and legs and feet and hands and toes, but we can move by float-ing, you would say. So we are quite involved in motion. About two-thirds of our physical body would be what you would call "brain." This is why we are so involved in study. If two-thirds of your physical body were brain, you would be involved in study as well, all the time. So I would not say that we are entirely mental, but this is a strong focus for us. Considering the nature of that kind of organism, you can see why the science and philosophy go so well together, because these are two fields that involve a great deal of thought, wouldn't you say?

Our Technology Helps Us in Our Studies

How do you study, then? Is it telepathic, or do you have technology there or is it past that into the spiritual stages?

We don't have technology as you know it—meaning there are not machines with moving parts. But we do have very small objects. If you were to see it, it would look a lot like maybe an inch-square box. If you could open it, you would find that it is hollow inside. But this is because it has the capacity to adapt to any task that a machine might do.

Say that on your planet food was needed. It would be possible to instan-taneously produce that food—not from the box, but the box, the object, the mechanism would be able to instantaneously produce the food needed, though it would take time to train the mechanism to get the food prepared just the way you like it or for that matter to get the food exactly the way it is on Earth. If the mechanism were there, where you are now on Earth, it would have to just sit there. It would be helpful for it to be moved about from person to person for a couple of weeks in order to access enough of a sympathetic vibration between the mechanism and human beings to understand what humans like to eat and the combination of foods, and whether it'd be appropriate to deliver foods already prepared or whether it would be better to deliver foods that were in their raw state, such as corn with the outer parts of it still attached.

So it's like a power generator that attracts particles, something like that?

No, no, that's too much of a machine.

That's too physical, I see.

This is something that will analyze what you need and simply produce it. It would not, however, be able to produce food that had what you would call Earth vitality, life-vitality energy. It would simply be able to produce something that would taste like food and you'd be able to swallow it and it would fill you up, but it wouldn't give you a lot of strength. In order to do that, it would have to be moved around from person to person on the Earth for many, many years in order to notice how food on Earth does give you vitality.

In that case, it would then probably tend to produce foods that you hadn't seen before that would be able to give you all of the vitality you need so that you would not get diseases, would never get sick, would not get angry, would not get old. The duration of your lifespan might stretch out to a thousand years. In short, it would tend to be a food that would be, not a cure-all, but close to being something like that which would give you everything you needed in order to survive and thrive.

Can you mail me one before you leave?

[Laughs.] That's a joke. We have humor.

You do?

You know, you might want to make a reservation to live a life here, because we have, in our trading, traded these objects. It might interest you to know that we did not create these objects; we acquired them from a trading partner. At the time the partner came here, our life duration was about 800 years. The partner came here and said, "You appear that you could benefit from this mechanism we have." That's why I used the food example for you—that's what happened.

They produced this wonderful food, and we all partake of it and it has had this amazing effect. We live for about 1,900 years now, and toward the end of our life, the 40 or 50 years before the end, we used to lose a great deal of capacity to think clearly. That doesn't happen anymore. Now, when one goes right up to the end of their life, they can think as clearly as they could when they were young.

That's wonderful.

Communicating with Our Trading Partners

So how do you produce what you trade, then?

We trade a capacity to see beneath the surface of the thought into action process in cultures so we can reveal knowledge to other cultures about their own beings, about how their thought moves into action and what they can do to improve the process, or in the case of some, what they can do to create like a dance that will improve their thought. This is two different variations I am exposing you to, because sometimes we have noticed in some cultures, especially the more physical cultures, that motion is profoundly important in stimulating certain types of inspiration or thought. Therefore, we are able to perceive motions that are missing in that culture. And if those motions are adapted into some form of pleasurable dance, for instance, then it is possible, simply through the performing of these motions, to vastly increase one's capacity to be inspired and to think various thoughts that can be used to improve the quality of life for that culture.

How do you communicate? You're five inches high and they're from something similar to ten feet tall or so.

There is a device that . . .

A translator?

It is like that, yes. We think in our thoughts and they think in their thoughts, and there is a median form of communication. When I'm hearing what they are communicating, it is not exactly in our language, but I know what they wish to say. I grant there is some loss, but it is not very much and they know what it is I wish to say. I would say that the loss has to do with cultural differences that are so significant as to have no similarity, meaning that there is nothing in the other culture from one culture to, to . . .

. . . to translate it to, right.

Well, sufficiently similar. So there could be as much as a 2 percent complete loss, which is . . .

That's not very much.

It is not. I have not yet seen anything that can make up for that, other than an educational process of, "We do this and I see you do that, and so let's understand that part." When we do that, then the device would work better because there will be some understanding of the aspect in their culture that is entirely not present in our own.

So you go there without ships? You just go there?

Right.

How do you get their attention? Describe some of the people you've contacted.

Oh, well, they invite us. So we do not go uninvited. The fact that we have these devices, the mechanisms I mentioned to you, is simply on the basis who we . . . I'm calling them trading partners, but in fact our society lives as it lived before. You know, 800 years, we're doing all right, but because we have offered these services, other societies wish to share something that is serving their culture with us, and we do not bill for our services, eh? [Laughs.]

But because they are grateful, they share something. I mentioned the mechanism because it vastly improved our society and our quality of life, which was a gift. Since we offered a gift, they said, "Well, please take this, and I'm sure it will improve your life," and they were certainly right.

I'm assuming you're talking about people we've heard of, like Andromedans, Arcturians, Zetas and all this. Or are the people who ask for your services, beings we've never heard of or what?

Most of them, I think, are not beings you have heard of before. They are beings who are interested in growing in their culture, advancing in their culture, doing something more with the culture that they have, but they do not wish to experience what I have heard your culture is going to do—meaning to offer them some slight sense of discomfort that they can then use to stimulate their growth cycle.

So they're able to grow benevolently.

Yes. This is a benevolent means of growth that involves a discovery about themselves within their own culture that they didn't know they had. So it allows them to discover a whole new area of their culture and their being that is new to them.

If I were to see them, what would they look like?

I understand your question. Mostly, they are not humanoids. I recall one or two humanoids, but this is not typical. So if you were to try to imagine them, we are not talking about people who bear any resemblance to human beings, for the most part. I do recall one that I am perhaps stretching by calling humanoid. They did not have legs, but they did have something not dissimilar to arms.

But personalities can create any form to inhabit. Can you just give us an idea of some of these beings—shape or size or something?

I think that if you examined your own microbiological entities on your planet, you would get a pretty good idea of the type of forms that exist in the larger sense. Your planet was supposed to be a microcosm of all the beings, oh, from about 1,200 to 1,500 light-years around you in the spherical. So if the beings could not be on the Earth or perhaps under the Earth, then the simplest way to depict themselves would be microscopic.

Or under the ocean. Yeah, they're everywhere.

Yes, but microscopic, you see. You can get microscopic beings looking in vast, many different forms. And if you want to have some idea of the different forms of beings on other planets who are not humanoid, all you have to do is examine a slide.

So they're . . . they're here! I never knew that. That's interesting.

Yes, because it is important. Your Creator wanted you to be exposed as much as possible to life forms from other places so that you would be surrounded by it and have your curiosity piqued all the time. This is part of the reason why science and philosophy go together. You see something, you're fascinated about it, you think about it and you might form a theory and try to prove it. But at the very least, your mind is racing and you might form a philosophy around the whole subject that you're exploring and maybe try to fit your science into the philosophy but just as often accept that the science and the philosophy might have many apparent similarities but are not exactly the same. So science and philosophy go together very well, I believe.

That is wonderful. I love it when we get a little beyond what we already knew here.

Our Bodies on Earth Are Disguised

So is the body you live in on your home planet, is that the body you're in now, but, like, shifted a little bit?

Not shifted that much. Our bodies are what I would call not exactly visible but in part visible—disguised, you see, disguised.

Oh, I see. But I didn't realize that the disguise part of it was invisible. I see.

Yes, but it would be like shading—meaning that if we were seen, we would usually be seen at night. And at night, one would not be surprised if one could only see part of something. It's not at all unusual to hear, say, a bird at night or to get a quick glimpse of feathers, perhaps, but to not be alarmed at all by not seeing the whole being.

Right, right. Then when you, in that same body, take off and follow a soul that is spirit . . . is that how it works? In your physical body you . . . ?

Yes, because we are able to travel in time loops, so speed is not a problem.

What an amazingly effective form!

We have found it to be so, and this is why our people tend to reincarnate within our civilization, though it is not unusual for people to reincarnate elsewhere. But it is . . . if I had to put a percentage on it, I'd say right around 55, 58 percent of our beings in our civilization tend to reincarnate in our civilization.

Philosophy Will Serve Your Science

What do you study? Give me an idea of the topics you study.

There is no limit.

Anything, all across the totality?

We are particularly interested, however, in other cultures and naturally, not unlike yourselves, how they relate to us, even in some obscure aspect. You might consider dreams to be somewhat obscure, since you do not have a well and thoroughly based philosophy about dreams that is universal on your planet, nor do you have a science of dreams that is universal. It is an area that is definitely ripe for research, however, because it is so profoundly involved in the actual motivations of your day-to-day personality.

But science would have to admit that spirit is real before they could study the true understanding of dreams.

Yes, and science would have to, as you say, admit to what scientists believe. I believe most of your scientists are either religious or cognizant that the unexplained belongs to a vast world that they might wish to know more about and would very much like to have permission to explore. So I don't think that scientists would have to make much of a stretch, but the accepted philosophy of science would have to grow a little bit out of its infancy.

And it will, I hope.

Oh, of course it will. It is only natural, because it is natural for science to want to know more, to want to expand knowledge, and there is some point eventually when it is necessary to expand beyond one's—how can we say?—growing clothing. Babies, eventually they wear other clothing. You get older, you wear other clothing. Eventually, you grow out of your early clothing and you want to go on and do more, and that's when the philosophy will serve the scientific. It's coming.

Why did you choose this time, or do you have groups of you at various times along the timeline?

Yes, there are a few in the past. Generally, the teams are usually about eight to ten beings. There are a few about 300 to 500 years ago—it varies in timing—and there are a few about 300 to 500 years in the future. Your planet is quite a bit different then.

I'll bet it is. That would be interesting if they would tell us what they see. Will they be allowed to do that?

I doubt it, because there are variables involved. I would say that they probably wouldn't allow it, because it might put undue influence to encourage you to pursue certain activities, believing at this time—without having a good foundational marriage between science and philosophy—that a pursuit of a certain type of behavior would ultimately lead to benevolence, whereas a pursuit of other types of behavior might, in fact, be the roundabout course that leads to benevolence. As you have noted in your culture, very often the roundabout course is the one that makes the most contribution, because when you travel roundabout, you meet many beings and you discover how very similar they are to you. Whereas if you travel in a straight line, you might not meet as many beings and therefore you would be more ignorant about the multiple cultural and personality varieties on your planet.

Slow Things Down for Yourselves!

You have perceptions, even in the short time you've been here, about Earth. Can you share some of the perceptions of how you experience us, how you see us, where we're going?

On the soul level, you are quite involved in imaging, in creating and in resolving. This you are good at, but you are as yet still struggling with the experience of—how can we say?—physical motion in the form of time that you are in. I believe there is a tremendous resistance by your souls, incarnated into bodies, to embrace the benevolence of the physical existence that does occur where you are in existence. This is something that I think has been slowing you down because you are attempting to speed things up. In the process, you are missing the whole point, which is that you are in your current physical existence where you are so that you can slow things down, study them as a slow-moving being, to see, to observe, to notice—not to speed things up and miss the whole point of you being there.

Do you mean that people who are trying to get off the planet and get out of here and get up to the next level are missing the point of why we're here?

No, I am talking about people getting into a four-wheeled vehicle and whizzing down the street. Your cultures are set up to demand that you be portable like that, whereas your bodies are made for doing exactly what you are intended to be doing here—that is, traveling from place to place slowly, stopping and observing things that you find interesting, not unlike what you might see a child do, stopping and watching the little creatures moving about or stopping and looking at another human being doing something interesting. Your bodies are made for doing what you came here to do on Earth. Your vehicles do not improve what you came here to do.

So walking is the best way.

This is probably why you have been on Earth in this current time cycle as long as you have, because of having vehicles. Without vehicles, you would probably have moved on from this place some time ago, as many of you do. Of course, people come to the end of their cycle and they move on and they rarely return to Earth, especially if they have walked about quite a bit. If they haven't walked about too much in a given life, then very often they will return to Earth so they can get that slower time experience.

Do you mean walking to work, or just walking around the block? Expand on that a little bit.

Your bodies are made for what you are expected to learn here. You can, most of you, walk. Even those of you who might not be able to walk often move about in small wheeled chairs and not quickly—about the pace of somebody walking—to observe, to see, to notice, to touch, to feel what is safe to touch and feel.

So the way we've set our lives up with going off to work and rushing home and rushing to the store . . .

Delay your experience to move to the next thing, as I see it.

Communicate More with Your Fellow Human Beings

We will have to end pretty soon. I will make a closing comment.

Please.

I would like to say that it is not my intention to criticize the manner and means by which you run your civilization on this planet. I would like to say, however, that I recommend that you communicate more with your fellow human beings. Some of you communicate better to animals you have around the house than you do to your fellow beings or even members of the house life—I think you say "family." I'd like to recommend that you talk about things that are philosophical or scientific to find common interests. This is something that allows one to explore personalities and details.

Your reason for being on Earth now, on your planet, as I see it, is to examine details and to understand where these details fit into a broader picture—in short, the combination of science and philosophy, how things work and how they fit into the vast working reality in which you live. I want to encourage you to talk to people, to consider speaking about things that might be of great interest, not necessarily political things, but things like what's happening in science or what's happening in philosophy, the thoughts of the time. This is something that is worth doing. Try to walk about more, if you can. That is something good. And if you see something interesting, stop. Look. Enjoy it, and take in the details and color and pleasure of it all: a tree changing colors, snow on a mountaintop. You are on this planet to observe details. Don't try to get it all in your dreams. Good night.

Good night. Thank you so much.

＊　　　　　＊　　　　　＊

Greetings.

Greetings.

I will not completely speak about all things today, but there are others of my group who may also come and we shall see the directions in which you would like to have conversation. What shall we talk about?

In Loops of Time, No Actual Motion Is Involved

Help us understand the loops of time. I mean, I know of one loop of time that we of the Explorer Race are coming out of, but help us understand loops of time. I didn't know there were lots of them.

My perception of "loop of time" means that travel, as you understand it in your world, is something that happens through space first and is measured in time. But our travel happens through time first and there is no quantum involved, meaning no amount of space. It would be as if you wished to go somewhere from your residence—say, to a planet far from your current location—and if you traveled in a loop of time, you would stand, perhaps, in a room in your home, and then focusing on that and with certain assistance, you would not move at all physically, but you would be there.

So no space in terms of actual motion is involved, but the arrival happens as a result of—how can we say, how to put it in your terminology without actually instructing your scientists how to do it?—it involves a layer superimposed over another layer, which allows arrival through a filter. The filter, in this sense, is all of those portions of your personality and physical makeup that are compatible with the place where you wish to go, come through to that place. But if there are any portions of your being, be it personality or even elements of your physical being that are incompatible with your choice of arrival, that will remain at your point of departure—generally, at your point of departure, or occasionally in some other space reserved for you.

When you return from that place you went to, you will reassimilate that which you left. This filter works to prevent any difficulty or trauma to those to whom you are going to visit and would not care to harm simply by the function of your existence. This way, much of this travel happens in something that you would call, perhaps, a movable portal. It is something that comes to you rather than something that you go to.

That's why I say there is no space involved. It is only a fold or a layer of time; it's not motion. It is like this: If you could make a formula saying how far it is from place to place, you would say, "Well, that's the space involved." But you could also make a formula or make your best guess of how much time it would normally take you to travel at a given speed to that place. The time that it would take to get there is actually more important than the distance because of how much time you have or the stresses and strains that it might put your body, soul, personality and spirit through to get to that location. But if you were able to travel instantaneously, leaving behind not only that which would be harmful to those whom you wish to go see or to the place where you wish to go, but also you might leave something behind that you would cherish, some portion of yourself that might not be safe in that location due to the nature of the beings or the place that you're going to visit, then this also would be safe for you. So the filter works two ways, but it always works in a way to make the visit benevolent for all parties.

You Travel Like This in Your Dreams

That's amazing. The stuff we get when we get out of here! [Laughs.]

No, this is not that different from your travel in terms of your dreams. When you dream, quite obviously you do not take your physical body with you, so your physical body is safe in your location, cherished and protected according to your society's culture or protected the best you can, given your available means and resources. Equally, your physical body might not be— how can we say?—safe in other locations, where your dream might take you. Or it might not be acceptable in those other locations for those whom you travel with or go to see because there is more that goes on, as you well know, in your dream than a scenario. There are visits to teachers and wise beings.

There is music of a sort. There is travel, there's beauty, there's profound harmony and there is reassurance of the continuity of life itself. This reassurance is essential in order that you would continue to pursue life in a place that is as difficult as this university, you might say, that you are living in, this school of Earth. Without that reassurance, it is hard to live your life through the many difficult conditions that you might encounter on Earth.

So the travel is not dissimilar, and when you travel, you immediately experience motion beyond your physical body, beyond your world, beyond your understanding and concepts of physical reality, beyond your understanding and concepts of thought, for that matter. And the travel is able to occur because you move in your soul essence, your spirit, which is always free, free to come to Earth and be in your body. It also requires freedom to travel when your body is addressed.

So the travel happens quite naturally in the same way you travel when you are not physically in your own body—after death and so on, before life, you travel in this way. You still have your personality, you have other characteristics about yourself—meaning you might have friends, family and so on— but you travel instantaneously. So it's quite natural, when you experience your dream travel, that you travel in the way that is most familiar to you. In other words, you travel in your normal, natural way, not unlike the way we travel—the only difference being that you have a connection to your physical body during your lifetime, your life cycle, your life existence. That's the only difference, but the way you travel is exactly the way you travel when you are not living on Earth and you have your spirit or soul. So you travel naturally in the most familiar way to your total being. It's not something you have to learn, is what I'm saying.

You Did Not Always Dream This Way

But if everybody does this, all beings everywhere, then why are you interested in the souls on Earth who go out of their body at night?

Since Earth conditions are so entirely different than the conditions on our planet, we did not understand in previous studies of human dream capacities that you could live in such a challenging existence. I grant, there are things about your life that are benevolent, but we did not understand that you could live an Earth life in an Earth culture and society with all of its challenges and difficulties, and continue to travel in the natural, normal way. We thought that some other method must be involved. But we were fascinated to discover that the way you travel is identical to the way you would travel in a disembodied state, meaning without a body in your natural soul state as Creator birthed you.

So you've studied us before, then?

Our people have; I have not. So there have been studies before, but there was always speculation that the method of travel could not be the way one might travel in other places that are more benevolent. But we have recently had contacts with other beings who have assured us that, yes, it is true, you travel exactly that way, but it is because you have moved as a society of beings—not in terms of this national society or that national society, but as a society, a greater cultural being (your great teacher calls it the Explorer Race)—to a more natural version of your own souls and spirits, and you have resumed traveling in that way. According to our studies in the past of human beings on Earth, you did not dream that way. This is a change.

Going back—in terms of your time, I'll have to measure it as perhaps 1,600 to 1,800 years ago—the only way human beings could dream on Earth living in your cultures and societies then was that you would pass through what I will call a doorway and the doorway created a filter both ways. This prevented anybody from beyond Earth being affected by Earth energies and experiences of conflict and so on, and equally you were protected because you were able to dream or pass through this portal or doorway that allowed you to take your lessons—-not all the burden of your life, but the lessons that you had—with you to places where your teachers resided out into the general area of existence without it going beyond the perimeters. It was almost like traveling in a tube; there wasn't really a tube, but you were traveling in something for which there was insulation.

But that changed. Now, granted, the filter is there, but it is not dissimilar to the filter that exists for other beings as I described before. You have made a shift.

When did this happen?

According to our tests and research, the shift started about 400 years ago and was completed, in terms of your time—I can give you an actual year perhaps . . . no—it was completed 67 years ago. Now, on Earth, there will be other motions that will allow you in time, as you move forward into a greater natural state . . . that will take place in the future. But this motion—a shift, if we can call it that—has changed things greatly.

Even though you might feel that your world is in desperate straits at times, there is still, according to our perception, a move forward in a unified energy so that your hearts and spirits, if not your thoughts, are much more unified these days. And it is the unity of heart and spirit that allows for the motion toward the natural state of being. Thought is something that is largely conditioned and cultured, but heart and spirit are immortal. "Heart" is another word for love, you understand.

So how would a person be then, when he or she woke up in the morning, versus someone today? Is there a difference in the way that person would remember the dream or the way he or she would feel?

No. There would be no difference in terms of the actual, if you're talking about somebody, a human in the past. No, no difference. No difference at all.

But I always thought the spirit, the soul, couldn't hold negative energy and that the spirit or soul itself needed to be shielded.

It doesn't hold it in terms of the . . . it doesn't hold it. The energy isn't negative, all right? It just . . . the lessons are not perceived of as negative. Granted, the experiences associated with the lessons on Earth might be unpleasant or difficult, but the actual lessons and the means by which to work on the lessons—all of this is benevolent, positive. The reason you are here—to fine-tune something, to discover ways of solution, a means to ameliorate problems and so on—all of that is completely positive. It's just that the experiences you have on Earth either acquiring that wisdom or in applying solutions might not be. But that does not go with you when you travel in the dream state.

What does is the intent for lessons and the modification based upon your experience so that when you go to talk with your teachers and guides and so on, there is a significant amount of modification, say, in the life of an adult. A child might—or other beings, a soul if you like—have a very clear idea of the lesson, but as life goes on and there is experience and wisdom and accumulation of these, then the soul's understanding (or the spirit's understanding) of the lesson might moderate. The lesson chosen might become more specific to a given life. It maybe will wait to work on this other part of the lesson in a different life because it becomes too much. That's just an example. Or it might be that, as a result of the wisdom gained, the approach to the lesson becomes entirely different—meaning that you might be something different in order to approach the lesson. It might take on a different approach to your own, the way you address your life, the way you live your lifestyle, as you call it, for example.

We're Here to Study Your Means of Travel

Now, if you would . . . I'm so sorry, but I really wanted to talk to you before you left our system here. Do you follow individual humans and watch them talk to their teachers and visit friends?

No, no. That would be invasive. The best we can do is observe at a distance. We always have a respectful distance so no one is in any way distracted by our presence. A "distance" would be quite a significant distance, and this way we are able to get the general idea. We're here to study the means of travel; we're not here to study the individual's lessons and so on. That would be invasive and not really part of an acceptable exploration of an individual soul journey. But as far as the study of the means of travel, in terms of how you—or your personality, you understand, your soul, your spirit— move beyond your physical body to the point where you are going to, that is acceptable to study.

Well, it's my understanding that you had to get out of your body and then fly up beyond the Earth or beyond the solar system. You're saying that's not true. At what point do you come to this portal, as you said, so that you're there and here?

You will have to change the word "you." You have used the word "you" in reference to humans and in reference to myself and beings, and the question is not understandable.

Okay. As a human being going out of his or her body, I had the idea that you literally flew up through the house, up through the clouds. How far do you actually fly and then when do you come to this portal?

There is no flight at all. It is instantaneous.

Really.

When people have experiences where they feel that they are flying, that is entirely different. That does not have to do with the dream; it does not have to do with the travel to one's teachers. It is an actual, physical experience—physical outside of the physical body. One takes the physicalness, the certain capacities of the physical body, with one. In that case, one is actually stretching in the physical body. The physical body itself can stretch that way, so this is not part of the same thing. That's my understanding of how that works for you.

You said before that a certain small percentage went into the past and some went into the future. Does that mean their teacher is in the past or the future, or are they just going out to sightsee?

They're studying to see if there's any difference. When one does a research study, one does not automatically assume that any given life form is exactly the way they are presently, throughout all time. One would naturally assume that there has been some change when you live in time and space, such as yourself—that there's been some change. So quite naturally, some went to the past, some went to the future and, from your point of view, I am here.

No, I'm sorry. I'm doing that "you" thing again. [Laughs.] Yes, I understand that some of you went to our past, our future and our present. But previously you said that some humans, when they went out, went into the past, and some went into the future. You gave me a percentage. And the rest of them went off to see their teachers.

I'm sorry, I do not recall that.

You gave me a small percentage. I don't know . . . 16 percent total or something like that.

I do not recall. I am not disputing you—I do not recall. To be perfectly honest, I do not recall our previous conversation at all. But I am doing the best I can to—how can we say?—diplomatically communicate here.

[Laughs.] You're doing great. There are things here that are new to us. So how can we say this, then? As humans, we go out of the body, we do this instantaneous connection to our teacher who could be across the totality or in a neighboring galaxy or anyplace, right? You're saying anyplace?

Remember, distance is meaningless. Granted, it has meaning, but . . .
In this case, yes.
It has no limiting factor whatsoever. As high as you can count in number to as small as you can go in percentages or fractions—it doesn't make any difference. If your teacher lives on the head of a pin, that's where you go.

You Have to Eliminate the Whole Concept of Space

[Laughs.] Some humans—scientists and also science-fiction writers—have come up with a word called "tesseract." We take that to mean that, like you said, it's a fold in space so that you're right next door to where you're going. Is that anywhere close to what you're saying?

It's not that far off, but it doesn't take into account the necessary filtering and it also assumes a fixed situation. It is not fixed; it is flexible. The means of travel, the means of point-to-point relocation (let's even eliminate the term "travel"), has nothing to do with the corridor to get there, because when one assumes the corridor to get there, one is quite naturally assuming a travel in space. You have to eliminate the whole concept of space if you want to travel, if you want to relocate great distances. The minute you start considering space, you are going to limit yourself, period.

You have to consider—how can we say?—the feelings and use the element of attraction. And you see, the attraction has to be on both sides. That's why there has to be total assurance for who ... "who" in this case could be a planet, could be beings, could be beings you don't even understand ... they must be able to feel absolutely welcoming of you—not just out of being naïve, but by knowing for certain that the "you" who will arrive there will be absolutely safe for them and that they might enjoy visiting with you. So they have to have that feeling, meaning that quite obviously, they know you're coming before you go there. And you, for your part, have to feel absolutely safe to go there.

This is the same thing we've been told about the lightships that we'll build in the future and how we'll travel in those lightships. That's fascinating.

Yes, only this other thing does not require a ship, nor does it require traveling in space. This is not to rule out the fact that you will enjoy traveling in space. This simply means to travel great distances as you travel now in your dreams, as you call it—or from my point of view, as you travel to communicate with beloved teachers, guides, Creator and so on, to be reassured that the continuity of your immortal life is guaranteed. Therefore, no matter what happens on Earth, you will go on benevolently. This is essential in all places, but particularly where you are in this challenging world.

So if you were to go to places that we've heard of—Andromeda or the Pleiades or Arcturus or something—and you would observe those beings ... do they ... I'm assuming they have some rest cycle. Do they do the same thing?

What beings?

Beings from other galaxies—humanoid types.

You are asking whether they sleep and dream like yourself?

Yes.

It entirely depends upon the culture and their own physiognomy of their bodies. If their bodies require that, then yes, of course. If their bodies do not require that, then no, they do not sleep and dream as you understand it. But they have that capacity to move in space as you understand it, or from my point of view, to relocate from point to point without having to sleep and dream, because sleeping is unnecessary.

Take Care of Your Physical Body

So these more benevolent beings ... [breaks off coughing].

Is there something you can take for your . . .

No. I took the antibiotic, and I don't have anything else. I'll get some more water. I'm sorry to bother you with this.

You're not bothering me. I am concerned for your health. You need to be concerned for it as well. I will say that where we live, before we are born (as you understand it, yes?), we as spirit, as soul, make a oath that we will cherish our physical bodies, and we ask our physical bodies to welcome and cherish us. The rest of the oath is that we will care for and nurture each other, and provide each other with the most benevolent form of existence we can offer. I do wish you to consider that. It is not a dissimilar oath than the spirit of human beings take, but you do not remember it because of the nature of your life here.

But you did take that oath, I assure you. All beings do when they come here. So if your body needs to rest, it is good to rest. Lie down or sit up and do something that amuses you and distracts you and is a comfort to you while your body assimilates the support it needs to get better.

Well, that's what you are right now. This is what I chose to do.

I understand, but I cannot interact with you indefinitely if you do not treat yourself well. When you do not treat yourself well, it gives me pain. This is important for you to know, because as a spiritual person, someone pursuing that for yourself, if you are ignoring your own physical needs and your body is announcing that it needs attention, then all beings around you experience the pain of that lack of attention and beings might tend to move off. You may notice you have beings there who are not of your race.

Right, cats.

Yes. Do they rush to you when you are making those sounds?

No.

They move off, yes?

Yes.

Because why? Do you ask yourself, "Why do they do that?"

Ah, it didn't occur to me before, but I see now that it's causing them pain. I didn't know that.

It's because you are not addressing your body's needs, not nurturing your body. I realize you might not have something to nurture your body with, but perhaps there is something, some drink, some balm you might have, perhaps something to serve your discomfort in a benevolent way. I am not here to lecture you, but my feeling is that your body is announcing its needs, and when you do not meet your body's needs, it's something . . .

Just a minute. I have something I'm putting in my water that should help; it's called a calming agent. Okay, that should help.

I feel that, given the nature of human tendency (quite naturally because of your school on Earth), many people might do what you do and ignore their discomfort if they're pursuing something they enjoy. But when you do that, you might not be aware—you were not aware and equally other human beings might not be aware—that your body then immediately broadcasts pain. This is not a cry; rather it is a request for help. And I am responding to your physical body's request.

In other societies that are more sensitive and alert to this—and in your culture in times gone by—the helpers come and perhaps they brew a tea for you. In the future, someone comes and would touch your chest, and you would lie down and rest, and the touching would calm your body and nurture it. This person might rub something on your chest, but more likely on the side of your head, and you would relax and in time your body would feel better. That's the future.

But in the present, you have other things you could do, or you could call a friend to bring something over to you (you probably do not feel like going anywhere). You could do that and take care of your body, and then you would discover that your local teachers who live with you would approach you again. But the reason they have moved off is because they cannot . . . they have no means to serve your body's needs. The cry goes to others. So they move off, and by moving off they give you the information, the message, that there is a need for you. It's not that they are afraid of the sounds.

This might be important, because sometimes people approach those with discomforts who can help, and if you're in a place where people can help you, they might know that you're uncomfortable because of something, even if there is no announcement such as you are making now, physically. And you might wonder, as a person with discomfort, why this person's coming over to help. How did they know?

They could feel it.

Perhaps they felt it, and then if they knew it was not their pain, they looked around and they realized on the basis of their own physical feeling where that pain signal was coming from. And if they are strong and sturdy, warrior healers—not to make war, but they have the strength of a warrior—then they might approach to offer what they can to help your body to feel better.

Yes, we have books like that, the Shamanic Secrets *series, where Speaks of Many Truths and Reveals the Mysteries have talked about their life 400 years ago—that's how they lived. If someone was in pain, they were in pain, and they needed to help that person, not only to help that person but also to help themselves.*

Your Dreams Are in Layers

How do dreams work? How come we remember our dreams in a sort of jumbled way?

Imagine, for a moment, that you have tables in front of you. Well, I refer to the method of travel as layers. So if you had a table in front of you and it was covered with documents, pictures, objects, sculptures, food—various things like that, all right?—and then on top of that there's another table with a different arrangement of objects, pictures, food and so on, and on top of that another one. So there are several layers, like that. If you traveled, say, from underneath that table and were able to travel straight through all the tables to the point where you went, you might have, perhaps, on each level of table . . . on the first table, you might meet a teacher, on the second table, you might meet a guide or friend and so on. And you would have an experience with each of them, you understand?

Yet when you came back, when you traveled, you would have that experience and it would be enjoyable and it would be from one thing to another and multiple experiences at once perhaps. But it would be not unlike how you might have multiple experiences now at once, meaning that you are in your physical body and you are looking around the room you are in and you are talking on this device—in short, you are doing more than one thing at once. So you might have multiple experiences on each of those levels, and you would have those experiences as you move toward wherever it is you are going in terms of space (considered here, since that is your word).

Yet when you came back, when you woke up, that would be instantaneous and you wouldn't have the recollection of the linear experience. You would just have the experience of whizzing back, if I can say that, through all of the tables simultaneously. So what you would have leftover is a recollection of bits of layers.

Ah. I see—all jumbled up.

No, not jumbled up at all, because you don't remember the entire experience on each level. You remember only . . . try to picture a hole through the center of the tables. You go through one table, one layer, and you have a full experience on that level. But it isn't all taking place in and around that hole. It happens in a . . . this is really a picture and you are not here, so you don't understand what I'm saying.

So it happens on the whole . . .

The whole plane. And you move onward to various layers like that. Although it might be a full and complete experience on the way to wherever you are going, when you return, in terms of waking up suddenly, perhaps to an alarm clock . . . if you simply wake up, if you wake up slowly, you have perhaps more that you remember. But if you wake up suddenly, it happens so instantaneously you can only get what is in and around the hole, so to speak—although there is no hole. That's why you don't remember things very well and why one thing seems to be juxtaposed to something else.

Do you think we'll be able to remember what we do on these travels while we're still in this physical body?

I do not feel that this is to your advantage, because it would be so fascinating it would distract you from what you came to Earth to do in the first place. You came to Earth to learn new ways to do things or to figure out through your experience and culturing or gathering of wisdom what works, what might work in different conditions and how you might bring about resolution for yourself or others in the best or most benevolent way. And to remember how you do things on other planes of existence . . . well that's something you already know how to do. What's the point of reexamining that since the whole purpose of your soul is that it's here to learn something new? If you immerse yourself in what you did and how you did it everywhere else, you'll be disinclined to learn the new thing because it doesn't have the touchstone, so to speak, of what you're familiar with. That is why people have difficulty very often staying in your Earth place.

Work with Those around You

We'll have to stop soon. You'll have to excuse me, but you see the channel, the being Robert, he is not as insulated and protected as he normally is because you are ill, and it is beginning to affect him and is causing him harm. We need to encourage you to look after your physical body, and therefore, I recommend waiting until you feel better. The discomfort you're in is unfortunately passing through . . .

To Robert. Okay, yes, absolutely.

Now, remember to work with your friends there who are with you. If they are fleeing, this means you need help from somebody else. Try to notice what they are doing. If they flee from your state of being, then you need help from somebody else. There may be some sort of medication you might need to serve your comfort zone. Don't do it for their sake. They are all right, but they give you the message that you are broadcasting pain. The pain is not being broadcast because of your body's condition; it is being broadcast because your body is not being served.

Thank you. Good night.

Reflective Zone Causes Sightings During Washington Earthquake

ET Visitor from Andromeda and Zoosh

April 1, 2005

On March 12, 2005, I heard on Fox News that fifteen miles north of Olympia, Washington, there was a 3.3 quake and at the same time there was a sighting there by many people. This is just my own awareness, but when I saw that, I wrote down that "the ship rides on the Earth's magnetic field, pushes down on Earth and causes a small quake." The answer from Speaks of Many Truths was, "Yes, Robbie. This is Speaks of Many Truths. Channel on this with Melody. There has been much talk about this, and I think it's important to confirm the sighting in Washington—there was one in another state as well—and to confirm that minor earthquakes can be caused by a ship riding on the Earth's magnetic field. It rides on and it pushes down unintentionally in a weak-structured zone. It is possible to produce a minor earthquake. Major earthquakes are not caused this way."

- Robert Shapiro

Greetings. I was an observer during the recent transit through your planet's reflective zone. There's a zone around your planet. I think this might be because there's so much water on your planet that it can at times, especially if there is significant magnetic energy present, create a reflection of passing ships.

Ships Are Often Not as Close as They Appear

There was a vehicle—and I wish to confirm this—that passed near Earth and was seen by many people in this location of Earth. The situation, though, was that the ship itself was not as close as it seemed, which is why those attempting to detect it for the purposes of self-defense for your country were unable to detect much in the way of blatant evidence, meaning fluctuations in magnetic fields and so on. Due to the reflective zone, the ship was really much further away from the planet than it appeared to direct observers.

This reflective zone fluctuates in its focus, not based upon a moving position but entirely based upon the reactive elements between the zone itself and the nature of the ship's propulsion system. This vehicle that was noticed did use magnetic energy, making it a bit of an older vehicle, older technology. That is why it was seen and, I might add, seen in a curious way. Many people saw it moving in a slow arc across the sky. Others saw it—and this was something that was less widely reported—moving across the sky and then it would be invisible, they wouldn't see it, and then again it would pick up and be moving again. Some people reported it as a dot-dash pattern, this having to do almost exclusively with their position in viewing the vehicle—not unlike, as a scientist might say, the focal refractive element, or to put it more simply, the distance between your means of perception and the lens effect.

This has been the cause many times in the past of mass sightings, simply because it is usually discouraged to fly through the atmosphere of a planet that does not have vehicles such as the one you are using or perhaps something more advanced—it is unkind to create a stir in the population. Yet because of this reflective zone, a great many sightings that have been observed did not actually involve a vehicle that was as close as it seemed. Rather, the ship was traveling, as in the case of this one, in an arc pattern that was almost identical in places to the curvature of your planet, though the vehicle itself was, in terms of miles away from your planet, about 350 miles away—quite obviously, then, living up to the desire to stay out of your atmosphere.

Yet because the ship was traveling in an arc that was almost identical with the curvature of your planet in that particular place and because it was utilizing a form of magnetic systems—not propulsion, but navigation—for a brief moment, it was visible to many, many people on the planet. If you studied the actual track of sightings over the past forty years, let's say, on your planet (by people all over your planet), you would often find the curious phenomena where people would say, "I saw it coming across the sky, and then it was invisible, and then I saw it again, traveling in almost an identical arc, but it disappeared for a time," or words to that effect. When the sighting takes place like that, it is always a situation of the reflective zone.

I wanted to make this comment to you at this time so that the people who saw this will know that they saw something real, but also so that the people in your community of observers who have difficulty in locating such an object will understand the physical situation that causes this. There is, I believe, a theory in some aeronautical scientific institutions (as well as with individuals) that such a thing is possible. It has not been given much acknowledgment, but I wish to acknowledge it now so you will recognize that oftentimes when one sees such a thing, you are completely safe, there is no immediacy in terms of potential contact; rather this situation does exist.

As far as the quake noted simultaneously in this particular area, it was not in this case associated directly with that vehicle, though as an observer—and I will explain more about who I am in a moment—I would have to say that, as far as I could tell, the quake was caused by underground operations of a nature associated with the extraction of elements from the Earth by . . . this is strictly a human consideration. There have been other Earth motions in this area, usually not as detectable. I do not believe that the extraction was in any way intended to cause alarm. It was unintentional.

I Am Here on Earth to Study the Reflective Zone

So here's a little more about myself. Somewhere in the next half-hour, I will be leaving your planet. But I have been on your planet for about forty days now, and I am here to study the reflective zone, which is why I have been here and have some knowledge of these things. For some time now, many ships have been queried, as it was noted by observing your patterns, your human behaviors, from a distance, that people were becoming alarmed or excited at seeing ships. So the ships themselves were queried as to their flight path. Everyone assured the querying parties that they were nowhere near the Earth at the time.

So a small group of us were dispatched to come to the Earth to study your atmospheric conditions—which, as you know, because of rain falling and snow on the ground and simply so much water on the planet, there is a lot of reflectiveness just simply noticed. You can look at the Sun beaming down on a pool of water, and sometimes it is so bright, it is difficult to look at. Our thought was that the reflective zone might be a factor, and we have been able to confirm this.

Our people are from the galaxy Andromeda. And my feeling is that it is perhaps going to be a comfort to those who saw this to know that they were seeing a real ship, a real vehicle traveling from one planetary system to another, but that it was not as close as it appeared.

How often do ships go in that area, 350 miles above Earth?

It's not just that particular area, though what I said might have left you with that impression. It has to do with a wide variety of factors. Sometimes it simply has to do with the fact that it's raining on the Earth. Other times it has to do with how much surface water there is, how close it is to the surface. And almost invariably it has to do with how much magnetic energy the ship is using or utilizing.

Now, ships, when they travel near a planet, might ride somewhat on the planet's gravitational field. This conserves energy for the ship if it's moving slowly, relatively slowly in that sense. In order to be able to do that, one must follow the exact arc of the gravitational pattern—which is not always the same arc of the curvature of the planet but in this case was similar, at least in places. This is done not to absorb magnetic energy from the Earth, but as I say, just to reduce the drain on the ship's propulsion system, whatever that might be. So the gravitational field does fluctuate in its density and in its radiation, meaning how far it radiates out or not. Therefore, most of the time, due to the fact that it is not in a perfect arc, one simply does not see the vehicle. So you might have to rephrase your question.

What would be the low point on the Earth and the high point from the Earth that this gravitational field would radiate? What would be the top and bottom limits in terms of miles from the Earth?

I do not feel I can answer that question at this time. But I will say that the range of sightings that have to do with the reflective zone on any part of the Earth as they've been seen in, say, since I'm arbitrarily picking the past forty years (I'm talking about how long the ships have been seen), the actual potential and what I've been able to research, what our team has been able to research in terms of sightings, have ranged from 260 or so miles from the Earth to almost 1,000 miles from the Earth. This has less to do with the gravitational range of Earth than it has to do with the variables of what the ship is doing.

You see, you might have a gravitational field that radiates out in a detectable fashion for so many hundreds of miles, but the ship has to . . . it is like a formula, you see? The ship has to be utilizing or emanating a certain amount of magnetic energy. If, however, the ship is utilizing a greater portion of magnetic energy, it might be seen in the reflective zone at a greater distance from the planet as compared to if the ship is closer to the planet but utilizing less magnetic energy. So it is a complex formula having to do with . . . I suppose the closest study you would have on Earth that could relate to this would be quantum mechanics.

Our Forms Are Seen More Easily as a Reflection

So you and your team are physically here on Earth?

We are preparing to leave.

Was your ship on Earth, were your people on Earth, or were you orbiting or what?

The ship is not here. We do not require an actual vehicle to depart. We can depart in what I would call component energy. Our physical forms—if I might use that term loosely—do not equate to your own. If you were to be able to see us at all, it would be somewhat reflectively, out of the corner of your eye. We do not have physical forms as you do. Our forms are more . . . how can I put this in your terminology? I believe our forms would be seen more easily as a reflection than directly—and this is why we were requested to do this.

Your vision is attenuated to a narrow band that allows you to see all that you interact with in order to learn and grow and experience your purpose on Earth. But you do not see the vast majority of what is here because it would have no bearing on your reason for being here and could only distract you from accomplishing your purpose. Therefore, occasionally you as Earth people might see something fleeting out of the corner of your eye, as you say—meaning in indirect view. These things that are seen are in fact there, but they do not bear upon your personal or Earth human purpose for being here. So I can only say that we would not be visible to you were you looking directly at us. We do not require a vehicle to leave, though there is a vehicle at some distance.

But we are visible to you?

Yes, because other forms of life—myself inclusive—do not visit the Earth as an Earth human, to live and accomplish your purposes here. I'm not trying to suggest that we are somehow superior, but rather since our reason for being here does not involve your reason for being here, we can see you and other life forms since we are visiting only. We are not in residence as you are.

That's fascinating. Who sent you?

Some other beings on the Earth, not human beings, have this same capacity.

Like cats?

Especially those beings who have been noted by your scientists as having what is, they call, a multiple eye, meaning a compound eye or a refractive or reflective eye. This has been studied, I believe, by those who study the very small creatures you call insects. These beings have eye structures that are considerably wide-ranging. They can see all life here. Sometimes you might see one of them sitting quietly somewhere. They're very often communing with life forms that are not native to the Earth, perhaps discussing with them Earth life or simply communing about life in general, personal experience.

There are other life forms who can see many things. Perhaps the closest life form that comes into contact with human beings in a familiar way is cats, but also many forms of wild birds can do this—not so much in the way of the so-called domesticated bird, which has very often been genetically altered to accentuate certain characteristics that sometimes unintentionally de-accentuate other natural characteristics. "Dogs," as they're called, are less perceiving of these things, because dogs are here almost exclusively to assist human being in your experience on Earth, to support and sustain you. Dogs, though, have capacities—not in vision, but in smell and hearing—to detect these other life forms.

We've talked to Andromeda beings and we've put a book out about Leia and her shipmates. Are you from a dimension similar to theirs, or from a higher one?

"Higher" is something you use . . .

Well, more expanded.

Differences in perspective?

Yes.

I see. We are not from that focus, but we are aware of that focus. I do not personally know these beings. From what I can glean from your memory, they do not appear to be familiar to me, nor does their culture have any familiarity to me. But we are, from our culture, aware of their focus.

So have you been to Earth before?

I have not.

Can you tell us something you've learned about us that we could learn from?

I thought I just did that by . . .

Yes, you did. [Laughs.]

We Are Here on a Diplomatic Mission

Who sent you? Well, let's put it this way—who queried? Who's the group or organization or person who asked you to come here?

There is a group that oversees to help insulate Earth from contact with too many life forms that have not been trained on how to interact with Earth humans. Many of what you call the animals on Earth have all been trained. But there is a group that is involved to help to insulate the Earth from contact from beings who might cause distraction. It is not anything more than a loose-knit group of beings who care about Earth and wish to support you to accomplish your purpose here. They are wide-ranging and many different focuses.

They requested it because they felt that this is an ongoing situation and at times it is creating excessive distraction for you as a people. Now, understand that some sightings are intended and they will usually be inspiring and nurturing or have elements of great beauty about them, and there are certainly some situations where individuals on your planet have been directly contacted. These are also, at times, intended. But these unintentional sightings, having to do with the reflective zone, have been considered by this group to be a distracting element. That's why they requested we come to research the situation and to make suggestions to be able to alter the situation in the future so that less of these sightings take place strictly based upon the reflective zone. And we will be able to make the suggestions as a result of our studies.

So tell me, why you? What is your experience, that they would call on you? Do you do this a lot, or is this something that happens on every planet?

Which one of those questions do you want me to answer?

Why did they call on you, or your team?

They called on our people, not me specifically. They called on our people because it is in the nature of our existence that reflectivity is how we are seen by many. We are not always seen directly, even by various beings with compound vision as I referred to, the small beings on your planet. Even on other planets, it is very typical for us to be seen in our reflectiveness rather than as a direct vision. So apparently it was considered that we would be the most likely beings to be able to detect something, since the group that asked us to come here believed that a reflective or refractive causal factor might have been a circumstance here. There have been others who have been asked before us and they were able to come forward with that theory, but we were asked to come here to get more details and perhaps offer suggestions to improve the situation.

How did you do that? If you don't have a ship or technology, how did you do that?

Strictly by observation. Since the sightings were taking place at a certain moment, we knew there would be certain sighting circumstances, because we, well . . . I do not wish to make it sound . . . well, I have to be frank with you. We came back in time because we knew there would be this particular sighting in this location as mentioned—in the Washington State area and, I believe, in a few surrounding states as well, as they're called. So we were fully prepared to observe the situation with all of the research done by previous parties that had come here. And because of lifetimes in our culture of interacting with beings on other planets, having to explain to them how they could see us and interact with us, it is almost like we were just as much of a diplomatic mission because of our experience here—not a diplomatic mission in the sense that you know it, it was not meant to contact Earth people, but a diplomatic mission in terms of our life and cultural experience. Due to the years and years, you might say, of communicating with other beings and trying to explain our existence, I believe that those who asked us to come here simply assumed that our cultural history would nominate us as the most likely beings to be able to perceive a reflective zone, if one did exist.

Yet you see each other clearly, right?

Of course.

And you go to many, many planets where the beings can't see you?

We have been to planets where the beings . . . I want you to understand what I am saying. We have been to many planets where the beings there can see us. We have also been to many planets where the beings cannot see us directly but they can see us reflectively. Sometimes, if they have a reflective material available, they can see us in that material. Sometimes it will be a natural form of their planet, perhaps a liquid not unlike water in which they can see us reflected in there. Other times it will be out of the corner of their eyes, so to speak, or out of a portion of their eye vision or their visioning portion of their body—a portion of their visioning, or let's say "eye" for the sake of simplicity—that they do not use very much but which they can use or can train themselves to use.

In your case, were we actually attempting to make contact with you, you would probably be able to see us. The simplest way would be to see us reflected in water—say, for example, on a moonless night or a night in which the Moon is in shadow. If there was a calm body of water and we were attempting to make contact with you, we would have to want to and you would also have to want to. The desire would have to be equal. Then you could, if we wished you to see us, see a reflection of our form in this water.

What would we see?

Of course, the water would be somewhat in motion. So you would not see a precise definition of our image.

And if I could see you, what would I see?

I don't think that's intended for me to say. I am not reaching out to make diplomatic contact. I am simply giving you an example of how you would see us if we were there.

We Were Not Intended to Make Contact with You

So do you walk around on Earth? Do you float? Do you see from afar?

Our bodies do not look like yours at all, so the term "walk around" does not relate. We are not humanoid.

Can you say anything about your shape at all?

I don't think that's intended at this time.

Could you say anything about what you do on your planet?

We have existence. I will give you an example that is very loosely associated with something you can understand, because it is something you can observe yourself. If you were to pick up a crystal and hold it up to a light source—be it the Sun perhaps being the best, or be it some other broad-spectrum light source—you might see the light reflecting in and around the crystal as well as perhaps even through the crystal to cause the color separation that you greatly enjoy here. The transit of the light through the crystal would very loosely describe some of the things we do in our culture.

You understand, we were not sent here because we are like you. We were sent here because we, well, as I described, have qualities to fulfill the purpose of the study—but not because we were intended to make contact with you. When you make contact as cultures openly on Earth, as Earth citizens, the beings will be almost identical to you in appearance in the beginning. And then as time goes on, some will just be humanoid but dissimilar.

Nevertheless, you will like them and they will like you. That is the whole point in creating such contacts, because it will create a greater feeling of welcome into the culture of planets.

Well, we're going to have to work our way up to you, right? [Laughs.]

No. I realize this is humor, yes?

Yes, yes.

But no, you don't have to work your way up. There is no need for you to meet us at this time. I have come through only because it was possible, though I am not now on the surface of your planet anymore. We have left during our conversation.

That's multitasking, talking through Robert while you're moving and leaving!

It is not a problem. We have not returned to our planet, though we are on the vehicle we enjoy traveling in—because the entire vehicle is a combination of our fellow beings and cultural elements from which we draw benevolence.

We're Not from the Andromeda You Know

Are you from our universe?

No.

But you said you were Andromedan.

But we're not from the Andromeda you know.

Really! There's an Andromeda in another universe?

Something that is close to that. If I were to pronounce it in our own way, it would sound similar to Andromeda as you know it. It is hard for you to imagine this, but sometimes when you refer to dimensions, your assumption is—and perhaps I can see why your assumption would be this—that all dimensions in your universe are . . . that your universe is inclusive of all dimensions. But this is not true.

I would prefer to say it as a focus, an individual focus. Your universe is not inclusive of all of these different focuses. We are from Andromeda but from a focus not within your universe. And while we do not pronounce it exactly like the word "Andromeda"—nor do the people, I think, in your universe pronounce it exactly that way—it is close enough. But our focus is different and not a portion of your universe, though I can state that we are, in fact, from Andromeda.

Well, if I remember, this universe is enclosed by the Void, and the Void is enclosed by the Creator of the Void, so we're enclosed within something, right? And you're part of an expanded sphere, or something like that?

This is how I will answer: Someday when you have accomplished your purpose and have benevolently affected, in the way that is intended, the rest of your universe, the insulation between your universe and the rest of your universe—which has literally become a different universe because of the conditional aspects (meaning, you would say, time, experience, but I would say, conditional aspects)—that the reunification will take place and it will become one universe. But right now you are insulated so that you can accomplish the purpose that the Creator of your universe has requested you to do. This has to do, of course, with nurturing and supporting benevolent and gentle growth in cultures beyond your own by learning how to adapt to the widest form of communication, interaction and cultural exchange on your own planet with species that are now present on your planet or have been present in the past or may be evolving toward a presence in your present or future. So the interaction (consciously, spiritually, yes, but also on the feeling and energetic level) is intended to allow you to, when you begin to move beyond the surface of your planet benevolently toward other places, to benevolently impact other life forms as they desire to be impacted in ways that will allow their own growth curve to expand. This way, no one's growth curve as a culture—meaning a planetary culture—is excessively stimulated.

Beyond their ability to handle it.

Stimulated to the degree that they desire in their own sense of, you might say, timing. Equally, your experience of reward from that interaction allows you in time to be as a planetary culture in contact with all life in the most benevolent way, feeling as a portion of all life, and all life feeling you as a benevolent portion as well. This is why you are here. It is a complex and involved task, and taken many false trails you have. But now you are beginning to ease toward the true path and trail of love and benevolence and necessary curiosity to allow you to move through otherwise foreign (meaning foreign to you) forms of existence and to generate safety based upon desire and trust, faith and appreciation of all life. Good night.

Thank you so much. Good life.

✻   ✻   ✻

All right, Zoosh speaking.

Thank you. So just as there's a veil around the Earth to protect the rest of the citizens of this galaxy and universe, there is also a veil around this universe to protect

the rest of the universes, which also then cuts our Creator off from knowing about his higher being?

It doesn't cut your Creator off, but the rest of your question is a yes. But it doesn't cut Creator off.

But there is a part of him that he's not aware of?

No.

There was.

He's aware of it.

But he's not in direct contact with it, because he wants to go join that part, doesn't he?

This is a very long answer.

Okay, we'll bring it up later. It's just that when this being said that it was like a flash of illumination, that there was . . .

Quite obviously, if you were able to be aware of it and you are a portion of Creator, then how would it be possible for Creator to not be aware of it?

That being's just wonderful. It was so beautiful I want to cry; it was just wonderful. Thank you so much for coming.

Good night.

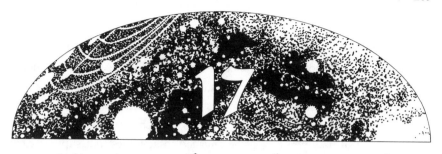

You Are in the Final Stages of Preparation for Contact

Antiquarian, Pleiadian Teacher
April 19, 2005

reetings. I am Antiquarian. My energy visited you today and did a dance on the computer for Robbie. My origin is from the Pleiades. I have chosen the name Antiquarian, because in your language it suggests age, value, beauty and perhaps humor. I come to visit you today because I want to make some suggestions for the people of Earth.

Your Time of Suffering Is Coming to an End

You are now in the final stages of preparation for contact with other beings from other places, times, origins and manifestations. Many of you even now are seeing things that you cannot explain. Others will see that soon. We will all try to manifest for you in the most beautiful way that you will find attractive. We will not be ghosts [laughs]; we will be of beauty, of different colors, of different shapes. We probably won't look like human beings, but there will be so much color and wonderful energy, which you will all enjoy no matter who you are, that you will feel appropriately safe and comfortable with us.

We are not here to take over or influence your lives. We are here simply to let you know that your time of suffering and strife is winding down. There will be a transition over the next forty to fifty years where the organizational structures that you have come to take for granted in the form of governments and even corporate entities will gradually merge into something that looks a lot like a global corporate government—not meant to cause strife but meant to connect people in cooperative ways, not unlike how people now come together who have similar interests. This will be the final stage that will allow you to become aware of your mutual interests, of each person's value to everyone else, and of how you can all be engaged in activities that support each individual and everyone.

Since you will have so much imagination and vision available to you all, and because it will be easier for you all to talk to each other with such unity, you will notice how many desires you have in common. Many of these desires will be more easily manifested by interacting benevolently with beings from other planets and even beings right here on Earth now who are part of the spirit world—often referred to as religion, but in fact, religion is an attempt to codify the natural love of Creator. Now you will be seeing Creator's natural love in its actual vision. You, Melody, have felt today this wonderful energy more so than you have felt it at other times, yes?

Yes.

And Robbie has seen the beautiful dancing lights on his computer screen and felt the energy as well. I am speaking to the world, you understand—this being inclusive of you too. So I want you to know, then, that this will be a wonderful experience. I know that many of you will not live for another forty or fifty years because you are already on in your age, but you young ones probably will. I'm not saying that struggle and strife are going to instantaneously go away. No, this will continue for a time, but it won't go on forever. I felt it was very important today to remind you of that.

One of the ways you will be able to tell that struggle and strife are beginning to fade away is that as individuals you will feel very calm inside and you will not feel in your body or in your thoughts particularly conflicted about anything. This way or that way; yes or no—a lot of that will go away on the feeling level. Oh, you might still compare and analyze things in your mind, but you won't feel that tension that comes from inner conflict. This is not because you are being controlled but rather because the natural calm, comfortable and well-loved-by-Creator state of existence that exists for all beings—except lately in the past few thousands of years on Earth where you are all going to school here—will begin to reinstitute itself here where you are learning.

At first it might be a bit unusual, because you are not used to it. But then it will feel perfectly natural very quickly, because in your deep-sleep states—which you will notice when you are just waking up without an alarm clock, just waking up slowly—you will notice this relaxed state just before you start to come up a little more awake. It is that very relaxed and calm state. It is your natural state, even when you are awake. I wanted to give you this little notice today so that you understand that times are changing, and even though there might be some struggles yet to come, it won't be forever.

Explorer-Race Time Must Be Slow to Fulfill Your Purpose

I am a representative of your nearest biological cousins from another planetary system. Pleiadians are very similar to you in their biological makeup—a little different, but not a lot.

Are they some of the first ones who will visit us?

Maybe. Probably not, because others you might find more fascinating. You'll be surprised at how much of a desire there will be then for extraterrestrials to look different than you. There will also be some considerable suspicion if the people who get off the ships look almost exactly like you. People will say, "Well, I'm not sure if they're really from another planet." But if somebody gets off the ships and they are quite obviously not from Earth, this will be a bit reassuring.

Therefore, it is not likely the Pleiadians will visit you first, at least globally. No, it is more likely that some humanoid species will visit you. They will not look like you, but they will look enough like a humanoid that the people will say, "Well, they're definitely not from Earth. But they're not very frightening looking, they're kind of interesting looking. I'll bet they'll have some wonderful stories to tell us: where they're from, what they're like, why they're here." People will be excited.

But you're not one of the Pleiadians who look like us, you're a being of light, right?

I am Antiquarian. I am one of the teachers there.

Just there, not here?

They know me there.

There's so much channeling and material out now that ETs are going to land at any minute, and I know from Zoosh that they can't come here for several years, that we have to do this ourselves.

That's right, but the desire is understandable.

Can you say a little bit about that? Where are these people getting their information? Who are these beings who are channeling through them and saying that ETs are going to land tomorrow and save them?

You have to remember that many times spirits will speak in terms of terminology, saying, "We'll be here soon," but that timing does not convert directly to your sense of time. I cannot speak for these beings, nor those who are bringing the beings through. But I do know that a moment on another planet might easily be several years here, just as time here does not equate to other planets—not because they are not in the same physical substance, but because they do not exist for the same purpose.

"Purpose" really casts a completely different light on the way time and even physical matter function. Purpose generally requires a given set of qualifying conditions, applications and the forms (meaning the beings) to live in that purpose for a reason. The Explorer Race is a purpose, and therefore, while you are moving through your purpose, applying what you've learned and still learning a little bit, you must have time in a very slow sequence because you need to be absolutely certain that you've not only learned something but that what you've learned applies to all of the circumstances you are likely to encounter. Therefore, time must be very slow here so that one can thoroughly check on his or her physical creative process of application.

So if spirit says soon, then "soon," in time away from the Explorer Race's experience on Earth, would be . . . soon, because time is very quick there. But that same "soon" does not convert to Earth Explorer-Race experience, because here time must move very slowly. To you "soon" might be a week, all right? But that same statement "soon" might easily be fifty, sixty, seventy years in that time off this place, out of the realm of interactivity of the human race as you travel to the Moon and even Mars while you experience your time—which is not slow because you are not wise, but is slow so you can examine, learn and apply.

So from my point of view, though I cannot speak for all beings, it is probably a difference in language—even though the words are the same—having to do with a difference in time sequence and, most importantly, to understand it, a difference in purpose.

We were recently told that this is the only planet that has this kind of time, this structured slow time.

Very slow, so that one can understand even the nuances of doing something or not doing something. It is a wonderful environment in which to learn, but it has no greater application than is being applied right here—

meaning that this type of time only works if individuals are engaged in this purpose. It does not have a means or even a reason to exist in terms of being lived in by other beings, away from the Explorer Race's experience, unless they are interacting directly with the Explorer Race and are therefore of the Explorer-Race cycle of learning and application. If they are not part of that, then of course there is no reason to experience that time.

The Common Heritage between Pleiadians and Earth Humans Is Cultural

I don't know if you'll speak to this or not, but the Pleiadians are similar to us and at one point they were on Earth. We have a common heritage here. Didn't they choose to be perpetually benign and not go through the learning process that we're going through?

I think you might have made the mistake of assuming that you were all on Earth, but no. You have a common heritage, but that doesn't mean you were on the same planet.

How did we get a common heritage?

This is a very long story. But I would say that the common heritage is cultural.

But we look alike.

Yes, very similar, but not identical.

Aren't there internal organ differences and other . . . ?

There is some difference. But with a casual perusal, you might say, "Well, they certainly appear to be very much like us."

But they have more of a perfected look, right?

I don't think I would use that term.

They don't need to take on some of the characteristics that we need here for our lessons, as far as age or weight or disease or things like that, right?

No. As far as appearance, they are not involved in your purpose, so they do not necessarily appear like you. I'll say that. But I won't use the qualifiers you gave, because one might still be able to, on the basis of your question, create a hierarchy there. They are not better than you; they are simply not involved in what you are doing.

Right. Well, in contact cases they're always said to be so extraordinarily beautiful and full of light. Were you their teacher at the time when there was a closer contact with the Explorer Race and Zetas?

Yes.

Ah! You're definitely coming back. [Laughs.]

Feeling Readers Are amongst You

What advice do you have for people to benevolently get through . . . to face what's ahead of us for the next few years?

For those of you who do not wish to engage this type of communication or culture or even self-examination, I would say that a loving, supportive, nurturing religion would be very helpful, as long as it is not a religion that attacks other people, whether they are engaged in that religion or in another. That's an important qualifier for a religion. If the religion or the leaders of the religion are attacking other people, then I'd say you might wish to either change leaders or you might wish to look around for a religion that is more benevolent.

What do you see in front of us between now and when it gets very peaceful? What do you see that we're going to face?

Mostly inner conflicts will be the individual's big challenge. The feelings that are difficult to define will be a struggle for some people who simply do not understand what their body's feelings are telling them. Fortunately, you have amongst you now human beings who can tell other human beings what they are feeling. Some people have been born to be able to not only know what they themselves are feeling and define it, but they can sit in front of someone else and can help that other person know what their feelings are physically. If you are visiting a person like that, you might simply come in, "Hello, how are you?" and sit down and have a cup of tea or coffee or something. Then you, as the visitor, would start to talk. And then they might tell you to stop or ask you to talk about something else.

During the time of your talking, they will stop you from time to time and say, "This is what you're feeling. This is what those physical feelings mean." You might even say, "Well, you know, I have this discomfort," and they may be able to tell you what feelings are there. They might also be able to say, "Oh, you have this feeling over here, and there may be some correlation to that." But they will not be intended to be doctors or even healers; they will simply help you to understand the physical feelings in your body.

Many of you—and this is one of the main reasons I'm talking to you today—already have this capacity, and it has very often been a complication in your lives. But now others will need to know what their internal conflicts are and what those strange physical feelings mean in their body. Is it just tension? No. Tension is always physical feelings combined, many together, to form a cohesive group with certain traits in common. Once someone tells you, "That feeling means this and this and this and this and this"—not interpreting what the feelings mean as a psychiatrist or psychologist might do, but simply saying that these are the feelings that make up that tension, meaning "Oh, you are feeling grateful, you are feeling unhappy," something like that— then that kind of definition is not really an attempt to analyze you but it's giving you . . . not a score either, saying you are good or bad, but simply saying, "This is what that feeling means."

If you know what that is, then when you have that feeling in the future, you will be able to say, "Well, I'm having this experience." Then if you wish to pursue it with a therapist or a psychologist, the therapist or psychologist might find that such information will be useful to help you come to grips perhaps with some difficulties you have or to possibly be able to help you work through it. And then, "Do you have that feeling now?" says the therapist, and, "No, I don't have that anymore!" "Well, this is good, then." From time to time, besides going to your counselor or your therapist or psychologist, you will go back to the feeling reader who will tell you what you are feeling and perhaps say, "Oh, you seem to not have those feelings anymore."

So feeling readers are all amongst you now. Many of the people who have certain conditions also have this capacity, but not all. One of those conditions is dyslexia. Not everybody who has dyslexia can do this, but many of you can. There are other people who have other traits. Sometimes they might be highly sensitive people, and other times they might simply have been born with their trait, which has caused them nothing but confusion because they have experienced, when someone is talking to them, an awareness of that person's feelings. In that experience of communication, the feelings are so much more prominent from that person than the words they are saying, they might even become confused about the communication.

Yes, and respond to the feelings instead of the words.

This has happened for some people, and it has created misunderstandings and conflict. But if you all know that these feeling readers are amongst you and if those of you who have this skill are aware of it, then you can perhaps be of great assistance to your fellow beings. This is a skill that goes through all nations and cultures. There is no nation on Earth that does not have amongst its group feeling readers.

So this is your time, feeling readers. See if you can hone your skills. Perhaps you can find other feeling readers and you can practice on each other, and when you feel you are ready, you can then say, "Well, now, whatever else I am doing, I am going to make my feeling-reader skills available to my fellow human beings."

So in my understanding, we're looking at . . . how shall I say it? It's been called Earth changes or Earth turbulence perhaps—a more negative interaction among nations while they get things straightened out. But you feel that this is the most prominent thing we have to work on, our own understanding of ourselves and our own feelings?

Yes, because so many of your conflicts from one culture to another simply stem from the fact that people do not understand their own drives and feelings. And when feelings are not understood and the conscious mind of an individual is unable to understand your own physical body's language to you, one can develop as a compensation a self-destructive behavior that might harm you or others. Very often this is the cause of conflicts.

Even sometimes our weather aberrations can be caused by our feelings too, right?

It has been known. But that would require many, many people having similar conflicts perhaps.

So that's wonderful—the most important thing we can do is to understand our own feelings.

Not only is it the most important, but it is something for which help is readily at hand.

How would someone living in a small town or a city even find a person like that?

It is up to those people who have that skill. Once they feel they have gotten to the point where they can help others, then it is important for them to find each other. Perhaps through your communication tools that are available today, it would be good to set up even some kind of a means to communicate with each other: a feeling communication or a feeling reader's communication network of some sort. This could probably be done through your computers but also through the telephone or even face-to-face. I will leave that up to you and your culture's ability.

Hopefully, this article will move out far and wide in some form. Many of you out there who might read this, please pass it on to others in order that the word can get out as best as possible by this means. If it cannot get out any farther than you normally get your articles out, well, that's a good start. After all, it's not something that must be completely resolved and healed tomorrow, but any time to start would be good.

Remember Your Own Extraordinary Capacities to Create

So you've been watching the Explorer Race?

No, I am the teacher for Pleiadians. It is not my job to watch you.

But you've been aware of us?

Yes.

What heartens you most about the present moment, where we are at present?

Many of you have the same needs in common. It is known and understood that you are all hungry, that you need shelter, you need clothing and so on, and yet many of you need to feel that there is a purpose in life that is greater than your own immediate needs. This is something that is found very universally on Earth amongst human beings. That's an example.

The idea that we're so close is so wonderful.

I will now give a closing statement. I am here today to support and nurture you, to offer you friendliness and hope, and also to remind you of your own extraordinary capacities to create. In recent years, in the pages of the *Sedona Journal of Emergence!* and in many books, you have heard about benevolent magic and living prayer; you have read about the loving heart-warmth that many of you can feel, and many other good things. These are all granted to you now so that you can explore your own capacity to create benevolently for yourselves and others.

Please practice some of these things as they feel comfortable to you. I assure you, they will not only improve the quality of your lives, but they will help to prepare you to be in an alignment that will feel comfortable to you and welcome to you, so that you may not only feel welcome on planet Earth, but so that you can welcome others to planet Earth as well. Good night.

Thank you.

BENEVOLENT MAGIC
& LIVING PRAYER

Benevolent magic can only be used benevolently, even if it is accidentally (or otherwise) said in some way that isn't benevolent. It will still only work as long as the experience for everyone is benevolent, including those who cooperate consciously or otherwise with bringing about your request. Benevolent magic is a request, not just words. Many of you will feel energy after you say the request. The fundamentals of benevolent magic are what you say and how you say it. Benevolent magic is provided by loving beings to help allow you and train you as a global community to begin doing things that will support each and every one of you.

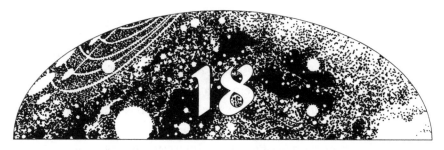

Sirian ET Studies Earth Tides

ET Visitor from Sirius and Arcturis
October 25, 2005

reetings. I am Sah-nahn-dah-nahnk'nunt'k'chah. It doesn't really relate to your alphabet. If we had Greek letters and numbers . . . let's just overlook that and say an ET visitor. I am now visiting your planet. I am not on the surface, but I have capabilities to observe the surface. I have been studying your tides. On our planet, we've been considering developing something along the lines of water. We have liquid, but we don't have water. We're not going to have saltwater as you know it, not even lightly saline water. It will be more like a clear water, but I'd say chemically speaking, it would probably be H_2O_2, possibly H_2O_3—but I think that would be a bit thick, so probably H_2O_2. We have not yet been able to artificially produce tides though, and I feel that this is the living aspect of water on your planet. So I've been studying tides for some time.

I can come through now because I'll be leaving your planet in about twenty minutes, but slowly, so my exit allows me to have this talk briefly with you. I am from a star system that is not that far away from your own, relatively speaking. It is in the Sirius star system, and because there are many planets with water there—though the water is not always the same chemical composition that you have—the idea of having water on a planet is welcome in that system. You might reasonably ask, why have I not studied the tides on planets there? Well, of course I have, and so have other members of the team. But the feeling is that the tides there are very slight, a difference perhaps of an inch or two. The idea of having a tide of, say, one or two feet, is much more of interest to the people of my planet.

The People on My Planet Are Interested in Contrasts

The people on my planet are interested in contrasts. That's what we're interested in. That's why we like to have the experience of contrast, somewhat of which you have on your planet. You have animals who crawl, walk, fly and swim. These are, you could say, varieties, but from our perspective, we would say they are contrasts. And of course, although your human beings all look generally alike, you have contrasts in some physical appearances. You have the female and the male, you have different colorings and, of course, you have quite a bit of contrasting personality groups.

Our planet is a little different. We have only a single sex, and reproduction is done through something not exactly mechanistic, but something that is a second or third cousin to cloning. Our approach to life, though, is one of a studied interest in contrasts. Our people do not crawl, for example, when they are youthful. There is an upright position immediately after the youth matures sufficiently to be mobile on its own. There is a marked desire for the accumulation of knowledge and wisdom. We are a thoughtful people in that sense. There is some interest in science, but the interest is much more so for social sciences. Therefore, if there is anything scientific being developed, such as the project I am working on, we always have consultants in the application and what you would call engineering fields that come in from other planets in the star system.

We are people who are different colors. We have a skin color that is blue, one that is green and another that is pale pink. We like that contrast. That's part of the reason we feel somewhat attracted to visiting your planet, since we feel a certain amount of kindred spirit there, even though the colors, of course, are not the same. Nevertheless, it is a similarity. We do not have what I would call male and female bodies. It is not even a cross between the two. We are humanoids, but there is no apparent sexual function. If you were to observe us, you would say, "Well, how do you reproduce?" and we don't, but we are able to have new generations.

The generations are not raised in a parental combine, such as you have, but they are raised in a loving, nurturing society not on our planet. They spend their first, oh, about one-tenth of their lifetime—what you would call a childhood—on another planet entirely, where there is something that is much more akin to a family environment as you would know it. This allows them to have more than one place to call home. They are not sent here at some arbitrary age, but rather they are allowed to come here to visit. And if they like it, then of course they are welcome to stay. However, if they prefer to stay on the other planet, they are welcome there as well. Of course, the people on the other planet look very much like us, but they do have a male and female of the species. So this is where we differ. I have tried to cover certain salient points. Do you have any questions?

Yes. What is your lifetime? What is one-tenth of your lifetime?

Well, in relationship to your time measurement system—of course, we don't experience what you experience, but trying to relate it to your years—we are in existence for about 940 years. Of course, since there is that existence, there is quite obviously no strain or stress as you know it, no discomfiture—that's the word.

If you like contrast so much, then how did you come to have only one type of asexual body? One would think you would have many types of reproductive possibilities if you like contrasts, if you like variety.

Variety is not necessarily the same thing as contrast. So that's different. We like contrasts, but we don't want to overdo it, eh? [Laughs.] So we are happy with the system that we have. It also avoids a certain amount of what we perceive to be pitfalls that other societies have developed. In our society, since everyone is the same physiologically, this tends to limit certain types of distractions. I suppose you could say, we've decided to avoid sexuality. That is one way of looking at it, but on the other hand, we simply prefer to put our efforts in other directions.

We Are Interested in the Water for Its Beauty

How do you live on a planet without water?

Well, you are assuming that water is necessary for all life. Of course, it isn't.

You don't consume liquids or have liquids?

We do not require liquids as something separate from the food that we consume. We consume a food that is . . . oh, I would say in the same general family as what you might call a fruit or a vegetable. And that has sufficient moisture in it for us. We are only interested in the water for its beauty; we do not need it for our personal consumption. We have noted in our star system the beauty of water planets, and of course, if we do include water on our planet, we will invite beings who live in the water, if they wish to come and live in places like that. Right now we have a fairly dry planet in the southern hemisphere, and we would probably have the bulk of the water down there.

You're social scientists. How would you get the oxygen and hydrogen to make water? What would you use as a source?

Well, you have to keep in mind that oxygen and hydrogen are in abundant quantity just about everywhere, but I understand that you want specifics. We have a form of mineral on our planet in vast supply—actually much more vast than we find compatible with our lifestyle—and that mineral does contain both of those chemicals. And with very slight compression, very slight, it immediately turns into something that is akin to water as you know it. But as I say, it would probably be H_2O_2.

Why do you say you have too much for your comfort?

Imagine a pile of stones every five or six feet in your cities. Would this not be inconvenient?

Yes! How did it get there?

This is the way the planet has always been. No one came and dropped it off, as far as I know.

[Laughs.] You have a sense of humor!

Yes! I like that about us. We feel that it is something we have in common. From my experience, those cultures that are interested in social science often have that. So the planet has always been this way, as far as I know. Thus the development of our cities has involved the moving of these stones, and it's a big job. Not long ago—oh, twenty-five Earth years ago—someone discovered that putting a very slight amount of pressure, not what you would call hand pressure, but a slight amount of externalized pressure on these rocks, turned them almost immediately into a liquid. This was a little thicker, as I say, than your water, something that resembles H_2O_3. So it was discovered that, with a small amount of chemical work by the other planetary engineers, it could be easily converted into H_2O_2, but not what you have.

So it was the engineers who suggested that instead of trying to figure out what to do with all these stones, we consider allowing them to place a small field of pressure around the stones, and then they would liquefy. They discovered that once the liquefaction took place, there would be, from their point of view, no apparent loss or what you would call evaporation. Therefore, instead of having piles of stones, we could have a large sea. And with a sea, it might be possible then to have vessels that go upon the sea and so on. And we could experiment to see whether we would enjoy that. If it did not work out for us within our social system, then they could always put it back the way it was.

Oh, that's amazing! There would be no byproduct, no debris laying around? The entire rock would liquefy?

The entire rock appears to liquefy. I have seen it done. The first time I saw it done, I was quite startled. It was a very small amount of pressure, something like twenty-five pounds per square inch or something. It wasn't much.

Do you have a moon, then? Because you need a moon to cause tides, I think.

Well, you see, we don't. That is why in order to have tides, we would need to have some artificial method to create this. We inquired of the engineers whether a moon would be something to consider, and they said that because it would have other effects on all liquids, it wouldn't be a good idea. It would be much more trouble than it would be worth doing this or engineering it. They recommended an artificial tidal system if we wanted it.

Like a motor in the bottom of the sea or something?

Well, it would involve a system. I don't really know; I'm not a scientist. It would involve a system that would create motion somewhere in the sea in various places. I don't really know how it works, but it would create a tide if we want it. It won't create surf as you know it. It won't do that, but it can create a tide. And the nice thing about a tide is that it's predictable. You know when it's going to happen; you know when it's going to go up, and you know when it's going to go down. But it would be motion that might be attractive.

We Are Humanoids

If I were to look at you, what would I see?

Well, we are humanoids. We don't look like human beings. Our eyes are a little bigger than yours, and our mouths are a little wider. We do not have much of a nose, but there is some—it is noticeable. We have very small openings for our ears with some tissue around it. We have a very small thumb and four long fingers. I am thinking that the thumb may or may not have the same purposes. You will press your thumb and fingers together to grasp and so on. We don't do that. Our thumb performs other tasks.

We do not have toes as you know them, but our forefoot terminates in three separate paths. And our internal organs are a little different. We do have a heart. Of course, we have a stomach. We do not have an elimination system like you do. We do not eat much, but what we do eat, we utilize it all. And if there is any waste material, it is exhaled either by our breath or through pores in the surface of our body, not unlike sweat to you, though it does not come out in a liquefied form as yours does. It comes out in a gas.

A gas! So a desert planet! How do you clean yourselves? You don't take baths or showers, right?

That would require water, would it not? We don't have much of a need for that, but from time to time we have sort of an ionic radiation system, for lack of a better term. That's the term I'm going to use. It is a chamber that you go into, and there is some radiation and it performs a function that you might loosely refer to as a standing bath. But there is no liquid involved whatsoever.

So your thumbs are not opposable digits, but you use them for something?

They are used for the plucking of an instrument and occasional other things. We do like music. That's another reason we are interested in you as a people—you seem to be very interested in music.

Yes! How tall are you?

Well, I personally am about four foot nine. But I am short compared to the rest of my people. Almost everyone is five foot five or five foot six or something like that.

Our Education System Is Available for All

Are you an elder, or did you just happen to be available?

I am about four-fifths of the way through my life span. But that would not be considered an elder in my society. Of course, we may not revere elders any more than we would acknowledge the value of young ones, so the accumulation of wisdom within an individual is not necessarily considered to be creating them to be of greater value, because our wisdom is available through our educational system. If someone uncovers something new, they immediately inject it into the educational system that is available for all.

Inject it . . . and then how do you get it out? How does someone else get that wisdom out?

It is technical. It is like if you inject something into your machines that . . . what do you call them?

Computers? Oh, I see! We would add information to the database, which would then be available to other people. But you don't have computers—what do you have?

It is only necessary to lay the palm of one's hand upon something that looks like a plate. It is not metal; it is akin to glass. Then one considers or thinks a moment about what you have either extrapolated or discovered, and it is then acquired.

We've heard that before from Andromedans and Zeta Reticulans.

Yes, I think we may have acquired that technology from other planets.

Do you then educate your children when they choose to come to live with you?

No, they get all of that education before they come. Of course, they can assimilate more when they arrive, but they get their basic education, acculturation and so on, on the other planet.

How do you think this happened? Are you a colony from that other planet that changed? Who's the predecessor, you or the other planet?

I think we are. The other planet might have broken off a long time ago. I really don't know. It's always been that way, according to my culture. It seems to be in what you might call the dim past. But from time to time, there are beings on my planet who enjoy going to visit the other planet and participating in family life, and occasionally the transfer goes the other way. But this seems to have been something that was chosen a long time ago. I really cannot answer that question in any reasonable, rational way.

How interesting. So are they, like you, focused on one thing? Mechanical experts or experts in science? Or do they have a variety of interests on that other planet?

Oh no, they are like us. Their only difference is that they like family life and they are interested in the raising of children. That's the only difference.

So then, they're not the engineers you were talking about?

Oh, no.

Ah, I see. I misunderstood. So you have access to other skills of people on other planets that you can . . .

Yes, yes, in our star system where there is a great deal of knowledge about water and so on. There are a lot of water planets here.

Supposedly ours came from there.

I have heard that, yes.

Or it was created exactly like one there. I'm not too sure.

I'm not either!

Music on Our Planet

You like music. So do you get together in groups, or does everybody play, or do some play and some listen? How does that work?

It is not unlike your planet. Some play and some listen. The instruments are different. We do not have woodwinds. The instruments are all involved with the pressing of various spots on the instrument itself, and then the instrument produces a variety of sounds. For example, one might take, let's say, the four digits of our hand, and one might press with one digit in a spot on the instrument, and that provides a great deal of variety of tone. However, in the pressing of another digit, while keeping the first finger pressed, then it creates variations of tone.

For example, you have a sharp and a flat. You might have a note, but then you have the sharp and the flat. It is something like that, where the pressing of different digits or multiple digits can produce variations of the same tone. So one still has to use a certain degree of skill to play the instrument, but it does allow the integration of multiple tonalities. I believe you have something similar on your planet.

Are these stringed instruments, like violins or guitars?

Oh no, nothing like that.

More like synthesizers?

We have a little problem with your stringed instruments, because sometimes they use parts of other beings. But no, it would be more closely like your electronic instruments.

Ah, right. Well, that's great! So how many people are there on your planet? Thousands? Millions? Billions?

Oh, let me consult my device here. It looks like we now have a little more than 430,000.

On a planet . . . in what proportion to Earth? Half as big? Twice as big?

About two-thirds the size of Earth.

Really?! So you have plenty of room! Do you all live in cities? Or do you congregate in smaller groups?

This is why we can turn the southern hemisphere, which is drier than the northern hemisphere, into an ocean, because nobody lives there. So we don't have that many people, and the idea of having an ocean on almost half of the planet . . . it will not impinge on the space where we live.

It sounds like a great idea.

We Study Other Cultures for the Sheer Pleasure of It

So what do you study? Do you go to other planets and study the inhabitants?

Yes, we go to other planets, mostly where we're invited. This is an exception, but I knew I would be able to come here and not impact your people by my appearance or anything. So it was considered acceptable to come here. I wouldn't be visible nor detectable, so in that way I would not create any problems. But generally speaking, we go where we're invited—to places, of course, where we feel a sense of kindred spirit. We are looking forward to the time when we'll be able to come here openly, but of course that won't be for a while.

Could we interact in the same room and see each other and hear each other?

Yes.

Ah! So you're similar in vibration to us, then?

We can have an experience of multiple vibrations. We could exist in the one you live in now, but we feel that you will continue to expand your capabilities there also.

Yes, absolutely. So you could interact with the Andromedans, who are . . . I don't have a new word. We used to call it eighth-dimensional. You could also interact with them, right?

Well, no. There is a range we can interact with, and I think you will eventually have the same range too.

Three, four, five—something like that?

Something like that, yes.

So why do people invite you? What is their purpose in inviting you?

Just to be friendly, that's all. We don't have much to offer. We just like to study how other people do things. We are attracted to cultures and civilizations where contrast is notable. That's our favorite thing, eh? So that's really it. We don't have much to bring, no box of Cuban cigars.

[Laughs.] So is your technology inherited or purchased?

Well, no, we don't buy things in our culture. I think that's fairly unique to your culture. In our world, people provide things for each other without buying and selling. The buying-and-selling thing is not typical to the rest of the universe, in my limited experience.

So it's like bartering, or if somebody needs something, they just give it to you?

It's not like bartering. Bartering is an exchange.

So if you need something and someone has it, they just make it available to you?

That's right. And we don't consider it ours. If they need it back, then they can take it back. We have not had anybody do that, but it certainly would be all right.

So your spaceships are given to you by whom?

The vehicles we travel in are not our own. We come in vehicles from others. And therefore, we don't have any vehicles of our own.

Who specifically provides the vehicles? Anyone we've ever heard of?

Other planets in Sirius.

So there's a lot movement back and forth amongst the planets, then?

Oh, yes. This is typical everywhere—other than Earth, of course.

Other than Earth, right. So I'm still trying to understand the social scientist.

Well, you understand, I am using that as an example because we study other people's cultures—not because we're trying to find things to do in our own culture, but rather because of the sheer pleasure of it.

So give me an example of someone who invited you to come, where you went, what you studied and if you enjoyed this.

There was a planet in a star system that I don't think you know about. It's quite a ways off. I was able to get a ride there. [Laughs.] They were interested in us because of our interest in studying other cultures—they also had that interest. So instead of studying their culture, we wound up just comparing notes, you might say. That was interesting, because we found that in the process of this communication, there were some beings we knew mutually. And the planet was very far. Traveling at a high rate of speed, it took us . . . oh, in terms of your time, it took us almost four hours to get there.

[Laughs.] Four hours?

Well, this is really quite a long time. And these people knew many of the same beings we knew. That was quite a surprise—I was intrigued.

A Culture of Fixed Beings

Say something about these beings you visited. What did they look like? What did they do? We're very interested in our neighbors, since we can't get out and visit them—yet.

They're not your neighbors.

Well, other people out there—since we can't get off the planet yet.

Well, these . . . they were quite different. They're not mobile. They're not humanoids. They remain in a fixed position.

But they communicate to you?

They communicate by touch, but they cannot touch us, since they do not have any arms, legs or appendages whatsoever. We touch them. They remind me of stone, but they are not that. So there's no similarity in culture to yours that I can see in any way.

So you touch them, and they communicate to you and you communicate to them?

That's right.

On a feeling basis? Or with pictures?

Yes, like that.

Like a communion.

Yes!

But they had traveled?

No.

The mutual friends had come to them?

That's right.

We've talked to beings like that before too. They can commune with others across the creation and not move.

This is not unusual. You can do that too. It's just that you don't necessarily believe it.

Well, we're beginning to.

Yes!

The Travelers Are Interested in Comparative Cultures

What about the third group that were mutual friends? What type of beings were they?

These are travelers. They are interested in comparative cultures, meaning that if they find beings who are lacking in something in a culture, they will try to create a tie between a culture they feel is similar and the culture they have found. Then that similar culture helps the other culture where needed.

They can learn qualities from each other that they don't have but the other one has?

That might be one situation. It depends what's lacking. You asked me something about that other culture that knew us both, right? That's what I can tell you.

So when you met them, what did you learn from them?

We learned that there was a culture that would be good for us to visit. This has happened several times.

Can you just tell me a little bit about the third culture, the travelers? What did they look like? What did they do? What are their interests?

Well, I don't know too much about them. They're humanoid. They're very tall; to us they were giants. They'd be quite tall to you as well—they're a little more than eight feet tall. They seem to be very fascinated with food. I don't think it's because they eat that much, but they are particularly interested in flavors. I noticed that when they spoke to us, they were quite keen to know if they could try our foods, just a sampling. And they would have the smallest amount. They were not looking to consume so much as they were fascinated with flavors. One finds this kind of thing in different cultures. One culture likes color, one likes flavor and so on.

They have arms that are not proportionately the same as your own; they are shorter. They have about ten toes per foot, and the toes are very long. They use their toes like you might use fingers. So the instruments and mechanization they might work a lot with their toes. They are wide but thin. I don't know what else to describe them as.

They sound fascinating. Do you talk to them, or is there some other means of communication?

It is a knowing and not really a spoken language. This allows, I think, for differences in language to not be a factor, not a block, you understand? I think this is not at all unusual, in my encounters with beings from other planets.

And among your own people, do you talk to each other?

Yes.

Can you also do the kind of communication you did with the tall ones with your own people?

Yes. We don't have to do it with our own people, but we can do it with others. This is not unusual, in my experience traveling. It is not at all unusual to come across a culture that speaks to each other but will commune with a foreign culture. It is much easier than learning a language that may not even be pronounceable, given your own language idiom.

And your physiological differences.

That's right—that's a big thing.

It would be wonderful just to find out the causes of how they got that way and how you got that way. We on Earth now were sort of created from samples of beings from the neighboring galaxies, you know? But it will be fun when we go out to travel to find out how each different group of beings got to be that way.

In my travels, I have found that there are usually specific groupings on different planets that meet to discuss such things with other cultures who come to visit. So these people would be trained and could answer such questions, usually with visual arts and so on, to give a complete full spectrum of acquaintanceship for those who are interested. There are always people interested who are travelers like that. We have someone like that on my planet, some group. I am not of that group, but there are those.

Life on Our Planet

Let's go back to your planet. You talked about buildings. Do you live in homes or apartment buildings? Or do you live close to the ground?

Quite close to the ground, and somewhat underground, because it is a dry planet and it gets a bit warm. So the underground aspect allows a place to go during the bright time—the sun time, you might say. During the hot part of the day, it is typical to go to this underground area that is . . . oh, by your measurements, eighteen or nineteen feet below ground, which is much cooler and not in the direct light of the sun (we have a sun also). So that's what our dwellings are like. The surface of the dwelling does not come up much more than, oh, eight or ten feet at the highest point.

Do you live alone? In groups?

Generally speaking, eight to ten individuals will live in a single dwelling, each having their own personal space if desired, and it often is. But we like to do things together. This is not based upon a family unit, but more on personal affinity—friends, you might say.

So you clone a particular person, and then the clone looks like that person?

No, we have a gene pool, and different variations in that gene pool are cloned. We don't have the idea of cloning identical people. We are not units. We have some variety in our personality and some slight variety in our appearance, not unlike yourselves. The difference in your appearance is also slight, when taking into account the vast similarity level of your appearance.

Yes. So someone is cloned and sent to the other planet, and then when they come back to live, how do they meet the people with whom they gain the affinity? Or do the young people bond on the other planet?

There are social situations, a lot of social situations. Groups gather to experience music and theater and things like that. So there are multiple opportunities for making friends.

You don't use money and you don't need to eat, so you don't actually work, right?

You have forgotten—we do eat.

A little bit, right?

Well, in comparison to you, but we don't consider it a little.

So do you have people who grow that food, or does it grow naturally? Do you have divisions of work on the planet or things that people are interested in?

We don't have divisions of work, but there are orchards where the food grows. The roots go down very deep, I've been told, and different individuals who like to do that kind of work choose to do it. And if they have times when they don't like to do it, then there are others who also like to do it. So there are usually more than enough people who like that kind of thing, and it provides enough for our needs and sometimes a little extra for the occasional visitors we have.

So like on most planets, then, people sort of do what they want to do, what they like to do, right?

Oh, yes. That is the most practical way.

Animals Are There for Consultation

What do you think when you look at us, with our having to go to work and our money and our wars and all that?

Well, of course, your wars and violence are very alarming, but from our perspective, we don't consider the variety of your choice of experiment in profession to be a bad thing. We realize that you do not have access to your full knowledge and wisdom, so all things considered, we feel you are doing quite well with what you have available for you.

Making it up as we go along, yes? [Laughs.]

Well, you do have to experiment. I don't see what else you could do, given that you are not in contact with other civilizations that are more stable. And the stable civilizations that you do have are generally not influential.

What do you mean by that?

Well, you have beings on your planet who live very much the same way and have lived very much the same way for thousands of years. They are just not humans. They are available for consultation as to how to create stability, but your people at this time are not in a wide embrace of that available education. There have been, over time, from what I have studied on your planet, civilizations that have assimilated that knowledge and wisdom, and in certain ways, have been able to practice a human form of that and were able to create stability for a fixed population—by "fixed," I mean very carefully not exceeding certain numbers. But those civilizations are not in as great a number as they once were, nor are they able to maintain stability anymore because of the inroads of external civilizations that have cut off their ability to support themselves.

Can we put some names on this?

Well, some of what I think you call native peoples have in the past established a very well-organized system that supported their society. And a lot of this was done through interaction of sharing wisdom from what you call animals.

And then other groups would come in and violate that, yes.

Well, they would come in and exert their civilization, promoting it as something superior. This seems to be a problem you are having at the moment with excessive energy in that direction. I think in time that will cease to exist, since that is not really in your nature but appears to be an aberration of your temperament for the moment. That is, you are not born with that quality. It is conditioned or in reaction to violence and aggression and control—all of these things. You're not born that way. None of you are born that way, as far as I've been able to observe in my short time here.

I Am Here to Study the Tides

Do you have the ability to travel in time? Can you look at us in various stages of our growth, like a thousand years ago or ten thousand years ago?

No. I can travel in a ship that may have that capacity, but I have not studied your people excessively. I am here to study the tides.

Right. You have sensing equipment on the ship that allows you to see humans one by one.

Well, when I was on your planet . . . I've already removed myself during our conversation, as I said I would. But when I was on your planet, I wasn't in a ship.

You were walking around?

No. I was underground.

And you brought equipment . . . your ship can go underground?

It wasn't my ship, as I have said. I was on someone else's vehicle to get here, and their vehicle could go underground, but not in a way that your society or technology could perceive. So that's why it was all right to come. The location where we arrived was also not in any way going to disturb your society, but I cannot reveal that location.

And either on the ship or in that location was technology that allowed you to study the humans on the surface?

No. It allowed me to study the tides. You seem to be confused. You think that I am here to study the humans, but I am not. I'm interested in your society, as far as contrasts go, but I am here to study the tides, or I was anyway. I'm off the planet now.

I just wondered how you saw the humans or how you saw the tides.

I do understand that. That's why I was giving you my observations. But I wasn't here to study your culture, nor have I made any effort to go into the past to study your culture, because I was not here to study your culture.

I see. I was just trying to get the method by which you were able to see us, that's all.

I understand, and of course I am avoiding telling you some of that [laughs] because the beings who allowed me to travel on their vehicles said that you're not supposed to be told that right now. The reason is quite obviously that you're probably developing that technology yourselves—not in a public way, but I am assuming that this is probably in the experimental stage somewhere on the planet.

I see. So you're a passenger on someone's ship?

Yes. We don't have our own ships—I said that.

I know, but I thought that you actually had borrowed a ship yourself. I didn't realize you were . . .

No, we don't know how to fly one. I wouldn't have the slightest idea.

Then who are the beings whose ship you are traveling on?

Oh, it's not anyone in particular. It's just whoever happens to be going this way who has access to facilities.

It's like a passenger ship or something?

No, whoever happens to be going this way.

What civilization has the ship? Is it somebody who . . .

You mean, the particular one I traveled on?

That you're on now.

That I'm on now? Oh, this is a different one, not the one I came here on.

Well, tell me about both of them.

I came here on a vehicle from Sirius, and I am now on a vehicle from the Pleiades.

And what was the vehicle from the Pleiades doing on the planet?

It wasn't on the planet. I cannot explain to you how I got from the planet to the vehicle, I'm sorry.

Is it like, "Beam me up, Scotty?"

"Cannot explain" means cannot explain. It does not mean that I don't have the knowledge.

It means you're not allowed to tell.

Exactly. And that always and only means one thing . . .

That we're developing it ourselves.

That's right.

Ah, in some mysterious, underground, super-secret place.

From what I've been told, it's not underground and it's not that secret.

[Laughs.] We'll have to look into that.

Appreciate the Variety and Beauty You Have on Earth

Well, this is extraordinarily interesting! What can we gain from you? What would you like to tell the people who read this?

I feel that your planet is profoundly beautiful, even now. When one approaches it from space, it is astonishingly beautiful. And on the Earth you have many beautiful people and a wide variety of plants and animals still. It is perhaps very easy to take this for granted, I suppose, living here and seeing many of these things day to day. I would say, appreciate and enjoy the variety and beauty you have on your planet, because in the many other lives you may have on other planets someday, you will not see that variety and beauty. You will see beauty of its own kind, but such variety is very rare in my experience. You will probably, if you travel around to different planets, long to go home to experience that beauty. So notice the beauty around you and cherish it.

I'm extraordinarily pleased and grateful that you took the time to talk to me.

You are most welcome. It was a pleasure, and I appreciate the cultural contrast of our exchange. Good night!

Good night, thank you.

❋   ❋   ❋

This is Arcturis.

Arcturis, I have a few questions about the being and the planet. Why were there piles of rock all over the planet?

I believe those were left in the past.

From mining or something?

That's right, from mining that had nothing to do with that culture. It was just left there. It wasn't left because of some digging in that planet, but the mineral was from another planet. That's why it was a surprise when the scientists from afar experimented with that rock, because it had no resemblance to anything on the planet. So it was a surprise when that stone liquefied. It was apparently from some other planet someplace else.

Which of the two cultures was first, the asexual or sexual?

You seem to be confused about that. They don't have a sexual culture, period.

Oh, they clone even on the male and female side?

Yes. I've looked at the culture. If they have male and female, it's not . . . I cannot perceive it. They look identical to me. Perhaps it is male and female only in feelings.

So which came first? That planet or the one of the fellow who spoke?

I think it was the family planet.

And then some of these beings just wanted to be . . . there must be a lot of feelings, because they didn't want the distraction of that.

Oh, I don't know if that it was that. I think it was just variety. The other planet where the family action is, is very small, meaning that there's only a very limited amount of space to have a culture. And on the planet where this being is from who spoke to you, there is much more space to have a culture. So the variety . . . I think they had to go to a different planet because there just wasn't room.

Right. Thank you very much.

You are welcome. Good night.

Good night.

Feelings Unite All Forms of Life

The Diplomat and the Observer
January 25, 2006

reetings. I am a representative of the first species that human beings will meet when your journeys into space become more oriented with the general population. These are not the military journeys that go out tentatively and cautiously, but the journeys that involve many people coming out into space for fun—you might call it commercial. In order for this to be allowed—meaning not only that you have the capacity to do so technologically and so on, but that the beings (the races of beings, if you like; the forms of beings is what I'd prefer to call it) welcome you and allow ourselves to be found—we have certain ethical moralities that we require from another species, especially one venturing out into the vast worlds beyond our own.

Are Humans Ready to Be Exposed to Other Forms of Life?

I'm going to say this because it has been said at the deep level to all contactees on Earth, and you will recognize it. I'm also going to say it so that the people of Earth have some general idea of the moral and ethical qualities that you are all striving for and how those qualities will coincide very nicely with the benevolent and loving forms of life in space beyond your own planet who will welcome you, assist you and support you on your ventures and adventures. This is what we require from all forms of life who meet us. We do not expect perfection, but we expect dedication toward these purposes. We require that you, in your own culture, have these tenets.

One is that you treat your children lovingly and supportingly. If treatment happens to children anywhere on the planet that is other than that . . . not just an outburst because the child has done something that the parent is concerned about, puts his or her hand too close to a flame or something, but the treatment on an ongoing basis of all children must be loving, supportive, nurturing. And regardless of whose children are involved, this treatment must be pursued. There must be no judgment of different cultures (the way they are with their family's children), and the cultural elements of families and different nationalities must be nurtured.

How do you treat your older people, those who are elderly? Are they treated lovingly and kindly? Are they encouraged to speak their wisdom? Are they supported to move through the difficulties that occur as the body gets older? Is there universal support—meaning, wherever they go or whoever they are exposed to, just like families with children, is there support available? Not just officially, but from families? Is there a sense of family on Earth—not an enforced culture, but welcoming all life so that what is needed is available? So that the elderly are not only encouraged to speak their wisdom but have the opportunity to speak their wisdom as long as it is something that provides benefit and benevolence? This does not have to be something instructional; it could be life experience. It could even be entertainment—that is acceptable. In short, are your actions based upon a desire to fulfill all people's needs, hopes and dreams, and to encourage them to be fulfilled?

How do you treat your prisoners who have committed some crime against another member of your planet? Not just a shortcoming, but how do you treat those who have committed a crime intentionally or otherwise? It is possible to commit a crime that hurts others that is unintentional, done in ignorance—how are these people treated? Are they nurtured and supported? Are they educated to become knowledgeable of the cultural conditions they have crossed over? Are they given the support they need during the time of this education? Are they treated humanely? This is most important.

How do you treat your people who have handicaps, whether they are physical or, as it is called, mental? Do you recognize the traits and qualities in them that balance these handicaps? Very often a personality trait becomes more pronounced and inspires others. One finds this typically amongst children who do not seem to have a desire to excel mentally or cannot do so but have some winning personality characteristics. Or one also finds that when people are unable to walk or see or some such thing, that they have some form of personality or even some physical characteristic that is often admired or appreciated. Do you not see these things right away? Are there people in your cultures and societies, perhaps many people, who point this out and say, "Look, this person has something wonderful to offer regardless of the great challenge that befalls him"?

Do you seek out each other's cultures as an enjoyable experience? You have made great progress there, since different culture's foods have become very popular, and as a result, very often the culture is appreciated more. You have made progress there, and we feel good about that.

Do you seek the planet upon which you are living to be whole and complete? You must live, you must exist—do you seek that the planet be welcome as itself? We do not expect you to have the technology that many of our forms of life have. We will, of course, support you in acquiring this technology that does not have very much impact on the planet upon which you are living, in order to sustain a very comfortable quality of life for all peoples. If you seek this, if you are desiring that the planet upon which you are living is whole and complete unto itself, if you are prepared to let go of what you take from the planet to make into what you need, this is also considered a desirable thing.

How do you welcome the skills and capacities of what you call the animals? Do you look upon them as strictly forms of life rather than lesser beings? Do you have a ranking for animals, considering some to be more valuable and others to be less so? This is considered a marker to know that you are not ready as a culture to be exposed to other forms of life.

Animals Will Prepare You to Meet ETs

Other forms of life will often remind you, at least in some remote way, of a form of life you may have on Earth. You will say, "My gosh, you look like . . ." and then you'll fill in the blank in your own mind. Sometimes it will simply be a cultural phenomenon, in which you as an individual are reminded of some other form of life (not a human being) when meeting a form of life in the beyond. And when you do that, it can unintentionally create an attitude within you. Practice meeting those forms of life who will resemble forms of life you now have on your planet, and know that all those forms of life you have on your planet now are intended to prepare you for the wise and welcoming forms of life. This will not only provide you with the means to have a much happier and more comfortable life on your own planet and in your travels in space, but also, we would feel comfortable if you would welcome us for our appearance and our culture.

You have on your planet now forms of life of the first hundred species you will meet, other than human. Granted, they do not look exactly like the forms you will meet in space, but in some cases, there is a distinct resemblance, and in other cases, there may be only a very distant and vague resemblance. Your artists sometimes draw suggestive pictures like this, and there have been those whom you call contactees who have also drawn pictures when they were able to or given descriptions when they could recall of the beings they met, and people have said, "This reminds me vaguely of . . ." meaning this or that form of life already on your planet.

We know that you are expected to be what is called in your English language the Explorer Race. This means that you will all have a tendency and a desire to migrate to space and explore, and that you have and are born with a natural curiosity. Given the nature of this obvious factor of all the peoples on your planet, regardless of their appearances, we must accept the fact that the Great Being who has supported all life in this universe must have a purpose here. We then are prepared to welcome you, to recognize that you must have some very important qualities that this Great Being we all love and respect has endowed you with. I grant that from a distance, this is not always apparent to us, but we trust that it is so.

Therefore, we prepare for your arrival in this way—not just, as I said, those initial probes out into space that are happening even now, but the arrival of families with children and the elderly who are flying out into space even for a few hours to enjoy the wonderful beauty, the sight of your own planet at a distance and the perhaps clearer pictures of the stars and your own satellite . . . the Moon, yes? These flights will truly herald the awakening and the desire to awaken to some larger quality of interaction with all beings.

Look toward what you call the animals as your opportunity to train for that and of course toward each other, to those who might look different or act different. Look toward the eyes of those beings when you see them. There is not a single being on Earth of these hundred beings and all of the animals I am aware of who does not demonstrate its soul personality, the personality provided by the Great Being, and who cannot show you with the looks and expressions in its eyes (sometimes significantly, and sometimes you have to look closely) of feelings identical to your own. This is intended so that you will know, honor and trust that these feelings unite all forms of life.

We have these feelings too. We want to know that you will be looking for them, just as we will be looking for them in you, so that no matter what languages or forms of communion you have with us, we will all be able to instantly recognize the feelings and know that we must move more slowly, or you must act more peacefully, or something like that. You all recognize certain feelings in the eyes of each other, such as fear or happiness, annoyance or pleasure—in short, basic feelings. But there are many others that you can learn by studying your own eyes and the eyes of your friends or companions.

We Are Observing How You Treat Each Other

There is one last thing that we look to your planet for to observe and wonder if you are truly ready to meet us: How do you treat each other when you are angry or upset with each other, regardless of the justification? I'm not talking about criminal acts here; I'm talking about feelings from person to person. How do you treat each other? Learn to treat each other based upon what works to create a more benevolent experience with each other—not just who's right and who's wrong.

There is no question that it might be provable who is right and who is wrong. But in my experience and in the experience of the elders of all forms of life beyond your own planet, regardless of such proof, the ultimate desire and the practical desire (in terms of the reality of living together) remains: Can you forgive? And can that forgiveness result in welcoming and restoring the personality of all beings? I know sometimes that people transgress in ways that harm you, and you must speak sharply. Other times people transgress in ways that you fear might be harmful—then it is time to educate.

I know you desire to encourage cultural benevolence—meaning within the family, within the community, within the world—and we encourage this. But how do you do it? Look toward how you wish to be treated. The Great Being of All always teaches that: how you wish to be treated as a person, how you wish to be supported and how you need to be supported and treated in your day-to-day life. If you can desire to do this, even if you have not perfected this—and we do not expect perfection, given the challenges that all life faces on your world—then we can welcome you with many ways to know and understand.

We believe and have seen at a distance that there are those amongst you who can, as you say, talk to the animals, who can understand the great teachings they have to offer you, who can even herald that their appearance has a great resemblance to the appearance of one of the forms of life you will meet in your space journeys. They can teach you not only about the culture, desires, needs and hopes of that form of life but about how you can best interact with that culture in order to be supported and encouraged, as well as what you can offer to that culture and what that culture can offer to you. Be alert to this, because you will have the opportunity to be supported.

We do not expect perfection, but we do hope that you will desire to have . . . not perfection, because you are constantly changing (and even forms of life in space change as well), but we do hope that you desire to have a form of perfection that strives for these points that I have mentioned today. There may be other cultural points that different cultures you meet hold dear, and they may even offer you technology or philosophy that supports you to achieve them if you find them desirable. And of course, there will be many forms of technology and philosophy offered to you, if you so desire, that will support great comfort on Earth and for your peoples to explore.

Do you desire this strictly in order to have more? Or do you desire it so that everyone on the planet can, be they human being or be they what you have in the past called animals, or be they even what you know to be microbes and other small or greater forms of life—massive trees, the planet herself perhaps? Do you desire that all beings are served by this? We will notice.

It is not our job to judge you, nor do we do so, but we must observe certain desires and hopes and true signs—yes, signs—of your striving for these qualities in order to welcome you as a brother or sister, a fellow traveler in space. We are watching. We have seen good signs, and we hope that you choose to emulate or hold these qualities dear. The beings you will meet will all be travelers like you—as you might do if you went to explore. You would not bring your culture with you; you would reach out tentatively and say, "Look, here we are." They will be from far away.

So we'll meet them at space stations or something like that?

That is up to you. You will meet them when they feel—when we feel, if you like—that you are ready. We will not spring it on you [laughs]. In short, we will not thrust ourselves on you until we feel you are ready. There have been others, the early pioneers into space by various cultures, who have seen beings in space and have been startled, and who reported this to their various scientific, cultural and political agencies. But this has not, in large part, been given to the greater cultures of peoples.

Most cultures of peoples have had to invent and create or imagine what forms of life in space are like. Therefore, there have been some kind and genuine inventions in your literature. But because there is so much surprise that is based in fear, so much challenge on your own planet and struggle, your cultures—and also those set up for profit, regardless of the cost culturally to people on Earth—will often portray beings from beyond as terrible and frightening.

It Is My Job to Make Initial Contacts

In my experience of being a diplomat, you might say, to use your word—an initial contactee, yes?—I was contacted by forms of life from other places when I was young. I learned the philosophies of this and how beautiful it can be. Through my contact with other forms of life, living on a planet as I did with very few people and having had little of that explanation to me—which says that things might happen in our remote part of the universe and that those contacts were made for me, with me, with these forms of life in such loving and supportive ways, in ways that were nurturing—I learned to admire this type of work. As a result, my life became a determination to learn these skills, and by my being—not by what I taught only, but by the ways of my being—I would then teach, being one of these contact individuals.

This is my job now, then, as an elder of my society, of my planet—though the population on my planet hasn't grown much. It is my job, which I love and embrace, to make initial contacts with societies and even individuals in societies of planets and cultures far, far away from our own, who are coming of age as a group of beings in order to be welcomed and nurtured into the community of all life in the universe. I have found this very rewarding work, and though I am near the end of my life cycle, I do still reach out in this form, though I no longer travel in space due to my advanced years.

Oh, so we're not going to meet you personally but some of your race, then?

It is possible when the time is right, according to our understanding of these things.

Can you say what your form looks like? What would we see if we saw you?

I will say only what I have said, and that is that we have representatives of our culture on Earth, whom you refer to as an animal. We do not consider any form of life an "animal." We recognize that you identify forms of life this way because you do not easily understand their way of life. You do not know their language nor their thought communion. But you can often, for those who truly observe, see the feelings in the eyes.

We do not look exactly like that form on your planet, but there is a resemblance. We would not wish to think that you would consider us to be animals when you meet us, nor would we consider that you would be such. I will say only that, because I do not wish you to say, "Oh, this animal is better than the others." Be alert that there is no form of life on your Earth that is an animal; there are only those who resemble the forms of life you will meet on your journeys.

Of course, the first beings you meet will look very much like yourselves on Earth, and there will be some characteristics about which you will say, "That quality of you reminds me of . . ." and then you will think of an animal on Earth. It may not happen immediately for you, but it will happen in time—in time, if we feel that you welcome that. We will be observing how you treat your own forms of life on Earth.

Remember that all forms of life on Earth are existing there to support and nurture you. They are not there to pursue some dream or learning experience for themselves. We think of them as astronauts in a distant place, living as best as possible, waiting for you to ask, desiring to teach you and welcoming those who make the effort to learn how to learn from them.

Practice Communicating with the Animals

How will we communicate with you, then?

The way you learn initially to communicate with the animals. If there are those around the house, you may look at them and they may look at you. If you can feel good feelings within you, they will respond in kind. If you feel frightened suddenly, then you can say, "Oh, I beg your pardon; I was startled," and then go into good feelings, if you can. And though they might move off, they may pause. Notice that if they pause, they are either trusting that you will go into the good feelings you have or they feel your relaxation from being startled, and then they will pause, perhaps somewhere even vulnerable.

Take note when another form of life pauses in a position where it is vulnerable to being injured by you or even by others. If it is doing this because it is feeling good feelings—you are not sending your good feelings to this being but simply feeling them—then it is showing trust and faith that you will not harm it. The being may even desire that you protect it from others, should that be a risk. Honor the being's courage and bravery by protecting it, if you can, and saying, "Do not harm it. We are attempting to communicate," or something else.

How long have you been watching us, waiting for us to grow up?

It's not to grow up; it's to find the qualities that you yourselves would welcome and to emulate those qualities. We have been waiting—our culture only, speaking for our culture—about a thousand years.

How did you know about us? You said you're from across the universe.

We were informed of this experiment going on, on this distant planet, and we were interested, so we journeyed. I was one of the first. We did not come too close, but we have the capacity to unite with those who are like us, about whom you would say, "Oh, that's an animal!" We have the capacity to unite with them for a moment and look through their eyes and see life on Earth and the human being.

When we do this, then that form of life on Earth whom you might call an animal will pause for a moment or perhaps be enjoined with us. It will be able to see us, and we will feel our brotherhood or sisterhood or union with it, and it will feel something like the wonderful feeling of home—seeing us, seeing our culture, perhaps even hearing a song or a story from home while we look through the being's eyes and observe through its means of communion. Perhaps it is hearing, perhaps it is vision, or perhaps it is sensing, what you call instinct—knowing, you might say—or any of these forms. And we will observe. That's what I did.

Make an Effort to See Differences without Judgment

You say there are very few beings on your planet?

Very few. In my youth, there were about forty-eight. It's a small planet, of course. Now there has been some slight change, and there are seventy-four. It is a difficult place to live—what you would call, if you looked at such a place, inhospitable. But we are able to manage it.

Why are you there if it is inhospitable?

Because it is home, and we love its benevolent qualities. Our desires and loves may not be understandable to you. The fact that you have asked the question, as a representative of your culture, shows what is needed. Think how many peoples in your cultures would look at an animal species and say, "Why does it live like that? Why does it not wish to live in more comfortable surroundings?" You are not alone in such a natural question for your species, and yet it does represent, unconsciously on your part, a judgment.

Recognize on your own planet that there are many animals (as you would call them) who do something or interact in some way that you would say, "Why do they live like that? Why would they want to?" A better question might be someday to say, "What is the pleasure they experience from this?" and to even notice, "How does it serve our peoples, their being here and doing these things?" This second part has, in fact, been noticed by many peoples in your cultures, and we feel good about that.

We do not admonish you for your question, but we bring to your attention a cultural condition, and that is, "Why do they . . ."—whoever they are, whether they be other human beings or animals—"Why do they live like that? Wouldn't they be more happy living like us?" It is important to note that many cultures on your planet, including ones that could be profoundly helpful to your preparations to meet beings from beyond who could welcome you and provide you with great gifts, have been lost because of that question: "Why do you look like that?" These cultures were cultures of humanity, and they were profoundly identified by others as being very philosophical and without judgment.

I recommend that you make an effort with the animals and with other human cultures. Instead of saying, "Why would you live like that?"—a perfectly understandable question by an Earth person at this time of your journey through your life—say something that sounds like this: "I'd be interested to know why you live like that." It's almost the same question, is it not? And yet it inflects a different desire and welcomes communication and communion in the best possible way available.

I would be interested in knowing why you live where you live, besides the fact that it's home. What pleasure do you get out of living there?

Our bodies are formed from the dust and elements of that planet. Therefore, our bodies are ideally suited to living there—much more ideally suited to living there than living anywhere else. You will notice this as you travel in space. And yet you do not have to wait to travel in space to notice this with other cultures. You can notice it right now on your own planet, with those representatives called animals.

You can notice how—and many of your peoples have studied this— a form of life might be perfectly suited in appearance, shape, philosophy (meaning actions) and interaction (meaning communion) with who and what it is doing or what is its natural tendency to do. And therefore, you will say, "How perfect it is, and what wonder the Great Being has bestowed, to show us these wonderful forms of life that are not only perfectly adapted to their bodies in their world, but also, their bodies are perfectly adapted to their world!"

So if I knew who you were, what your species was on this planet, would I say the same thing? Would I say, "Why does your species live in that . . . ?" what we would consider an inhospitable place on this planet?

That is a reasonable question. I will not answer it, because I feel that has been established. I will compliment you on your question, however. You have a quick mind.

I'm just curious as to who you are! [Laughs.]

[Laughs.] But there is no advantage for me to tell you. Why? Because there is no advantage for your culture to say, "Look! These animals are special." I recognize that as a contactee—which I consider you to be since we are having this communion—you will have certain qualities about you that do make you a representative of your culture, and I expect these things that you have shown. And yet you are showing many wonderful qualities, which is why we are prepared to welcome you when you demonstrate to us, at a distance from our perception, these qualities that are desires—not because you want to qualify for traveling in space, but because you want to improve the quality of your own life and you want to improve your knowledge and wisdom of how you may be inspired to live your own lives more comfortably and happily by seeking out, in the most hospitable way, communion with forms of life on your own planet.

Sometimes on your planet these forms of hospitality might mean that you will have to go where these other forms of life live. Often your people will go for a walk in the woods, for a swim in the ocean and even attempt to fly in the air. These flights with machines are not always benevolent to forms of life in the air, but there are some forms that you have created that gently glide quietly through the air, allowing the individuals operating them to feel for a moment like a bird. This is something that the flying beings have noted. Recognize that at the deep-dream level, when your bodies rest, you often fly very much like they do in order to move about the Earth, seeking experience to learn and even to teach, and that you will have that feeling sometimes as a recollection from your sleep time.

Yes, like an eagle.

Seventy-four people . . . how many are out in your spacecraft now, watching, close to us?

One.

One? Are you in communion with each other? Do the other seventy-three on your planet see what the one in the spacecraft sees?

Do you do that on your planet? We are individuals. We commune with each other on the basis of desires, but we are not in constant communion. That is a reasonable question, however.

One is out here. I think you said that you were on your planet, right?

I am on my planet. There is one nearby, like a person nearby, but not in your solar system. Still, that is close enough to observe your culture in great detail. If it is important to have some sense of what the people feel in your culture, it can be done through a representative on your planet—whom you would call an animal. You might even have another name for some of these representatives.

You live, what, 1,200 years, 1,500 years? How many years do you live, in our time?

According to the way you measure time, our life cycle is about, oh, around 1,200 years. It is not fixed—around that.

Are you born? Do you desire to manifest a body? Or do you clone? What is your process? How do you come into being in the physical?

I cannot say too much about that right now. I will only say that we come into being in a way that you would identify with one or more forms of life on your own planet. So it is not so very foreign to you.

Do you have families?

Yes.

Are you male and female?

Well, I do not wish to say too much. I will just say that we have representatives there, and although they do not diplomatically represent us, since they have lives, they would be, as I said, what you might consider at your now philosophy levels of pursuit to be animals.

If there are only seventy-four of you, then are there very many of them here?

I cannot say. Be alert to the fact that your planet, even under the strains it experiences now, encourages life and encourages the thriving of life. You seem to think that there is one being for every one of us. They have their own lives. When they pass over, they go their own places, but they are—how can we say?—cousins.

So they might be from another planet?

They might be, but we have communion. They might also be from our planet. I feel that this is not necessary for you to know in order to appreciate forms of life that may or may not always receive acknowledgment for their own value.

Do you remember your life on other planets? I don't know what your level of awareness is.

I do not put much energy into that. Sometimes I dream of them, yes, when sleeping. But I know that my job requires a great deal of being alert to subtle communion; therefore, I do not think of those things much. The fact that your peoples do is another clue for you that your tendency to explore goes beyond your physical parameters into your thoughts, hopes and dreams.

When you come to the end of your natural cycle, do you deliberately . . . do you step out of your body? Does your body go back into the soil, or does someone come in to inhabit it, like a walk-in?

What I have seen in this passage, on our planet, is simply that the body begins to make that motion before the end of our life. You would call it, perhaps, not unlike your own—a sort of wasting away. And then the personality departs to join its next venture. Now, if you wish to have further communion through this channel about some subjects, we will have to bring this to a close, because the channeling cannot go on much further today.

You Have Many Beings on Earth Who Are Ready to Teach You

What brings you joy? What particularly brings you joy, as you look back over your life?

What I am doing right now: communicating with those beyond who are almost at the point of readiness for communing with the Great Being's children, which we all are.

You mean what we call the Creator, right?

Yes.

How many other awakening civilizations—or whatever you want to call it—have you contacted? How many times have you done this in the past?

Depending upon how you count it, about six hundred.

Six hundred! There are six hundred planets out there with people just getting ready to go into space?

No, no. Remember, when I was contacted, I was not getting ready to go into space. I was simply receptive to knowing and meeting other forms of life from other places. That's all.

Oh. So you have contacted six hundred kinds of beings in various stages of growth, right?

In various stages of existence, yes. Sometimes they were just happy to know we were there, and other times they were surprised, and there were all kinds of other reactions one might expect when one discovers worlds not only within worlds but worlds beyond.

Six hundred. Oh, I can't wait until we get out there!

What is the rush? You have many wonderful astronauts and cosmonauts in cousin form on your planet right now who have wonderful teachings for you, many from which, when you are able to learn how to commune with them—which is similar at times to the form that is going on here, but there may be other forms, such as dreams and so on—you will learn their philosophies, which will all be very benevolent and hospitable. And that philosophy will prepare you for the philosophies and hospitality of those you will meet beyond your own planet someday.

Would you recommend that we ask for one or several of them to speak through Robert as you're doing? Would that allow us to talk to them and receive their teaching in a way that is understandable to us?

It may be benevolent and bountiful, yes. It is most important to understand the points of similarity between their philosophies and your own so that you will not have the stress, as you say, that you would have to give up something in order to be accepted and that you could notice how everyone's dreams, hopes and desires are so very much alike in the hospitable sense. Hospitable, to my understanding, means the welcoming of all life.

That's a wonderful title: "ET Astronauts and Cosmonauts Living on Earth." [Laughs.] [See the 2007 Animal Souls Speak book for more information.]

Training to Be a Diplomat

How are you trained as a diplomat? Through the experience of meeting other civilizations?

Yes. Initially I admired how gently and nurturingly this was done with me. And while I was living a comfortable existence on my planet, I spoke . . . not to the first one who contacted me or even to the second or third, but over time I gradually spoke to these beings and said, "This seems like an admirable thing you are doing. Would you speak to me of your own desires to do this beyond the great philosophies and teachings you are offering me?" In time they did, and I noticed that they had similar traits to my own in personality. This ultimately provided for me the insight that I would not only be good at this but that I might find a form of personal satisfaction in doing it.

Were you the first one on your planet to be approached like that?

No. Our peoples live individual existences at a distance from each other. I had heard of contacts like this, but they were not contacts that I identified in the same form as those who contacted me. You must remember also that this occurred when I was very young and not as knowledgeable in the ways of the universe.

Can you say the form of the beings who contacted you? Have I ever heard of them?

I will allow you to have such contacts, without creating expectations.

[Laughs.] Okay. Why do you all live apart from each other?

It is our way of life.

Do you come together in certain seasons or rituals or times?

We do not consider them rituals, but there are times when we are more joined.

Sometimes I see pictures, but I'm not seeing a picture of you.

Space Travel Is Beginning for You

Do you see that we can go out into space using the technology we have now?

Well, as far as a journey into space for a couple of hours for the general population, it is not quite there yet, but soon, very soon. Within a few years, this might be available to the initial beings who choose to do it. But in time, there are those who desire to bring all types of human beings at least the distance of maybe sixty, eighty, one hundred miles from your planet in order to enjoy the beauty and the moments—just to enjoy the moments would be wonderful. So this is really the beginning for you. It is becoming, for many of you in your lifetimes, something that you will see, and for the younger ones amongst you, something you may choose to experience.

So you're saying we'll start with commercial flights into Earth's orbit and then maybe to the Moon before we actually start going out to explore other planets?

That will be up to you, but at the very least, I would expect that there would be a great desire by a great many people of Earth to do this. If they could fly up into space in some comfort and enjoy the wonders of the feelings in some comfort, it would be profoundly desirable, especially if they knew they could return in a couple of hours and perhaps do this again another time, bringing friends and family.

This is the beginning. It is not what I would call making it an ordinary experience, because it is not in your body's physical properties to do this.

You will require great protection to do it, as well as guiding and teaching, in order to get the most out of the experience. But it will become not only something that people will strive for in their imaginations but also something that they will feel is possible. And that will excite the very nerve endings of your physical body and become, not just a dream, not just a reality, but a universal principle.

Philosophies will spring forth: "What is the best way to be in space?" And many of your great thoughts and philosophies will say, "Look! Emulate us!" But there will be others who say, "Wait. We have made, with the best of intentions, mistakes on our own planet, some of which were irretrievable: forms of life were unalterably changed, or forms of life were even unintentionally destroyed, to say nothing of intentional destruction. How can we do this exploration with the knowledge of our lack of knowledge? How can we even go into these places and know what we might experience? Perhaps there will be profound spiritual encounters, inspirations, that will be seen by some or even seen by many? How can we prepare ourselves to do this? What might we encounter? And won't it be something we wish to do again? How can we create in those who do encounter us in dreams, in spirit, in joy . . . how can we make the best impression so that they will want to do this again, if not as individuals, then other members of their being?

"Perhaps we can begin to learn on our own planet by becoming more diplomatic with other human beings and with other forms of life, by studying them not only as a scientist but as a philosopher, as an astronaut, as a diplomat: 'How do you live? Do you have anything to teach us? Any advice? If you do, can you not make it more available?'" And so on. In short, don't wait to go into space to have these encounters. Begin now on your own planet, which is ripe with possibilities.

You have inspired me to start a book about the truth of the beings we call animals on our planet: the astronaut and cosmonaut book. [Laughs.] You are wonderful; I thank you deeply. I thank you very much.

Seek No Further Than Your Own Planet Right Now
Are you the one who will meet us? It depends on how soon we do this, right?

I will probably have finished my life cycle before your peoples are venturing out at greater distances. But there will be other members, and perhaps my friend, who is beyond your solar system observing, will be one of your contacts someday.

Was he trained as you were? Was he contacted? Or did you train him?

It would be best if you asked that being yourself.

Does he want to speak for a few minutes? The channel is probably tired.

I feel that there may be the opportunity for him or her or something else, in terms of form of interaction, to say a greeting, but that is all. For myself, I will say, I look forward to your welcoming and to your embracing of each other and your own value, and to the welcoming and hospitality by the human race for all other life forms on your Earth. Seek no further than your own planet right now to learn, to appreciate and to be appreciated. And someday soon, you will have the opportunity to meet wise and wonderful beings who will help you, who will guide you and who may be interested in your teachings as well. Good night.

Thank you very much. Good life.

※   ※   ※

Greetings.

Greetings!

I am the observer of that which my friend mentioned. I have noticed many fine qualities in the human race. I have noted that in order to get the best out of yourselves—meaning, in order to excel—you sometimes drive yourselves or each other excessively. Learn through patience as well. Patience often offers opportunities for observation and inspiration. I have made it my life's work to strive for patience, and this has allowed me to observe many qualities in the personalities of other beings who realize that I have no purpose with them other than to welcome them. Thus, in time, they relax and reveal their personalities, their wishes, their hopes, their dreams and their actions.

You can do this too. You can observe, note, appreciate and, most importantly, learn the value of approval. Approval often provides great permission for all beings to be themselves. Learn that being humble does not require subservience but rather can simply provide for you the feeling of equality between all the forms of life on Earth. They all have great wisdom to offer you, and many of them are interested in your wisdom. Learn to expect such communion, and such communion will then seek you out. Good night.

Thank you very much. Good life.

※   ※   ※

[Melody, speaking to Robert after he came out of channeling mode:] **Did you see a picture?**

[Robert:] Yes. I saw orange and white and gold, and a form of life that can be seen or not seen as it chooses.

ET Synthesizes Network of Inspiration to Help Stranded Space Travelers

Eech-en-ah
August 10, 2006

am Eech-en-ah, a visitor from another planet. I have been visiting for some time.

Eech-en-ah! Welcome! Tell me about yourself.

I am not exactly of physical substance, but I can accommodate physical substance. I most often attach myself to stone outcroppings, because the makeup of my physical being is not crystalline but is sympathetic in vibration to crystalline. If you were to consider the auric field of rock, I am like that—meaning the makeup of my being is like the auric field of stone on your planet. Therefore, my connecting to stone in whatever form it is in is comfortable for myself and for the stone.

I have come from a distance to understand the nature of your planet's capability to produce responses—in the long range and the short range—to the needs on a soul level of any population that establishes itself here for more than a few hours of Earth-measured time. I have studied the temporary stranding of populations, usually one or two, sometimes up to one hundred or one thousand, that have occurred around this general part of the galaxy for some time, because I believe that it's possible to coordinate a form of communication that can be established beyond technology to support individuals who may be stranded on any planet through simple spiritual connection.

This is particularly helpful to beings from other planets who will occasionally get stranded here, but it is just as helpful for beings from any planet who get stranded on any planet, if the local population either is not helpful or cannot be contacted for assistance, as you have here on Earth. This planet is well-known in the galaxy as a planet that is profoundly responsive. It is responsive according to people's needs, not only on their survival level—meaning you as beings need water and food and so on, and the planet is capable of providing that—but the planet is also highly responsive to the lessons any soul has when it comes here, including visitors or those who get stranded temporarily here from other planets.

Almost everyone who has been stranded on this planet has reported when they returned how their personal lives were totally altered—not from the stranding (after all, occasionally one gets stranded for a short time), but they were totally altered because whatever they experienced as a life lesson or even an interest that led to growth for them greatly expanded and accelerated in all kinds of directions. Depending upon the nature of the personality or the culture of the beings, they would either make huge strides forward in assimilating and adapting new ways according to whatever it was they were trying to achieve as a soul, or in some cases they would require a considerable amount of gentle care after the stranding, because that acceleration of personality was well before the time that one would have normally reached that in one's life span.

I Am Creating a Waveform to Connect Those Who Are Stranded

My intention, then, I believe can be served over the next few days of your time, and then I can depart. I've got an initial test going on now whereby the personal capabilities of Earth can be assimilated into a means of communication that will cater to all beings' needs—meaning an energy that initially, where there is a connection to Earth and a connection to all those who have been stranded in this galaxy for a time . . . where they feel that they can receive all of the wisdom of others who have been stranded and that their own personalities can accelerate and grow to adapt to their immediate problems of being stranded by being connected to the Earth. It works, but it's too strong. I've had to tone it down quite a bit.

I believe that I can, through the use of an artificial synthesis, create a waveform (meaning adapt a waveform) by which all these beings who have been stranded on Earth and other places can be connected. And most importantly for the future, anyone who is stranded somewhere can tap in to this waveform without the need for instruments—because very often the big challenge for people when they are stranded is that the equipment is not functioning properly or they wouldn't have been stranded in the first place.

So this will likely take place as a connection. You would call it a telepathic connection, but to me it is a feeling connection connected to energy, or "quadrated." I don't think you have that word, but it means "through the use of four"—the inner, the outer, the perceiving and the perceptive—and the synthesis of all of those four. That's the basis of the energy, and it is an energy that is imitating that aspect of the personality of Mother Earth to create almost immediate adaptation, growth and stimulus on the level of which the recipients, the other populations, can comfortably accept. That's why I'm here.

Earth Has Almost Every Quality of a Deity

That's absolutely wonderful! So we owe so much, then, to the energies of Mother Earth for responding to our needs and accelerating our growth?

I do not think that it would be possible for you to achieve your intended purpose on any other planet. I have heard that you, as a population, have traveled on soul levels, sometimes in this form or in that form, and have attempted to achieve your purpose on other planets. These planets were good planets and so on, but they didn't have the tremendous spiritual capabilities that Earth has. This is a planet that in many cultures would be considered a deity. By "cultures," I do not refer to your Earth cultures, though I believe there may be some Earth cultures that feel that way. Perhaps they are not in the present; I do not know your history that well. But the planet herself has almost every quality of a deity.

So how did this start? How did you get interested in beings who were stranded?

I was stranded myself, and I was stranded in a planetary system that had no magnetic energy at all. It didn't, as a result, have much in the way of electrical energy. To you it would feel stagnant; you would be very lethargic. But in my case, it was difficult to connect energetically to anything. I am simply fortunate that other beings knew where I was and were able to find me, because I had a life signature that was totally different than the surrounding matter. And even though I had, because of exhaustion, blended into the stone there—what would look like stone to you (it looked like stone to me, but it turned out not to be)—they were able to find me on the basis of checking my life-sign energy as compared to what I was connected to.

Granted, when they took me back to the vehicle (because that's what they used), they accidentally brought some of the planet with me, so they had to make a second trip back to take that back, because they weren't sure what was the planet and what was me. But they were able to rescue me. I really felt I would come to my end there.

What were you doing there? What was your purpose?

Research. I was looking for what I found here. You see, what I found here on this planet, on Earth, is something so rare. As I explained in my opening statement, I had been searching for this kind of thing my whole life. I am toward the end of my life now, and I have found it. I was stranded when I was in the early stages of my life, and now that I'm in the late stages, I have been granted the opportunity to visit your planet and therefore have been able to find what I need to do and synthesize it, based upon the personality of your planet. I believe it will be a contribution I can feel good about when I come to the end of my natural cycle, which will be coming up pretty soon. [Laughs.]

I Found Earth Strictly by Feeling

How did you know about Earth? Did you have a feeling that such a planet existed? Or had you heard about it?

I heard about it.

Ah, but you didn't know where it was?

I found it strictly by feeling. I focused on my need. Because I had heard that the planet is so responsive to needs, I focused on my need and tried to find the general area of the planet. The best I had of the general area of the planet was a little larger than your solar system, so I searched the solar system for a while until I landed on the stone of this planet, eh? What a great joy!

How had you originally heard about it?

From survivors. Several survivors had been stranded: one on Earth, one on what you call Saturn, one on Uranus and another one a little closer on . . . I believe you call the planet Mars. They had already come to the end of their cycles, but they left records, which I studied. And they felt this energy—not on those planets, but they felt it nearby.

So I explored most of the moons first, because after a lifetime of searching, I did not think it was possible that a planet itself—an entire planet—would have such energy. So I explored the moons, and then I explored a lot of the smaller pieces of matter. And then I just focused on my need and allowed myself to be drawn here. But I had to focus on my need totally and nothing else, and I felt myself being drawn here like an attraction. Of course, it did not occur to me that it was the whole planet. It took awhile to discover that it was the planet herself in the way I explained in the beginning.

Are you in a vehicle?

I have a support vehicle. Due to my advanced time of my life, I require a support vehicle. Younger members of my culture do not always need a support vehicle. They can travel, and if you saw it, it would be something that looked like a condensed light—meaning that if it appeared briefly, just for a split second, it would be very bright. You wouldn't be able to stare at it for a long time. That's why it only appears to the human eye for just a moment, so that it does not damage your vision. But at this stage of my life cycle, I require a support vehicle that has been loaned to me by other researchers who are from other planets and other cultures, and they are also in occupation. They cycle in and out, but there are three or four in occupation on the vehicle in order to support my searches. And of course, we are all very happy to have made this find.

None of them has ever even been in your solar system (of course, I've been here for a while). But they usually cycle on and off the ship and back to other vehicles and back to their home planet—in terms of your time, about once every two or three weeks. Most of them have very close family ties, and to be away from their families for too long is a burden for them.

So will you be able to get home now? Do you have enough time left to get home?

Yes. That's why I'm leaving in a few days of your time, so that we can get back to my culture, which occupies numerous planets in a distant star system. Even with this ship that they have, it will take us several more of your Earth days to get there. We do not travel instantaneously on that vehicle. When I was younger, I could do that on my own, but now that I am at the end of my life cycle, that's not possible.

How long is that cycle in Earth time?

Oh, perhaps approximately 51,000 years.

You've spent most of 51,000 years looking for this energy?

Closer to 48,000. It was a worthy search. This will make all the difference in the world to beings who are stranded anywhere, possibly even your own as you begin to explore other planets. It happens. Technology breaks down, some of your people might be stranded, your instruments might not be functioning and you might not be able to contact your people or those who help you.

But if you are trained in focusing, you may be able to access this network through the means of communion—not exactly what we're using here, but something where you would hear words and be inspired to take certain actions. So without any knowledge or capability whatsoever in the field of repair of your ship, you might be able to synthesize the repair of your ship using technology not native to your own culture—meaning another culture, if they were there, could come and fix it, but it wouldn't look like anything you have in your culture.

So this kind of capability would be wonderful, wouldn't it? You could be stranded somewhere and say, "Well, that's the end. This is where I'm going to die." And then you get this feeling, you get this inspiration from others who have been in a similar circumstance. And they, working with you, will help you, using your inspiration. You see, you will be using your own inspiration, and you will just feel stimulated to make these repairs, some of which will look totally outrageous. You'll say, "That can't possibly work!" But it will.

You're saying that you're going to set up a network, almost like a channeling network, that has information that the stranded being can tune in to?

Yes, but it won't be channeling. It will be inspiration, meaning that you might hear some words, but mostly you will feel physically inspired to make certain motions. They will be inspired motions. You might even walk around on the surface of the planet and just know what elements you can use and what not to, and be able to make repairs with technology that is not native to your culture.

And this energy that you're tuning in to is a combination of Mother Earth's energy and other people who have been stranded?

No. Remember, I told you that the Mother Earth energy is too strong. It will be a synthesized version of Mother Earth's personality. As I said, it won't be Mother Earth's energy, even for those from Earth. It's too strong.

And by synthesizing . . . ?

It makes it possible for all races, all cultures, all types of beings who are likely to get stranded—obviously many beings wouldn't need it, but all kinds of beings—it will be comfortable for them. And it won't be as intense as Mother Earth's capability . . . well, you don't need to be able to move your entire planet, you see? Mother Earth can move huge masses to adapt to her own needs and the needs of others. But you don't need that.

You would simply need some energy that would function with your capability to spontaneously act and react in order to know how to repair something that is not repairable because of the materials you have at hand, or because you don't have the skills to repair it, or because the function of your equipment is hampered by the planet itself in some way. So the equipment itself might be working fine, but the planet or whatever the environment is might be hostile to your technology.

That is awesome! Will this function within this whole universe, or just in the Milky Way?

Within the galaxy, and it will be available, of course, for others to study if they feel that they might wish to adapt it. Perhaps they already have it, but I've never been beyond this galaxy, so I don't know.

The Idea of Synthesizing Is Part of My Culture

So your star system is in the Milky Way galaxy?

Yes, not quite on the other side, but close.

Tell me something about your life there.

I'm a little more dense in my own planetary culture. I'm adaptable to other planets' conditions, and that makes it more comfortable. But at home—and this may not help you very much—I am thicker, meaning I have more substance, but not as much as you would consider yourself to have in order to be solid matter with flexibility.

And you move because you want to be somewhere else?

We move if we feel the need—yes, of course. Just as you do. Our forms are adaptable. We do not have arms, legs, a head . . . we are not humanoids.

But do you move with a physical body, or do you float, or are you attracted to where you want to go? How does that work?

I'd say mostly it functions through attraction and others' attraction as well—meaning someone may have an attraction, want us to be present, and if that's possible, then we allow ourselves to be drawn to that.

Have you been mostly away all these 48,000 years?

Mostly.

So you don't have a family?

I have a family that I became one with in the beginning, but it has more to do with my point of origin rather than anything that has come about through the rest of life. We are not born as you understand it but rather synthesized— not technologically, but through spirit—into form on the basis of our family's desire for a certain personality type to be amongst them.

Oh, so that's why you can synthesize this energy—that's part of your culture!

Yes, it is at the deepest core of our being, the idea of synthesizing. That is how we procreate, so it is our nature to be able to see things in that light and offer it not only to our own kind but to others. But I see a parallel in your culture. You also are adapting kinds of people.

We are very adaptable, yes.

Yes, and you tend to appreciate your technology the more uses it has. Even in your language, very often you have words that you use more than one way. So it is very appealing to you, the idea of adaptation and synthesis. Even for your foods, you do not have, say, this kind of fruit and that kind of fruit, and you eat them separately. Very often you will put them together. So that's a synthesis of complementary foods. You see, we have similarities.

That's great. So you're sort of called into form and . . . how do you learn what your culture knows? Are you born knowing it, or are there teachings about that?

There is no teaching process because the beings are a family of personalities that are mutually complementary. They don't really sit, but they are in a circle form, and in the center of their sphere is the desired personality form, and it forms in reaction to the desires of those who are present. So everything that they know is known by the personality that is manifested through spirit form. Therefore, no teaching is necessary.

Then how do you share what you learn over your life span? Is there some other coming together and sharing?

The way I will share when I get back is that I will join that circle that is desiring to manifest another personality. By joining that circle, we all become one, and when we welcome the new arrival, that being will also be synthesized with that wisdom. So it will be instantaneous. It's very easy to share.

But that's in your family. How does it spread to the rest of your culture?

The entire culture is involved in welcoming every new being. The planets we occupy are all one family. I just used that term since that is a term you use.

That's exciting! So they'll all know everything that you have learned and everything that everybody else has learned in their entire lives?

That's right—there is no loss of wisdom.

For Us, Being Old Is about a Desire to Move On

So as you prepare to end your cycle, is that the time they choose to replace you, then?

Yes, but I don't think they think of it as a replacement.

No, but I mean, you have a fixed number.

We have a number that we find is adequate.

You're trying to get one of Robert's lozenges out of the package [laughs].

It's awkward. If I were on my home planet, it would just float to me. We don't eat, so that's not a factor. [Laughs.]

So you have a fixed number of beings on your home planet?

We have a fixed number. And of course, some come to the end of their cycle, so new ones are welcomed, as you say, as old ones move on—"old" in terms of just coming to the end of our natural life cycle. But there isn't the experience of change that you have here at the end of one's cycle. It's a feeling, mostly presenting itself as a desire to move on to the greater One.

Do you have a memory of doing this before?

No.

You don't remember your past life?

No. And if you consider it, you can see why. If we were to remember our past lives, we would be remembering information, knowledge and wisdom that probably would not fit into our culture. But since we are all synthesized with the same wisdom, we would simply be permeating our culture with things that we don't need and that may be obsolete or inappropriate.

So do you communicate with your home planet when you are away?

No, but the helpers who are assisting me will do that. When I was younger, I could communicate at a distance, but now that I am older, I'm going to say— even though that's not a factor of our culture and we don't think of ourselves that way—that I need assistance, and those on the ship will do that for me.

How does this oldness manifest? Everything just slows down or what?

The capabilities we have when we are young are no longer available. This is not dissimilar from yourselves, but there is no pain, and the basic necessities of life still function very well. But some of the abilities of youth are not present, such as . . . as I mentioned, the long-distance communication, the ability to move as a single being or perhaps united with one or two good friends. And now I need to fly on a ship. [Laughs.] But it was worth the trip.

This Is My First Trip to Earth

So what did you communicate to your planet?

I first communicated the Mother-Earth aspect, and then I communicated that actually I realized that this was too strong. In short, I communicated the research level. We've already got the model going for the synthesis, but I'm here mostly now confirming. We don't make [snaps fingers] snap decisions.

So you were here before, and now you're back. This isn't your first trip, then?

It is my first trip to Earth.

Oh! But you're staying here until you know that everything works perfectly?

Yes, but I have only been here a short time.

But you came here to make sure everything worked?

This is my visit here. No, I . . . you . . . we're having a breakdown in communication here. I have been here for about two and a half weeks of your time. I've never been here before. I'll be leaving in a couple . . . in three days of your time.

So you discovered the effect of Mother Earth before you came here, then?

As I said before, I heard from those who were stranded in this solar system, and I found the planet the way I described.

So after 48,000 years of searching, in two and a half weeks you have found what you were looking for and you have begun the synthesis process. That's awesome! You have your glorious invention or creation.

Well, I already had the understanding of how it could work, but there simply weren't the means. But because of the personality of your planet, I could see how it could be done. Your planet volunteered, and we used the energy, but it was too strong for everyone. So then naturally it occurred to me that a synthesis of the personality aspect of Earth would work just fine. So what we did was synthesize and blend, you might say—you would probably say "blend"—that personality characteristic.

And you are the one culture that would know how to do that?

Well, we're good at that. [Laughs.]

So people on your home planet must be enthused for you; they must be excited for you.

Well, they appreciate the project because it will not only help our own beings, who on occasion get stranded—though I think a lot was learned from my getting stranded—but it's a wonderful thing to be able to offer such a gift to travelers in general. I believe it will get a lot of use, perhaps saving a great deal of suffering and loss.

The Stone-like Substance That Stranded Me

So your culture is a space-faring planet? You live on many planets, but you go out . . . ?

We travel, yes.

What other kinds of things do you travel for, besides what you were traveling for?

There are only two or three other projects—again, beings who are trying to solve something, a need that we were unable to solve in our own part of the overall physical place. I do not know much about those projects. I've been focused on my own.

When you were on that planet and were stranded, you said you thought it was stone, but what was it?

It was not a matter you have here, because of course, everything here has an electrical or magnetic charge. So it was something that looked exactly like stone, but as I got closer to it, I realized that it didn't have those characteristics, those qualities, nor did it have a crystalline characteristic either. It was more something that was taking in energy, drawing energy, instead of something like your planet, for instance, that radiates energy. And I feel it's in the nature of the electrical and magnetic to do that. But this was something that looked exactly like stone anywhere else, yet as I got closer, I realized that it was this other . . . more like drawing energy. And then it was drawing so much of my energy that I couldn't get away.

Even though I was right on the surface, I couldn't get away, and I looked exactly like the other matter. It was just because of the determined efforts of those who rescued me that they found me at all. I thought perhaps that this would be where I would finish up my life cycle.

And you were so young! [Laughs.]

[Laughs.] I was a bit discouraged!

At that time, were you already on this project?

No, I became inspired to do this project as a result of being stranded, because I could not communicate. I was stuck. I could not communicate with my people because my energy had been drawn. If they hadn't known where I was, they couldn't have found me. I was unable to communicate with them. So, you see, I became determined to find some way for those who get stranded to be able to commune and to have the means to either be rescued or assist in their own rescue.

What were you doing there, anyway?

Traveling as the young do, even in my culture. Traveling, looking, exploring, trying to find things that were familiar or interesting or fun.

So you do that even though you don't have projects?

Oh, sure! Not everybody does, but it generally happens when one is young. Early in one's cycle, that is more appealing. Often groups of two or three travel, but in this particular case, I was on my own. It isn't always that groups of two or three travel; very often individuals go, and in this case, it was an individual. After that, for quite some time it was rare to find individuals going out.

As I said, we have individuals out now, but this is because of the advances that have been made, not only in communications, but in the project I've been working on. So now individuals can go out, at least to places that have been visited before and where our beings normally travel to and from. Therefore, if an individual is missing, that being will be quickly found.

Do you get a Nobel Prize or . . . ? [Laughs.]

[Laughs.] No, but the result is enough of a prize.

Our Great Joy Is Contributing

So your great joy is in discovering things, then? Is that one of the joys of your life?

Discovery is fun, yes, but I feel that our great joy is contributing something for which there is a need and where that need has not been fulfilled. Even if it is only a small portion of a contribution, we find that satisfying. This is not unusual, though. In my travels, I have found many other cultures that have that same pleasure.

Are there other innovations or inventions that your culture has created or synthesized that have helped people?

You have to understand that I have not been there. I have been totally devoted to my project, so I must say that I am ignorant of that because I have not been there since I was very young. I have not been back to my culture.

Never?!

I was stranded, I was rescued and I was taken back to my culture. Then I went out on this mission, and I haven't been back since. So, therefore, I don't know. I was determined, and I am very happy to have been rewarded with this discovery. That's the way I see it. And now after this project is done, I will go home. I haven't been home in a very long time.

But when you were younger and you communicated with your home, everyone encouraged you to continue, right?

Oh, most of them discouraged me. They said it would be better to just be conservative, so to speak, in travels—to travel in numbers and to be careful and so on. But I was determined—not only for our own beings but for others, because the experience of being stranded alone was not very pleasant, and I would not want others to go through that if it's not necessary or if there is a means to make it possible to improve the return to one's culture and friends and family. It seems valuable.

Oh, it sounds wonderful!

We Will Teach This through Communion

How will you then communicate this to the Andromedans and the Arcturians and the Zetas and all the other space-faring cultures? Will they just all know what you've done?

No, they regularly visit and they will often sit—by "sitting," you understand, I'm saying that for your sake—not in the circles to welcome new beings, but in other circles to commune. They like the way we do things. We don't sit, but many of them do. Many of them are humanoids, and they will sit or recline as they sometimes do, and we will be amongst them. We will go into our experience of synthesis and what you might call union, and they will join that to the extent they can.

And by doing so, they will learn what you know?

They will be exposed to the many things that we know, and if they come across something that will serve them, that they might find fits into their culture (such as my project), then they will have what they need to know about it so that they can adapt it to their culture and teach about it—or at least make it available as information to others in their culture. When you have cultures like the Zetas, particularly, who are very enthusiastic about travel and interacting with other cultures and supporting things on a discovery basis—not only with science but other means to discover (they love that)—they will be very happy to communicate this to anyone and everyone who wants to know. There are other cultures like that too, and some will simply come and share it with their own culture, and of course, some won't need it.

So you already have the knowing that even though you might be leaving your body soon, your project and its value are going to get out all over?

Oh, yes. That is a great reward. I will return home and come to the end of my natural cycle pretty soon, but it will live on after me. And to know that I have not only fulfilled my own quest but will leave things in a better condition is a great joy.

So you have other visitors to your planet, then?

Regularly, yes. Granted, we interact . . . we have life, as I said, on more than one planet. Generally, the visitors come to only a single planet in the planets where we function, where there are extensive visitor services available: everything they need to service their vehicles and to have what they need in replenishment, including the capability for them to have a permanent establishment there if they wish so that they can have all their necessities fulfilled. And they know they are welcome there.

Your people built that?

We made it available for them to build or create in the manner that they create—not to have a vast population there, but whatever they need in order to provide for the cultures. It's not like what you would call a colony; they are not expanding their numbers. It's more like what you'd call an outpost, where the people who are there come and go so that they're not there their whole lives.

But they come and go, and they come to you because of your wisdom?

Yes, as they do with other places. We do not claim to be any wiser than any other beings they travel to, but it is typical for travelers to establish a means of support wherever they travel. I believe your own people do that when you explore.

Since your beings are all over several planets, when the visitors come and they want to join you in your synthesis, do they come from all the other planets to this planet where the visitor's center is?

No, no. This is one of the planets we occupy. So if they wish to join that, then they will simply just come out of their centers and join in our community experience—like that. They don't have to go anywhere; they stay on that planet.

But if you're on a different planet, then how do you join?

Why would I need to do that? Remember, synthesis is complete.

You don't have to go anywhere because you can join the synthesis from wherever you are!

Yes.

You Must Be in Sympathetic Vibration to Be Welcome

Do your people have a history of coming from somewhere else, or have you always been where you are now?

As much as I know, yes. We have always been in that part of the galaxy.

So your beings, when they go to planets where the Zetas or the Andromedans or the Arcturians live, they don't need an outpost because they can just come and be there?

Yes. We don't eat, so we don't have any needs like that. If there is a need, then the beings on that planet will simply communicate that we have a need, and someone will come and acquire us, and either take us home or serve that need. And then one goes on.

We are looking forward to being out of quarantine [laughs].

Ah! You feel you are a prisoner on this planet. It's true, I have noted that your people cannot travel off the surface of the planet here without great effort, and you of course have the desire to do so. It will perhaps take a little alteration in your culture to be welcome. The reason, of course, you cannot leave by being drawn somewhere is that that place would have to welcome you on your personality level, as well as for other reasons.

You could be bringing the greatest gift they'd ever needed, whatever that was, but if your personality was not in sympathetic vibration with them and you weren't comfortable with your own personality in every way, then of course you would not be drawn to a place. You would not be totally welcome. Therefore, you have to use a mode of force that pushes you somewhere rather than something that draws you.

Until we become more benevolent, right?

To be more specific, yes. But you are making progress. [Laughs.]

Do you know where you are on the planet?

Yes, I am in an area of gray rock. Oh, you mean as in a map? Oh, I really don't understand those things. I am in an area of gray rock and it is Moon time, nighttime, yes?

Is it cold and icy, or really, really hot?

It is comfortable—not cold, not hot. But the stone, you understand, is almost exactly the same temperature as the ambient air, perhaps a little cooler, slightly cooler.

Why were you drawn to that particular place?

That's the area that attracted me. It is an island.

Can you can communicate with Mother Earth? With our planet?

Not on a thought level, but I can feel the feelings I know. My understanding is that given the deity-type personality she has, I'm sure she has many more feelings that I do not know.

But you feel . . . you somehow requested permission to use her energy, and that was granted, right?

The planet seemed to know my needs. You see, that's her whole expression—that's what she does. She knows my needs, so I found my needs accelerating; I found my personality accelerating. In short, I had the experience of Earth. And I was able to achieve the goal because of my personality, because everything accelerated for me.

That's how it is for Earth here—everything's accelerated. That's why you as individual personalities—even with your short life span here—can grow and have tremendous life capabilities. Within a single life, you can go through vast changes because the personality-growth lesson cycle is being constantly accelerated since Mother Earth is adapting to your needs.

I'm so glad we talked this long, because I didn't understand that the reason you were able to get this in two and a half weeks was because of the acceleration you experienced by being on the Earth. That's awesome!

That's right!

Maybe others of your culture will come here to accelerate their progress on other projects?

Oh, I don't think so. There are not that many who are comfortable spending the bulk of their lives traveling. It's one thing to travel for the sake of the adventure or exploration, and entirely another thing to make it your life's work.

But they wouldn't have to make it their life's work just to come and visit.

You want more visitors, eh? [Laughs.]

[Laughs.] Well, if we can accelerate people with their great inventions, why not?

Well, they will know that as the result of my experience. I don't know that this will necessarily draw others. We will see.

My Experience of "Suddenly" Anything

Describe your feelings. You came to Earth almost at the end of your life, having searched all of your life, and you finally experienced this great realization or inspiration—how did you feel?

I noticed it in an unusual way. I was blending with the rock and resting, going into a cycle not exactly like your sleep, but a rest cycle, and I noticed a flavor I had been missing—we don't eat, but we do experience flavors. I couldn't exactly recall where I had missed that flavor, but suddenly it was there! I had been attempting to recall it for the last third of my lifetime, and suddenly I knew where it was and what it was. Now, it's not like me to suddenly do anything. The experience of "suddenly anything" got my attention.

So that's when I began to consider that the stone itself had something to do with that, because I'd been to a lot of other planets with a lot of other stone and other forms of physical matter, and this had never happened. In short, the experience of "suddenly" had never happened in my lifetime. I had never experienced "suddenly" anything. And so it got my attention.

How long had you been here at that time?

Oh, just a few moments. Perhaps in terms of your clock time, three or four minutes. I hardly had a chance to relax when I had the "suddenly" experience.
And then what?

Then I started paying more attention to what I was relaxing on. And I wondered whether it had to do with the contact the stone had with the plants, the animals and the occasional peoples. That's where I looked first. It took me a little while to realize that it was the stone itself—meaning the planet. I didn't learn that right away, because after a time of rest and relaxation, I went to the waters to commune with water beings, and I had another experience like that. I won't go into it, but it was something simple like that.

I thought it was the water being, but the water being suggested to me that it wasn't, that it might be the planet itself, and suggested a place deep under the water to go and feel. So I went down there, and it was a place where the Earth moved and I felt it, but the motion was uncomfortable. So I returned to the surface and continued my search. But I liked that spot on the rock to rest, and I would return there to rest, and I had more experiences like that. That's when I eventually realized that it was the planet herself.

And then eventually you got the idea of how to do the network?

That's right.

For You, Much Will Be in the Feeling

That's wonderful! Thank you for sharing that with us. Maybe somebody will read this book someday who can use it.

I am hopeful that your space explorers will read it and be inspired, because space exploration can be so much easier without having to push yourself somewhere. Also, you will find what you are looking for much more quickly if you can be pulled somewhere on the basis of your needs and on the basis of that place—or those peoples, perhaps, desiring to have you be there and pulling also. Therefore, if two things are pulling, you'll get there very quickly, and that will happen when your personalities are benign and benevolent. You will still have your humor, you will have your individual personalities, but there will be nothing hostile.

Yes, that's the goal.

I feel it will be more easily reached than you imagine. I don't think you're going to have to change your minds. If you had to change your minds, the way you think, it would be very long indeed. But from what I have observed in my short time here, it seems to often be entirely in the feelings. And there will probably be a little less thought and likely more of a sense of feeling.

The good thing about your culture is that much that is in your culture will support that. You will probably have more experience of food taste. Your senses—taste and touch and things that you really don't think much about, that you take for granted—you will suddenly find to be much more enjoyable. These things are physical but are also wonderful feelings. But there won't be questioning; there won't be value judgments based upon a limited range of information. There will simply be, "Well, how does this taste to you?" "Salty." "It tastes sweet to me—we're different!" This may seem simple and uninteresting to those of you who like to think, but as wonderful as thought can be, it is also thought that has created some terrible things.

You've learned a lot by just being here a short time!

I learned this before I got here.

How did you learn it?

By visiting planets that had wars on them. Planets do not easily get better after that.

There are planets out there that have war? I thought we had the only discomforting energy in the universe here on this planet, because of the Explorer Race experiment.

There are planets out there that had wars on them. These planets are attempting to recover. They don't have populations anymore. I have communed with the stone.

So there are no wars out there now?

Not on those planets. But there were when there were other cultures on them not of the planet—cultures that came and stayed, and then moved on or were destroyed.

But there aren't wars out in this galaxy now, right?

You mean beyond your own culture? No. My understanding is, this is where your culture was before you got here to Earth.

This is where . . . oh! So you're saying that the Explorer Race people are the ones who had the wars?

I do not know for certain, but that's my understanding because of seeing what I saw. These planets are not that far apart.

So where are these planets?

I'm being constrained. I can only say, not that far.

I knew of two or three of them, but I didn't know there were more.

I have noted four, possibly five. I'm not certain about one of them. One of them looked like it suffered war damage, but the planet itself was uncommunicative, so I do not know. It might have just been the appearance of the planet and not war damage. I couldn't tell.

There are some things the beings whom I talk to through Robert don't tell us.

It is that way for me as well, but I noticed that it is important for your peoples to know things on a gradual basis because you have to try out all of the various functions of those things. And if there are too many things at once, you get overwhelmed, and then you get self-destructive. So it is apparently part of your protection to not know too much at any one moment. I think we ought to end on a more cheerful note.

Look for the Similarities

Your culture on this planet and our culture have similarities. We each like to learn more so we can do more. We like to apply what we've learned in ways that improve quality of life for others. We like to discover new uses for the things that are already here, including the personalities of our friends and family and our own. We like to interact with beings we don't know and have never met in order to experience the joy of discovery and the joy of similarity, and thereby feel reassured that the continuity of life—no matter how far away or how unusual—is supported by similarities, some of which we consider to be at the core of our very being.

These similarities between our culture and your own I have found to be very similar to other cultures. Our feelings, what nurtures us, what supports us, what we quest for, what we treasure—this is all very much the same as your own. Know this and understand that in your travels on this planet, in your explorations with other species on this planet and in your study of your own planet yourself, your planet has these very same personality characteristics, including many more. And when you travel in space and discover other civilizations, look first for those personality characteristics so that you can build on something that both of your cultures will embrace and feel as a strong sense of home. Build on home, no matter where you are in the galaxy, and you will be welcomed. Good night.

Thank you very much, and congratulations!

Thank you.

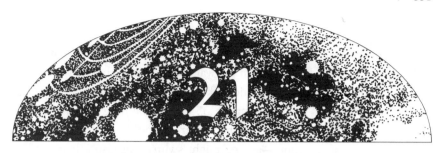

Embrace True Magic and Become Time Doctors and Harmony Specialists

ET Visitor from Mars and Zoosh
March 13, 2007

am Ee-chee-dee Rah-gsh'da. I am available for a short talk about our civilization on the planet you refer to as Mars.

Mars Was Once a Water World

Our civilization existed before human beings arrived on this planet you reside on. We did not emigrate to this planet—Earth, as you say—as has been considered and speculated upon by many. We did not emigrate anywhere in this dimension. We emigrated to the past. We had many years, in your terminology, to create our civilization, a few portions of which are still visible in your time, though perhaps not so clearly from a distance. We had a high degree of mechanized civilization before we moved on to something past the machine age. We evolved into a civilization highly focused in the creation of creation.

This caused a few difficulties at first, because as you can well imagine, different peoples wished to create different things. And although sometimes one could superimpose another, other times they were incompatible. We believed at the time that we were being trained to create something past what had been created on that planet before. We believed that we were to create a seagoing world. It might be surprising for you to imagine now, looking at our planet, that it was once a water world. It was *the* water world of this solar system, and we thought at the time that being on the water was going to be a way of life.

We did not have a vast population like you do, in terms of our type of beings, the humanoid. We had maybe 35,000, something like that. We started out with the understanding that water, being life-giving, could not only be a means of transport—as one might swim—but also a living substance itself and a substance that supports life. It made every bit of sense to be something that one would live in, as on your planet fish live in water and are supported by it. You, being fish out of water, so to speak, must find water on land, which is harder.

We Consumed All the Water on Mars

In our world we believed we could consume water. You may think you consume water, but it passes through you and only a small amount is retained, and even that passes through you. We believed it was possible to create all the nutrients necessary to live, as long as one lived in the water, and we did derive those nutrients. We assimilated what we needed from the water. But we made, as I said, some errors. We did not realize that the more we became like the water, the more we would attract the water. So we unintentionally began to acquire the life-giving properties of water so much that the water—those portions we didn't use—began to migrate from the planet itself.

What occurred is something I feel is important for you to know. You are not living like we did, but you are having water problems. Our water that we lived in was what you would call fresh water. It existed on about four-fifths of the planet. There is still water there now, but it has been changed in composition. Some of it is frozen, and some of it is under the surface of the planet and would be hard to get to. But the most important factor for you to know is that we unintentionally assimilated all of the oxygen from the water. We were able to live on it, you see, but by acquiring it that way, it caused the water to break down and become something other than the form of water you know. If you took oxygen out of the water that you have on your planet now, you would leave something behind that is not really water.

In our world, then, we gradually . . . it happened so slowly that we didn't really realize it until it was too late. We gradually consumed the water and thus were consumed, since we were so much of water. We only were able to escape through the assistance of others who came to help us. We could only escape to another planet where water existed, but of course, no one would have us because of our bodies being built in such a way that we were required to essentially consume the water. We did not realize that, but there we were, and that's who we were. So those who came to assist us felt that they could create a loop—you might call it a loop in time—where we cycle back to our planet as it once was. And then we can live, for there is much water. We go forward in time until the water just begins to leave the planet because of our actions, and then we cycle back in time again. We are caught in that loop of time, you might say, but it is not really that we are captured. It is rather that we—to our shame, because of our creation—have been placed in that by those who rescued us, for we would all surely be dead had they not come across that idea. But we are caught, as it were, in that loop, because that's how we can survive. We are slowly, gradually—it takes a vast amount of time—migrating to some other way of existence. We have been assured by those who came to help us that we would be welcome somewhere, even to live in the water, as long as we did not consume it. And we are gradually coming to this. So that is what we will do.

You Are Facing Hazards on Your Planet Now

I have come in today to speak to you because you have much water on and in your planet now, and more is being created for you with the melting of the surface. But there are hazards, and I will name several of them. One of the hazards is that you are doing—not in the way we did, or for the same reason—a breakdown of water to create something that is of its component parts. You are doing this to a degree for fuel, and this is with the belief that there is so much, that there is plenty. But even if your population was much less, eventually that plenty will be reduced.

There is another much graver hazard, and that hazard is that Mother Earth, as you call her—a delightful term—is also trying to protect herself. She does not wish to harm you, but because your civilization has been slow to accept the kind of creation I believe you call magic—but it is really just creation by another word—thus Mother Earth is considering how she might save herself from so much digging in her body and the impact on her body from your other ventures, including your wars and so on. In the past, she has always done this by simply increasing the water level on her surface. Some would survive. Those who are water beings—not all, because of what occurs, but some—would survive. But land beings would have difficulty.

Embracing True Magic

This does not represent an irreversible phenomenon, but you must embrace a kind and gentle form of magic to cure your problems. Some of that has come through this channel, and there are others. The magic is intended to effect change of all that is problematic on the planet. First, you must start on the planet herself, to bring her into balance and comfort. It is natural to think of your own survival and the survival of family, friends and others, but if you are going to survive and thrive, you must do more than think about bringing Earth to balance. You must be able to regenerate parts of her body that have been removed and are still being removed in your now time—for example, coal, oil and other various minerals that you use, since you are in the machine age. To your world they are but commodities, and yet, consider, does one really destroy one's host and survive? At some point, the host says, "That's enough."

Yet you have been granted great powers and abilities, though you have been slow, as they say, to embrace them. This thing called benevolent magic is a good thing, but there is much more. True magic is naturally benevolent, because its function is for the betterment of all beings. I'm calling it true magic because it has a lasting effect. It ultimately invites like to like, and like to like feels a natural attraction, just as the cells of your body achieve like to like at least on a temporal basis, and therefore your body functions as well as it does. You see this in the animal world, as well as in other parts of your world. You do not have coal falling from the sky; it is rain—like to like.

So I am here to suggest that you embrace what you call the mystical and that you use it to regenerate your planet first. And then as the planet is complete with all of herself, in herself, and all that you have removed and have displaced by utilizing it in the machine age . . . it will not disappear, but your machine age will be maintained in somewhat of a temporal loop, though you will not be stuck in it—only the machines, until they are assimilated into Mother Earth in the past. You will not have to go into the past, nor will most of you want to. You will simply go forward, having restored the planet to its former state of balance.

This magic can be accomplished. It is not meant to be kept to a select few but is meant to be taught slowly and gradually. The book that you're going to put out about benevolent magic will be helpful. It will help those who are in the mental world—meaning focused into thought as an ideal—to create actions that produce results, to move on the bridge across thought to the creation abilities of the physical, which most of you have yet to tap.

There will be a magic book that will follow. Of course, true magic is discussed now in this being's [Robert Shapiro's] blogs, but the true magic book that will follow will provide in words as best as possible and perhaps in some demonstration through visuals, if possible, how the average citizen can perform magic to bring about the most benevolent and desired results to restore Earth to complete harmony. None of this will harmfully impact in any way any life form on the planet, including humans. You do not have to give up your happiness and comfort that Earth might live in harmony. You are here on this planet to create solutions to unsolvable problems, and through true magic, you will do it.

Don't get caught up in what we did. We thought we were creating an ideal world, but you can see the Mars that exists today. Our belief came about as the result of using an ability in a way that was an extrapolation of the machine age. Even though we had magic available to us, we still thought in terms of products. We weren't creating products, but we were creating along the same line of belief that that thought promotes, as I mentioned before. So you must move past that to something that is more involved in the result. You must be able to leave the past. How? To what? True magic allows that, because it does not require that whoever causes the magic to take place—meaning, brings the parts together—understand anything about the way Earth functions, because you cannot know it all. Mental knowledge is not sufficient, as you have discovered, though it has vast reservoirs yet to be discovered. What must occur is a great deal of trust.

You Just Might Become Those Who Rescued Us

The magic must be done on the surface of the planet by those who can do it, and it must be done by your peoples. Those who have caused the problem must always be the ones who bring balance. Otherwise there is a vast gap, as in our civilization. We caused the problem, and we were unable to bring about the balance for the planet, so we continue to cycle through our loop of time so that we can change and be welcomed elsewhere. But those who came to help us felt that we did not have the capability in our way of thinking to bring the planet back to balance.

When we leave the planet, then those beings will return, and they will bring that planet back to balance, and it will become a water planet, not unlike your own. It might have an atmosphere of a slightly different color than one sees on your planet—the beautiful blue planet. Mars, as you call it, will probably be tinged with green, this having to do with a more chlorophyll-based atmosphere. But this will be only temporary while the planet recovers its true nature.

If you are good at what you do on Earth, you might just become those who rescued us. Time is so very flexible. The hearts of all beings, so very much involved in a desire for beauty and balance, will tend to seek out places where it is needed, as it was in our world, and help to balance things out in as much time as is necessary, time being the great healer. We are involved in a journey of time. We have come to believe that your peoples, in your time, evolve to become those who came to rescue us. We have come to believe this because of clues they gave us about their identity. They would not tell us where they were from, but they always said, "We came from nearby." That was the biggest clue, you see? We looked around and we could not imagine who that would be, but that's because we didn't look into the future. We only looked at the present.

We believe that because of what you are learning now, you will in time become those very heart-centered beings who came to help us and who—we were always struck by this—seemed to feel that time itself was the great curative, even when it seemed to be interminable. We are enjoying our life. We are not being critical, but it takes so very long to do what we must do, and it will take time to restore Mars to its original condition. Yet we have developed a respect for time that we never had before contact with those who came to rescue us, and we believe that your peoples will evolve a philosophy based upon your understanding of time and its healing properties. I have come to warn you, yes, but I have also come to praise you and thank you for the path you have chosen, to be the rescuers of this universe, to be representatives of the philosophy of the value of time and its many different facets. Thank you.

Thank you very much. Will you take questions?

A few.

This Universe Has Many Different Focuses

How long do you live? What is your lifespan within this loop of time?

There is no ending.

You're still the same beings who went in? Far back in the past, compared to where we are now?

Yes. Before human beings as you know them, including what you think of as evolution—which is not real, by the way—were on Earth. A long time, eh?

A long time. Do you look like us? What is your appearance?

No, nothing like you. It is hard to describe, but we are very big. That's all I will say.

Ten feet? Twenty feet? Fifty feet?

Bigger.

Bigger than fifty feet? What did the people who came and helped you look like? Were they humanoid?

The beings who came to help us, we could not see. Occasionally there would be a glint of light. We only heard them and felt their effects, but we could not see them. If we could have seen them, we might have been able to understand who they were and where they were from. But because we could not see them, that was the mystery.

So there was a difference in focus, then? You were in the same focus we're in now?

No. We were in a different dimension.

Can you say which one?

Which one? We were in Nah-keez-dee-ah. Does that mean anything to you?

No. Was it similar to us? Or was it more expanded or more dense?

None of those—it was different. There are so many focuses. This is how so much life in different forms can live in our universe. The Creator of this universe is very fond of different types of life, and the universe was only given a certain amount of space to be used. So one must consider how one can create all the vast possibilities in a given space. This Creator has been very . . . well, if I may say, creative.

[Laughs.] Are you familiar with other universes? Do they not have so many focuses?

We have a little familiarity, because when we asked to migrate, when no one welcomed us in this universe—for good reason, eh?—we tried to feel our way a little bit into exploring other universes. But because we were so out of balance, you see, no one chose to take us. So those who came to help us felt that we would be welcomed if we could learn, through the assimilation of the constant, how to migrate into another form. This migration, though, requires purposefulness on our part. We have to want to. And of course, we are highly motivated since we can exist in the world we thought was going to be so wonderful [laughs]. But it is not the existence we desire. You yourselves have some of this too, I believe. You exist, but not in the way you would like. So there are similarities between us.

What kind of form are you trying to assimilate into?

Into one that would be welcome elsewhere. It is not for us to create a form that would be welcome. It is for us to change ourselves so that we would be welcome, so that we are not going to consume other worlds. This is why I have been allowed to speak to you, because your peoples are consuming your world. Therefore, you as a people will not be welcome on other worlds until you change, just as we are not welcome on other worlds. Why would other worlds wish to have us if we are just going to bring about problems? We must change in our world, yes, and you must change in your world, because you have common traits with us that will make you unwelcome. Your fondest desire, many of you, is to see what is beyond, and some of you will want to go.

In order to go there, you cannot consume their worlds. You cannot harm their worlds. You must actually want to maintain the harmony of their worlds more than you want to consume. You must desire to maintain it. I'm not saying sign a pact to maintain it or promise to do it—I am saying it must be a natural desire in you. You will evolve this desire by bringing about that harmony on your own planet, discovering why that is valuable as a personal experience for each person and experiencing the reward of living on a planet that is completely in harmony.

The reward, of course, is that since you are cycling the planet through your physical bodies so that your physical bodies are made up of the planet, you yourselves will feel in complete harmony. So you gain by bringing about the best for the planet. As souls, you have chosen, we believe, to be in the position you are in now, because only your actions can save the planet, and in doing those actions, you will make yourselves welcome on other planets and even welcome to yourselves.

So you are changing within in the same way that you describe as what we must do?

Yes, but we are doing it over a great deal of time, and you will have to do it more quickly.

Are you using true magic to do it?

No, we are using time.

But we have to use true magic?

You must use true magic. I have come today to make the issue clear to you, so you will be able to consider whether you wish to use true magic and what you're prepared to do about it. You will have many stumbling blocks, because some people will wish to use the magic for short-term effect—meaning how it might improve the quality of their lives and of those whom they care about. But you must use it in ways that will benefit all beings all the time. The construct mentally, and its attendant energetic support in benevolent magic, does work that way, but you must go beyond the current practice of benevolent magic to achieve true magic, which incorporates more energy and less thought.

You can do this, we believe, because we believe that you have done it in order to come and save us and our planet. You have developed—and are developing, perhaps even now—a great respect for time, and you seem to be examining it very thoroughly, not only by living your lives as a people, but also in examining time and its effects. This fascination with time will serve you well, I believe.

Well, you know that we plan to go to Mars in the next twenty-five or fifty years.

You will find what you see now through your telescopes. But true Mars is a water world, and your succeeding generations, sometime in your future, will see Mars that way. Your peoples now will describe Mars as a rocky world with little water and many enticing suggestions of past civilizations. But look closely—you will see the way the stone is. Look for the signs of the water.

Your civilization . . . are they the ones who created the artifacts we will find?

Only some of the artifacts you will find.

Other civilizations created others of them?

After us.

Oh, after you! When you left, was there still an atmosphere?

Oh, yes! But we didn't leave. You said, "When we left . . ." We haven't left. We are still there.

But you're back in time.

Well, that's how we experience it. You experience time differently. To us, where we are is current. To you, where you are is current. Is one more current than the other? If you were to answer that in the mental, you would say that your current is more current. If, on the other hand, you were to answer it from the position of a time doctor, you might say that both currents are equal. Now I am getting into philosophy. You must ask your questions.

You Must Develop Magic That Is Benevolent for All Beings

When the beings whom you take possibly to be our future selves rescued you, they created the loop of time?

They helped us to do it. They couldn't do it for us, because then they would have had to stay. They taught us to do it ourselves. They taught us true magic. We thought we were practicing magic, and we were. Remember what I said? But the magic was in conflict, and different forms of magic created the problem.

You must develop magic that is benevolent for all beings. You must stress *all*—"all" meaning past, present and future, since you are so devoted to time— and must also honor all forms of life on your planet, from the tiniest to the largest, whether they live in water, underground or in the sky. Whether they be microbes, whether they be other trees, it matters not.

But it does not have to be so difficult. If it is of a benevolent energy, it can be felt in your physical body, and it feels good. If it is of an energy that is not harmonious—and this is the way to think of it, not as good or evil, but just not harmonious—your body will tell you, because your body will feel uncomfortable.

It's really very simple. Remember, don't stray too far from the simple. It is uncomplicated, because all forms of life are in benevolence with that energy, since it is the energy that attracts like to like. You have been confused about that. You think like to like has to do with appearance, but it doesn't. Like to like is what makes that which makes up a tree want to be a tree, or a portion of the tree, or a rock, or rain, or even lightning. Human beings have different appearances, but that which makes up the human being is like to like. And trees have different appearances, don't they? You have fruit trees, nut trees, huge tall old trees, little trees. They look different, but they are trees—like to like.

Variety, remember, is what your Creator likes to do and is fond of. Human beings have variety—maybe not as much as trees or fishes or birds, but maybe someday you will, since you are growing more fond of variety as time goes on. You are missing some beings whom you believe are moving on: plants, animals and so on. You will welcome that variety very much, especially as you embrace harmony, as it can be easily felt in energy. And you will let go of your acceptance that disharmony—which feels uncomfortable—is natural. It isn't.

Yes—you are very wise! So you are able to view our planet and know us?

Not as you would. You would, as you become, be able to observe at a distance. I am looking through something you might call imagination but that we would call a window—something like that. I can see at a distance, but I am not there. I do not know your lives individually, but I can observe at a distance. I have been allowed to do this because we have extrapolated that it must be you, in some form, who came to help us. The more we discovered that and came to believe it, the more we can see you as you are now, but not as you become.

This is because we have so much in common. It's not that we look like you exactly but that our traits on the personality level are similar. You see, how we got into the trouble we're in now are the traits that you are struggling through now. We did not recognize the lack of harmony because we were so caught up in our new creator skills. You will learn magic, if for nothing else initially than to save yourselves, and you will come to embrace harmony and the need for harmony. We believe you will move through the seduction of the temporary use of magic for personal gain, because you will recognize that the feeling is one of disharmony.

No one need suffer using magic. Your current belief says that some have more, so they can enjoy life. But this creates others having less. You believe that based upon the world you have created. But you will, as you embrace harmony, discover that everyone can have all that they want and need when there is true harmony for all. This will be not just a philosophy but a practiced lifestyle that moves you beyond philosophy and patterns of philosophy into harmony of existence with one another. You can do much as individuals, but together you can do so much more.

Harmony Is Your Ultimate Purpose on Earth

What was your path to Mars? Where did you live before you came to Mars?

No, we will not go into that now. The purpose of this chapter is to address your needs and to point out our similarities, not to give you our history. We do not wish to deny you this curiosity, but we feel that the urgency must be addressed. If you do not embrace this true magic, there can be only one inevitability. It will not help you; it will not help us—and going past that, you will not live to achieve your ultimate purpose for being on Earth, which I have come to believe is to learn how to help others and to do so because of a desire to perpetuate or to stimulate harmony. You will seek out places as you travel beyond your planet someday that do not have harmony, and you will find an eternal joy in creating harmony on worlds that you do not need to understand in order to create that harmony.

In order to create that harmony, you will simply know what energy feels good and what doesn't, and through the interaction of the physical feelings of that energy that you can note in your physicality, you will be able to support life on those other planets to experience the harmony that you have come to love, even though it will look different and be felt differently from planet to planet. But harmony is always felt as a physical comfort that you can feel and that other life forms can always feel. You will come to be the time doctors and the harmony specialists.

[Laughs.] I love it! That's so wonderful!

This is perhaps something Creator intended for you. All creators must have those skills, we believe, and because of your appreciation of time and what it can do, you will espouse those personality characteristics in the most benevolent way, which is to demonstrate them and to simply be that which comes to be admired, appreciated and honored by others. This path will lead you to your ultimate goal: to become a benevolent creator from which springs only benevolence. Good night.

Thank you so much. Thank you and good luck. Good life.

✻   ✻   ✻

Zoosh here. Those of you who have read that citizens of Mars consumed their water as fuel and that's where it went, understand that this culture you are reading about preceded those citizens, preceded their culture.

We Are Observing and Waiting for Human Benevolence

Zeta Reticulan Hybrid on mile-wide ship seen over London
June 30, 2007

reetings. I am from the vehicle. I am a being that has a balance of the human genome and the Zeta genome.

Greetings. Oh, wonderful.

So we have not been too close to your planet for a time, but it is our belief that the time approaches soon where contact between us and you might be possible. Also there has been a desire by certain entities to reach out to make contact with—and this desire to make contact is a real thing—I believe you call them governments. It is clear to us that these individuals in the governments are building vehicles to travel into space—granted, space close to your planet . . . relatively close—that are designed to make contact with peoples in other places with the knowledge that we have what it would take to set your planet to rights. But in order for us to make that contact on a frequent basis, not only will you have to be peaceful in your actions, but you will have to be peaceful in your souls, for that is how we are.

It will be possible—on a limited basis, as with contacts in the past—to meet an astronaut on a one-to-one basis, or at least us and one astronaut. But I feel that most governments, as well as most individuals, might feel uncomfortable with that. It has been done, however, in discreet ways that are not widely known or understood by the public. But many times these governmental institutions, or even to a degree corporate institutions, feel that they are protecting the public, since they are afraid, or they have told themselves these stories that the public will panic (although I do not feel that is true). But I bow to their knowledge of your own people. So we are making ourselves more visible now, so that you will be reminded that your tour through the realms of the imbalanced on Earth is coming to an end and that the source of your being within each and every one of you cries out to be united with the flow of interplanetary life as it exists for all other beings everywhere else.

Many of you living in the bodies you are in now do not feel comfortable in your physical bodies because you feel like you are not at ease with yourself physically. This does not surprise us because most of you have had many more lives on other planets than you have had on Earth, and it is not your actual nature to look the way you do in a physical human body. So for those of you who feel that way—and I know there are a great many of you, from my observations—that is what is going on. And the thing you are missing that you can't seem to put your finger on is your family and friends whom you have known in other life forms and in other focuses of your being on other planets where you undoubtedly looked different.

We Are Here to Remind You to Balance into Your True Nature

I am . . . I cannot put it in . . . I will put it in years so that you can understand it. From my perspective I am about 900 years old, and I have studied the human being for a time on Earth, you understand. There are human beings all over the universe, but the Earth human is a bit different. From what I have noticed, there is an urgency felt by you to move beyond this study on a day-to-day basis of living in a world not balanced and to be balanced in your true nature. From my observation I believe that you will accomplish this more quickly than it took for you to establish the machine age. So it does not have to be something lengthy.

We have allowed ourselves in our ships to be seen lately to remind you that you are coming out of your time of imbalance and into your natural true selves. As you do that, we will be able to more closely connect with you and meet, as you might say, across the table, to discuss how we can help you. But (speaking to entities of government and corporations) if you would, don't offer us anything. If we want something, we will ask. But we may desire to help you, just because it is in our nature and everyone in the universe helps everyone else, just as many times in your own cultures people help without being asked and without a need for compensation. The reason I am making a point out of this is that in the past there has been unintentional offense given by governments and corporations interacting with us and negotiating. [Laughs.] If we want something, we will ask. Leave it at that. Question?

A mile wide! Are your ships a mile wide?

The small ones are.

What did you have over London? What was the size of those two ships? They were seen a week ago.

They were not that . . . the beings who saw them as they would appear in your space and time . . . they were about that big.

If they are a mile wide, how long are they?

No, no, that description, it is not a length by width by height. We are not measuring cubically. The description is adequate to know how big they are. You have to keep in mind that there are lots of individuals inside the ship, and the vehicle itself was interdimensional, meaning that the vehicle was not entirely in your focus. That is how we are able to remain safe. But it is enough in your focus so that you can see it. It's present. It's observable, but it is also completely safe for us by being only partially engaged in your existence. That is why you might see the vehicle as a blob of light, instead of a vehicle like you would recognize, such as a truck or a bus.

The only report I read said it was a cigar-shaped, mile-wide light with some green in it.

A good observer!

How many beings are on . . . you had two ships side by side, right?

They weren't side by side, but two, yes.

Two. How many people on each one?

Individually speaking, about 30,000. But you have to recognize that when it is in our focus the vehicles are much, much bigger. That is a hint as to what your focus is about. Your focus is looking at things close up, and when you look at things close up, your experience of life is smaller—literally, not just philosophically.

I didn't know that. You are a Zeta hybrid, right?

I am that, but everybody on the ship is not.

Innate Capacities, Recognizing Communication,
Gender and Reproduction

Are you the captain?

No, there is no captain. It is important to note with these vehicles that fly, the whole thing about captains. This is a nice little story I think some individuals might have said to other individuals on your planet to make it as simple as possible. But no, there is no captain. Everyone does the job they feel that they can do. On your planet, people are born with certain innate capacities. Some people can do something naturally very well. Other people do something else naturally very well. And it is easy, simple and comfortable to do it. It's the same for us. We do what is natural and easy for us to do. We might even get a little extra training from those who also find it easy to do, and that's what we do on the vehicle. But there is no hierarchical authority.

What is your function?

My job is to teach the children how to be able to recognize qualities in each other and in other life forms that represent an attempt to communicate. You know, where you are now, this kind of teaching is often given from mother to child. Sometimes it's given from father to child, but mother usually is with child more and is more likely to teach the child when others are attempting to communicate with them. And if mother is very observant and helps child to be observant, this will help child to understand when other species are attempting to communicate as well—and child becomes observant. Is dog trying to communicate? Is cat? Is beetle? Then one can live in one's Earth more benevolently.

Hmm. Do you function in genders?

Explain.

Male or female?

Ah, we have male and female.

Which are you?

Female.

Aha, I thought so when you said about the mother. Do you create children through reproduction like on Earth, or do you clone?

We don't clone. We don't really like cloning too much because it has a tendency to repeat errors. By that I mean it's very easy for one group to say, "This is the perfect being, let's continue to re-create that being." And that is how civilizations stop—stop meaning don't grow. So even though we have that capacity and it can be done, most often we prefer to re-create through physical contact, although we do not have a gestation period such as you. But for us, the birth is pain free. And it's often ceremonial, although it is also a reality. But there is no pain or discomfort. And the reproduced being, the offspring, is very small, but we have the capacity to incubate the child outside of mother, so mother does not have to suffer at all.

Ah, that's how you do it. The child is born at what, two pounds, or three or four, or what?

Relatively speaking, you know, it's not about pounds, but mother does not have to suffer in any way. The child is born into a vessel that holds the child and the vessel has—how can we say?—an insulation quality to it so the child is protected and can grow but mother also has the means to be in that vessel or contact that vessel in such a way that the child is nurtured. So the mother stays close to the vessel so the child is loved.

Is that where we're going to attain pain free birth?

It is a way. You may choose something else. I think initially you will have a tendency to become enamored with cloning. Most civilizations, when they discover how to do that, become highly enamored of that. Not only because it is pain free, because that's very important, but also because of the desire to eliminate disease. Of course, very often in the process benevolent things are eliminated unintentionally. Therefore I'm going to suggest—even though you'll have plenty of people saying this anyway—that you proceed with cloning cautiously. It will be like a toy, in a sense. You'll be so excited about what you can do with it that you might accidentally throw out the good qualities as well as ones that are painful.

And you lose the incredible diversity, right?

Well, you could lose some diversity of personality. You know, sometimes you will find individuals that you meet to be annoying. This is not to say that everyone will find them annoying, but you may find them annoying, just as other people might find you annoying from time to time. And yet, when your neighborhood or your family or your group of friends or your nation needs something that you can do better than other people or that you and a group of others can do better than others, suddenly everybody notices your good qualities. So sometimes the good qualities are not always observable. But other times when they are observable, then the wide range of personality is appreciated.

We Are Waiting and Observing

Yes. This is just my curiosity, because we haven't talked to anybody for so long. Are the Zetas all in their gold lightbodies? What happened to the parents?

I do not speak for them. You'll have to ask them.

Okay. All right. How long have you been on Earth . . . or how long have the ships that you're in been on Earth?

They're not on Earth.

How long have you been in the vicinity of Earth observing us?

Ah, yes. In terms of your years it's difficult, because your time is not the same as what I would call natural time. So let's just say, the only way it makes sense to state it in your time is . . . we've been coming and going for about forty years. But we've been here all the time, even though you have to super-impose "coming and going" on that because your time as you live it, not as it actually exists, is not real. The only real part is night and day. That's real.

And your purpose for being here, is it other than to observe us? Are you doing other things?

Well, we're waiting. And when one waits, one naturally observes. I am not here on a job to observe you. That's not my job. It's nobody's job on the ship. We're waiting. We were advised some time ago that you were getting ready to come into your natural state. So we're waiting.

And what are the other beings' . . . what are some of the functions and jobs and occupations and whatever of the other beings on the ship?

I don't know where to begin.

It's like a city, right?

Yes, it's a city in that sense. Everything you can imagine and more than you can imagine. I'm sorry; I think that's too wide ranging.

Okay, never mind. So you are 900 years old out of a lifetime of approximately what in our years?

For my species, maybe about 1,300.

Thirteen hundred—now this is where time gets really gnarly. Because in our time it's only maybe sixty years ago that the Zetas were here doing . . . are you a hybrid of people on Earth or other humans?

Earth.

It's only about 60 years ago when the Zetas were doing this, but yet you're 900 years old so . . .

But our vehicles can move in natural time, which exists everyplace else in the universe. You have a fixed linear time that you are living in, so that you can observe and experience and examine—which is why you are living in this artificial version of time, so that you can do that. But imagine . . . imagine that like a highway. We can fly to any point on that highway, in a smaller vehicle of course, and we can access any sequence in there. So I can be 900 years old. Also, of course, in years ago, a thousand years ago or what have you, many of the people on Earth had no difficulty in interacting with people from other planets.

Feel Comfortable Communicating with Other Beings

It isn't in your nature. Think about it. Think of all the different beings you see. Do you scream and run away when you see a bird? A bird is not a human being, but it doesn't make you scream and hide. It is not in your nature, out of your simple nature, to run and hide when beings look different than you. I grant that if they are frightening, such as a grizzly bear, then running and hiding might be a good idea, but I don't know that they would recommend that. I'm not claiming to be an expert on such things, but hiding from a grizzly bear might be a good idea. But you don't hide from a bluebird. So meeting people in the past, they didn't scream and run away. They said, "Oh . . ."

How are you? [Laughs.] Yes.

"Who are you? Where are you from? You're not like us."

Yes, yes. Have you . . . have any humans been on your ship in the time that you've been on it?

A few, a few. Not many.

Recently? In our time, or not?

About twenty years ago.

Twenty, yeah. Do you have plans to . . . what is your plan? Let's say someone determines that . . .

We're waiting. That's our only plan.

So there is no, "we'll contact this government or this person, or we'll show ourselves here, or . . ."

We're waiting to see when you have the appropriate physical feelings so that we can contact you.

Safely.

If you are conscious and speaking, you have to feel comfortable with yourself, and you can't be frightened when you're talking to us. Think about it. And you can practice this by talking to a bluebird, or talking to a pigeon, or talking to any other creature. You can practice this with your dog or your cat if you like. Talk to them just as if you were speaking to an astronaut from another planet. Just because they don't answer back in your own language doesn't mean they don't understand you. Those of you who live with beings who are not humans know that there is a degree of understanding. And because they do not follow your orders does not mean they do not understand you. I think that's something that would be good to remember.

[Laughs.] Yes, I know about that one.

But I'm really speaking here to governments and corporations. If you are training your astronauts, an important aspect of training is to talk to beings who don't look like humans. You don't have to assume that we will look like beetles, although we may. I'm not looking like a beetle, but you have all these different life forms. Talk to a goldfish. Talk to a bumblebee. You don't have to say, "Where are you from and what planet are you from?" but you can begin by saying some greeting. "Hello I hope you are having a good life, and may you have a happy day." I realize that sounds like something you'd teach a child, but it is that basic, that important. If it is a being, make sure they are in their natural state. Try not to talk to beings who are in a prison, like chickens in a coop, because they may be uncomfortable and unhappy. Talk to someone who is free. That's what it will be like when you're talking to someone from another planet. They will be free.

Yes. What was the impetus to show yourself at that particular place and time in London?

The beings who could see us had the courage to speak of it. I salute them. I think it was very brave in your culture. I do not comment as a critic. I recognize that it is brave to speak the truth when the truth is frowned upon.

Mothering, Family and Community

Well, I know that one, too. Are you a mother?

I am a mother, yes.

If you live 1,300 years, at what stage do you become mothers?

That's entirely up to the individual, but not when we are very young, of course.

What is "very young" in your . . . in that range of age?

You have to remember that you are getting attached to how old we are in years. Youth, you know that you are ready to have a child when you desire to have one and are prepared to do what it takes to take care of a child. Not just as a child might play with dolls in your culture and then as you get older get interested in other things. But rather, to speak of your culture, when you are done playing with dolls and when you are living your life and have the desire to have a child and raise the child and care for the child, it's the same for us.

Do you form units of man, woman, child, or do you . . . ?

Not just like that, no. We have a wider community of friends and family. If I am doing my work, then one of friends, one of my friends or family will take care of the children if they are able to move about on their own. When they are very young, of course, they come to work with me.

That's wonderful. So there are not nuclear families? There are no . . .

Ah, family unit? Not in the strict sense of one of each. It's a wider community. I believe some of your cultures have that too. A wider community, more family, more friends, more uncles and aunties. And there are some people who aren't related but are still called uncles and aunties. It's like that for us too. My people have a lot in common with your people, but we are not bound by the rules of your culture. We have been exposed to many of the wonderful things of your culture. The arts, for example, and we tend to be artistic. I think you would find us that way, and that would be something we could enjoy together.

Oh, it will be wonderful when this isolation and imprisonment is over.

You have to do your part. But it's preparation that will serve you well.

Yes.

Travel to Other Planets and Galaxies

So have you gone to other cultures in other planets, galaxies, civilizations?

Everybody does who's on the vehicle. I have done that, yes, and I have found everyone to be very pleasant—a wide, wide variety of different people and places and cultures, but everybody is pleasant.

Other than being told to wait for us to wake up, what is the purpose of your traveling? Is it some sort of cultural exchange, or trade, or what?

No. No, we're just waiting for you. Travel at other times is, from my perspective, just because you can do it.

Let's go out and see the galaxy?

Yes. You can do it, and you have a desire to do it, and there are always others who have a desire to do it, so you do it together.

So the common thread among the 30,000 on the ship is that they had a desire to travel?

No. We're waiting. They had a desire to be involved in meeting Earth humans and helping you to come into your natural beingness. That's why we're here waiting.

So this is a particular trip to this particular place. This isn't a stop from one place to another. You were sent here, or you chose to come here.

We chose to come here. We weren't sent. And we've been waiting for forty odd years or so but we're not always in that exact spot waiting.

So if someone wants to see you or be aware that you are there, can they ask you to appear, or . . . ?

No, we're not a magic trick. But prepare. Prepare by becoming more aware of your own feelings and addressing yourself as you might talk to yourself in the mirror. How do you feel when you're talking to yourself? Know how you're feeling, because other people—other beings from other planets, to say nothing of your own kind—will be reacting to your feelings. If you're feeling uncomfortable when you're talking to yourself in the mirror, other beings, especially nonhumans, will feel all of that. It's not as if you're not surrounded by nonhumans. You have lots and lots of nonhumans. Perhaps you go for a walk and you meet a friendly dog, and because you are feeling happy, you pat the dog, and the two of you go for a walk together. That is an example—just as you may meet a dog who is not so friendly. How are you feeling? Granted the dog might not be feeling good and that's why he's not so friendly, but how are you feeling?

Because he may be mirroring your feelings?

He may be reacting to your feelings. If you are frightened, upset, unhappy and so on, many things, dog will react to your feelings on the basis of his being or her being. You will be interacting with beings you have not met before. If you are not able to naturally feel calm and comfortable in interacting with other life forms who are maybe only slightly like you—breathe air, eat food, in short, very much like the other beings that you have on the planet with you now who breathe air, who eat food, who sleep, who have families and who love their kind and interact with the world around them and so on—if you're not comfortable with them, how can you be comfortable with us? We're waiting.

We Are Waiting for Humanity to Have an Unobservable Agenda

We talked at length in the past to members of the Fawn group who are half human/ half Zeta. [See Shining the Light *and the* Explorer Race *books for more information.] Are you part of that?*

A moment. I'm stepping in something here. I'm becoming aware of the physical surroundings here.

Have you ever done this before?

No.

Ah. You volunteered. How did it happen that you are the one who is talking to us?

I'm available at the moment. And I am comfortable with it, and it fits into my job description.

Yes, communicating. Are you a member of the group called the Fawn?

We are like them, but not exactly.

Different how?

I don't know how to describe it to you because you don't know what they're like and you don't know what we're like. So how would you know how we are different? We are similar.

The Zetas don't eat, and I don't know if they breathe or not as humans do. So where do you fit in that spectrum?

I just said that in the beginning, when I said I was made of the human genome, meaning Earth human and the Zeta.

Yes I know, but do you eat? Do you breathe? Do you digest? Where do you fit in the difference between the Earth human and the Zeta?

I don't want to tell you too much, but we eat, we sleep, we have families.

I don't understand why you don't want to tell us too much.

Because you're not ready yet. I will put it in a way you can understand. If you weren't sure about another being's intentions, would you tell them everything about you? We are waiting until you do not have unobservable agendas.

And waiting until somebody doesn't try to shoot you down. That is so reprehensible.

Well, it is understandable in your times because you don't know who you are, but the more you become aware of who you are, the less likely you will be to overreact.

Were you related to any of those who were shot down in the past or that had accidents?

No, but we hear about it, and so we are cautious.

Cautious, yes.

The Physical Appearance of a Zeta Hybrid

So you are about five feet tall. Can you say if you have hair or not? Or you don't want to say too much.

We look . . . not completely like you, but we are humanoids. We look more like you than the Zetas look like you, as you understand the Zetas to look. But we don't look exactly like you. We could not possibly pass for human beings.

But in height, you're between Zetas and humans—about five foot or something?

Something like that. But of course we're not all the same height.

Tell me about the other people on the ship. Are there Andromedans or Arcturians or Pleiadians and others?

They're not all one thing. We don't really think of ourselves in a geographical sense. I realize that you think of yourself in that way because you are in this focus of examining the minutiae of life. They feel themselves as who they are on their personality level. But to answer your question without attaching tags to people, I will say that they all have similar feelings. They are travelers like myself. But they come from different cultures, many from different planets, and most do not look like everybody else. If you're asking of the varietal types of beings in terms of appearance, not counting personality . . . at any given moment—because it changes; people are not attached to being here, and they're not bound to be here—it moves back and forth from being about thirty-five different varieties to ninety-five, roughly.

Life on the Ship, Life at Home

So you have other ships that interact with yours and come and go, and personnel changes?

That's right, and it isn't always travel by ship.

Well, some beings don't need ships, of course. We just put a book out called Animal Souls Speak, *and I spoke to the personalities of beings who are what we call animals on Earth. And one of them (who was very interesting) was a dog diplomat. So many of the species, many of the beings on your ship are not necessarily humanoid, right?*

Yes, that's correct. A great many of them are, because thus do they have a built in interest in other humanoids, but no, they're not all.

It would be fun to go up there and meet them.

I am sure you'll have that opportunity in some way.

So where is your home? Have we ever taken a picture of it with our telescopes?

Our home and our culture are largely associated with these vehicles. Some of them are larger. This may have something to do with the human aspects of our genome, but we have found that we like to travel, and we don't really have permanent civilizations. I feel that this is not caused so much by a restlessness within us, but rather by an innate curiosity about what is.

This is part of our Zeta Reticulan self, because Zeta Reticulans are always curious about what is. But it's also part of human desire, the Earth human desire, to discover. And this is probably why we don't become particularly attached to a planetary home. Most of us are traveling from place to place, or on vehicles that might, in my case, generally park themselves someplace.

Were you born on a ship or on a planet?

On a ship.

Ah. So you have parents? You have an extended family there?

Yes, but my parents are not here. They are on another vehicle. I'm here because I'm interested in meeting Earth people someday, the way I described. And I know that you are, many of you, interested in meeting us.

Absolutely.

And I'm quite certain that the parent race, the Zetas—and to a degree the human beings—are also interested. And of course human beings on other planets are very interested. We have quite a few people here from the Pleiades. They're keenly interested. They look just like you, and in the proper circumstances would be very difficult to identify as being anything but you. They have no desire to live among you, but if they did, they'd look like any other human being. You wouldn't be able to tell the difference. Except they would be able to tell, and they would not be able to live easily with people with strong feelings.

I've never asked this of anyone and you may not know. Once we come into our natural selves, I imagine everyone's going to leave so Mother Earth can clean this place up, right?

I believe that is what's going to happen. Most people will want to go someplace that's more pleasant, and they'll want to be with friends and family they have known in other lives, because your life on Earth is artificially short. This is so that you do not have to experience too much discomfort. After all, if you were living a lifetime such as my own, it might sound attractive to you, you see: "Oh, I'd like to live to be 150 or 250," but think of all the discomforts you have. If you were aware of those discomforts—as you get more aware of your physical surroundings and pay attention to what you are actually feeling and broadcasting, because you are always broadcasting your feelings—then living 250 years in the culture you have now wouldn't be so wonderful.

No, but if we were all benevolent, this would be a very beautiful planet.

Yes, but it needs help. You will have to help—sometimes passively, sometimes actively.

Helping You Move toward a Benevolent Earth

When did you learn about humans on Earth? When did you learn about the experiment here on Earth? Have you always known it?

I haven't always known it. I think that when my parents felt I was ready to know, they told me. I was fairly young. I naturally asked, "How come I look the way I do?" as all youngsters do. Well, many youngsters do. I have met people in cultures on the ship here who never remember asking that, but I did. So they explained the reason for our existence. This was of course explained to my parents from the parent race, that we existed for a reason, since we were a hybrid between two cultures that might not otherwise meet in an intimate way. Our purpose for being—aside from living our lives in our own way and enjoying our lives in our own way—was to help these individuals on Earth bridge from an insular Earth life to being citizens of the universe. And we would be very helpful in that way because we would understand some of the desires, since we were partially that ourselves. So then I understood. While they were talking with me, I was seeing pictures and so on.

Do you look like your parents?

My friends say I look more like my mother.

I've never asked this, either. When the Zeta extracted DNA from various volunteers on Earth to start your experiment, did they use it from all the different races and species on the planet? I mean, do your people look alike or do they look as diverse as humans?

I'm not a scientist, but my impression is that there was a synthesis of DNA. Your basic DNA is from every single type of appearance of human being. And of course these different appearances of human being on your planet are a small but definite representation of the way human beings look like on other planets. You have human beings, as I've said, all over the universe. And so the appearances have to do with conditions and desires of appearance on those planets. But the basic human genome is almost identical, with very few subtleties affecting appearance. You have a big nose or you have small eyes or something like that.

So do all of your people look like any particular race on Earth, or some sort of, as you said, combination of all of their features?

We look like ourselves. We're not humans. I don't know how to describe it. I think you will find us attractive.

Oh, I'm sure we will.

We're very artistic.

What are the various ways that you express your artistic natures?

We like to express on an individual basis: the way I might dress, the way I might walk, the way I might talk, the way I might sing and so on.

So how many people of the 30,000 are of your race or group?

Oh, a few hundred.

Oh, just a few hundred! Is there any group that is more predominant than any other?

Some are more—how can we say?—dedicated to being involved with that process. Yes, some groups have 1,000 or 1,500 or something like that, if that's what you're saying. Yes.

Can you name some of the groups?

We had problems with this before. You want me to say, "Oh, they're from this planet or that planet." So no, they're all united in that they're interested in you. I do not function that way. No, I can't, because on your planet that's how things are separated. I want you to consider that. If you're separated, that's it, and we are not about separation; we're about inclusion. And if you say that someone is this or that, then you have a preconceived notion of who and what they are, and you separate them into that group. So I have found that this is fraught with more pitfalls than value.

We All Volunteered

How did you all come together on this ship that you are on?

The ship is immortal in that sense. It was known—it wasn't a secret; there aren't secrets in the universe—that this project was coming to a head.

And then you all volunteered.

And then you could participate in it if you wished. Not permanently, but you could participate in it as long as you wished. And that's why I say people come and go. I've been here for a while but some have been here for much longer.

Hundreds of years, in our time?

No, no, no. In your time it's not relevant anyway.

[Laughs.] But that's all I got!

That's what you have, and I do understand that. There's a tendency to use that, but I think you will have something else soon.

That's so wonderful to look forward to. All right, I'm running out of questions.

It's time to come to an end anyway. I'm going to say this: Pay attention to the things in your culture that are universal from one group to another—parents, children, friends, what you like . . . a beautiful flower, a passing friendly squirrel, even though you might not understand what the squirrel is saying. It might be very friendly and it might be saying something like, "Greetings. How are you? So nice to see you." And you feel that, since it is beautiful, and it is not harming you, is it? It is just going about its life, living, as it must. Say, "Greetings. I wish you well on your journey." Begin talking to other species.

After awhile, you'll notice that you're no longer nervous doing this. If you feel shy, you can whisper. But I feel it's good to do it out loud. That way, it is a way to prepare, to prepare the children. Who can say whether it will be your children or your children's children who will travel to the distant planets and interact with all life forms? But it would be good to get them ready now. If your children are talking to spiders or birds, don't stop them. Maybe they can understand. Maybe they noticed that spider changes how it moves when they talk to spider. Maybe they notice how bird cocks its head a little different when children are speaking. Maybe children don't even use your exact language. Maybe your children still remember a little bit of who they are. Pay attention and cull from that experience the best you can to put into your life. Goodbye for now.

Thank you very, very much. And we hope to see you soon.

Being Benevolent Is Your Access to Zero-Point Energy

Zoosh

November 23, 2007

reetings! Zoosh here.

About ten years ago, you said that the secret government's fifty-year secrecy pact on ETs and UFOs was over [see Introduction], but the secrecy lid is just as tight now as ever. And now Dr. Stephen Greer is saying again that those beings who control the secrecy on UFOs are also keeping the technology on zero-point energy secret and unavailable to humanity. He says they should have given out this technology long ago—that we have been damaging the planet using oil and coal because we don't have it—and if they don't release it now, we will destroy the planet. Is there something you want to say about that?

Other Countries Report ETs/UFOs, but Not the U.S.A.

For one thing, the secrecy *is* over in a lot of places. There is a tendency to believe that your experience, no matter how well read, is the experience globally, but this is not so. There are many countries where UFOs, when they are spotted, are reported in the newspaper, just like any other news. That's been going on for some time. This is not just this little country or that little country, but many countries! One does not always hear about it though, because one reads English. Interestingly enough, countries where languages other than English are spoken widely report these events. But the curiosity is that in the English-speaking countries, those individuals who are influential with the press have by and large been able to control the output of such things and to maintain the editorial policy that the sighting of such things is a joke. But the odd thing is—and everybody in the press knows this whether they are in any form of media in these countries all over the world—this is something that is a strange situation associated with the English-speaking press. I am not saying that you necessarily find that all other countries that speak other languages predominantly have exposure in the press of UFO sightings just as a daily fact all the time, but generally speaking, this is the case.

Now, if you could assign somebody to go online and monitor normal reportage in the news of events associated with UFOs and even phenomena, you would find that there were a great many such events reported just as a fact and often in a balanced way, as is best for the press. But you see, those who are attempting to influence are trying to control that in certain parts of the world. So it is an odd thing for people in the professional press in English-speaking countries, because this is one of their big embarrassments when speaking to their colleagues in countries where the news is the news and it is reported.

As far as Dr. Greer—I don't rule out what he has to say. I wouldn't say, however, that there is ever a situation where "have to" comes in. Also, you must keep in mind that almost every species on Earth, including some rarely seen, has been trying to tell you all that something is going on, that beings are here from other planets, that the architecture of new technology is available for the asking. You have seen this in crop circles; you have seen it in unusual behavior from animals, including pets; and you have seen it in phenomena in the sea and on the land and in the air and all kinds of things. People are reaching out, and you don't necessarily have to be a sensitive like Robbie and be able to speak with inspiration like this to have these senses.

Sometimes when people feel a tension that they cannot put their finger on— "Is this wrong?" "Is that wrong?"—they check up on everything. "No, everything seems to be okay, but I still have this tension." It is because something other than your usual way of acquiring information is trying to get your attention. So this is what I suggest: For people who are having that sense of tension for no apparent reason, speak out loud as if you were talking on the phone to somebody and say various scenarios [some true, some false]. Say, "This is going to happen," or "That is going to happen," and see how you feel. If you feel worse, that is not it, but then say things like, "This is happening," or "That is happening." For instance, say, "UFOs are real. They are filled with benevolent beings who want to tell us things that will improve the quality of our life." That is generic, but see if your tension eases.

This is a very interesting thing, because you will often find that you will feel better physically after you say such a thing and that then that information will present itself. For instance, in the case of the desire to know how the drive systems work in simple ships—not the big, big ships, but the simple ships that are able to travel just locally—most of them work on a simple basis of magnetism. And if you can amplify magnetic interactions, you can essentially—and this has been done—create an ability to float over something. This has been done for some time and is available now.

You have to remember, a great many things are being experimented with by various governments of the world that are accomplished and working pretty well at all times, and eventually these things percolate into general society. So it is not as if there is an individual cabal trying to keep one or two essential things from you. But I will say that for a long time—as President Reagan suggested when he departed office and as others have said as well—there has been an idea floating around here or there: "What if there were some strange threat from afar and it united the peoples of the Earth against this strange threat?" I grant that this was essentially a justification for the Star Wars defense system, as it has come to be known, but in reality, there are still a lot of people talking about how to stage such a thing.

So let's just say this: I don't think that would work anymore, even if the phonied-up ship arrived floating in space, as it were, with fake scary aliens on it who fired with their laser guns—which nobody uses anymore, by the way—from those places where benevolent beings come in their ships. They don't use anything like that that has to do with electrical. So any fake weapon from that scenario . . . if anybody tries to pull it, if anything is electrical or has explosive results, you can be sure that it has nothing to do with benevolent ETs who do want to come and help you, okay? If that should be staged, then you will know it is a phony. I am putting that out there just to clear the air a bit.

Don't Blame; Instead Ask What We Can Do

Well, the point Dr. Greer was making is that if the group on Earth that has kept back the zero-point energy would release it, everyone could have a little gadget to put on their roof and we would quit depleting the oil and gas, and quit ruining the planet. How can we get the beings who control this information to do this? We can't unelect them. We can't get a petition. I mean, what can we do to get access to the technology they got from the ETs and their ships?

Well, for one thing, it wouldn't make very much sense, would it? I am not trying to argue with Dr. Greer. I am saying that, "Oh, yes, that will certainly happen." There is no question about that being the case in the Third Alignment. But, in fact, even though you are overlapping into the Second Alignment right now, you are going to find that that technology—which is being negotiated to apply here and there and all over—is going to be distributed initially through your normal distribution system, and that even though it is not obvious, you have to remember that new technology always phases in and that those who are in control of the old technology resist it. But I think Dr. Greer is a wise man, and he knows this. If his question represents, "When are we going to get what we want and need so we can have a nice life here on planet Earth?", putting it in the simplest possible way, it will take awhile.

Three Alignments to Bring the Explorer Race (Human Race) to Benevolence While Leaving No One Behind—The First Alignment, Using the Corporate Model as a Method of Unification, Leads to World Peace on Planet Earth

The First, Second and Third Alignments are gifts to humanity from Creator. They are designed as safety mechanisms, as a last resort to bring all human beings on the planet into benevolence in the event that you as a planetary society stray too far from a benevolent path, even temporarily. But the First Alignment is not an objective, something you're striving for, something that you want to do as a global society. It was always meant to be not just a last resort—yes, that—but also a safety mechanism so that no matter what path you take, no matter how twisted or tortuous the path becomes, no matter what way you go, at the very least you will all get to where you need to go by the First Alignment, the Second Alignment and the Third Alignment. So it has been granted: the First Alignment, world peace; the Second Alignment, happiness; and the Third Alignment, fulfillment. That's the way I see it from my time.

—Preamble to the First Alignment
The Professor through Robert Shapiro
January 13, 2004
Shining the Light, Vol. 7
©2005 Light Technology Publishing

But I think it's important to not say "they"—whomever you want to refer to as "they"—are the bad guys and they are stopping this. Don't do that, okay? That is just like what you did when you were a little kid, and you went to Mom or Dad and said, "Look, he did it, she did it," and Mom or Dad most of the time made trouble for whoever "he" or "she" was. In other words, it doesn't really pay to do that, because it is just going to create trouble for someone, and as you all know so well, even with a casual overview of history, blaming doesn't make for peace.

So I am not saying to just let everybody off the hook no matter what they do. I am saying, find something else other than blaming, okay? And it has to be benevolent—ETs are not going to come to your planet and save you all because they love you. They love you from afar unconditionally but also impersonally for the most part, and you can't expect them to be as the prover-bial lion tamer going into the cage and cracking a whip and saying, "You, get in line there! We are going to make your life happy." You can't expect that. They are generally going to wait to see certain things that you must do—not to qualify, but to let them know that they will be safe.

ETs Are Waiting for You to Show Benevolence to All

Why should they die trying to save you? Really! It is something that they have done in the past, many of them, not unlike how sometimes the best of intentions by Earth humans to save others have caused you all to die trying. And while that may look good in martyrdom, the practical aspect of it is not appealing. So my recommendation is this, as it has always been: Pay atten-tion to how you treat your elders, your children, your animals, the plants and all life. Generally speaking, those from other planets will be happy to provide the technology that exists, but they are waiting to see if you are ready. They are not expecting you to turn Earth into Eden. They are expecting and wait-ing for you to show that you want that and that you are willing to do your part individually to treat animals, plants, children, the elderly, those who are mentally infirm, criminals and so on benevolently in some way—not just with respect, not just "apologize and then off with their heads," but to find ways (and a lot of those ways are already known) to treat people better and to treat those issues as if they are much more important than the latest, greatest bomb or the latest, greatest technology that is destructive.

It will take an act of faith to do that as an individual, and I am not saying to just offer the other cheek to be slapped. I am saying, get together with people; talk about it: "What can we do? What do they want? How much can we share? What can we expect from them?" In short, talk it over, work it out, make a commitment and do what you can. That's all you can do. Try to do it with your neighbors and others in your town. A lot of people are doing that now, so you are not going to have to spearhead something that is unknown. And in time, those who have already shared that technology—and it exists on the planet in the few scarce places—will make the effort to share it again.

But they are not going to come out of the sky like superheroes, land on the UN lawn, so to speak, and say, "We are here to save your world!" That would be interference. You know, many are the parents and grandparents who are held back from interfering with a youngster, watching a baby or a youngster getting ready to make some mistake—not something that would be life threatening, not something that would result in pain or injury, but something that they can remember seeing all kinds of other youngsters doing and can maybe even remember themselves doing—and now discover that the child just goes, "Oops, that's not it," and then he or she goes on and finds some other way. Or perhaps Grandpa or Mom or Dad or Grandma comes over and says, "This is how to do it, dear," and eventually the child figures it out. It is fairly complicated, you know, tying a shoelace, and it takes practice. And not everybody can ever accomplish it, but you accomplish things as children that are more complicated when communicating with each other.

You put a bunch of babies in a room—say toddlers—and they are usually pretty happy to see each other. It doesn't make any difference where they were born, or what culture they are raised in; they can work things out on their own, usually. But if you supervise, it's handy. Learn to appreciate the natural friendliness of babies. Watch them when they are eying each other in the store in this or that carrier. I think those pictures have gone around, and you will notice generally how happy they are to see each other. Don't teach them how to be unhappy to see each other. I know there is plenty of justification for that, and you can present a clear case to me just as children often do, talking to Mom or Uncle or Auntie: "He did this. She did that." I am not denying the truth of what you are saying. I am just saying, it doesn't solve problems. It doesn't make life better. If you want to say, "He did this, she did that," add this: "What can we do to work it out benevolently?"

Natural Magic Is Benevolent Magic

Okay. You have pretty much said all of this before, but that's . . .

Why have I said it before? And why am I repeating it?

I suppose because we haven't done it, but that wasn't even my question. My question was not when will the ETs give us that technology—that technology is already on the planet. My question is, what can we do to get those who have it to share it before we destroy the planet?

You are doing your part, but if you are saying you want a benevolent magic, you want something like that, well, you have already had the training in that, and I am sure many of you have done so. I will say this, though: Some of you have also had training in magic—and I am talking about natural magic, which is benevolent for all beings in its application and its results. Keep in mind, those of you working on magic out there—nothing can suffer to say or do the magic, and the result requested must also be benevolent *for all beings!*

Still, you have been trained, and it has been exposed to you, the magic of life on this planet. Beings can fly. Beings can stay under water for great time. I know what you are asking. I am putting your question simply here, Melody, as a representative of the human race and the outraged community of "Where is it, and why ain't we got it?" The simple fact is that what I said before is a fact. Why am I talking and using analogies of children? Why? Do you think that I think you are children? It's that the childlike way is *the* way. It is even in your Bible. It is the way. You have to be able to let go of attachments and approach this innocently. That is the way of communion, meaning communication heart to heart.

Every place else on the planet and even amongst many species on your planet now . . . plants have got that down, and many animal species and biologics as well. But it is up to you who have the capacity to do this and that, to not know who you are, to discover who you are or to have faith that you can do things. It is not for me to teach you too much magic; Grandfather and others will do that. But I will say to those of you who have been waiting for the sign, who desire the perfect technology from which you can draw all the energy you need to do anything you wish to do with that energy—*that is not the sign!*

The Sign You Are Waiting For

Now, this is the sign I know you are waiting for. It won't be some spectacular sight in the skies; it will be all over the world, pictures you see in the clouds. There are spirits in the sky all the time, and they often allow themselves to be seen temporarily as a cloud passes by where they are. Don't question the way they look. They will be able to—in that illustration—often give you hints, suggestions, the kind of thing you might do if you were going to give a hand sign to somebody else. They will be able to do this, but not in a fluid way—just a picture, a hand sign or a body stance, suggesting something that you would all need or want or understand. Look for them to do that symbolically all over the world. Some of those signs have been given, but when you can, keep your eyes on the sky and know that no spirit in the sky who allows itself to be revealed briefly by the etching of a passing cloud will ever give anything having to do with violence.

This desire for the energy unit, as benevolent as that may seem—can you not imagine what some people might use that for? If you had an inexhaustible device that would give you all the energy you needed, do you think that everybody would simply sit back, put their feet up and watch their favorite TV program? I think that some people might just use it maliciously. That is not the sign, all respect to Dr. Greer. I do appreciate very much Dr. Greer campaigning for that to be available, and it will in time, my friend. But look around the world! Do you really want everybody to have an inexhaustible supply of energy to do with whatever they wish? I don't think so. And that is because of what I said before.

People must demonstrate—not to negotiate, but from their hearts—that they need things to change more benevolently for everybody. It won't be easy, but it can be done. Pay attention to children, little ones, how happy they are to see each other, and ask yourself, "I don't know this person—must I assume he or she wants to hurt me?" You have tools now at your disposal if you communicate from one person to another, one country to another; you may never meet this person, but perhaps you will. Very often you form friendships that way—instantaneous communication, how wondrous! I know you will do the best you can, and I fully expect you to succeed, but even though most people would use that free energy in benevolent ways most of the time, many people would use that free energy in ways that would be harmful to themselves or others all the time or some of the time, and that is just not going to happen now. This is for your protection.

You can keep asking the questions if you want to. I am perfectly happy to answer them. This is an important issue, and I am glad you brought it up. I want people to realize how important these things are and that it is not something you can just allow the other guy to do. It is going to be tough, but it could be a lot easier for youngsters. Make it easier for them. Yes, teach them discernment, but don't teach them prejudice and bias. Life itself has a tendency to do that a little bit, but you can counsel them. You can help them. Do the best you can, and recognize that the best you can must be applied to all beings. You won't always be able to do it, but if you can form a consensus— which will not be as difficult as you believe—it can happen more easily now.

It Is Easier to Start Something Than to Stop

Let's go on to another topic. Things that Mother Earth must do to maintain her own health will be continuing to happen. There will be earthquakes, volcanoes, tornadoes, hurricanes and typhoons, as you call them in some places. This will happen, so given that, this is what to train for. Now, I have encouraged Robbie and other beings who work with Robbie . . . I have encouraged them to put out some of that training on the Benevolent Magic and A Mystical Man's World blogs. You can find it there—do a search or . . . you know what to do, those of you who have computers. If you don't have a computer or don't have access to one, ask somebody who does to print it out for you. Read it. Think about it. Consider it. Try it. No homework is given there that is not benevolent for you to do.

This is the challenge: Mother Earth must do these things to maintain the health of her body, and I know you want her to be healthy because, of course, if she dies, so do you all. And of course, that's Dr. Greer's great concern. We agree on that and on many things. But what you can do, what you can be truly influential with these days—those of you who want to practice benign, natural magic—is to modify the weather to the best of your ability. Don't try to stop it, but modify it. If there is drought someplace, invite the rain. If there is too much rain, floods, invite the sun. Don't fight the thing that's happening; rather, invite the thing that is needed! See, it is always easier to start something than to stop something—never forget that!

So I am going to send you toward the blogs. You don't have to like everything that is on there, but the training will be there, and for those of you who are unable to acquire that training, the blogs will be reprinted in book form in time, when Melody is able. They will be reprinted in total so that you can study all the various things that have been taught there and will be taught there, because that is the laboratory. It is instantaneous, and it doesn't take time to put out like a book. But you will find that soon you will have books available on your Internet that will come from this company, and you will be able to click on the links and all of that, and get that training built-in. That's the whole point here—they want to make it available to you. We are not trying to sell you something here. We are not going to sell you the means to influence the path of a hurricane so that it goes someplace where it's not going to harm people. The hurricane is part of Mother Earth's health system, just as the tornado is. It may not be easy to live in and around and near, that's for sure, but if you know how to move that tornado . . .

It's not your job to stop them. Don't fight against them. Just move them around people, animals, property, if you can, so that they can ease around on the land. If you know how to do that, it can be done. In the past, people were able to do that. Then you can make it easier for Mother Earth to take care of herself and show not only what you can do to help all beings but also demonstrate your desire to work with Mother Earth, not against her. How many times have scientists said, "Oh, how I wish I could trap lightning in a bottle. Then we would have electricity, all we wanted and needed." While you can't trap it in a bottle, it is certainly possible—oh, yes it is!—to be able to harness it in a benevolent way.

You will see how to do that someday on either the Mystical Man or Benevolent Magic blog, because there and in the *True Magic* book we will give instruction on that—Grandfather will, I will, Isis may. It is intended to provide you with the skills to learn how to work with the building elements and the building blocks of life to support, maintain and create life in the most benevolent way here on the planet. This is what you are here to do. You are here to learn how to create. You are not here to learn how to control. You are not here to learn how to stop. You are here to learn how to start and to create, and I have complete faith in your ability to do so.

I did not think of using zero-point energy for weapons—just heating houses and running vehicles and equipment.

Of course, but do you think if you had all the energy in the world in a little cube that you could flip around in the palm of your hand . . . just think, if you were holding that for a moment—magic. Here you are holding a device, or it's in the room, or it's hooked up to your house, and you get mad. Temporarily, you get mad at your brother or your sister or your friend or someone you actually love; you are temporarily mad at this person and you have all this energy available. How might you misuse that and bitterly regret it later, to say nothing of people who are mad on a regular basis for various reasons that they can completely justify, and some of whom are mad because life has caused them to be corrupted in their heart and soul and even perhaps in their body? Think of the damage they might do and, only after life when they see things clearly and have their life review or talk to their teachers and angels, bitterly regret that. No, as every parent, every grandparent knows, you do not give children knives to play with.

You Have Moved Beyond 3.5

There is one more thing: Can you say a little about the wondrous, magnificent fact, which I was just told last week, that humanity just went over 3.5 (on the journey from 3.0 dimension to the fourth dimension). [This terminology has not been used by the Explorer Race *teachers for many years—as they say, the shift from one dimension to another is not like a vertical elevator trip to a higher floor but is more of an awakening to who we are, or who we were before we volunteered to forget who we were to become part of the* Explorer Race *project—but that they had to start somewhere with concepts that were familiar to us. See the* Explorer Race *series, books 1–15 for more information.]*

Yes, you have done that on your own. Nobody came from space to say, "I am going to make it all right for you now, *poof!*" You have done it on your own, because people have a desire, a real desire—and the news services have helped out here in a way sometimes [laughs]—that people feel better, that people feel happy, that animals are treated well, that trees and other plants are appreciated and loved. This is growing in the land, or I wouldn't be talking to you in this article this way. This is growing in the land, meaning in the people all over the planet.

There are huge amounts of people all over the planet who desire that life be better for all beings, and this is what has done it. This is not something they changed their mind to do. Many of them have this in their heart, though their minds are confused. They are pulled this way and that way, because sometimes evidence that you are presented with—though not necessarily the whole picture, as judges, juries and defendants in courts, as well as others, know—evidence to the contrary of this and that, can create confusion in a mind. There isn't usually that confusion in the heart, but the heart can be in conflict with the mind—not destructively, though that has been known. More often, the mind is in conflict with the heart: "Why did you do that? I thought we already learned that. Here we are doing that again. Oh, no."

That is why therapists, counselors and often good friends are so valuable, because they can help your mind. You must help your hearts, and you can do that. The love of a friend, the companionship of a beloved pet, the love and tolerance of family . . . even though they might think their family members have gone off the deep end: "Eh, what's the matter with her? Is she crazy?" But, in fact, she just thinks differently, acts differently. Go with heart. Learn to practice tolerating your family. You might reasonably ask, as many family members have since the beginning of the human race on this planet: "Why in the world was I born into this family? I don't get along with these people most of the time, or when I do, it passes too quickly. Why was I born into this family?"

Well, you were born into the challenge so that you could learn what you are here to learn. You are not here to have fun, though fun is allocated to everyone. You are here to learn, and sometimes that learning is fun—when you go to school, for instance, or when you go out of your home to meet children in the neighborhood, or when you go out of your new home in your apartment to explore and meet your neighbors, some of whom you like, some of whom like you, and some of whom could take or leave you. But that is just the way it is, because you are here to learn, to discover. It's not only the new children—as they are called in various texts—who are here to learn, who accept certain things that even previous generations of children couldn't accept, and who have a sophistication beyond their years as parents and grandparents have noted. It is also many, many adults who want and desire that life be better for everyone.

You have done it yourselves. Pat yourselves on the back, and keep on striving. Know that many times you will be learning things that you thought you had done, but sometimes you don't learn these things again for yourself. You might just be learning them again in a new way, because you are going to teach that new way to somebody whom you are going to meet someday, you see? And the way you learned it in the past won't work for that person, but the way you are relearning it now . . . when you are with this person, you say, "Now I know why I had that experience," and you go on to show him, or explain, or a combination of both, and he gets it. And you know in your mind very clearly that if you hadn't had that experience again, you never would have had this way to teach him that he can hear, which improves the quality of his life immensely—not just something that you know will work for him but he can't hear it, because it has to be spoken in a certain way accompanied by feelings so that he can feel good about hearing it, not just threatened to do it or die.

You are wonderful! Thank you.

We have to give people who like old Uncle Zoosh (sometimes simply known as Zoosh, eh?) a little taste of "Zooshalizing," as Robbie's dear friends used to call it. I am happy to do that from time to time, covering all the bases in my own way. I don't want to discourage Dr. Greer. He is a good man. I am glad he is campaigning for these things, but I must speak the truth as I know it.

Yes, and I am sure that many people think of zero-point energy as something to heat the house or run the car, but not as a weapon, so this is going to help many people to see a bigger picture.

Well, that's my job, to help expand your view. I am glad you are interested in these things, and as I say, I have worn many hats as end-time historian, grandpa, uncle or friend, and I wear other hats in the future. But for now, the hat I am wearing is the salutary one. I say, greetings, good life and bon voyage on your pathway to the charter-member certificate you will receive during or after this life here. Someday, as I like to say, we will all sit around the pickle barrel and talk Earth stories. Good night!

[Laughs.] Good night! Bless you! Thank you.

Here to Help, an ET Diplomat Encourages Benevolence

Diplomat from ET Ship Seen in Stephenville, Texas
January 16, 2008

reetings. We are getting used to the vernacular. I am on that vehicle that was seen by your peoples.

Wonderful! Who are you? Where are you from?

I cannot describe myself as a named being; there are many different types of beings on the vehicle. It was felt important to briefly bring the vehicle close to Earth and to allow citizens of Earth to see the vehicle that has been parked at a distance from your planet for some time. It was always intended to do this. I am thankful, as with others here, that your government did not interfere. Although they could not have stopped us from being near the town and other places nearby, it was nice to not have to interact too much—though there was a brief interaction, but it was resolved peacefully. Perhaps your government felt that our visit was prolonged and wanted to suggest, "Okay, that's enough, eh?" We are from beyond this galaxy, and my job is as a language expert—but not of Earth languages, so I am struggling a bit.

You're doing great.

I am attempting to access your sayings as well as the linguistics, so I will do the best I am able. We are from a galaxy that is approximately two billion light-years from your present location, but we are able to cover these distances in the means of travel well diagrammed by other beings that essentially involves traveling through time. Your abilities are still focused on speed, meaning speed of light and so on, but we are hopeful, if you welcome visitors from afar such as ourselves, that we can help you skip over that step of

UFO Investigators Flock to Stephenville, TX
Investigation Opens After 30 Residents Claim They Saw a UFO Flying Over Their Town
By **MIKE VON FREMD** Jan. 18, 2008

UFO investigators, flock to Stephenville, Texas!
A team of six investigators from the Mutual UFO Network will be interviewing citizens of Stephenville, Texas, who say they spotted a UFO at sunset on Jan. 8.
The Mutual UFO Network is a nongovernmental group interested in documenting UFOs. State director Ken Cherry says that the network has received calls from 50 citizens who say they witnessed the UFO and that the number and credibility of the people is exceptional. The rural Texas town has attracted worldwide attention after the sightings.
(for the rest of the article visit: http://www.abcnews.go.com/GMA/story?id=4142232&page=1)

Stephenville eyewitnesses discussed their experiences on the Larry King Live show–Aired January 18, 2008 at 21:00 ET

propulsion and move directly to the more feminine approach of attraction. Attraction allows one access to travel that can take place almost instantaneously, allowing for long distances. When one approaches a planet or occupied solar system, especially if it is well and thoroughly occupied, one slows down a bit and does not use that same method but still travels in a fashion that is fairly quick.

You Are Moving toward a Group Identity

My reason for not providing a name is that in my group here—there are about seventy of us on the vehicle, though there are many, many others—we function as a group identity, so we do not embrace duality as you must on your planet. We understand that you must do this, since that is a portion of the way the planet is set up, although you have many species on the planet that do not do that—although they appear to be individuals, they are more comfortable with a group identity, such as the way we are. And of course, when you are in your natural state, the group identity is much more comfortable to you. Individuality does tend to foster competition, but when individuality is less of a factor, competition is also less of a factor. If you have a planet like the one we come from—where there is no individuality but there are, as you would perceive it, individuals—we all tend to work toward the same general goals. Although we might have personal likes and dislikes, when there is no competition, the general goals are readily achievable, no matter how difficult they may seem.

I feel that you have done as much as you can do with individuality and its attendant competition to rescue competition from what it became on other planets. On other planets that have experienced competition that I am familiar with—either from having been there or, more to the point, having studied about them and others' experiences there—they ultimately wound up very similar to the current state of affairs on your own planet, where the striving for this or that ultimately leads to some form of battle or at least argument. So we feel that your ultimate goal in the transformation you are undergoing now on the physical level to help you become more in alignment with your natural state of being will allow you to let go of some of the more extreme expressions of individuality and will allow you to achieve goals that may be impossible for you to achieve at the moment.

You all know, of course, that teamwork can bring things about—many people striving toward a singular goal. I feel you appreciate that, so don't think I am trying to talk you out of something or into something that is foreign. I am stating these things because you asked me something about myself and I felt that rather than describe my height and weight, I would simply tell you something about what my peoples believe and practice.

I shared these things with you because you, as a global society, are returning to that point of view yourselves. It will be difficult for you, I believe, to let go of competition, because there are so many forms of entertainments, even self-imposed entertainments, that individuals do that have to do with competition, and I recognize that many people believe this brings out the best in an individual. And while I can understand this rationalization and the attendant proof that might be offered, it also tends to bring out the worst, and this is a problem, isn't it? So if you could only use it to bring out the best as occurs in teamwork to achieve a goal, that's fine. But it's the other part that is problematic, and I am sure your history, even with a casual study, to say nothing of your current events, would prove my point.

So I do not wish to compete, with my civilization compared to yours, eh? Rather what I am truly saying is that your natural state of being is, yes, teamwork, and also a joined state of being that allows you to be many different things, many different personalities, with the widest variety contributing and no one excluded, and yet no inner or outer conflict. This is your true nature, and you are easing back into that—or should I say, easing forward into that, eh? But it is a complete circle.

You Are Recovering Qualities on Earth That Didn't Work Elsewhere

You have volunteered to come to your planet to accomplish, from my point of view, the recovery of qualities of other things that have been tried and did not work elsewhere. But these things had good qualities, good capacities, that no one wanted to just throw away. So you volunteered to rescue and glean the good qualities from functions, philosophies, ideas and practices that otherwise had significant aspects to them that were not so good.

That is an interesting way to put it. List some of the qualities we are recovering.

Discomfort comes to mind instantaneously, because no one really likes discomfort. But you use it on a low-key scale to accomplish things, to simply even stimulate your motivation to do something. Something is a little uncomfortable, and so you perform an act perhaps to return to stasis or comfort. What does your old friend Zoosh say? "You close the window and the draft is no longer on your neck." That might seem to be perfectly obvious to you, but on other planets it is not a factor of their existence because there is no draft on the back of anyone's neck. This does not mean there is no wind, but there is no discomfort and therefore no need for motivation of that type.

There are other qualities that you have gleaned the best out of. Competition I mentioned because it has brought forth the application of teamwork and this is competition's best quality, from my perception. There are many others— you can look around and see things that you don't like in society, but then if you distill them down to their original expression, you might say, "Well, I don't like this and this and this, but this is good." You may not approve of the way your food is grown, raised and, in the case of animals, treated, but that does not mean there are not food items you do approve of and enjoy eating.

You see? Polarity on your planet has affected everything, but you have to have a planet that has polarity in order to accept these things, unresolved in other places, that come with the full package of discomfort and comfort—to glean out the comfort aspects and say, "Let's not throw this thing away just because it has discomforting aspects; let's glean these things out and find a way to synthesize them into a societal philosophy that can be practiced benevolently, and then we will be able, with these structures, to set aside the discomforting aspect of all these things." You have actually done this; you have accomplished it. Now you are striving toward a global societal function to test all of what you have done and to set aside everything associated with discomfort. It will take you awhile, but not an infinite time. During this time, though, you will have more and more visitors.

Is this the first time your ship has been seen?

No, but it is the first time it has been seen so closely. There are many ships, many standing off at a distance. We must do that so that we do not interfere with your project. That is the way we see what you are doing on Earth: It is a project, a worthy project generally, but we could interfere if we are too present, couldn't we? Still, we must announce our presence so you realize that you have allies who are prepared to assist you once you gravitate to a more benevolent state of being and are prepared to consider that what you call feminine science has not only value but greater value, since it does not involve discomfort, uses the attraction principle and has at its core and foundation and framework benevolence as an expression of all aspects.

It will be difficult for your science to accept that because of the competition angle in there—the desire to succeed and be recognized with all that goes with that recognition. Once your society recognizes all individuals, treats them benevolently and develops support systems for those who do not fit in but may be the herald of something new . . . though their socialization process, for example, may not work in your society. It is all right to have a place of their own, isn't it? To be treated well and cared for and perhaps gently observed to see if this something new or if it is strictly an anomaly that needs to be cured.

You have much of that now. Many of the children are expressing these things, and it will happen more and more. I know that your medical science will be concerned that you are having a wave of birth abnormalities, but one might reasonably say, using science as a benevolent analogy, that many technological inventions were considered abnormalities to the point of being laughed at. But you take many of them quite seriously now and use them well. And even pathological aspects of modern inventions are considered laughable by some, but not quite as laughable as they once were—as in the famous steamboat, which was quite a joke at the time, but the inventor definitely had the last laugh.

How many of you are on this ship and how long have you been on the ship?

It varies, but at any given moment, perhaps 20,000. My group has been on the ship about . . . now I am going to use your years. They do not really relate to our sense of existence. But from your way of measuring, about nineteen years. And we live . . . I am going to have to calculate this to your time. We live about 700 years. Now, I am not talking about everyone on the ship; I am talking about my group of seventy. I will always be doing that. We have time, but it is measured by experience, not by night and day. Your time is measured by night and day.

You all have different jobs aboard the ship? Are you one of the diplomats, since you are the one speaking to us?

Yes, mine is diplomatic, and when there is no diplomacy needed, then my group simply studies the likely places we might go or the possible ramifications of this and that associated with whomever we are likely to be involved with. That is why we have a considerable amount of information to study about Earth beings, since we have been in and around your planet for some time, using your timing.

And you have equipment that can scan the events on the planet, so you can keep up with what is going on?

I don't want to say too much about that, but the answer is yes and no. I can't really say too much more about that.

What is the original purpose of your ship? Is it to explore and discover, or is it to travel and trade, or what?

I would say that it is to welcome. It has a tremendous amount of diplomacy, yes, but ultimately sharing capabilities. There are a great many peoples—from all over the nearby galaxies to your own—on board this ship, which allows us to offer, when welcomed, a great deal of support to planetary civilizations that would welcome us. And I would not wish to say that we need anything from you. We might from time to time request a scoop of this or that portion of your planet—perhaps a little sand, perhaps a little water, something like that, that we might use in various ways. But we would never ask for any personal sacrifice by anyone—and by "anyone," I mean any form of life on the planet. We would certainly make certain that there were no creatures in the water or in the sand.

Do you have the ability to land, or do you have small ships that would land?

Generally, we would have a smaller vehicle. We made an exception in the recent flyover because we felt and we were advised by those who know more about Earth's civilization that an announcement of our presence was important. Therefore, we chose a place that was not too big and that would be perhaps reasonably friendly, where we thought the children, as well as many of the young people, would be happy to see us. Generally speaking, what makes your newspapers and what might make a sensational story is not the bulk of the story. The bulk of the story is that the people there who saw a ship . . . it really reminded them of the continuity of life. Needless to say, there is no more question about whether there is life on other planets. These people, at least, know what they saw, and that's that. No one is going to talk them out of that. And also many of their children will become excited about space travel, which we feel is a good thing.

Do you plan to show yourselves more?

I cannot answer that question at this time.

Of course. You said there was an interaction with the government—did they send up fighter planes?

Yes, just the kind of thing you have done before, but there wasn't any battle or anything. They just mostly said, "Okay, that's enough." They didn't send them immediately, and we thought that was quite diplomatic, but when the planes came up, it was like, "Okay, we honor your expression."

There Are Hundreds of Different Groups on the Ship

The report I read said your ship was a mile wide.

Well, you know, if there is no resistance, one can build things. Think about that. Your engineers, when you build structures, have to take all of these different mathematical formulas into account, don't they? How tall it is, what is the load per square inch, and the whole business. But if you're building something in a place where there is no stress, one can build something in a different way. Also, if every single molecule and atom desires to be a portion of this ship and desires to be exactly what it is doing, then the vehicle—this is more advanced—essentially creates itself based upon the needs, wishes and desires of those who may occupy it, as well as those who might invite the creation of the vehicle and invite all of the participants, including the atomic and subatomic particles that wish to join in the adventure. One does not have to give up adventure, you see, just because one is no longer competing.

It is possible, when you have such a vehicle, that the form of the ship, the appearance, can be altered. When you have the makeup of the ship, what it is, when it is cooperating to be something, it can appear within a certain range—it is not infinite, but it can alter its appearance slightly.

I think I read that it split into two pieces?

Let's just say that it is possible.

There are so many people on the ship—so there are hundreds of different groupings from different planets?

I think that is a good estimation—hundreds. It depends how you count. If you are counting a single person as a representation of a planet, then we might have to go into thousands. But if we are talking about groups, which is more in my comfort zone, then hundreds would be appropriate.

Before you got on this ship, had you met many of the different citizens of the different planets?

No, it has been an adventure meeting certain groups of peoples that I had heard about or read about or studied about, and here they are—I am meeting them. It is exciting, yes?

How did you happen to come on this ship? Did you get a notification or an invitation or what?

I was not personally involved, but our group was asked if we would like to participate, because such vehicles often encounter the need for diplomacy and those who embrace diplomacy, which requires an interest in history and those social functions of large groups of citizens and so on, and that is really something that we like doing on our planet. So it was some time ago that a request was made: "Would some of you like to volunteer for these ships, to be on them—perhaps a few of you on a small ship and many of you on a larger ship?" Well, we were less enthusiastic about "a few of us on a smaller ship," because we prefer groups—that's our thing, eh? And so we were more inclined to favor a minimum of three individuals from our group to do our work. That tended to rule out a lot of the smaller ships. It was generally decided that the larger ships would be the best place for us because we are much happier in groups of, say, fifty or more.

Does everyone on your planet focus on this linguistics and diplomacy, or just your group?

No, it was our field of endeavor—not unlike one might go to a school, a university, and say, "We need some historians," and you might get a lot of historians to volunteer to do something if they were interested in it.

Is everyone on the vehicle from various focuses, various dimensions?

Everybody is comfortable in the same focus. We are comfortable in the same dimension.

Which one is that, or which range?

I do not . . . do you have numbers?

How would you describe it?

Oh, I do not know—my tendency would be to use atomic weight, but I would say something akin to the weight of copper.

I see. These are just terms that we are given—that we live in the third dimension or focus.

Ah, I am accessing that now. You're using that . . . that's based upon mathematics. But you're not in the third dimension; that is simply a mathematical expression. No, you've always been in the fourth dimension—you have to take all of your dimensions and bump them up a number. We don't use numbers.

The Appearance of These Beings

Would I see you if I looked at you?

A simple answer is, if you were on the vehicle, yes, you would, but you would be altered on the vehicle. You would not have one iota of discomfort in your body. This means that a great deal of what you could remember would not be present. Anything associated with a memory of discomfort would not be present. This would include thoughts in the present, worries—no worries, because anything associated in the slightest with discomfort would not be present. This is fairly typical for people on ships unless the ships are performing a biological function or something like that. I don't know much about that, but I have heard about it. If you were on this ship, yes, under those circumstances . . . you could only be on the ship under those circumstances. You couldn't be on the ship otherwise.

Let's put it another way: Could you exist in our atmosphere, in our discomfort, or do you need to stay on the ship?

We need to stay on the ship, but in time, we will be able to exist with you and walk around with you. But this will take awhile, because your planet will need to heal itself, and by that time, you will not be on this expression of this planet anymore but will likely have moved on to a different expression of this planet.

How long will you be here?

We will be here as long as we are here. I am performing my job, but I do not pilot the helm.

Who does?

Think about it: If we were picked to do what we are doing, civilizations are picked to do such jobs as navigating, but people are not picked because they make good bosses—we do not have that. We would have groups of people who are good at, say, navigation, so when I refer to "pilot the helm," using perhaps not well your sayings, the peoples who would do that would be good navigators. They would be interested in such things.

What are some of the functions or talents or trades that people were asked to do on the ship? What are they doing?

I don't know where to begin—just everything you can imagine and more. I realize this is vague, but I don't know what to say. Not science as you know it, but more science as I described it before. In that sense, science and art are one thing, which they actually are to a point on your planet now. Many practices that involve sciences also involve art. As for the other people, you would have to ask them. I see them coming and going, and they seem to be doing things, but I haven't ever stopped anyone to say, "What are you doing?" We have social things, but we don't tend to speak about work.

Can you all communicate with each other? Do you have some sort of common universal language?

Oh, yes. You would know it as feeling. Some of you would like to call it telepathy, but you are caught up in words, so I would call it "one knows what the other person is communicating based upon the feelings one receives and the memories that are jogged, even though the memories that are jogged on the basis of that feeling may not be associated with the memories the other person is communicating." They would be as close as the feeling can incorporate. So it would be that kind of communication. If you're asking if we sit down and drink tea and discuss politics, no, but there may be peoples on the ship who do.

I was thinking more of a universal translator.

I think that might be on the ship, but you would probably find such a device with those who might actually walk on the surface of planets not their own and use such a device, if the people on the planet are comfortable with it.

Our Ship Tends to Go Where We're Needed

How many planets have you gone to since you started adventuring?

Since I have started doing this, about twenty-three planets. Not that many.

What is an example of an experience with a planet—do you interact with the beings?

Only in so far as that is desired. First contact is not made by our group. First contact is made by those who are trained in not only perception but in understanding the feeling nature of the beings. We don't necessarily do that. We do some of that, but we're more in . . . I am going to come up with a saying here. We're in middle management. We are the people who actually go out and do it, but we don't make first contact.

What are the purposes for which you go to these planets? Do they need something?

Usually we're in a follow-up. We are doing something that others have started, and we're just coming by to offer what's needed or to commune or just to visit. Most planets are quite social with others. This is considered a plus, but there are a few planets that are less comfortable with visits, and that is when our ship comes along, because not only do they have us for diplomacy, but there are others involved in diplomacy, so we are therefore more able to provide the nuances that that civilization might need to accept a visit which might be to their benefit.

So you see, our ship tends to go where we're needed. That is the foundational principle of our travels: We go where we're needed. Sometimes we are able to communicate with such planets and civilizations when they are not exactly embracing visitors because of the diplomat abilities of many peoples on the ship. But in the case of your planet, where you are involved in extraordinary attempts to do many things, it is too soon to expect to fly down and land in some vastly open place, to announce our presence and say, "Here we are. Now bring us your problems." It is not like that.

But you are in a time now when you must be aware of other civilizations. I grant that there will be some on the planet who will be afraid of such things, but I can assure you that we are all benevolent beings. We believe in a Creator, and we have reason to believe it, and we will be interested in sharing our stories about Creator with you and hearing your stories about Creator, and so on. So we are not that different. We may look different, but we have personalities. I'm sure you will find many of us pleasing.

You Are Not Ready for Our Help

Can you say what you look like?

I will say only that we are humanoids. There are others on the vehicle who are not that, but you will always and only, for the first 500 years or so (perhaps 600 years) of your interaction with other beings, largely be interacting with beings who are humanoid so that you will get comfortable with the interaction with other civilizations. This is not to say that it won't be brought to your attention that other beings look differently, but you won't be expected to interact with them—meaning that you will be able to say, "This one, not that one," essentially. But after 500 or 600 years, the youngsters, the new generation, they will be tired of the old stuff. They'll say, "Come on, I want to meet these other guys."

If you were to look around your ship and see people coming and going, give me some examples of what they look like.

Different shapes, some lightbeings who do not have a physical form. If you're asking if there are creatures on your planet that might be compared to those on this ship, I must be vague. I will only say, yes. I can only say . . . you know, we're not just talking about civilizations and sitting drinking tea. We are talking about a vehicle that flew close to your planet recently, so there is only so much I can say. We are talking about something that is beyond philosophical discussion. You are not ready to hear it; you are not ready to recognize that the other forms of life on your planet are equal to yourselves. None of your major religions accept that yet. But until that happens, we won't be able to help you as much as we would like. You must accept that.

You must accept that there are beings who live in the sea, and while your ships are tolerated moving across the waters, it is not something welcome to have fluids and other matter discharged into the home of the sea, just as you would not appreciate having these matters discharged into *your* home. With your civilization, the more individuals you have . . . your science and industry and businesses are working overtime, you might say, to figure out how to deliver everything you all need to live as well as possible, and it is a major struggle because your vehicles are limited by what they can do. You're doing as much as you can and more, and of course, there are accidents, because people feel pressured to get there on time, to say nothing of other problems. We would like someday to show you how various things can be done in various ways, and you won't have to give up your basic economy the way it works.

Do you have discussions on the ship as to how you could communicate to us in ways that we could learn faster, so that people who aren't aware of this yet . . . but that's why you're showing your ship, that's one of the steps, right?

That's right. And other material you are putting out about what the so-called animals and the so-called plants have to say—these books are also a contribution. The whole point is to remind you that you are living on this amazing planet with these amazing beings from all over the universe. They are all here to do one thing, and that is to help you, because what you are attempting to do on this planet is so important. You are literally rescuing things that did not work well in other places and caused harm in other places, and they are causing harm here as well on your planet. But you are gleaning from them the good and will attempt to find a way to set aside the other without too much difficulty. The next five to ten years will tell the tale there.

It's not easy to glean the good from discomfort and say, "Okay, let's leave the rest." It is kind of like pollution, isn't it? You have to move it from place to place, and it doesn't get any sweeter.

There Has Been Some Contact with Earth Governments

Has anyone on this ship attempted to communicate with the various governments?

I can only say this: You understand, we're getting into territory I cannot discuss. But I can only say that there has been some contact, and it has mostly been a good thing. There is some shyness by some groups on the planet and some welcoming by other groups, but that is all I can say at this time.

So there has been interaction—how do you choose who to talk to?

It's very, very simple: We are able to feel at a distance, just as you are able to feel close up, and we approach that where we feel welcome. Have you ever gone into a room crowded with people and approached the ones who looked at you and smiled and nodded, and you walked over to them? We are able to do something similar, although not with that exact technique. But ultimately it has to do with feeling welcome. It is really so simple; it is not complex.

So do you bring them up to the ship, or talk at a distance?

Well, you are talking again in areas that we don't really wish to talk about, but you are also asking me to speak for the ship, and a lot of what you are asking I do not know. Generally speaking, our peoples on this ship do not come to the surface of the Earth, as far as I know. I do not claim to know everything. I am talking a little beyond my field as it is, but I recognize that you do not understand my field very well, so you are asking innocently.

Well, I ask a lot of questions that don't get answered.

I am not offended, and perhaps you are not either.

No, I get used to it after a while, but I'm still curious.

I am sure there are people in your government whom you could ask many questions of, and very often your government person might not be able to answer. I do not claim to be in a government, but as you say, you get used to accepting that people cannot answer for whatever reason, and you say okay and on you go to the next question. It is not that different, you see?

Yes, some things you don't know and some things you can't say. I understand that.

There are times when you do not tell what you know, but I am not saying your people are children—there are just things you are not ready to know yet. And the reason you are not ready to know . . . it has nothing to do with your intellect; it has to do with timing. You are ready for something, meaning that you have moved toward something. Then something might be ready for you, just like on your planet. But if you are not ready for something and you haven't moved toward it, if that thing moves toward you, you might get frightened and run away.

Why do that? That would suggest impatience on our part. We do not have an agenda to get to know you and to do things for you. We are simply volunteers. We are available, but we do not wish to thrust our civilization upon you. We wish to support your civilization. We are not here to take your civilization away and give you ours, nothing like that. We are not competitive.

Helping Two Planets Share Materials

To get a better idea of what you do, can you give me an example of what some of the civilizations that you've contacted needed? You said you respond to the need.

I will give you one example. I did give you an example already, but I will give you one other. There was a civilization that was attempting to establish trade routes and reach out to another planet that had something they needed. At that time, the other planet had an abundance of it, but they weren't comfortable seeing anything of their planet being taken somewhere else because they felt a sense of personal identification with everything on their planet. We were able to set up an energy that would allow something to be taken from their planet but to remain connected to their original planet and not ever be used up. It also would have the means of returning to the original planet when desired, either by the civilization on the original planet or by that which was taken.

Now, you realize that I am being very careful here, but the reason I am being so careful is that you, in your space travels in your first few hundred years, are going to meet these people. That is why I am being vague—I don't want you to get caught up in this and that. There was no competition, but if someone came to your planet and said, "We want to have this and that from your planet, and take it away," you might be a little shy also and say, "Wait a minute."

That was brilliant. All of the people on the ship came up with this, or one group?

Everybody comes up with a solution and says, "Why not try this?" or "How about this?" And if the people on those planets have not considered some of those things, then they say, "Oh, well perhaps this could work." Then it is not so much trade as it is sharing—the materials are not actually traded, one thing for another. Rather they are shared and are able to return to the original planet at any time.

That is wonderful. It was really satisfying, wasn't it?

It is a comforting thing. My group had something to do with that because it was necessary to have a means to understand the other planet's general philosophy. Where one planet didn't feel attached to the planet itself, the other peoples on the other planet felt the planet was just as much a portion of their bodies as their bodies were. It would be as if you were to sit on a rock and say that you felt about the rock the same way as you felt about your body. You would then be less inclined to have someone come along and say, "Hey, can we have that rock?" You'd say no. Some people on your planet might feel that way now.

Do you ever go some place so that all of the people on the ship can get off the ship for sightseeing or for recreation?

Yes, that happens. We don't necessarily get off, but we could, and yes, this happens. It's not necessarily for recreation, but to explore. Yes, I have done that on a few occasions. On one planet was a place . . . I can only describe it as the art planet. I can only describe it that way because the planet was solid, but at the same time it was also light—colors of light I had never seen, and the light responded to music and it also responded to feelings. Therefore, it was popular to exit the ship, go out and be in the light, and have different feelings, and the light would do things—amazing! As a diplomatic historian and language expert, of course I was attempting to learn if something was being said, but it was beyond my capability.

Were there beings or people there?

We assumed the lights were beings. We were there for only a short time—we were attempting to grasp what it was about, and after a while we thought that we needed teachers to explain it to us. But they have not been forthcoming yet. A moment.

You Are Not Alone on Your Planet

Have you ever done this before—talked through an Earth human body?

No, and I think we are just about at the point where we are going to have to stop. I did not realize it was necessary for the physical self to drink water, and I may have taxed the physical body a bit there. But it seems to be recovering well. And when I put the speaking instrument [telephone] down, I apologized to the person's body.

But if no one told you, how would you know?

But I did not grasp, you see? Here was the water nearby, and I did not grasp the reason for it. This is not good. This is perhaps why I am not involved in contact on planets.

Have you ever talked through another being like this?

It is the first time, but I see I need to improve my technique. I must make a closing comment now. The channel is tired.

As a member of the diplomatic corps on a vehicle, I am asking you to forgive us if our appearance over your planet frightened anyone. That was not our intention. It was rather to remind you that you are not alone on your planet. There are a great many beings from other planets who love you from a distance, of course (because we haven't met you), who feel very good about you and who you are and what you are doing, and who are looking forward to helping you in any way we can.

Please do not encourage your children to be afraid of us. We are here to help you, not just to do things that we think ought to be done, but rather specifically to help you in the ways you desire to be helped. We are not here to support your wars against each other, but we are here to help you to have all that you need so that wars are unnecessary and so that you can have the comfort you deserve with other beings and have livelihood and things to do and to discover. We are hopeful that you will understand that this is our purpose for doing these things, and we have seen those desires in you, wishing to help others as well as your own family and friends. Often we have noted that you have even wished to help others unlike yourselves, as those who would help other types of beings. So that is my apology as well as my promise, and for now I shall say good night.

Thank you very much.

Navigator of ET Ship Reminds You That You Are Not Alone

Navigator of ET Ship Seen in Stephenville, Texas

January 19, 2008

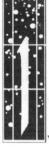I am a portion of the navigation crew of the vehicle. I understand you want something exciting.

Yes.

There is no one on this ship who is excited. Let me tell you why. The emotion of excitement is based entirely upon the experience of that which is withheld. If you cannot have something or can only have it rarely, then there is an excitement about the opportunity, even if it's unfulfilled. But that does not exist in our world or in any of the worlds of any of the beings on this ship. So although we understand your request, there is no one on this ship who is excited.

[Laughs.] Tell me something that will excite me.

You will have to ask questions.

We Make a Connection to the Places We Visit

Tell me about yourself: who you are, where you're from, as much as you can tell.

We're from a planet where what you might refer to as mathematics, having more to do with geometric than numbers, is a source of interest, although not the only one. As a result, we seem to find that navigating in vehicles is something interesting to us, even though the bulk of the navigation that's involved is profoundly simple. Once you have the means to get from one place to another, then the capabilities of navigation are not in any way problematic. In your world, I understand that navigation is problematic and has been for some time, though perhaps it is less so now.

Our job is to be able to form relationships with one or more beings on the planet we are going to. If this is not possible, such as on your planet, then we need to form relationships with nonhumans, or if necessary, portions of the planet itself. When that relationship is established, usually from a distance, then it is simply a matter of focusing on those individuals or those places and acquiring . . . in that sense you would say "desiring," but we don't have that either. But acquiring means creating a closer proximity.

This is done simply by focusing on the feeling and/or the pictures of those entities or those places and simultaneously having a connection to the means of motion of the vehicle. It doesn't make any difference if the vehicle is tiny or if it is massive; the size makes no difference. Weight is not a factor either, including that of those in the vehicle. Of course, those in the vehicle have all been chosen carefully, not unlike your own astronaut programs. I might add, in your own astronaut program, I do not know that there are too many people who exhibit excitement.

Generally speaking, the people on vehicles like this are professionals. Now, I grant that there are some dependents, as you might call them, or extended family members on board such a large vehicle. But even those individuals are nurtured from an early age to have certain personality characteristics that might not otherwise be heightened in them so that they can travel in such a vehicle and have the appropriate feelings and actions. Those are necessary.

So the ship is alive and you connect to the ship with feelings?

We don't, but some people do. The ship is alive in the same way your ships are alive, except the main difference is—and this is an important difference—that every portion of the vehicle, including all that it is equipped with and every other portion that it is next to and in the continuum (meaning on and on), is completely at peace and comfortable with contacting every other portion. Whereas your ships are just put together by force. But you will get past that. You have only adapted to that because you are not conscious of the rest of your being. But that will change.

So our job is not to concentrate on the personal connection to the vehicle—one can only do so much. It is rather to concentrate on the place we are going. To make the connection to the ship, you might say, is personal. So it would be like, for example—I don't do this, but one of my fellow beings in this group does (I'm going to put this in your terminology)—you might put one hand on your heart and one hand on the vehicle. There is a place to do that. But I am not that person.

We have a group and we all connect to the same beings or objects to get to that place, but we do so as a group. This makes it easier, perhaps, for such a large vehicle to move about. But also I think the main reason is because there are so many places we go or could go that there needs to be at least one member of the group who has been there, who has made a connection with someone or something there. And if that is the case, you see, then every other member can utilize a similar feeling to amplify the individual who has made the connection.

So even if you haven't been there, you know the feeling that you have to function in that attracting capability. And you can connect with the other members of your group, especially ones who have been and are making the connection to amplify that.

Are you the one who had been here to the planet or who made a connection to the planet before?

No, that was someone else.

Who have they made a connection to? Or was it to the planet?

They haven't been here, but they have been close. They traveled in a small vehicle on a previous expedition and got close to the planet. They didn't actually get out of the vehicle, but they got close enough so that they could make a connection to several long-lived creatures. And since life forms come and go where we live too, then those beings would usually make a connection to some portion of the Earth, in case they had retired from life on this planet— your planet, eh? In this way, they would leave some of their energy on some portion of the Earth so that that connection could be made if they were no longer present on the Earth. As it turns out, one of the beings is no longer present, but another one is. And the bulk of the beings made the effort to put some of their energy on the same place on the Earth.

So there are no pilots per se, then? You connect, and then you sort of look, and then the ship moves?

No, no, there are people who can fly the ship if necessary. But I don't do that. I think if you talk to pilots and navigators in your time and on your planet, you will find that good navigation is pretty important.

[Laughs.] Or you're going around in circles. Absolutely. Is navigation of starships a profession amongst many on your planet because of your interest in mathematics?

No, just a few. It is one of the things we're interested in. But because we're interested in it, we have a natural talent and ability for navigation. If it is not possible, you see, to make a personal connection to a being on the planet, then it must be done to make a connection to the planet itself. And this sometimes involves mathematical principles, because one has to be able to use the angles, quadrants and reflective energies associated with crystalline forms. Planets are often associated with crystalline forms, whether they be larger or microcrystalline. So the idea of having some interest in and being able to follow along threads, so to speak, of angular reflectivity is useful.

That's wonderful. So how long have you been doing this?

On the vehicle?

On any vehicle.

In terms of your time, eh? A moment. Maybe twelve centuries.

What is your life span?

Maybe three times that.

So you're one-third of the way through your life?

No, I did other things before I did this work.

Can you tell me about your home planet? Is it a place we've ever heard of?

No, you haven't heard of it. And I think it would be better, considering our proximity, to not say too much about that.

Oh, you're not from too far away?

No, no, the ship.

Oh, I'm sorry, the ship, yes.

Clues Have Been Left on Earth to Connect You to Your Point of Origin

Can you tell me some of the adventures you've had on other planets?

Define "adventure."

What has most interested you about your interactions with either the planet or the beings on the planet in terms of other places you've gone?

Wouldn't you be more interested in this planet? Because of our connection to the being on your planet, we are able to utilize not only that being's full capabilities—because that being is trusting us and allowing that—but also some of that being's capabilities that they might use on the home planet. One of those capabilities that interests us is to see through things, as long as there is a means of angular refraction or reflection. So the being can see something, perhaps a stone, and as long as there is a means, it is possible to see through things. You might not find that interesting, but we do.

We are able to look inside, for example, what you call mountains and look for life forms not on the surface, not interacting with your peoples. The interesting thing about stone, especially crystalline, is that sometimes it retains personal memories—not always, but sometimes it does, especially if the stone has been in compatibility with those life forms.

There was a race of beings on your planet—they are not there anymore—who left such memories. I'll mention just a little about that, since you seem to be enthusiastic about others. I'll say this: This race of beings has left clues for you on your planet to find the mathematical connections so that you can coordinate yourself through your (meaning human beings') point of origin. These mathematical objects are all pyramidal, most of which are underground in order to keep them safe. Very few of them have been discovered—only one or two. One, I think, was damaged, but there are so many more of them.

They cannot actually be discovered. You can be standing five feet away from them and not see them, not be able to detect them in any way. This is because you yourself, as a being, have to be of a certain feeling or capacity—I don't want to say "vibration" because that's vague, and you can identify more with the idea of being of a certain feeling—because sometimes when you have different feelings, you are able to perceive different things. You not only become aware of what another person might be thinking or feeling, but you also become aware of your surroundings in a different way—perhaps briefly, but you can have the experience.

So mostly these things have simply gone unnoticed, though they are there. In order to see them, you will have to have those feelings. It is more likely that the up-and-coming generation will see these things, and perhaps the generation after that will know what to do with them. But they are meant so that you can find your origins. Of course, the people on your planet all look pretty much the same, with some slight alterations. So your origins are not that far-flung.

Some peoples originally came from certain places, though, and therefore, it will give you markers as to where you want to go once you start exploring the vast reaches of space. I'm not talking about the kind of vehicles you have now, but once you have vehicles shared by others, perhaps you will be able to explore places that are so far away that you would have to travel in much the same fashion as we do.

How big are these pyramids? Two feet or fifty feet or two inches or what?

They are big enough to notice and not so small you trip over them.

Do you need different feelings to contact different ones or one feeling to contact all of them?

You wouldn't necessarily be able to touch it, but in order to see it and perhaps retain a certain amount of memory of what you've seen or felt, which might be the case also, you would have to be completely at ease with yourself at that moment. You'd have to have a relaxed feeling, perhaps a feeling of welcoming of life, all forms, and generally have the means to experience a natural altered state. By "natural," I mean no artificial means. So you can understand what I'm saying. People do what you call meditations there, which is a natural altered state—though I'm not saying that that is the one. That's all I can say for now.

Can we find these by going down into caves and under mountains?

Most of them are under the surface, but there are quite a few on the surface.

Oh, on the surface of mountains. I thought they'd be down under. So we could just be walking around and run into them?

You could notice it. And then another time you might not see it even having the same feeling, because it would have to welcome you as well.

So they have the feeling of different planets, or are they from different planets? I know that various star systems all over the place have had colonies here and have seeded or have had people be here.

They are made entirely of materials from Earth.

So they are made? Somebody made them? Formed them into that shape?

Somebody welcomed them to form into that shape. Remember, anything built by force will necessarily return to a different form, if not necessarily its original form.

So when you look at the great stone bases under Jerusalem and the Sinai and in South America—these huge, huge multi-ton stone blocks—were they cut and placed there, or were they formed? Were they asked to form?

I've never looked at that. Do you want me to?

Yes.

It will take awhile.

How long is awhile?

In your time? About a year and a half. I would have to move from one angle to another on the crystalline level.

You Are Starting to Wake Up

Can you say anything about your shape or your form?

We're not human beings.

Can you tell me what you look like?

It's hard to describe that, isn't it? I will simply say that we are not human beings; we are not humanoids.

How many beings are in your group?

Seventeen.

And you all came from the same planet? Or are you together because you all have the same interest?

We came from the same planet, yes. Some of us are from the same family group or extended family.

So it's a talent that runs in the family then, or an interest—both, right?

No, it's a planet-wide interest.

How do you decide where to go?

We are invited. In this case, the vehicle was invited to come because your peoples are . . . the term we were told was "waking up." This is happening on a planetary scale for you now, so you need to see things, you need to have experiences. In short, you need to be able to utilize the sensitivities that are present within you now.

Sometimes you are experiencing these sensitivities in ways that are uncomfortable—meaning, for instance, from friend to friend, you might never have had an argument, but suddenly you're having arguments because one person is more sensitive or both people are more sensitive. In short, some of you are experiencing discomforts and sensitivities together. But you need to also be reminded of your capabilities. For example, some people who saw the vehicle over that area of your country saw some things and other people didn't see those things, because some of the people who saw things but in greater detail were, at that time, simply more sensitive. They could see more. It wasn't simply just what was available due to the light; they were just a little more sensitive at this time.

On your planet, in some cultures, the idea of being sensitive is not considered to be a good thing. Yet that will all change, you see, because sensitivity in this case has to do with perception, and perception can be very useful. Think

Figure 25.1: The Hand of Creator.

about all of the things that are available to be seen that people don't see or feel, and if they did see or feel them, then life would be infinitely easier, to say nothing of there being considerably less misunderstanding and hence fewer battles.

I want to say two things about that. Recently we were shown a picture of what Zoosh said was the Hand of the Creator bringing us energies to make us more perceptive. [See Figure 25.1.] Also, the climate is changing in the United States, and there were people on a national television show talking about having seen your ship.

Ah, this is a good thing, yes?

This is excellent; this is wonderful. Instead of hiding it, it's starting to be something that people talk about.

It's more likely that seeing various vehicles, not necessarily ours, will be a planetary phenomenon this year. Some people will see things that are just unusual. They will not be certain whether they will be vehicles or not.

We Go Where There Is a Need

So who invited you? The consciousness of humans together? The planet? Or teachers? Who specifically invited you?

An emissary. That's what I've been told.

From?

You don't ask. It depends how the emissary feels to us. Generally speaking, no emissary who doesn't feel good . . . such emissaries would not be able to see us. But the emissary felt good, came and explained the value of helping you all to achieve your natural state, and we said, "Of course."

Was it an emissary from the Creator, you think?

I don't think so. Not directly.

And he came to all of you on the ship?

Yes, he came and explained the value of your peoples: who they are, what they are doing. Up to that point in time, we had heard things that were alarming about your peoples. But then they took the time to explain why you are the way you are—in that case, why you were the way you were—and what you are attempting to accomplish (albeit mostly unconsciously up to this point in time), and your need to move beyond your current existence quickly and benevolently. So we said yes.

So that's how you came to be here. How do you decide where to go to other places?

It's not that different. Since we don't need to trade—granted, there are vehicles and peoples who go around trading and so on, but that's not us—then it generally has to do with the need (you might say "priority") and how welcome we feel and how good we feel about the need. It's basically the same. Sometimes an emissary is involved, sometimes some other form of communication.

What are some of the things that interested you that you have done in all this time you've been doing this—some of the interactions with beings or the planets or whatever?

I can only think of one that might remotely interest you. There was a planet where the life forms are entirely composed of plants. And they requested our presence because they needed to have a little change in their atmosphere as the plants were growing out.

If you were to see such plants, you would consider them . . . now, they're not trees, but they do have something that looks like leaves. Imagine if you would, a "tree" that is about forty miles tall. These plants were growing out into layers of their atmosphere that were not supportive for them. And they needed to have their atmosphere changed so they could continue to grow out farther.

We were able to accommodate that. But in order to accommodate it, we had to develop some personal relationships with some of the "leaves." So I had the opportunity to experience myself as (I'll have to use your terms) a capillary in a leaf. These beings on this planet explained that the plant life they represent is not dissimilar from plant life around the immediate universe. Since this is in your galaxy, I'm bringing it up. It's amazing that a single capillary in such a leaf was conscious of the entirety of the plant.

Of a forty-mile plant.

I found it interesting. Also, I found it interesting that on the surface of the leaf, there was an energy that to me . . . I'm still not certain to this day whether the glow from the leaf had to do with its personal energy, because it was like light, or whether it was acquiring the light. You see, I'm not certain whether it was taking in the light or emanating it—I don't know that. Since it was happening so slowly, it wasn't clear to me. In any event, I managed to form that relationship with that leaf, so if we ever go back there, I'll be able to go back because of my relationship with that leaf—I'll be able to acquire, understand?

Yes.

Even when leaves grow out from the plant, the other leaves remain vital. They don't seem to absorb sunlight. That's why I'm interested. You asked if there was something I was interested in. I'm interested because they don't seem to absorb sunlight; I think they are actually giving off light.

Does the whole tree glow?

It's not a tree.

Does the whole being and the leaves on it—do all the leaves glow?

It seems to be going more up than out.

So what did you do to the atmosphere, then?

We were able to alter it so that it was more enriched in the ways they requested.

Use certain gases or something?

Yes.

The Place for Mystery and Adventure Is on Earth

So what about first contact? I think the diplomat mentioned that you did first contacts sometimes.

First contacts—what do you mean by that?

You contact beings on the planet who have never interacted with anyone from off the planet before.

Yes, but that's not my job. Do you mean the vehicle does that? Other peoples on the vehicle?

Yes, other peoples on the vehicle.

Oh, you were speaking to the Diplomat?

Yes.

They would do that. You'd have to talk to them about that. I had to do this with the "leaf" because of orienting, in case we went back.

So you might go to a planet but not necessarily usually interact with the beings on them. You can see them, right? You have technology to see what's happening on any planet, don't you?

I understand that on your planet now, technology is something that is almost deified. But if you were to be on our vehicle, you'd be surprised at how very little technology is present.

So you have the ability and the sensitivity to interact with beings at a distance.

Yes, and so do you. You just don't know that yet.

So it must be fascinating to go to all these different places and feel the feelings of the beings who live there, right?

We go where we're needed.

But it's very educational and expansive in your understanding of creation, isn't it?

You see, you are speaking from someone . . .

From a limited point of view.

You're not limited, you're just restricted at the moment, because your job is to look down, so to speak. Your job is not to look up—other than, of course, to look up at the stars and so on, and enjoy the beauty. But what I'm saying is that once you know (and this is your natural state of being) . . . fascination is not exactly the word I would use. You'd have to come up with some other word. It is pleasant. It is enjoyable. But mystery is no longer a factor. And I believe mystery is a portion of fascination, isn't it?

Yes.

You're fascinated because you're trying to solve the mystery, but if there's no mystery, you're not fascinated.

There is never a mystery? Ever?

No. If you're looking for the mysterious and you want adventure, you're on the planet now where the mysterious and adventure exist. Really, I'm not joking with you here. If you're looking for the mysterious and fascination and adventure, you'll never find more of it than on the planet upon which you are now residing.

If you expect to find that once you become your natural being and start traveling in space, you will have to find it in your memories. Because the planet you are on is the place that is intended to fulfill those desires in you as a soul now. That's why you are where you are, because you have those desires, regardless of whether you qualified to be on the planet. If you don't have those desires in some way, you see, then you're not going to be able to tolerate the conditions of the planet as a balance to the opportunities, from your point of view.

That is very interesting.

I wanted for you to be aware of this, because a lot of people want to go to other planets to discover this or that. But once you go there, you no longer have the same desires because you are your natural selves and mystery ceases to exist.

I don't know if I like that or not.

That's why you're on Earth.

[Laughs.] I know that we'll be off here at some point.

You will have things to replace it, you see. The things that fascinate you, if I may use your word, are things that seem to be out of your reach, yes? But when they are in your reach, you will have other things that you are interested in and that you enjoy. Life beyond Earth is filled with wonderful things. But you may not find mystery, fascination, adventure and excitement—that's on Earth.

But will we have deep interests and be able to do interesting things as you are doing? We will have an interest in something that we will pursue, right?

Yes, but you will not have ignorance; you will not "not know." By ignorance, I do not mean stupidity, you understand. Ignorance simply means you don't know and you can't know. That will go away. The reason you have the "don't know/can't know" on Earth is so that you will solve the unsolvable, and that has to do with the Explorer Race project. That is why you must have those stipulations in order to be able to have the mysterious and the exciting and the fascinating. But if you no longer have those stipulations, things change.

Earth Is About Balance

So that was the only case, with the atmosphere, of an interaction with beings on the planet that was something we would understand?

That's the only thing I can think of, and the fact that it's in your galaxy is important. There's not much point in talking about things beyond your galaxy because it would be totally different and there would be huge gaps in what I could tell you because you wouldn't be able to relate to it at all. I see no point in getting you fascinated, as you say, with something that you are unlikely to experience in any way in your life on Earth, including your dream life. But in your dream life, you often see plants or are amongst them—this is typical in dreams for you.

I believe that on Earth, human beings do not often realize how you cannot live without plants. Earth is about balance, you see. And when life forms disappear, as they are doing so now, life for all other life forms becomes more difficult. This is why the more of a human population you have—and of course, human beings need room to live and so on—the more other forms of life are disappearing and plant life is dwindling. Of course, the most obvious result is that your oxygen supply is dwindling.

So if you don't know what to do, I recommend that you have a garden or, if you can, perhaps encourage houseplants. Plants, after all, breathe in some of what you breathe out, and it's very balanced. It's no accident; it's not just a fascinating aspect of science. Your science, at the moment, likes to take a distant look at things that are close-up, meaning to not be involved on the feeling level. But the feeling level has everything to do with life forms. Plants that exhale these gases that you breathe are not on Earth by accident.

They, like you, are all volunteers. The only difference is that they know who they are and they know why they're there. They are volunteering to exhale what you need. I think it would be better to treat plants, especially those that grow on their own without being planted by humans, much better and not to be cutting them and harming them. They are there because they are volunteering to support you.

I do not understand this strange fascination with destroying those who keep you alive. It is a curiosity. I've been informed by others on this ship, especially the diplomatic group, that it is a phase you are going through and that in the past you did not do this, but because of your fascination with technology now, you are doing this. And they assure me that it will pass.

You Need to Learn to Relate to Other Life Forms

Okay, so you can't tell me any more about your experiences. In the beginning you said that the children on the ship are trained to accentuate certain feelings. Can you say more about that?

This is not really my job, and I do not have children of my own. But this is only insofar as they're encouraged to enjoy other life forms, because here they are on a ship with multitudes of life forms, even though on their home planet there may not be as many. So their socialization skills are accentuated. That's the main thing.

Can you say anything about your family? I don't know if you're plant-based or what you are, but how do you reproduce? What is your family situation on your home planet?

Well, I'm not going to say much about that, and there's a reason. The reason I'm being vague about certain things is that the diplomatic group has assured me that it's most important for you to know about the type of beings you are likely to be meeting in time and that these beings are going to be humans or humanoids. You're not going to have too much interaction for a time with beings who are not humanoids, mostly because you don't know how to treat them.

You don't know how to treat beings on your own planet who are not humanoids, and you will have to learn on your planet how to treat them first before meeting or encountering them beyond Earth. Otherwise, of course, you could very easily just treat them as you might a species on your own planet, without realizing that you are causing yourself harm as well as others.

We're doing a book on talking to plant beings, and one of them said that if we don't become aware that the major life form on the planet could be plant-based, we might come and land on the very people we're trying to talk to.

Yes, and this is why diplomacy is such a vitally important level of your astronaut and cosmonaut programs—diplomacy and science, yes, but the social sciences as well, such as anthropology. Your anthropology is essentially the study of different groups of people and how they live, but it needs to go beyond the human being. A good anthropologist in the future on your planet will know how other life forms live and their socialization process. You can do that on Earth right now, with sea creatures and so on.

Many life forms that you consider to be lesser beings . . . I think this has evolved in your modern times because of religions and philosophies that have not taken on the full range of experience of life forms. I grant that religion or philosophy might not feel that this is of primary importance, and I've heard the argument to advocate that. But ultimately, when you begin to go out into space and explore other places—which you've all indicated you wish to do on a soul level—you will have to know how to relate to other life forms, which is why you still have quite a few on the Earth to learn from.

But I don't understand why we can't learn about the form of life you have. What is the reason why we can't know that just as a fact of life?

This is the reason I can give you. I have been guided by those aboard ship to not say—that's why. I can't give you the reason—that's the reason I have. I have been told that, and that is what I must do. I'm not following orders; I'm following advice by those who know better than I do. They must know you. They must know you as creatures. They must know that this conversation we are having is not just between the two of us, that it will go beyond the two of us.

That's why I wanted to talk to somebody else besides the Diplomat, so I could get more information.

Yes, I understand, but how much do you want?

As much as I can get.

Yes, well, you will get what we have to offer.

This Ship Has Everything to Do with Teamwork

So what excites you, what interests you, what gives you the most feeling of joy in your work?

I believe it is in cooperation, doing things with others to accomplish a common goal. You would find on this craft something that is a little different I think than on some others, and that is that everything on this craft has to do with teamwork. There aren't singular individuals doing singular things on this craft. It is entirely groups of individuals doing tasks, and this is apparently intended for this ship.

I do not know who set it up like that, but I enjoy doing something that involves others where we do it together to achieve. In terms of the navigation, I suppose in a small vehicle I could do it by myself, but I wouldn't enjoy it as much. So that's something—I enjoy doing my work. I believe there might be people on your own planet who might enjoy doing their work and perhaps there are even some situations that you can think of where people accomplish what they're doing because they are working with others to accomplish a goal that they all share.

Oh yes, look at the teamwork it takes to land our little primitive attempts at space travel: to land a probe on Mars or to send something out beyond the solar system. I mean, that's an incredible amount of people working together.

Yes, that's an example. I'm sure there are more mundane ones.

So do you get a chance to interact very much? I think the Diplomat said there were about 20,000 beings on the ship. Do you get a chance to interact with them and to learn from their experiences or to share with them?

Sometimes other beings come into our area, but I do not generally go into other areas. It is a factor of the form of life that I am that we do not move about much. But other forms of life do come in, and we are able to communicate and speak of matters.

So you are plant-based, I'll bet.

What makes you think that?

That you don't move. Or you could be floating in a tub of water, too.

You have beings who are not plant-based on your own planet who, as you say, do not move. I move.

Oh, okay.

But you are trying to figure it out.

[Laughs.] Yep.

You could explore your own beings on your own planet who don't seem to move around very much.

Rocks, stones, yes.

No, no, those you would identify as life forms—not just that which would for all intents and purposes appear to be inanimate to you.

Like crystals? I must have a hundred crystals in this house.

So you're saying you cannot think of a single life form on your planet that is not crystalline that does not move around too much? I think if you explored animal life, you would find such things.

So it's not like a TV series where they have like a great common room where everyone goes to sort of relax and maybe eat or something. How do you guys eat?

We all have our own.

Your own chef, or your own food?

We have our own means to—how can we say?—receive nutrients. I have not traveled much beyond this space, so I can't tell you too much.

You Will Have to Develop a Means of Communication beyond Technology
All right, I guess I've run out of questions you can answer.

You have asked to speak to somebody else because you weren't satisfied with the last person you spoke to because they weren't Earthlike. But I am not Earthlike either, and you would not find anybody on this ship who is Earthlike. The irony of the situation is that you are not Earthlike either. You are an adapted life form. The bulk of your true nature is not with you at this time. Therefore, it is not unlike if you were some small portion of your own body—pick anything—and the rest of it has to do with an encapsulation in which you are living. So it is not unusual that you might come to identify with the encapsulation as compared to the "you."

So it is not surprising, you see, that you are asking these questions and would assume certain things. But this is something that is a bit difficult for you, and that is that there's a tendency to assume that the life forms on vehicles might relate to you in some way. This is perhaps because previous contacts or communions—communications, you see—with other beings would suggest that that's the case.

But there will be many times when you will have at least some form of distant communication with beings who have no relationship to you whatsoever. And even the questions you ask will not interpret very well—meaning your questions are going to be based within the realm, not only of your own vocabulary and intellect, but also within the available experience that you are consciously able to be aware of in your now home.

Do not feel that I am criticizing you. I'm simply stating that as you travel to other planets as a culture, you will have to be alert to the fact that there will be times when you will meet beings who may not even be in vehicles. Maybe they'll simply just be in space, and you'll find it hard to believe—"How is it possible?"—because you will be focused on the idea that beings, even humanoid beings, would be air breathers. But this is not necessarily so.

You have to study more, and by "study" I do not mean pick apart and destroy. You will have to study on the socialization level—the way an anthropologist or a sociologist might do—the way other life forms live on your own planet. Recognize that it's perfectly possible that you will meet other life forms who might look like what you would refer to as animal life on your own planet—or simply, with a broader description, as nonhuman life. And what will you do then?

You will have to develop a means to communicate that goes beyond technology. I feel inspiration is the best. And it is vitally important that you move past prejudice. So even if you've been told that this kind of being is that and that kind of being is this, don't assume that that's true. Just say, "Well, it may be so in what is known now, but perhaps there's more." That's all. Develop an attitude of, "Perhaps there's more," as you have. You have that attitude—I think it would be good for others to develop it as well.

So do you have access to your total . . . what we call the immortal personality? Do you remember past lives?

Yes, but only if they are relevant. There's no point in remembering something that might be more interesting than what I'm doing now, that would draw me into the past and, more importantly, draw me out of the present. How could I possibly do any good for anybody if I'm not in the present?

Do you know if you have incarnated into other life forms before?

Yes, I know that I have. As you have.

We presume we have. We just don't remember. Our teacher Zoosh calls it "the gift of ignorance." We have to leave our memories of who we are at the gate of the planet.

Yes, and for what you are doing on this planet, it's a gift because it has positive aspects: the joy of discovering a flower, or the joy of meeting someone you've never met before and you have a new friend. That is joyful, and it is dependent on ignorance to experience it. So yes, I understand that it has its positive qualities. It also has more challenging qualities, and that's the main challenge right now in our communication. But you did ask to speak to someone with a different personality than the last being.

I did.

That's the way it was interpreted in your request, not because the desires of your request did not relate at all. So the best we could do is to offer someone who has a different personality.

Well, you did. I'm not slighting the diplomats; I love diplomats. I just wanted another perspective.

You Too Can Make This Personal Connection

Have you ever done this before?

Yes.

You have? With other life forms? You've communicated through them?

Well, you understand how I described my contact with the "leaf." I'd have to be able to make a personal connection as a person in navigation work, the way I do. Everyone in my unit has to be able to make a personal connection in order to get to where we're going—so yes, of course.

Of course. I hadn't stopped to think about that. You have to practically become the thing that you're going to connect to.

Well, we just need to be able to feel it, and it has to welcome us and we have to welcome it. It has to be sufficiently personal so that we are able to . . . how can we say?

Make that connection.

If you were to welcome someone or something, you would be drawing it toward you. And when we make that connection, our group—I can't say "I"; it's difficult—draws ourselves to that being or thing. That being or thing draws us to them because of the welcoming. So it's an equal attraction—it's attraction to attraction.

So in 1,200 of our years, you've done that hundreds of times? Thousands? Ten? How many?

Hundreds of times.

Then you have a vast personal connection and appreciation and knowing of these beings, right?

Well, I just need to have enough of a knowing so that I'm able to feel them personally. Not because I take over their bodies—speaking of my group as "I." We don't do anything like that. But "I," our group, we have to know how the other being functions, whether it is a mountain or a stone, a waterfall or a being, a creature. We have to know how the being functions so that we do not misuse them in the process of navigation. Very often for a being, it has to be gentle. It's not like we're tying a rope to something and pulling.

No, but I think this is so wonderful that of all the people who travel, you have such depth of connection, of communion with these various creatures of the planets, right?

Yes, but it is not anything that you cannot do now. You can do this. By "you," I mean the human race. I pick you as representative. You can do this.

We seem to spend so much time going to work and doing what it takes to keep alive that we don't allocate much time to that.

Well, we understand that, and that is because you do not have the support that is offered to you—meaning, you are not at this time relating to all the life forms personally. Were you to be doing that, you would have the wisdom they are waiting to give you. You might have to receive this in spirit form, which you are attempting to provide with these books and at some point something a bit more active, perhaps something more visual and so on. But the intention is that you do not have to work so hard.

You are having to work because you are basically using the masculine principle. You are essentially involved in force—creation from a push rather than creation from a pull. A pull is equalized by the other, which is pulling also—in short, attraction versus propulsion. That has to change. When that changes, then you won't have to work period, as you understand work to be. Work will become something more natural, more simple, where you use your individual abilities. And many of you will form together in groups and use your individual abilities in groups, kind of like what I'm doing with my group. It will take time, but you will do it because you are on your way.

Time Is an Idea More Than an Experience

You travel in time. Do you sometimes go to different eras of what we call time on this planet, or do you always come to the present?

We do not exactly go to different eras, but sometimes if we need to study how it is that you came to be in a certain way, we have access to what you might call a living history, filtered somewhat so that we are not too shocked by things you have done. But you understand, I think there's a little confusion in your mind about time travel. We do not travel in time, and I do not know of any other vehicle that does. But we would have available to us the awareness of different moments of experience and have access to that. Time, you see, is an idea more than it is an experience. And I have no . . . I do not know how to explain it to you.

How is this living history stored? Do you access it on a feeling level?

It isn't. It's available to everyone—it's available to you. It's available, and it can be accessed. The reason you don't access it too much is that you would begin to identify with it. And then you'd begin to process it in your present. This has created a considerable amount of problems for you in the past and is an ongoing difficulty. You call this history, but for us it is something we can do when we need to do it. But it isn't stored in any way, meaning on the ship.

Oh, on the ship, no. But I mean, do you access it through feeling? Is that a desire to know or something?

That is a necessity. That's not our job. The diplomats might do that if necessary, if it will allow them to communicate better so that there can be certain thoughts or words or word forms that they would avoid, because people might be offended or hurt by them, you see. So they are careful.

How do you communicate with the other beings who come into your area of the ship?

We are aware of what we . . . we do not speak.

Is it a method of communion?

Yes, it is a method of what you might call telepathy. But there are beings on the ship who communicate by speaking.

In the book Animal Souls Speak, *we talked to a dog diplomat and he spoke a little bit about a ship sort of like yours, although it had more scientific purposes, I think.*

Our ship is not really meant for scientific purposes, but we can influence things, as in the support of the change in atmosphere of that other planet I mentioned. I suppose from your scientists' point of view, you might say,

"Well, that sounds scientific to me." I can understand it from their point of view, but we didn't use science as you know it.

You invited the gases to come that wanted to come, or you invited particles to form gases, something like that?

The closest way I can describe it is to say that we encouraged that to be which was prepared to be that. You like to call that magic sometimes because it is a creation of something that is otherwise unexplainable.

Well, but I understand we're going to need that to get through all the stuff we've created here.

Yes, that will be a requirement, but it is not so difficult now.

So you've learned an awful lot about us by being in the vicinity, you might say.

I am learning about you as we are speaking.

Oh, say more about that.

It is because of access to the channel's awareness, access to your awareness, access to the planet because of proximity. Proximity is always a factor, and therefore, someone like myself—meaning my group—we understand the idea of personal connection.

That's your life; that's your work.

That's the work, yes. But if you're asking, "Do I have a large storehouse of information about your peoples?" then no. But then, there are no storehouses like that on the ship at all. I have heard that other ships are different and they do have such things.

The Zetas do, yes, and I think the Andromedans do whom I've talked to, but heaven knows who else has that.

This is the type of ship that has many beings the likes of which your peoples will never meet in your now form. But there are some beings on the ship the likes of which you may meet at some point. We have, as you say, some humanoids. I believe the diplomats were humanoids.

Yes, they wouldn't say what kind, but they said they were humanoid.

The reason they don't say what kind when that comes up is that you don't understand that kind. You have no knowledge of it, and it is considered a good idea to keep it that way for a time.

[Laughs.] You guys seem to be obsessed with keeping us ignorant sometimes.

Well, you see, we are guided as to what we can say.

Your Lives Are Expanding Now Exponentially

We need to stop soon.

I really appreciate you very much. Go ahead and say what you want to say to the people reading this.

Your lives are expanding now exponentially. You don't see it in your day-to-day life, although sometimes you can look back a few years and see how different your life is and your capabilities. Over the next two to three years, you will all become more aware, not only of other peoples on your own planet, but you will relate to them differently.

You will also be reminded on a regular basis that there are life forms beyond your planet. At first, the reporting of such things will be rife with various forms of media coloration or opinions and so on. But after a time, peoples will accept the fact: "Well, there are life forms from other places who are visiting us." Don't expect this visiting to be associated with contact, but you will see more vehicles and you will see things that you don't always know are vehicles.

The main thing is to remind you that you are not alone and that someday you will be meeting peoples from other planets who love you, who appreciate you, who want to help you with things that you want. That's the thing to remember. They're not going to be thrusting something on you that you don't want. They're not going to be commanding or demanding. They're not even going to expect or allow reverence on your part. They will make themselves known only insofar as you are prepared to ask for what you need and receive it, as long as it is benevolent to you and others. So start making a list now and combine that list with the lists of others so that you can come up with a hundred or even a thousand things that you would like, that you need, that would help your peoples. Perhaps someday you will have a chance to have some of those items fulfilled. Good night.

Thank you from my heart. Thank you very much.

Supporting Microbes on Planet Earth

ET Emissary to Molecules and Grandfather
November 13, 2008

reetings. I'm living in the land of the almost transparent. I'm visiting from a planet that is not that far away. I cannot say which one it is; I'm constrained. But I will say that it is in your solar system. I am taking various forms, usually microbial in size, but I have also taken the form of a jellyfish, also appearing almost transparent.

Our world is one in which beings are seen or unseen but whose energy, personality, is always present. You have many beings like that in your world; therefore, I'm able to blend in—though other earthly beings who might look like the form that I take or similar do know that I am not of this planet. They are not always too friendly at first, but they accommodate me or use as an introductory an emanated energy that allows me to feel welcome.

Generally speaking, most life forms, including your own, do not feel very welcome on this planet right now. That is why there is so much self-destructiveness, not only of one's own kind, as seen in the human race, but also a shortening of one's individual life cycle, as seen sometimes in other types of beings on your planet. There has not been any mass self-destructiveness seen except mostly in the sea, for people who live in the water are sometimes doing such things.

Often this goes unnoticed, because I've noticed that water people will often be self-destructive by allowing themselves to be caught—as you would say, fishing. Therefore, their self-destructiveness is not obvious, except sometimes to those who are fishing. Sometimes they have curiosity: "Now, they knew we were here and they could have gone away but they didn't—why didn't they?" This is a question that has often been asked by those who fish. The answer is because they don't feel welcome on this planet and they'd just as soon get it over with as quickly as possible.

This was not something that occurred in the distant past, though fishing, as you call it, became popular in a mass way (with nets and so on) only recently. I'm not counting the fisherman who might throw a small net from shore or even a ways out in a body of water. I'm talking about what you call commercial fishing. So in the past, if someone started fishing and caught one or two members, that was always a shock to that community. But gradually, as it became more popular to do that, water people have felt less welcome.

Sharing Advice and Welcoming with the Beings of Earth

Many ancient cultures of human beings did not fish. Even when one is very hungry there's a tendency to believe—especially if you are in balance energetically with yourself, your people and your world—that all beings who have even some features like yourself (say, a mouth, an eye) are like you. They are just from another world. So many ancient cultures on Earth, including ones that were well established in terms of just a few hundred years ago, did not fish. They felt that water people were their equals and they would sometimes go someplace and consult with them if possible, meaning if they had a means to communicate.

Advice would often be given from the water people, not just in regard to how to survive—meaning when might the next rain come, how to get along with water, when might the next flood come and so on—but also sometimes just wisdom about life, family and so on. Such advice has not been asked very much by human beings lately, though there are some on the planet who know whom to ask and how. Such asking is worth doing. Even if you do not get an answer back in your own language immediately, even if words do not pop into your head right away, you might ask, just standing looking at a lake or a river or the sea, a question like this: "If there are any water people who can offer any wisdom for me now in any form of inspiration or even physical demonstration or in my dreams, I would appreciate it," and then go on and say what your question is.

Don't make a long explanation. If you want to say just a couple of words that define your situation, you can. But then just ask a simple question, the simpler the better. This way your feelings about what you are asking do not run all over the table, so to speak. You'll have one feeling, and then an answer might come. You might hear a couple of words in your mind as it were, like a thought, or you might even find that the fish will jump out of the water in some way and then you'll get an inspiration or even an idea of what the fish might mean. Or you might have a dream that you remember and interpret. This kind of contact between peoples of the land, meaning walkers, and peoples of the sea, meaning swimmers, is useful because it honors everyone.

Sometimes, those of you who are near bodies of water might have a question pop into your head and you say, "What is that? I know the answer to that—why am I thinking that?" It might not be yourself. Maybe you're not thinking that. Maybe a person of the water or even a bird, a person of the sky, or another type of person would be having that question. If a question pops into your head that you absolutely know the answer to and you are able to speak out loud or even whisper, then go ahead and explain, give the answer in the simplest and most direct way. Try to go beyond yes or no, but the simplest and most direct way would be helpful. Then just go on with your life.

If possible, when the question pops into your head, if it does, it would be good to stop and make that answer. But you might be in a moving vehicle perhaps. If you can't stop, then just put your hand up to your mouth and whisper quietly the answer that you know. If there are other people around, if you are not alone, you can speak quietly. This way the peoples of the Earth are reminded that they are welcome, that there is a place to go beyond one's own kind to get answers. It might not be the only answer, it might not be the solution, but it might be supportive, and whatever answer it might be, it might give you ideas, even if it's not the perfect answer. Maybe you hadn't thought about things that way: "Oh, that's interesting; it makes me think of this and this," and so on.

So it's important to feel welcome isn't it? These days, with so many human beings on the Earth, one does not always feel that way. And it's the same for the people of the sea or the people of the air or the other nonhumans of the land or under the land. It's important to honor all peoples.

If you don't have a question and if one is not asked of you, as far as you can tell, then if you're near a body of water, whether you can see water people or not, you could do this, if you like: You could say, "I honor this water and appreciate its life-giving qualities for me and others, and I honor all those who are in this water, who live in it, who are born in it and who move under, around and through it, and I'm grateful for your existence." Be sure you say this with sincerity; don't say it just because I am suggesting it.

After you say such a thing, wait for a moment. You might feel a corresponding energy. Maybe someone swimming by will feel comforted and appreciate knowing that a land person has said this. They will feel good and you might share that feeling with them for a moment. So wait until that good feeling passes, if it's present. If you don't feel anything, it's all right—maybe they were busy. You know how that is; you get busy too.

So then you've said it. You can say it from time to time if you like; don't do it every day. Don't even do it more than once a week, if you find that you have the opportunity. You can say it to the air. You might not always see birds around, but just look up if you want to say it to the air people. You can say it looking down at the ground for other people who might crawl or walk or dig into the ground. You can also say it to land people, your own kind. If you don't say something like that to a friend or if it feels sort of too formal, then you can stand or sit some place, look in the general direction where people are, and you can whisper it if it's embarrassing to say out loud. If it isn't, then you can just look at people in general rather than one person and say it.

Adapt it to people of the land, all right? This is something in your language, you see, that is said generally when people visit from one planet to another. It's a formal way of acknowledging and appreciating other life forms. It is what you might call diplomatic, but it's important to have the feelings to back up what you're saying, because all beings, especially those beyond Earth—or nonhumans, let's say, because you have beings on Earth who are not as complicated as humans—all beings will hear what you have to say with their feelings first. So if the words do not match your feelings, they will either be confused or they will assume a lack of sincerity on your part. If your feelings are very strong about something else and you're saying it as you would say something without thinking, it's going to disturb them. So center into the feelings you want to project before you say these things. Then they will be understood. If you want to say something like this, center into that feeling of welcome or welcoming, or respect, if you prefer. That would be good.

Microbes Are Here to Help You Learn Transformative Magic

What would be the danger if you said what planet you're on? Are you visible even though you're transparent?

I do not know. I would normally say, but I have been asked not to say. So it isn't any danger that I'm aware of.

Ah, they're playing games again.

Well, when this is done, it is always done for your protection. You must know this, and please include that statement that you said, because we think it might be something that is a truth expressed by others, a genuine feeling, you see—not necessarily logic but a genuine feeling expressed in words. And I honor that feeling. I would be happy to tell you perhaps even later in this session; it might be possible, I do not know. But for some reason, you are being protected from knowing. Perhaps you can ask at another time and get the answer you wish. But I believe it must be for your protection, for there is no risk to our peoples that I can perceive.

What caused you to come here? What was your motivation?

I did not have a motivation to come to this planet, but I was asked by the type of people whom I am appearing to be. I was asked by what you call microbes. And I was asked, I was also welcomed . . .

By the jellyfish?

Yes, by a couple of types. I don't know what they're called, but they're basically transparent, at least in ways. You can kind of see through them. I came along with a few others, and we are on your planet. We are in existence in the water. Even with all of the dangers in the water, there is basically also quite a bit of safety in various places and a great deal of beauty, though I know this will change because of the dependence you have on various substances that you dig around for. Still, in time you will not use those substances anymore; you will use other means that do not have hazardous side effects.

Is the runoff from mining? Is that what's you mean when you say "dig around"?

Well, I'm not excluding what you just said, but I was thinking more in terms of the fluid—"oil" you call it.

Oh, oil.

There is always quite a bit of destructiveness with this. It might not always be visible in the water, but sometimes some of it is. But below the surface, it's experienced. I'm not saying those who are looking for this fluid are doing that intentionally, but it seems to be a hazard associated with the process.

So it gets down on the bottom and makes like a tar or something like that?

It's a pollution that destroys life. It has various forms; I do not know what you call these things.

What particularly were the microbes looking for? What was their reason for asking you to come?

They wanted to leave and they asked if there was any reason to stay. They had the impression from those they interact with—teachers and so on—that the beings they were originally intended to support were also leaving, and many of them have left, water people. Therefore, they wondered if there was any reason for them to stay. So rather than just departing, meaning not continuing their ongoing life cycle beyond themselves—they would just not do that, and then when they departed they would be gone—they asked in general, beyond their own teachers, if there was any reason for them to stay. They were told there was and my group was sent as emissaries to explain the possibilities.

So they're staying for a time. But they know that the only reason for them to be here on the planet is to function as a respondent in your learning, consciously, how to use magic, I think you call it. Transformative magic is a means to request that life changes its form in order to be more benign to other forms of life. Microbes can do this.

You have this transformative capability in yourself, but it is not something you are conscious of. Most of you cannot consciously transform something in your body, and yet you are in the transformative process all the time. You breathe in air, and from the air you take certain things in your body and it transforms to other things and so on—your body is constantly transforming food, air, etc. But you don't necessarily do this on your own.

Say you've got a wound on your arm—you don't consciously look at that and transform the wound quickly into a healing that is as good or better than it was before. Though you can do this, you need to learn how. It would be a re-learning, because when you're inside mother, your mother, you are conscious of the transformation going on inside her. You start out as this very small thing, and you are constantly transforming into something that eventually looks like a little human being. But as a baby in there, you are very well connected with your total spirit and thus with all life. You enjoy the transformation process, but you forget about that when you are coming into the world of land people.

You do not consider yourself to be a land person when you are growing inside mother. I feel that this is a large portion of the reason you don't remember who you are. I know I've been told that this is intended—you're not supposed to remember who you are in your larger sense of yourself. But I feel that the function of that, the mechanics of that (if that's a term), is that when you are inside mother, you are not a land person, you are a water person. So you are conscious of being a water person and you never think of yourself as a land person until you suddenly become one. Then because your growth and transformation did not prepare you to be a land person, it's like having to start all over. And so you forget what you always knew being a water person.

If you don't know the name, can you ask what sea beings left that the microbes were supporting?

What you would call some kinds of fish.

So there are whole species that have left completely?

Oh, yes. But you know, that's not surprising; I think your science acknowledges that. And of course, they also acknowledge a rarity in species. Due to the inconvenience, naturally, for you to explore species of water beings, you don't really know all the species that have left because you didn't know they were here in the first place.

You Are Learning This Magic

So the oil is damaging everywhere in the water, not just where it sinks to the bottom.

Well, it's a natural substance, you know. In some places it just seeps out. But because it seeps out very slowly, one can see it coming, and you're able to get out of the way. Or the knowledge exists that there is a seepage there— "Don't get caught in that stuff," eh? Just like if you were walking along and you saw a big pothole, it would be, "Oh, I better not step in that; I don't know how deep it is." But certainly if the water was upon you, you wouldn't be able to do that, would you?

I see, yes. You talked about how one of the reasons you were asked to come as an emissary to tell them to stay is for our use of transformational magic—can you say a little more about that?

There are only a few amongst you now who can do this, but you are learning that magic isn't—and doesn't have anything to do with—theatrical magic with people on a stage and doing entertainments. That's not the kind of magic

I'm talking about. I'm talking about a true form of magic that is beneficial to all beings but very often requires or requests, let's say . . . the desire of the magic is to require at least a temporary change in one's being so that you go from one form to another form, or perhaps you might simply transform the way you survive. Instead of eating this, you eat that; instead of emanating this, you emanate that. In short, there is some temporary—or even permanent, depending upon one's life cycle—form of transformation that is more benign to this or that species of being. So it is possible, you see, when doing a form of this benevolent true magic, as I'm going to call it, to request that certain things take place. A moment . . . [Sneezes.] A strange experience, that.

You might ask that an organism that might normally produce a disease in people, in human beings—not because it is malevolent, but just because of its existence—that that organism in general transforms itself at least temporarily, so that those diseases or that disease is not experienced by human beings for a given amount of time or in general. And if those organisms, those microbes, are able to do that and still live, they might—at least, some of them might.

So this can happen. And it can be studied how to do it. You have to be able to invite benevolent energies to be with you, because the human being cannot always feel benevolent in every second. But if the benevolent energies are with you—spirits, you understand—and they have kindness and love for all beings and you can feel that energy, it does not mask your own feelings because you must be completely devoted to what you're asking for, but it supports your benevolent feelings. Then you can ask in some fashion that those microbes transform themselves or even mutate (which would be a permanent transformation) to become benign to all those whom they touch, for instance, or specifically to the human population at some place or in some part of one's being. It can be done individually for a human being, or considering the motion of matter into a human being and the transformation and then that matter beyond the human being, it can be requested in general for that which affects human beings.

You are gradually learning to do these things, because there are a few amongst you, I can see, who are doing these things that way. It must be done with respect, because you are asking beings to literally change their lives. Imagine if somebody came up to you and said, "I am asking that you no longer eat. You can drink all the liquids you want to, but don't eat anything, don't chew anything, because it would be better for this or that form of life." That's a pretty major request. You have to consider it like that. Some beings will do that. Some human beings might even do that if asked. I'm not saying you ought to; I'm saying that it is similar in terms of the impact on that life form. Still, these microbes have been requested to stay here while you are learning that. But they do not have any other duties, so mostly they are waiting and just living as well as possible during that time.

Where will they go back to? Did they come from all over or from a particular place?

I think all over. But you know, in other places, of course, they do not cause any harm by their existence, nor are they exposed to any harm from others.

Our Culture Is Entirely About Motion

Tell me about your existence on this planet. What is your natural life like?

Well, that's what I do . . . we don't talk the way you do, but we still communicate. Microbes communicate too. So when we meet the beings who requested us, we don't just talk in general to a group like you would speak to a group of people. We talk to them individually, and they communicate a bit to each other, but we have to travel around and talk to them about these things. So that's what I do. We communicate to this form of microbe that is covering quite an amount of territory. And the others in my party . . . that's what we're doing full-time, communicating this. We can't be everywhere at once, so some of them have already left.

How long have you been here?

By your calendar, eh?

[Laughs.] Since I don't know yours.

No, you don't. Let's see. Depending on how you measure, maybe eight to ten years.

Oh, that long? And how long do you plan to be here?

As long as it takes. I don't know how long that will be.

So you've communicated with over half of the microbes—or is there a percent?

I do not know. I know I've communicated with thousands of them, but my understanding is that there are quite a few more than that.

Yes. [Laughs.] I think they're everywhere. So this is what you've been doing for ten years. But is this what you always do, go out as an emissary?

I've never done this before.

How did it happen that you did it now? You were called?

Well, yes, the call went out, so to speak. That's the only way I can describe it. And some of us answered. We had never worked together this way before, so we had to be trained. It was shown to us how we would appear on your planet, and we were comfortable with this because it wasn't that far from our natural appearance. In our natural appearance, we are more of what you would identify as a gas.

Without a particular shape, then. You sort of flow. Do you have boundaries?

I cannot say more. It is important for you to know that an individual, a personality, a being and many beings can be in that form.

Many beings can be in that form on your planet or anywhere?

Can be in the form of a gas. That's what I've been allowed to say.

Did all the beings who came come from your planet, or do they come from different places?

No, they all came from my planet.

Can you say anything about your life or your society or your culture or your activities?

The only other thing I can say is that our life and our culture is entirely about motion. So we are always in motion. This was one of the things that made it possible for us to adapt to being in the sea, because in the sea, one is also always in motion. Even if you are at complete rest, the water itself is moving. So one never really is stopped. Even if you are not moving with the water, if you manage to hang onto something, so to speak, the water is at the very least moving beyond you and all around you so that you are in a world of motion. In this way, we adapt well to this environment.

Is your awareness such that you're aware of all the people on the planet, or are you only focusing on your mission?

I'm focusing on what we were asked to come here to do, but I have a certain limited knowledge of other beings on the planet insofar as it might correlate to what we have been asked to do when we came here. So that is why I have a certain limited knowledge of the human being. But I do not know, I can't answer much about you. If you asked a question about the intricacies of human nature, I would not be able to answer that.

On the planet you're on, are there other consciousnesses you can interact with? We probably wouldn't see them, but . . .

I am only aware of the personalities in the form of gas.

Of your people, yes.

I don't necessarily refer to them as my people, nor do they refer to me that way, but it is the life cycle that I am familiar with.

Are you familiar with life cycles before that?

No.

Aren't there microbes, not just in the sea, but I mean in people, in animals, everywhere?

I believe so, yes.

How are you going to talk to them?

I don't have to talk to them because they didn't ask.

Only the ones in the seas did.

The specific ones who requested are in the sea, so I don't have to do the other. That's just as well because I feel more at home in the sea.

My Joy Is in Motion

Do you have teachers you talk to?

Before we came here, we were instructed at length how to exist and function in this world. But while we're here, that doesn't seem to be necessary, at least it hasn't been for me so far.

Now, the beings come to this planet and then they go home, and because there's discomfort here, they don't always get to remember what they did here. Will you be able to remember this and have it as part of your experience?

I won't know until that happens. It was not told to me that I would. It was said to me that what I would do here would not have any applications at my home when I return there. So they said I might or might not retain those memories. That's how much they said. I did not take that to be a requirement, a fixed principle, but rather a simple statement of fact.

Well, usually they say that the feeling of discomfort can't leave the planet.

I see.

So what is your joy there in the movement on your home planet? Do you see colors?

Yes, there are many colors and they are constantly transforming as one might see them from a distance. But when you are within it, you can see that the colors are all fixed to specific individuals or groups of individuals, and the apparent transformation of color as one might note from a distance is simply a representation of the motion of beings. So yes, we see colors.

So it's like a big dance!

Yes, and my color on my home planet is like yellow—you'd say yellow. But there are other beings of other colors, and it comes pretty close to matching the colors you have on this planet, though without the variety you have here. I have never seen anything like the variety you have here.

Do you see what's on the planet too? Do you see beyond yourself?

I am only aware of the gases. I am not aware of any firm substance of a planet, though it is certainly possible that there is a firm substance. One would assume something like that, given a certain amount of gravity.

Do you have life cycles there? Do you have a fixed length of time that you inhabit this substance?

I cannot say our life cycle is eternal, but I can identify my awareness on that planet. The first time I was aware of myself, there was apparently just as much gaseous substance on my home planet as there is now. So that would suggest that our life cycle is not eternal, because it was already there when I became aware of myself.

Do new beings come in, or are you all the same?

There seems to be some transformation, but I cannot tell you how many of your years it is. It's longer than you live, though.

[Laughs.] Everybody, everybody, lives longer than we do.

But this is understandable, because your life is so difficult—and by "difficult," I mean that you do not have the normal memories one might have other places nor the access that you would have beyond the planet in some other form. So my understanding is that your guides and teachers and Creator Itself have pity on you.

Yes, plus we have the discomforts and the lessons and all this stuff.

You are like soldiers, though. You volunteer for this mission not knowing what is to come.

I know, they've told me that. Some soul says, "I'd like some adventure," and suddenly that soul is on planet Earth [laughs].

One must be cautious.

[Laughs.] Yeah, they don't tell you much. What are your joys? You're conscious all the time. You don't rest or sleep or anything like that?

Exactly. And my joy is in motion. Perhaps this is why I live on that planet. But being on your planet in a world of motion is almost as good, if it weren't for the substances that . . .

The pollution, yes.

Yes, that's the word. If it wasn't for that, it would be almost as good as being on my home planet, without the familiarity, you see.

Practice Welcoming Others

Do you have time to communicate with fish going by or turtles or sharks or octopuses or anything?

No, that's not why I'm here. I'm here to communicate with microbes, and that is what I do. We do not know if other forms of life are aware of us, but we are aware of them, so perhaps it is mutual.

I just thought maybe you could sit down and have a chat every once in a while.

That's not why we're here. We are mission-specific. Do you chat with turtles and other forms of life?

I would like to, but I don't.

I mean as a people.

Oh no, you're right. Some shamans might, but I haven't learned how yet.

You can always do it. You can speak, but speak politely at first. Say a form of greetings and then introduce yourself. Say this someplace where you feel comfortable, not in front of a crowd of your fellow humans. Let's say you are talking to a turtle. Just say your name and who you were born of, maybe your parents' names or the family from which you come. Then say something that is welcoming of its presence. Don't ask it any questions, though. It is up to it if it wishes to respond. If it wishes to respond, you will probably get words in your mind. Don't push those away, waiting to hear something out loud that is the response. It might not be any more than that.

Even if you do not get those words in your mind, it might look at you, which means it is hearing you and perhaps what you are saying. You must say the words out loud in some fashion, whispered perhaps. If the being doesn't get the words transformed into its own language, then it will be acknowledging your feelings. So you must, first and foremost, have good feelings of welcome and kindness. If you are just saying the words and feeling other things, then it will not listen. It will have to maintain that boundary of energy it maintains in order to live as well as possible, you see.

But generally speaking, human beings do not do that. They do not focus in the feelings they have. Feelings are the first form of communication, especially in a world where there are so many different sounds and forms of sounds by beings. Your peoples are getting used to the idea that there are sometimes ways of communicating for which language is not a barrier. If you have some happy feelings, very often a physical demonstration shows that. If you have sad feelings, one demonstrates that. There are certain universal feelings that are recognized by certain physical demonstrations or even an acting out or something.

Generally speaking, the human being is still getting used to this. It's important when you ask for something that your feelings match that, especially if you are introducing yourself so that the turtle, in this case, whom you are talking to feels a sense of welcome. "Welcome" is easier to accomplish as a feeling than, say, "greetings." "Greetings" is a little hard to create in yourself, but "welcome"—you know that feeling. Perhaps you have felt welcome some place or felt welcome from someone. Then you know the feeling, so you attempt to establish it. Also, it's important to actually be welcoming of that turtle. If there are other forms of life that you feel you ought to introduce yourself to but you are not happy to see them, you won't be able to maintain the feeling, so don't introduce yourself in that situation. Just let them go on and pass by or do whatever, and wait for beings you would genuinely welcome, other forms of life.

You said so many people want to leave the planet because they don't feel welcome. Is it that the humans aren't welcoming, or the planet?

I'm including those human beings wanting to leave the planet because they don't feel welcome. It's not easy to feel welcome in environments that are not pleasant. And if you are constantly in such an environment, you might long for someplace where you would feel welcome for being yourself and not expected to perhaps act in some authoritarian manner, for example, if it is not your natural way. This can sometimes take a form that is unexpected. For instance, a human being might have grown up in the desert, and say he or she is in a mountain community with snow temporarily, eh? It would be hard to feel welcome in such a place, even if the people were friendly. You might not be used to such cold and such weather conditions, and you would long for home. See, sometimes it's like that; it's that simple. And that's what I mean—the authoritarian existence might be a demand of nature. To feel at home in such a circumstance might not work for you, or you might enjoy it for a time but not to spend the rest of your life there and having to live as well as possible in an environment where you don't feel at home. I use such an example because this is something you can understand; it is not complicated.

So people really won't feel welcome and the animals won't feel welcome until we're all in a more benevolent vibration, is that correct?

No, that's not true. You can, if you make the effort, create welcome within yourself. You can practice it—that is, the welcoming feeling. You have perhaps visited a human being here and there who has said "welcome" and meant it. Have you had that feeling where someone said "welcome" and meant it?

Yes.

You actually felt welcome?

Yes.

Well, then you can practice doing that yourself. This may not help someone to feel at home, but it might be a comfort. And if you can practice the feeling of welcome and welcoming—"welcome" meaning "feeling welcome" and "welcoming" meaning "transmitting that feeling that others might feel welcome"—then you can perhaps at least make things more pleasant.

It Is in Your Nature to Welcome

You have many wonderful things to say. Did you always know them? How did you learn them?

This is something that is understood by a great deal of life everywhere beyond this planet. You know this too. I am just reminding you of something that causes you to feel the truth in it; at a deep level, you know this. That is why you acknowledge its value. So on your own planet, there are many beings who know this as well. I feel that all human beings know this too, but it is easy to forget giving the complexity of your human cultures.

Well, how's our channel?

Tired.

Maybe we'd better stop. Do you want to finish up? After you go I want to ask for someone to come in and see if he can say what planet you're from.

I am certain you will not be told, but you can ask. I will finish by saying, it is in your nature, you are born to this, to be friendly and actually even to welcome experience. For to live on Earth as a human being is unlike any form of life you will ever know anywhere else. Everywhere else you will be quite conscious of other forms of life. You will be careful of their existence and respectful, and they will be the same to you. There's no chance of being stepped on by an elephant somewhere else—there's a chance on Earth, but it's not likely.

So try to give that feeling of welcome as a free gift. If you don't know what to give to people for a special occasion, and perhaps you do not have much that you are able to offer in terms of the exchange of physical gifts, then I suggest that you create an arrangement between the two of you where if they are unhappy, even somebody at your workplace, that they can come to you at some convenient time for you both and that you will welcome them. You will say with sincerity of feeling, "I welcome you and I am hopeful that your life here will be a joy."

You will have to practice the feeling of welcome to say that, and you might have to practice the feeling of joy, because when you end with that statement you will need to transmit what it is so that they can be reminded of it. This is a gift of your personal work, but it is something worth receiving, and if you are on the receiving end, it is most definitely enjoyable. I recommend that you practice these gifts, as they are things you will find useful in your life and in your lifetimes indefinitely. Good night.

Good life. Thank you very much. Thank you.

❋   ❋   ❋

Greetings. This is Grandfather

Greetings. Where did this fellow come from?

I cannot say, but you can ask Robby if he has any impressions.

❋   ❋   ❋

[Robert]: Hello?

Do you have any impressions of a planet or anything?

[Robert]: Well, I know what I saw.

What did you see?

[Robert]: I saw that spot . . . you know that planet where you see that spot and there are like clouds or something swirling around the spot?

You mean Jupiter?

[Robert]: I don't know. I think so.

Humans Are Going through Rapid Changes on Earth

ET Traveler Focused on Rapid Change
August 7, 2009

am a visitor to your planet.

Welcome, welcome to our planet. What would you like to talk about?

You Are Going through Rapid Change

I travel more to the outer planets these days, especially yours, because there is so much happening here. My culture is very focused on rapid change, and from our perspective, your planetary peoples are going through a rapid change that is not typical of that which is found elsewhere. My peoples are not embodied physically the way yours are, so we traverse space through what you call portals or windows. I believe, as I've noticed, that there is a great deal of such traversing on this planet now. Some seems to have to do with previous humans who have lived here and are getting a last look at what was, because you are apparently just about at the point where you will transfer over to being on a future-connected course of travel and life rather than a past one. So as near as I can tell, those particularly affectionate toward the past (and who have been human on this focus of Earth) are coming to Earth, as much as they get permission, to look about and see what is and the change.

I feel also that there is quite a bit of particle visiting. By "particle," I mean material, mass, not bodies or souls—personalities, you would say. Some of the greatest interest comes from materials. Well, your race, the human race, is an adaptive one, and you are particularly good at adapting to whatever is available to form it toward your needs. From my point of view, materials would fall under the heading as anything that human beings use to form to their needs, though I rule out nonhuman beings who people your planet in that case, even though you use them also. I rule them out because, from my point of view, they are just like you, only you do not know that—meaning most of your peoples do not know that these are simply other life forms from other planets who are exactly the same as you but look different, as one would find in traveling beyond Earth.

So the materials I'm talking about might be what you would call minerals. I've seen a lot of visitation from a mineral world to your planet, because when you get on this new path and are locked on to it, everything changes. Gradually, yes, but some things will change more rapidly—not necessarily the human soul and personality, but the other beings on the planet, including the materials themselves. There will be very rapid change in, say, buildings, which are made of minerals. The material, the composition of the material, will change quite a bit. You will not notice because everything will change relative to everything else, but if you were able to stand back and look at it, everything will be bigger.

So molecular structures will transform to being about one-third larger than they were before this change. This has less to do with the so-called dimension than the fact that in order to live through such a transformation, it is necessary to have more room to be able to flex, you would say, and thus materials need to do that as well. I have looked ahead to see what this would look like, and it's quite different. Imagine, if you could, that your buildings will be one-third larger, though you will not notice that and it might not even be observable to your contemporary science. thoughHowever, I do feel the science you are developing will, in about eighteen to twenty years, be able to detect that on the basis of . . . well, you'll be able to look into the past a little bit then scientifically in terms of sequenced past as compared to momentary past, which you can do now anthropologically and scientifically, to a degree.

So that interests me: the expansion of materials. But then there's the other factor, too. When you get on that future-anchored track of travel and motion, something else happens, and that's that the other life forms besides the human soul will rapidly transform into their more natural state. This does not mean that they will necessarily be one-third larger [chuckles]—because everything will be that, relative to everything else—but it means that they will have less interest in being on the planet. So other than those life forms you consciously welcome as human beings, you might find that many of the life forms you are dependent upon for your very lives will simply depart.

Some of them are departing now, such as honeybees, but these are not really natural bees. You will have to either learn to accommodate natural bees, which are a little more aggressive—meaning learn how to get along with them, which simply means you have to give them their distance—or you will have to welcome honeybees. They do not feel welcome. They have been oftentimes confused with the more natural bees and eliminated. You cannot do that to a species as gentle as honeybees; they will just leave, and they are doing that now.

Other species wish to leave because of feeling mistreated. Cows and a lot of beings whom you consume or who are vital to your existence, such as honeybees, are leaving. So if you want them to stay, you will have to consciously welcome them and treat them as well as possible, meaning better than you do now. It might be good to gather less honey from honeybees and recognize that [chuckles] the honey is meant for the young bees—it is their food. If you want honeybees to stick around and multiply, you're going to have to find a way to welcome them.

My Peoples Are in the First Loop of This Galaxy

My peoples have been in and around, not the very center of this galaxy, but perhaps if you were to look at the galaxy from a different perspective— science has speculated on this and it's pretty accurate—our planetary system is within the first loop, coming out from the center of solidified mass. However, when our culture (which is not only associated with a planet) has in the past been in what is now in the second loop, we simply moved to the first loop, because we find it more comfortable to be as close to the light of emergence. We like this better than being in some of the more outer loops.

The centers of galaxies like this contain the emergence of substance, coming directly from creation outward. It is an immortal thing; it will always be. But it is very much light and not substance. Substance happens afterward. The closest thing I can come to here, scientifically, would be like a precipitate. But to put it in more conventional terms, it would not be unlike a very light steam vapor condensing into a droplet of water, which you could feel but you might not feel. So just translate that into light. When it comes away from the point of emergence far enough, it gradually condenses into mass, which eventually becomes planets and suns and so on.

There are many peoples associated with my culture—"personalities" might be a better statement, but our personalities are revolving. This means that we are not focused only as one personality, as you would identify each other on this planet, but rather at any given moment, a hundred or so personalities would pass through us. Therefore, in order to communicate, it is necessary to tap into that portion of ourselves that might be more capable of such communication as is going on now. But even during this now time, fully 90 to 95 percent of my being is doing other things—some of them here, some elsewhere.

You Are Moving Much Faster Than You Realize

Your culture, the human race on this planet, is moving much faster than you realize. Of course, you are aware of the physical motion you make and you are at least dimly aware of the planet's motion—since you see night and day, and the motion of the stars in the sky and so on. But the actual traversing of different focuses of being is happening very rapidly within the context of such transformations. I have had the opportunity to observe another such transformation many, many, [chuckles] many structures ago, as we would say. This was in a Pleiadian galaxy—the third galaxy, as they call it—and the peoples there, also a human race, very rapidly transformed from one focus to another. So this process is not unknown, but the difference is that in the Pleiadian situation there was not the polarity. So the transference happened very quickly but in a way where people were conscious of it and they could experience the change within themselves.

You are mostly having this transference going on, on an individual basis at the deep levels of sleep. Otherwise it would be so very distracting for so many of you that I think you would find it hard to cope. But this is only for the human being; all other materials and all other beings on the planet, including particles and so on, are doing this rapidly. You might reasonably ask that if particles are doing this rapidly, then what about the particles inside yourselves? They *are* doing it rapidly. You catch up—meaning your total physical being, yes, but more your mind, your personality as you understand it—ou catch up during the deep sleep, when you are less resistant to change and transformation. I do understand why you are resistant to change and transformation, because as a physical being, as a human being, you have had to adapt from very fast life in your lightbodies to what your lightbodies would perceive as an exceedingly slow life in the physical body. But you are here to learn about physicality, so you must adapt.

So you can see that, at the deep levels of sleep, when your lightbody and soul travels about, your physical body automatically makes the shift—and since your lightbody and personality is in its more natural focus, it easily makes the shift. That is why this takes place in the simplest way at those deep levels of sleep. This does not cause you any immediate sense of discomfort and, more to the tune of an attunement, so to speak, happens with relative ease.

You Are at 40-Percent Discomfort

Perhaps you have a question?

Yes. I didn't know that any other species had moved in this way while they were alive in their body, but you're saying that one did in the Pleiades?

Yes, and the reason I bring that up, you understand, is that they were human beings also, so I feel it has relevance.

Absolutely. I just thought we were the first ones to do it without dying and then coming back in a different vibrational body.

But the really big difference, you see, is that these beings from the Pleiades were not experiencing polarity—nothing discomforting, you understand—so this might be why you have this impression. well have, if they mentioned this to you before, other beings may well have felt that it wasn't relevant. But the reason I feel it is relevant is that these were human beings. Granted, they were not identical in physical makeup, but they were so close that if you were standing next to one, somebody else, an observer would say, "Well, two human beings!" They wouldn't necessarily notice much difference. There might be a little noticeable difference, but short of a physical examination, it wouldn't be obvious.

They shifted to a different timeline? How did they transform?

Well, they didn't transform in the same way you did. They shifted to a different focus, and from my perspective, that's what you're doing. I realize that others have told you it's a different timeline, but that is because it's easier for you to understand things within the context of time than it is for you to understand things in the context of space. Space seems very understandable to you—you walk across the room; you walk around the block—but I'm talking about vast reaches of space. You don't think about, "Oh, you walk over to the next galaxy." (I might think that, though walking isn't involved.) I mention this because they shifted focus from one focus of existence to another, allowing them to . . . oh, I can't say too much, but allowing them to migrate here and there with greater ease.

"Travel with greater ease"—what does that mean?

As I said, I can't say too much.

Are we moving to a different focus of the same planet, or are we moving in space to another focus somewhere else?

No, you are moving in focus to the same planet, but it will be a different focus of that planet. When you get to that point where you're, from your perspective, fast-tracking—meaning everybody notices changes every day when they wake up from deep sleep—then you will have dropped a great deal of your polarity. The first thing you will notice, though you won't be measuring it, is you will drop down to about 12 percent discomfort.... The next big shift goes down to 8 percent, then 4 percent, then 2 percent, and it kind of stays at 2 percent for quite a while through the next focus. So that's the big change that you'll notice.

Right now there's a little pause, because everybody is now involved in waking up. Before there were some people doing it, and they were sort of pioneering, but the whole point of pioneering is to createcreate a pathway for others and to try to create it in such a way that the others who are coming along will be able to traverse that pathway without the problems the first ones encountered. The job of the first few thousand or so that traverse any pathway is to discover what the problems are and come up with at least workable solutions (and ideally, flexible solutions), which can then be adapted by the others as they come along and have that in place. So now that the rest of the people are coming along, you have to kind of slow down and wait up for them.

Will I be able to see 12 percent discomfort while I'm in this human body?

Oh, no. I wouldn't think so. It could happen "tomorrow," but . . .

It probably won't.

If you were, as a physical person ensouled with your personality, present to be experiencing the change to about 12 percent, you would basically no longer identify your persona as the person you were. It would be a dim memory. So even if you were alive for that, you wouldn't be able to get excited and say, "Wow! Here we are at 12 percent! I can remember . . ." In short, you won't be able to remember. Your memory will change entirely.

Right. What is the percentage of discomfort right now?

Let's see if I can get that figure. [Pause.] You understand, this isn't a constant, but taking into account the entire human race, what everybody is experiencing all the time and then averaging it, that's what it means. I suppose you know that. Ooh, it's about 40 percent. It's a big difference all right, because it used to be 47-percent discomfort. The range has changed during the past twenty years or so; the past twenty years have seen that change.

But the way the memory process works, it just falls away; it's just not even available. It's just like, "Well, it's always been like this." Is that's how we will feel?

That is how you'll feel, but there will be a dim sense of it being different. By "dim," I mean that there will be a feeling that it was different before, but you won't have images and you won't have thoughts. But the feeling of there being a change and that things were different in the past will be present at 12 percent. By the time you get to 8 percent, you won't have much of that feeling left; by the time you get to 4 percent, you won't have any of that feeling left; and by the time you get to 2 percent, you will be looking forward to the next focus, eh?

Fantastic.

You All Have Multiple Personalities

Tell me a little about yourself. Have you been physical in your past, or have you always been lightbeings?

No, our people have never been physical.

If I could see you and I looked at you, what would I see?

If you were able to see, you might just see a varying shape of light.

You're not a particular color or anything?

I will say no more.

That's a secret, too?

[Pause.] t, as I have been instructed by certain beings that it is important not to get you too excited about who and what I am so you get distracted from who and what you are!

All right. This hundred-personality thing—tell me about that. Is that unusual?

You think it's unusual, but it really isn't. When you are in your natural state, you will have available to you the essence—granted in its completely nonpolarized fashion, completely benevolent—of all the personalities you have ever been focused in, in any given life, anywhere. So you think it's unusual, but it really isn't. It is something you are totally familiar with at the deep-sleep level when you are traversing around here and there in your soul self. It is also typical of lightbeings, but it is not necessarily spoken of. ... Well, pPerhaps you had an encounter through this method of communication, where one day you spoke to a being who went by this or that name temporarily, and the next time you spoke to that being, you had a definite sense that his or her personality was different. That's an example of that situation.

They were speaking from a different part of themselves.

Yes, that's right. So this is something actually normal. It's true that in your world there is a sense of self-discipline and even a sense of demand amongst friends and family that you remain who you were. For anybody who has ever moved away from home and made new friends and got a new job, got a new life, you become yourself, whoever your *self* is. But even with new friends and a new life, old friends and family expect you to be who you were. Over time, naturally, you change. But then you go back to see those friends or you go back to see family, and there is an expectation, almost a demand, that you be who you were.

You see, in your life you actually have multiple personalities going on now for every physical person: you have your youthful personality, you have your young years, your middle years, your old years and so on. You think your personality has not changed, but you find out. The quickest way to find out that your personality has changed—and this happens; you can totally identify with this—is when you are with your blood family, because they talk to you the way they remember you and the way they were. Everybody becomes their children again, and as dysfunctional [chuckles] as that might seem in moments, it is a clear-cut reminder of how you are more than one being.

Yes, I understand that completely. I am from a large family.

We Travel with Other Portions of Beings within Us

How does it work, then, as a lightbeing? Have you always been in this galaxy?

I've always been, yes.

So if you're immortal and you stay the same (a lightbeing), how do you get a hundred personalities? What lives are you drawing from?

No, no. You're assuming that what I say is true for you is true for us, but it is not so. We get a hundred personalities or so, or more—I just picked that number out of the air—because it has to do with the rest of our culture, the rest of the beings. We have hundreds and thousands of us in our culture, but we're not comfortable being one. We're not comfortable unless there are at least a hundred, several hundred, maybe a thousand. It is like this: If you are a human being, it might be exciting to go out and travel in space, but after a few days, you'd be missing other human beings. Do you understand? For us, we travel all over time and we also are like that. We would get lonely. So then we travel with other portions of other beings within us.

It doesn't mean that they are then stuck inside us and can't be themselves. Right now, I am inside other beings as well, you see? It is a matter of being: - I would be lonely without them, and they would be lonely without me. It is not the same. I explained something to you about how you are, and you extrapolated that this is how all lightbeings are, but it isn't so. I just utilized that as an example so that you could understand it. I know you're trying to make classifications, but it isn't that way.

So all of your beings are one culture, and you can become one of them, or they can become one of you, or a hundred of you can be together and you can switch your focus amongst different ones of you and you're still you?

Yes, but that is an extremely simple way to put it. It's much more complex than that. Imagine a simple molecule. And tThat would be the individual. But then you think of a more complex molecule, and it would have many portions of itself, the atomic structure and so on. It's like that. We are complex beings. We have many portions, but they are not fixed. At any given moment, I might have revolving through me hundreds of different personalities that are associated with different beings in my culture. They don't travel in me as one might travel in a bus—it's not like that.

Okay, but you can experience, you can be one of those or one of these or anyone at any time?

Yes, that's a good, simple way to put it.

Okay, I don't know a more complex way. [Chuckles.] It sounds like fun!

Well, the reason I'm saying that's a simple way to put it is that I consider it to be an advantage. It's better to have it spoken simply in a cross-cultural frame of reference like this than to attempt to break it down into its formulaic complexity.

You come in through a portal, you said. Did you come from your own culture to get here?

Yes, you might say. Yes.

How do you know where the portals are? Do you see them? Do you feel them?

It's not like that, but I understand that you're speaking about spatial reference again. In our world, I have an interest to go to some place and then I am in that place. I am slowing down how I get there for you to understand. I am saying to you, "I get here . . ."

. . . because you want to be here.

Yes, it's like that. It is like a navigational aspect not based upon time and space but temporal need. It just so happens that I'll pass through a portal to make it comfortable for me and not harmful for others, but I don't look for the portal. It's just part of the process. If you were able to see the portal—and some human beings on Earth can do that now—you might see that traversing of a being through the portal, or you might simply see a being, or you might simply see a portal. I know that this channel sees such things all the time, but you know, there are others who see it too.

So you know an awful lot about us. Had you ever been here before?

No, but I know about you because I am here now. When I go and do other things, I will not know that. I'll only know it again if ever I come here again. So the knowledge I have is purely temporal.

Yes, I think we're trained to call it vertical wisdom: you know what you need to know when you need to know it.

Yes, that's a good description.

What other things interest you? You travel every place in this galaxy or beyond?

No, I'm just interested in rapid change. Our peoples are interested in rapid change, and when any rapid change happens anywhere, we're very interested in that and we tend to migrate there for a short time. This is why I am here, and I am not alone—there are a few others around in different parts of your planet. But we do not have difficulty. can, if we need to go someplace... Say I need to go someplace. From your point of view, a surface measurement would be, say, 3,000 miles away. But instead of going through the surface, I just go through the planet.

Why would you need to go there? Do you know where you are now?

I am inside the planet.

Ah. Why would you need to go from one place to another, for example?

It may be because I was curious. I wanted to see what was going on.

That's a trait that I highly admire.

[Chuckles.] I can understand that.

You're not one of the beings we will run into when we start traveling, are you?

Well, you won't see us, so you might run into us and simply not know about it.

Right through you, yes. You mentioned the Pleiadians. What other species or life forms have gone through rapid change? What are some examples of that?

When I mentioned the Pleiadians, I had meant that they're . . .

That was ... because they are human, yes.

Yes, even though it hadn't been mentioned to you before, but there are others. But to put it in a simple way—I am sort of on the borderline of what I can talk about here—all the others, including the Pleiadians, went from one focus to another without polarity. I'm only really allowed to slightly mention the Pleiadians, because they were humans. The others were not.

It's probably because you got it in there before anybody knew you were going to say it [chuckles].

No, that's not true; they always know. The reason you are not being told many things is that you—the human being on Earth—are a species who is very easily distracted. It is very easy. Just take a look at your day or take a look at the people around you: they are very easily distracted. Since you're doing something very important for yourselves and ultimately perhaps for others, we are not encouraged to distract you. It is felt that you already have enough distraction.

You Have to Redefine Comfort

When we are down to 2 percent discomfort, can you talk to us and talk more?

Oh, we will be talking to you more when you are at 12 percent. But when you're at 12 percent, then you'll be locked in and moving, but you'll notice. You understand, when you pass through the main point of change, you won't . . . when you drop to, say, 30 percent and then slowly down, it won't be "clicking" from 30 to 20 or anything like that—they'll go through notch by notch. When you get to 30-percent overall discomfort on the planet as an average, then you'll start to release a lot of distraction and you'll notice that something good is happening, and people will be excited and want to participate.

The reason for all of this talk coming through this being for the purpose of these books and articles and ways of sharing is so that when that time comes, that hopefully people will know what they can do. You won't be able to speed up the process, and there's no point in doing that—why speed it up if you've got beings who have to come along? Everybody has to go, so what's the point of stringing the line out? You want to go as a group; otherwise it doesn't work. So the whole point then is that you'll need to be informed of what you can do to welcome the change. It's not about stopping being polarized; it's about welcoming being in comfort. You have to redefine comfort. Some people might consider excitement and wild, violent movies to be comfortable, but in fact, they're not a good influence.

I think of the Zetas and their calm and peace, and that might truly be very boring for some people.

It would be boring if you were raised on that kind of excitement. But, you see, when you are born as a baby, that kind of excitement frightens and upsets you. You are conditioned to like this or want it or need it. So it remains a distraction your whole life.

How can we uncondition ourselves?

You can't. You can only welcome comfort, ease and love—"love" meaning a good feeling between all beings. I'm not speaking about physical love here.

Benevolence we call it.

Yes, you can welcome that. Welcome it for yourself and welcome it for others—you might say for all beings.

Have you been anyplace else where there is discomfort in this galaxy?

No, there isn't any in the rest of the galaxy.

While you're here, you can see it and observe it, but it doesn't affect you, right?

Certainly not. If it affected me, I wouldn't be able to go back. I know of several beings from other planets who have become caught up in the discomfort, and alas, tragically, they had to stay.

Just for the life they're living?

Oh, I cannot say. You'd have to talk to them. It might be worth talking to them now.

That's a good point.

Your Passage Toward Benevolence Is a Natural Motion

If you were a human on the planet and you wanted to somehow contribute toward everyone moving comfortably through this transformation, what would you do?

Well, for starters, I would do that living prayer process. Live as well as possible, in the most benevolent way. Be the example for your own sake. If others comment on the way you live, you can say why, but don't tell them that what they're doing is bad. Just say:

> *Living Prayer*
> "WHAT I'M DOING SERVES ME, AND I FEEL GOOD ABOUT IT AND MY LIFE FLOWS IN A BETTER WAY FOR ME."

But you will have to come up with examples, because people are going to want proof. In some cases, you would be simplifying your life; in other cases, your life may be more complex. It depends upon the individual. We are going to have to stop.

I came here today because I wanted to let you know that you are not alone in your passage. The passage that you make toward a more benevolent world is a worthy goal, but in a larger sense, it is a natural motion. For many of you who are very young—two years old, maybe—you might very well live to have a natural life of, say, 120 or so as the lifetime potential grows longer, and you might very well live to at least the point of an overall average of 30-percent discomfort—which will seem, overall on average, like a big change. But it's also possible that some of you will live to see 12 percent. So enjoy your life now, pay attention to the moment, live as well as possible in the most benevolent way, and help others when you can. Good night.

Happy traveling. Thank you.

ET VISITORS SPEAK, VOL. 1

THROUGH ROBERT SHAPIRO
Book 11 of the Explorer Race

Even as you are searching the sky for extraterrestrials and their space ships, ETs are here on planet Earth—they are stranded, visiting, exploring, studying the culture, healing the Earth of trauma brought on by irresponsible mining or researching the history of Christianity over the last 2000 years. Some are in human guise, some are in spirit form, some look like what we call animals as they come from the species' home planet and interact with those of their fellow beings we have labeled cats or cows or elephants. Some are brilliant cosmic mathematicians with a sense of humor presently here as penguins; some are fledgling diplomats training for future postings on Earth when we have ET embassies. In this book, these fascinating beings share their thoughts, origins and purposes for being here.

CHAPTER TITLES INCLUDE:

Stranded Sirian Lightbeing Observes Earth for 800 Years
An Orion Being Talks about Life on Earth as a Human
A Sentient Redwood
Qua Comes to View Origin and Evolution of Christianity
Qua's Experiences Studying Religion on Earth
Qua on Mormonism
Observer Helps Cats Accomplish Their Purpose: Initiating Humans
A Warrior of Light, The Ultimate Ally
Penguins: Humorous Mathematicians
Xri from the Ninth Dimension
Sixth Dimensional Cha-Cha Dances with Humans
Starlight for Regeneration of Earth's Crystal Veins
ET Resource Specialist Maps and Heals Planetary Bodies
The Creation and Preparation of the Resource Specialists' Ships
Future Zeta Diplomat Learns to Communicate with Humans
Sirius Water-Being: A Bridge between ETs and Humans
The Rock-Being Here to Experience Movement

$14.⁹⁵

310 P. SOFTCOVER
ISBN 1-891824-28-7
979-1-891824-28-8

SHINING THE LIGHT II
THE BATTLE CONTINUES

Current status of the sinister secret government and those who want to usurp its power. Actual cosmic photographs of hidden crafts, beings and events. Photon Belt "Doctor" comes to save Mother Earth. The truth becomes even stranger as the story of alien involvement in Earth history continues.

SOFTCOVER 418P.

$**14**95 ISBN 0-929385-70-5
978-0-929385-70-9

Chapter Titles:

- Update on Humanity
- The Light Is Returning Home
- The Sinister Secret Government Is Back in Sedona
- Zoosh Explains the Sightings
- Nineteen Time-Space Anomalies
- Time-Space Anomalies Explained
- Contactee Children
- Bringing the Babies Home
- Evolution of Earth and Humanity
- Sinister Secret Government Moves Entrance to Underground Base
- Awakening to the Master within Your Physical Form
- Xpotaz-Sinister Secret Government Shootout over Grand Canyon
- The Face of God: Robert Meyer's Photos Explained
- Interdimensional Entities Become More Visible

- You're Getting Shifted to the Center
- The Creator and His Friends
- Cosmic Holograms (photos)
- The New Vortex
- Interlude with the Planet—Your Lady
- More on the Sinister Secret Guerrilla War
- The Awakening of Humankind's Dreams (photos)
- You Can Now Integrate the Fourth Dimension
- Earth: A Planet of Peace
- The Photon Belt: A Planetary Troubleshooter
- The Earth's New Dance Partner
- The Photon Belt "Doctor" Is In
- Return of the Ancient Lemurians (photos)
- Nefarious Computer Chip Activated
- The Ancient Gods in You Are Starting to Move

Epilogue: Book III
Shadow Government Attempts to Mine on Hopi Reservation

MAURICE CHATELAIN

Author Maurice Chatelain, former NASA space expert, has compiled compelling evidence to show that a highly advanced civilization existed on the Earth approximately 65,000 years ago. Further, his work indicates that the knowledge of the advanced civilization had been "seeded" by extraterrestrial visitors who have aided mankind with advanced information in mathematics, electricity and astronomy.

OUR COSMIC ANCESTORS

Our Cosmic Ancestors is a dynamic work, unraveling the messages of these "universal astronauts" and decoding the symbols and visual mathematics they have left for us in the Egyptian Pyramids, Stonehenge, the Mayan calender, the Maltese Cross and the Sumerian zodiac.

SOFTCOVER 213P.

$14 95   ISBN 0-929686-00-4

Chapter Titles:

- The Apollo Spacecraft
- The Constant of Nineveh
- The Mayan Calendar
- The Secret of the Pyramid
- The Maltese Cross
- The Rhodes Calculator
- The Kings of the Sea
- The Signs of the Zodiac
- The Polar Mysteries

- The Universal Calendar
- The Four Moons
- The Mystery of Atlantis
- Extraterrestrial Civilizations
- Mysterious Visitors
- Conclusion

ROBERT SHAPIRO

the
EXPLORER
RACE

Zoosh, End-Time Historian
through Robert Shapiro

Book 1...
The Explorer Race

You individuals reading this are truly a result of the genetic experiment on Earth. You are beings who uphold the principles of the Explorer Race. The information in this book is designed to show you who you are and give you an evolutionary understanding of your past that will help you now. The key to empowerment in these days is to not know everything about your past, but to know that which will help you now.

Your souls have been here for a while on Earth and have been trained in Earthlike conditions. This education has been designed so that you would have the ability to explore all levels of responsibility—results, effects and consequences—and take on more responsibilities. Your number one function right now is your status of Creator apprentice, which you have achieved through years and lifetimes of sweat. You are constantly being given responsibilities by the Creator that would normally be things that Creator would do. The responsibility and the destiny of the Explorer Race is not only to explore, but to create.

SOFTCOVER 574P.

$25.00 ISBN 0-929385-38-1
978-0-929-385-38-9

Chapter Titles:

THE HISTORY OF THE EXPLORER RACE
- The Genetic Experiment on Earth
- Influences of the Zodiac
- The Heritage from Early Civilizations
- Explorer Race Time Line, Part 1
- Explorer Race Time Line, Part 2
- The Experiment That Failed

GATHERING THE PARTS
- The ET in You: Physical Body
- The ET in You: Emotion and Thought
- The ET in You: Spirit

THE JOY, THE GLORY AND THE CHALLENGE OF SEX
- Emotion Lost: Sexual Addiction in Zeta History
- Sex, Love and Relationships
- Sexual Violence on Earth
- The Third Sex: The Neutral Binding Energy
- The Goddess Energy: The Soul of Creation

ET PERSPECTIVES
- Origin of the Species: A Sirian Perception
- An Andromedan Perspective on the Earth Experiment
- The Perspective of Orion Past on Their Role
- Conversation with a Zeta

BEHIND THE SCENES
- The Order: Its Origin and Resolution
- The White Brotherhood, the Illuminati, the New Dawn and the Shadow Government
- Fulfilling the Creator's Destiny
- The Sirian Inheritors of Third-Dimensional Earth

TODAY AND TOMORROW
- The Explorer Race Is Ready
- Coming of Age in the Fourth Dimension
- The True Purpose of Negative Energy
- The Challenge of Risking Intimacy
- Etheric Gene-Splicing and the Neutral Particle
- Material Mastery and the New Safety
- The Sterilization of Planet Earth

THE LOST PLANETS
- The Tenth Planet: The Gift of Temptation
- The Eleventh Planet: The Undoer, Key to Transformation
- The Twelfth Planet: Return of the Heart Energy

THE HEART OF HUMANKIND
- Moving Beyond the Mind
- Retrieving Heart Energy
- The Creator's Mission and the Function of the Human Race

To order call 1-800-450-0985 or 928-526-1345
or use our online bookstore at www.lighttechnology.com

Book 2...
ETs and the EXPLORER RACE

In this book, Robert channels Joopah, a Zeta Reticulan now in the ninth dimension, who continues the story of the great experiment—the Explorer Race—from the perspective of his civilization. The Zetas would have been humanity's future selves had not humanity re-created the past and changed the future.

SOFTCOVER 237P.

$14⁹⁵ ISBN 978-0-929385-79-2

Joopah, Zoosh and others
through Robert Shapiro

Chapter Titles:
- The Great Experiment: Earth Humanity
- ETs Talk to Contactees
- Becoming One with Your Future Self
- ET Interaction with Humanity
- UFOs and Abductions
- The True Nature of the Grays
- Answering Questions in Las Vegas
- UFO Encounters in Sedona
- Joopah, in Transit, Gives an Overview and Helpful Tools
- We Must Embrace the Zetas
- Roswell, ETs and the Shadow Government
- ETs: Friend or Foe?
- ET Presence within Earth and Human Genetics
- Creating a Benevolent Future
- Bringing the Babies Home

Book 3...ORIGINS and the NEXT 50 YEARS

This volume has so much information about who we are and where we came from—the source of male and female beings, the war of the sexes, the beginning of the linear mind, feelings, the origin of souls—it is a treasure trove. Then in addition there is a section that relates to our near future—how the rise of global corporations and politics affects our future, how to use benevolent magic as a force of creation and then how we will go out to the stars and affect other civilizations. Astounding information.

SOFTCOVER 339P.

$14⁹⁵ ISBN 978-0-929385-95-2

Zoosh, End-Time Historian
through Robert Shapiro

THE ORIGINS OF EARTH RACES
- Our Creator and Its Creation
- The White Race and the Andromedan Linear Mind
- The Asian Race, the Keepers of Zeta Vertical Thought
- The African Race and Its Sirius/Orion Heritage
- The Fairy Race and the Native Peoples of the North
- The Australian Aborigines, Advisors of the Sirius System
- The Return of the Lost Tribe of Israel
- The Body of the Child, a Pleiadian Heritage
- Creating Sexual Balance for Growth
- The Origin of Souls
The Next 50 Years
- The New Corporate Model
- The Practice of Feeling

- Benevolent Magic
- Future Politics
- A Visit to the Creator of All Creators
- Approaching the One
Appendix
- The Body of Man/The Body of Woman
Origins of the Creator
- Beginning This Creation
- Creating with Core Resonances
- Jesus, the Master Teacher
- Recent Events in Explorer Race History
- The Origin of Creator
- On Zoosh, Creator and the Explorer Race
- Fundamentals of Applied 3D Creationism

ROBERT SHAPIRO

Book 4...CREATORS and FRIENDS
The Mechanics of Creation

Now that you have a greater understanding of who you are in the larger sense, it is necessary to remind you of where you came from, the true magnificence of your being, to have some of your true peers talk to you. You must understand that you are creators in training, and yet you were once a portion of Creator. One could certainly say, without being magnanimous, that you are still a portion of Creator, yet you are training for the individual responsibility of being a creator, to give your Creator a coffee break.

This book will give you peer consultation. it will allow you to understand the vaster qualities and help you remember the nature of the desires that drive any creator, the responsibilities to which that creator must answer, the reaction any creator must have to consequences and the ultimate reward of any creator. This book will help you appreciate all of the above and more. I hope you will enjoy it and understand that maybe more will follow.

SOFTCOVER 435P.

$**19**95 ISBN 978-0-929385-97-6

Chapter Titles:

- Andastinn, Prototype of Insect Beings
- Kazant, a Timekeeper
- Founders of Sirius, Creators of Humanoid Forms
- A Teacher of Buddha and Time Master's Assistant
- Designers of Human Physiology
- Avatar of Sea Creatures; and Quatsika, Messenger for the Dimension Makers
- The Empath Creator of Seventeen Planets
- Shapemaker of Portals
- Creator of the Inverse Universe, Our Creator's Creator
- Creator of the Void, Preamble to Individuality
- The Tornado-Shaped Creator of Creators
- The Center of Creation
- The Heart Council
- Creators of Gold Light and White Light
- Creator Talks About Itself and the Explorer Race
- Creator Talks About Friends
- Creator Speaks of the Stuff of Creation
- Creator Discusses Successes and the Outworking of Negativity
- Synchronizer of Physical Reality and Dimensions
- Master of Maybe
- Master of Frequencies and Octaves
- Spirit of Youthful Exuberance
- Master of Imagination
- Zoosh, the End-Time Historian
- Master of Feeling
- Master of Plasmic Energy
- Master of Discomfort Speaks of Himself and the Explorer Race
- Master of Discomfort Discusses Light Transference

Appendix: The Lucifer Gene

Book 5...
PARTICLE PERSONALITIES

All around you are the most magical and mystical beings. They are too small for you to see as single individuals, but in groups you know them as the physical matter of your daily life. These particles remember where they have been and what they have done in their long lives. We hear from some of them in this extraordinary book.

SOFTCOVER 237P.

$**14**95 ISBN 977-0-929385-97-6

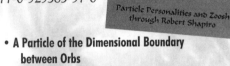

Particle Personalities and Zoosh through Robert Shapiro

Chapter Titles:

- A Particle of Gold
- The Model Maker: The Clerk
- The Clerk; a Mountain Lion Particle; a Particle of Liquid Light; and an Ice Particle
- A Particle of Rose Quartz from a Floating Crystal City
- A Particle of Uranium, Earth's Mind
- A Particle of the Great Pyramid's Capstone

- A Particle of the Dimensional Boundary between Orbs
- A Particle of Healing Energy
- A Particle of Courage Circulating through Earth
- A Particle of the Sun
- A Particle of Ninth-Dimensional Fire
- A Particle of Union
- A Particle of the Gold Lightbeing beyond the Orbs

Book 6...EXPLORER RACE and BEYOND

With a better idea of how creation works, we go back to the Creator's advisors and receive deeper and more profound explanations of the roots of the Explorer Race. The liquid Domain and the Double Diamond portal share lessons given to the roots on their way to meet the Creator of this Universe and finally the roots speak of their origins and their incomprehensibly long journey here.

SOFTCOVER 360P.

$**14**95 ISBN 978-1-891824-06-7

Explorer Race Roots, Friends and All That Is with Zoosh through Robert Shapiro

Chapter Titles:

- Creator of Pure Feelings and Thoughts, One Circle of Creation
- The Liquid Domain
- The Double-Diamond Portal
- About the Other 93% of the Explorer Race
- Synchronizer of Physical Reality and Dimensions
- The Master of Maybe
- Master of Frequencies and Octaves
- Spirit of Youthful Enthusiasm (Junior) and Master of Imagination

- Zoosh
- The Master of Feeling
- The Master of Plasmic Energy
- The Master of Discomfort
- The Story-Gathering Root Being from the Library of Light/Knowledge
- The Root Who Fragmented from a Living Temple
- The First Root Returns
- Root Three, Companion of the Second Root

Book 9...EXPLORER RACE and JESUS

The immortal personality who lived the life we know as Jesus, along with his students and friends, describes with clarity and love his life and teaching on Earth 2000 years ago. These beings lovingly offer their experiences of the events that happened then and of Jesus' time-traveling adventures, especially to other planets and to the nineteenth and twentieth centuries, which he called the time of the machines—the time of the troubles. So heart-warming and interesting you won't want to put it down.

$**14**^{95}$ ISBN 978-1-891824-14-2

Chapter Titles:

- Jesus' Core Being, His People and the Interest in Earth of Four of Them
- Jesus' Life on Earth
- Jesus' Home World, Their Love Creations and the Four Who Visited Earth
- The "Facts" of Jesus' Life Here, His Future Return
- The Teachings and Travels
- A Student's Time with Jesus and His Tales of Jesus' Time Travels
- The Shamanic Use of the Senses

- The Child Student Who Became a Traveling Singer-Healer
- Other Journeys and the Many Disguises
- Jesus' Autonomous Parts, His Bloodline and His Plans
- Learning to Invite Matter to Transform Itself
- Inviting Water, Singing Colors
- Learning to Teach Usable Skills
- Learning about Different Cultures and People
- The Role of Mary Magdalene, a Romany
- Traveling and Teaching People How to Find Things

Book 10...EXPLORER RACE: EARTH HISTORY and LOST CIVILIZATIONS EXPLAINED

Zoosh reveals that our planet Earth did not originate in this solar system, but the water planet we live on was brought here from Sirius 65 million years ago. Anomalous archaeological finds and the various ET cultures who founded what we now call lost civilizations are explained with such storytelling skill by Speaks of Many Truths that you feel you were there!

$**14**^{95}$ ISBN 978-1-891824-20-3

Chapter Titles:

- Lost Civilizations of Planet Earth in Sirius
- Ancient Artifacts Explained
- Ancient Visitors and Immortal Personalities
- Before and after Earth Was Moved to This Solar System from Sirius
- The Long Journey of Jehovah's Ship, from Orion to Sirius to Earth
- Jehovah Creates Human Beings
- Beings from the Future Academy
- Sumer
- Nazca Lines
- Easter Island

- Laetoli Footprints
- Egypt and Cats
- Three More Civilizations
- Medicine Wheels
- Stonehenge
- Carnac in Brittany
- Egypt
- China
- Tibet and Japan
- Siberia
- Natural Foods/Sacrament of Foods
- SSG's Time-Traveling Interference in Israel

WES BATEMAN, FEDERATION TELEPATH

Wes Bateman is a telepath with direct, open contact to ETs from the open state, who are not subject to Earth mankind's Frequency Barrier-caused closed brain and limited consciousness. Bateman has 30 years of ongoing information on the open state; the Federation; the Frequency Barrier and how it affects humanity; ETs and evolution; a wide spectrum of technical and scientific information, including mathematics and the universal symbolic language; and the three trading houses of this system—all part of the Federation's history of this part of the galaxy and beyond.

THROUGH ALIEN EYES

The accounts given by extraterrestrials in this volume are about events that occurred in our solar system many millions of years ago. In that ancient time the solar system consisted of four planets and four "radiar systems" that orbited the central sun. The four planets of the solar system are known today as Venus, Earth, Mars and a now-totally shattered world that was called Maldec.

The term "radiar" applies to the astronomical bodies we presently call Jupiter, Saturn, Uranus and Neptune. The original satellites of these radiars are generally called moons by Earth astronomers, but the extraterrestrials prefer to call them planetoids.

This book reflects the personal views of a number of different types of extraterrestrials regarding the state of the local solar system and the state of the Earth.

SOFTCOVER 507P

$1995 ISBN 1-891824-27-9
978-1-891824-27-2

Chapter Titles:

- Sharmarie, a Martian
- Trome, a Saturnian
- Churmay, a Venusian
- Thaler, a Neptunian
- Ruke, a Jupiterian
- Jaffer Ben-Rob of Earth (Sarus)
- Nisor of Moor   • Tixer-Chock of Gracyea
- Doy, a Woman of Maldec

PART II
- It Has Begun
- Serbatin of Gee
- Tillabret of Emarin
- Rendowlan of Nodia
- Petrimmor of Caitress
- Ombota of Mars

- The Great SETI Con Game

Plus:
- The SETI Messages

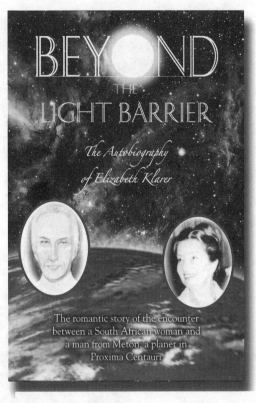

Shamanic Secrets Mastery Series

Speaks of Many Truths and Reveals the Mysteries through Robert Shapiro

This book explores the heart and soul connection between humans and Mother Earth. Through that intimacy, miracles of healing and expanded awareness can flourish. To heal the planet and be healed as well, we can lovingly extend our energy selves out to the mountains and rivers and intimately bond with the Earth. Gestures and vision can activate our hearts to return us to a healthy, caring relationship with the land we live on. The character of some of Earth's most powerful features is explored and understood, with exercises given to connect us with those places. As we project our love and healing energy there, we help the Earth to heal from human destruction of the planet and its atmosphere. Dozens of photographs, maps and drawings assist the process in twenty-five chapters, which cover the Earth's more critical locations.

498 p. $19.95 ISBN 978-1-891824-12-8

Learn to understand the sacred nature of your own physical body and some of the magnificent gifts it offers you. When you work with your physical body in these new ways, you will discover not only its sacredness, but how it is compatible with Mother Earth, the animals, the plants, even the nearby planets, all of which you now recognize as being sacred in nature. It is important to feel the value of oneself physically before one can have any lasting physical impact on the world. If a physical energy does not feel good about itself, it will usually be resolved; other physical or spiritual energies will dissolve it because it is unnatural. The better you feel about your physical self when you do the work in the previous book as well as this one and the one to follow, the greater and more lasting will be the benevolent effect on your life, on the lives of those around you and ultimately on your planet and universe.

576 p. $25.00 ISBN 978-1-891824-29-5

Spiritual mastery encompasses many different means to assimilate and be assimilated by the wisdom, feelings, flow, warmth, function and application of all beings in your world that you will actually contact in some way. A lot of spiritual mastery has been covered in different bits and pieces throughout all the books we've done. My approach to spiritual mastery, though, will be as grounded as possible in things that people on Earth can use— but it won't include the broad spectrum of spiritual mastery, like levitation and invisibility. I'm trying to teach you things that you can actually use and benefit from. My life is basically going to represent your needs, and it gets out the secrets that have been held back in a storylike fashion, so that it is more interesting."

—Speaks of Many Truths through Robert Shapiro

768 p. $29.95 ISBN 978-1-891824-58-6

THREE BOOKS BY NOTED UFO EXPERT
STEVEN M. GREER, M.D.

DISCLOSURE

573 P. SOFTCOVER
978-0-9673238-1-7

$24.95

For the first time ever, over five dozen top-secret military, government, intelligence and corporate witnesses to secret projects tell their true stories, which disclose the greatest covert program in world history. This explosive testimony by actual government insiders proves that UFOs are real, that some are of extraterrestrial origin and that super-secret programs have energy and propulsion technologies that will enable humanity to begin a new civilization—a civilization without pollution, without poverty—a civilization capable of traveling among the stars. This is not just a story about UFOs, ETs and secret projects; it is the story of how 50 years of human evolution have been deferred and how these secret projects contain the real solution to the world energy crisis, the environmental crisis and world poverty.

EXTRATERRESTRIAL CONTACT

526 P. SOFTCOVER
978-0-9673238-0-0

$24.95

Steven M. Greer, M.D., an emergency physician and Founder and International Director of CSETI (The Center for the Study of Extraterrestrial Intelligence) -- widely regarded as the world's foremost authority on UFOs and extraterrestrial intelligence -- has written a definitive account of the UFO/ET subject in his book Extraterrestrial Contact.

Relying on first-hand knowledge from his CSETI research experiences and direct sources from covert projects, Dr. Greer brings a unique combination of scientific knowledge, credibility, vision, humor and inspiration to the subject. Arguably the most insightful book ever written on the subject of UFOs, ETs and government secrecy.

HIDDEN TRUTH, FORBIDDEN KNOWLEDGE

325 P. SOFTCOVER
978-0-9673238-2-4

$24.95

Why did an emergency physician who had been chairman of a busy ER leave his career to get out to the world the information that we are not alone?

What had Dr. Steven Greer personally experienced -- from childhood onwards -- that gave him the knowledge of cosmic cultures, cosmic consciousness and a glimpse of the wondrous future that awaits humanity?

What are the new energy and propulsion technologies that can give us a new world, free of pollution, poverty and conflict? What is the nexus where Mind, Space, Time and Matter all come together -- and how might this be used technologically by an advanced civilization?